Retirement Plans
for Employees

The Irwin Series in Financial Planning and Insurance
Consulting Editor Jerry S. Rosenbloom *University of Pennsylvania*

Retirement Plans for Employees

John J. McFadden
The American College
Bryn Mawr, Pennsylvania

1988
IRWIN
Homewood, Illinois 60430

© RICHARD D. IRWIN, INC., 1988

All rights reserved. No part of this publication may be reproduced, stored in a retrieval system, or transmitted, in any form or by any means, electronic, mechanical, photocopying, recording, or otherwise, without the prior written permission of the publisher.

This book was set in Times Roman by Weimer Typesetting Co., Inc.
The editors were Larry Alexander, Waivah Clement, and Jane Lightell.
The production manager was Bette Ittersagen.
The Maple-Vail Book Manufacturing Group was the printer and binder.

ISBN 0-256-05588-2

Library of Congress Catalog Card No. 87-81436

Printed in the United States of America

1 2 3 4 5 6 7 8 9 0 MP 5 4 3 2 1 0 9 8

to Rhoda, Susanna, and Diana

Preface

According to recent Department of Labor surveys, more than 90 percent of full-time employees in medium and large firms are covered under qualified retirement plans. Qualified plans are also an extremely important benefit for smaller employers, covering a large percentage of employees of such organizations. Nonqualified retirement plans are also a widespread employee benefit, particularly for executives. At the end of 1985, private pension funds amounted to $1.3 trillion. In short, retirement plans are one of the most important employee benefits, fully justifying textbook treatment.

Because of the significant tax benefits for qualified plans, federal legislation affecting these plans has increased greatly in complexity, particularly over the last decade. Ongoing changes in legislation continually cause shifts in the focus of retirement plan design. This text reflects the current climate. It incorporates all recent legislation including the Tax Reform Act of 1986 and the 1986 age discrimination amendments.

The approach of this text is to regard retirement planning as a practical rather than a theoretical discipline. Full coverage is given to important policy issues, but the text emphasizes planning and problem solving. The emphasis given various topics and the type and order of presentation reflects the author's experience since 1974 in drafting and designing plans, working with planners, employer-sponsors, and plan administrators for large firms as well as small closely held businesses and professionals, and teaching graduate- and undergraduate-level employee benefit courses.

The text was designed to be useful for a broad range of retirement planning and employee benefit course structures. With regard to topics covered, a rule of inclusion rather than exclusion was adopted. Each chapter is designed to cover a single topic and is as self-contained as possible. Thus, specialized course offerings can be designed around this book by choosing chapters as appropriate and omitting chapters that are not directly relevant. For example, a retirement planning course that does not emphasize the needs of smaller businesses could omit chapters 18 and 24. On the other hand, for those programs emphasizing application to small businesses, the relevant material is presented together in several chapters to highlight the types of planning currently in use by specialized consultants in the small business area. Finally, certain material is placed in appendixes to indicate that it is primarily for reference or for use in particularly specialized course structures.

Tax Reform Act of 1986

The main body of this text fully incorporates the Tax Reform Act of 1986. However, the fact that certain provisions of the act do not take effect until after 1988 presents two problems. First, this text will be used for a period of time during which the old law is still in effect. Second, because of the delayed effective date the IRS has not yet given its full attention to certain aspects of the new law (the social security integration rules for example) and some issues are unresolved.

The approach taken here has been to incorporate in Appendix A the most important features of pre-1989 law. This way, the user can readily obtain information about these still-effective provisions without cluttering the main text with confusing transitional provisions. In addition, the IRS and other interpretations of pre-1989 law can be used by the student for reference and guidance as to the probable interpretation of the new law.

Note on Terminology

Unfortunately, the term *pension plan* is ambiguous under current federal law. Under the labor law including ERISA, pension plan is a generic term referring to any employer plan of deferred compensation, thus including virtually all qualified plans as well as many nonqualified arrangements. However, in the Internal Revenue Code, a pension plan is a specific type of qualified plan, contrasted with a profit-sharing or stock bonus plan. In this text, the term *pension plan* will be used in the specific, Internal Revenue Code sense; the term *qualified plan* will be used to refer to qualified (as opposed to nonqualified) deferred compensation plans; and the term *retirement plan* will be used to refer to all these arrangements in the generic sense.

Note on Legal and Other References in This Text

A textbook is not a legal treatise, a research paper, or a reference work; furthermore, the author of this book happens to dislike footnotes even in written works of the type where they are generally considered acceptable. Nevertheless, it was concluded after some deliberation that the usefulness of this book to all audiences would be greatly expanded if important points in the book were supported by references to the law or other sources for the reader who wishes to investigate further the point at issue. In the qualified plan area, such further research is much more difficult without such references. Therefore, appropriate references are in footnotes or occasionally in the body of the text.

References to Internal Revenue Code sections or similar items should *not* be construed by students as indicating that the Code section number (or other reference) is itself something to be memorized. However, students of retirement planning generally find that the more notorious section numbers and other references quickly become unforgettable as they delve further into the substantive material.

In this text, the term *the Code* will often be used in referring to the Internal Revenue Code, and the Treasury Regulations will be cited as *the Regulations,* with other citations given more fully. ERISA Section 000 will be used to refer to the indicated section of the Employee Retirement Income Security Act of 1974.

No attempt is made to provide a complete citation of authorities for all of the propositions set forth. However, the general discussion in this text should be adequate to enable the interested reader to obtain citations of the necessary legal authorities from one of the loose-leaf qualified plans or tax services or one of the handbooks in the field of qualified plans. (See the Bibliography section at the end of this book.) If accurate legal references are to be obtained, it is important to have thorough and up-to-date materials, because the legal authorities are extremely voluminous and subject to very frequent change.

Acknowledgments

The author gratefully acknowledges the assistance of colleagues at The American College and from the pension consulting fraternity who have helped in developing a level of knowledge where the writing of a textbook seemed feasible, if foolish. In particular, special thanks is due to Burton T. Beam, Jr., of The American College who prepared Chapter 2 and who read the entire manuscript and made many helpful suggestions. Thanks also to Kathleen Maphis who not only typed and proofread the entire manuscript but in so doing corrected many of the author's mistakes.

Certain material contained in this text has been adapted from material originally prepared by John J. McFadden and Burton T. Beam, Jr., for course materials at The American College, and the College's permission to adapt this material is gratefully acknowledged.

John J. McFadden

Contents

1 Retirement Needs of Employees   1

Sources of Retirement Income: *Earnings from Employment. Social Security. Savings. Private Retirement Plans.* Income Needs after Retirement. Effect of Inflation.

2 Social Security Retirement Benefits   10

Extent of Coverage. Financing. Eligibility: *Fully Insured. Currently Insured. Disability Insured.* Types of Benefits: *Retirement Benefits. Survivors' Benefits. Disability Benefits. Eligibility for Dual Benefits. Termination of Benefits.* Benefit Amounts: *Calculation of AIME. Determination of PIA and Monthly Benefits.* Taxation of Social Insurance Benefits.

3 Introduction to Qualified Plans   25

General Characteristics of Qualified Plans: *Eligibility and Plan Coverage. Nondiscrimination in Benefits and Contributions. Funding Requirements. Vesting Requirements. Limitations on Benefits and Contributions. Payout Restrictions. Top-Heavy Rules.* Tax Benefits of Qualified Plans. Classification of Qualified Plans: *Pension and Profit-Sharing Plans. Defined-Benefit and Defined-Contribution Plans. Specific Types of Qualified Plans.* Plans for Special Types of Organizations: *Plans Covering Partners and Proprietors. S Corporations. Multiple-Employer, Collectively Bargained, and Multiemployer Plans.*

4 Government Policy and Regulation of Qualified Plans — 35

Policy Issues and Their Resolution: *ERISA. Post-ERISA Policy Issues.* Application of the Law: *Federal Tax Law. Tax Cases in the Federal Courts. Federal Labor Law. Pension Benefit Guaranty Corporation. Other Regulations.*

5 Designing a Plan to Meet Employer Needs — 44

Design Orientation: *Compensation Policy Approach. Retirement Plans versus Cash.* Tax-Sheltering Orientation.

6 Qualified Plan Eligibility and Participation — 53

Age and Service Requirements: *Maximum Age Limits and Coverage of Older Employees. Definition of Year of Service. Breaks in Service. Other Eligibility Criteria Related to Age and Service.* Overall Coverage Tests: *Features of the Average-Benefit Test. Plans for Separate Lines of Business.* Coverage of Employees in Comparable Plans. Service for Predecessors and Other Employers. Commonly Controlled Employers: *Controlled Group Rules in General.*

7 Vesting and Benefit Accrual — 64

Vesting Rules: *Vesting at Normal Retirement Age and Termination of Employment. Choosing a Vesting Schedule. Vesting on Plan Termination.* Benefits at Termination of Employment. The Accrued Benefit: *Benefit Accrual Rules.*

8 Pension Plan Design: Benefit Formulas — 70

Structure and Design of a Pension Plan. Retirement Age: *Early Retirement. Late Retirement. Age Discrimination.* Benefit Formulas: *Defined-Contribution Formulas. Target Plans. Defined-Benefit Formulas. General Characteristics of Defined-Benefit Formulas. Types of Formulas. The Cash-Balance Formula. Definition of Compensation.* Sex Discrimination. Inflation and Pension Planning: *Preretirement Inflation. Postretirement Inflation.*

9 Integration of Qualified Plans with Social Security — 89

Purpose and Effect of Social Security Integration. Integration of Defined-Benefit Plans: *Offset Approach. Integration Level Approach. The Covered Compensation Table.* Integration of Defined-Contribution Plans: *Multiple Plans.* Adjustments for Additional Benefits and Benefit Forms.

10 Death Benefits and Other Incidental Benefits — 99

Required Spousal Death Benefits: *Qualified Joint-and-Survivor Annuity. Preretirement Survivor Annuity. Subsidizing Survivor Annuities.*

Employee Death Benefit Planning. Incidental Death Benefits: *Coordination of Death Benefits. Survivorship Benefits. Designing Incidental Death Benefits.* Disability Benefits from Qualified Plans: *Disability Benefit for Smaller Employers.* Medical Benefits from Qualified Plans.

11 Funding a Pension Plan   107

Actuarial Methods and Assumptions. Basic Pension Calculations: *Annuity Purchase Rate. Present Value. Installment Savings (Level Funding).* Actuarial Cost Methods: *Basic Principles and Terminology. Amortization of Past Service Cost (Supplemental Liability). Actuarial Assumptions. Choosing Actuarial Assumptions. Some Specific Permissible Actuarial Cost Methods. Choosing an Actuarial Cost Method. Ongoing Actuarial Valuations.* Minimum Funding Standards: *Exemptions from Minimum Funding Standard.* Deductibility of Pension Plan Contributions: *Timing of Deductions.* Summary: *Actuarial Cost Methods. Minimum Funding Standards. Tax Deductions.*

12 Qualified Plan Funding Instruments   132

Funding Agencies and Instruments. Trusts. Insurance Contracts: *Allocated and Unallocated Funding in Insurance Contracts.* Insurance Contracts Using Allocated Funding: *Individual Life Insurance and Annuity Contracts. Group Permanent Contract. Group Deferred Annuity Contract.* Insurance Contracts Using Unallocated Funding: *Group Deposit Administration (DA) Contract. Immediate Participation Guarantee (IPG) Contract. Current Trends in Insurance Contracts for Pension Funding.* Separate Accounts Funding and New Money: *Separate Accounts. New Money. Specialized Insurance Products for Pension Funding.*

13 Profit-Sharing and Savings Plans   146

"Nonretirement" Qualified Plans. Qualified Profit-Sharing Plans: *Eligibility and Vesting. Employer Contribution Provision. Allocations to Employee Accounts. Forfeitures. Integration with Social Security. Deduction of Employer Contributions. Section 415 Limits. Investment Earnings and Account Balances. Participant-Directed Investments. Withdrawals during Employment and Loan Provisions. Incidental Benefits.* Savings Plans: *Mandatory and Voluntary Contributions. Design of Savings Plans. Advantages and Disadvantages of Savings Plans.*

14 401(k) Plans   159

General Characteristics: *Advantages and Disadvantages.* Major Types of 401(k) Plan Design: *Pure Salary Reduction Plan. Bonus 401(k) Plan. 401(k) Thrift Plan. Other Possibilities.* Coverage Requirements. Vesting of Employee Accounts. Limit of $7,000 on Elective Deferrals.

Actual Deferral Percentage Tests: *Designing a Plan to Meet the ADP Tests. Distribution Restrictions. Investments by 401(k) Plans. Social Security and Employment Taxes. 401(k) Plans as Tax Shelters for Small Business Owners.*

15 Stock-Bonus Plans and ESOPs — 171

Using Employer Stock in Qualified Plans: *Advantages of Investing in Employer Stock.* Types of Plans: *Stock-Bonus Plan. Employee Stock-Ownership Plan (ESOP).* Creating a Market for Closely Held Stock: *Tax Benefits for Shareholder Sales to ESOPs.* Stock Valuation.

16 Qualified Plan Distributions and Loans — 182

Designing Distribution Provisions: *Normal Form of Benefit. Optional Alternative Forms of Benefit. Distribution Restrictions.* Federal Taxation of Distributions: *Payment over More than One Taxable Year. Payment in One Taxable Year. Taxation of Death Benefits from Qualified Plans. Excess Distribution Tax. Federal Estate Tax.* Qualified Domestic Relations Orders. Loans from Qualified Plans: *Limits on Loan Amount. Terms of Loans. Should the Plan Permit Loans?*

17 Plan Investments — 199

Fiduciary Requirements of ERISA and the Internal Revenue Code: *Prohibited Transactions.* Unrelated Business Income. Investment Policy: *Investment Vehicles. Investment Strategy.*

18 Plan Restrictions Aimed at Highly Compensated Employees — 210

Significance of the Restrictions Discussed Here. Limitations on Individual Benefits or Annual Additions (Section 415 Limits): *Defined-Benefit Plans. Defined-Contribution Plans. Combined Limit.* Top-Heavy Plans: *Ceiling on Compensation. Additional Vesting Requirements for Top-Heavy Plans. Minimum Benefit Requirements. Modification of Section 415 Combined Fraction. Effect of Top-Heavy Rules on Integration.* Qualified Plans for Owners of Unincorporated Businesses. Early Termination Rule for 25 Highest-Paid Employees. Federal Estate Tax Treatment of Qualified Plan Benefits. Excess Distribution and Excess Accumulation Penalties.

19 Qualified Plan Installation — 226

Plan Installation: Its Role in the Process. Steps in Plan Installation: *Adoption of the Plan. Plan Year.* Advance Determination Letter. Master, Prototype, and Pattern Plans.

Contents **xvii**

20 Plan Administration   **232**

Who Administers a Plan. Administrative Forms and Procedures: *Forms and Procedures for Typical Profit-Sharing Plan. Other Procedures.* ERISA Reporting and Disclosure and Other Requirements: *Plan Administrator. Claims Procedure. Reporting and Disclosure.* Accounting for Pension Plans: *Employers' Accounting for Pensions. Plan Accounting.*

21 Plan Termination   **241**

Plan Termination: *When Should a Plan Be Terminated? Premature Termination. Other Types of Termination.* The Pension Benefit Guaranty Corporation (PBGC) and Its Plan Insurance: *Plans Covered. Benefits Insured. PBGC Funding and Premiums. Plan Termination Procedures.*

22 Individual Retirement Plans and Simplified Employee Pensions   **251**

Individual Retirement Plans: *Historical Ups and Downs. Eligibility for IRAs. Deduction Limit. Spousal IRAs. Nondeductible IRAs. Other Restrictions. Excess Contributions. Timing of Contributions. Limitations on IRA Distributions. Taxation of Distributions. Funding of IRAs. Rollovers. Employer-Sponsored IRAs.* Simplified Employee Pensions: *Eligibility and Coverage. Contributions and Deductions. Salary Reduction SEPs. Other Requirements. When Should an Employer Use a SEP?*

23 Special Plans for Tax-Exempt and Government Employers   **264**

Section 403(b) Tax-Deferred Annuity Plans: *Eligible Employers. The Annual Exclusion Allowance. Salary Reduction Plans. Catch-Up Alternatives. Types of Investments for 403(b) Plans. Distributions and Loans from Section 403(b) Plans. Taxation of Section 403(b) Plans. Regulatory and Administrative Aspects.* Section 457 Deferred-Compensation Plans for Governmental Employees: *Other Rules.*

24 Qualified Plan Design to Maximize Benefits for Key Employees   **274**

Planning to Maximize Benefits. Maximizing Benefits from Defined-Benefit Plans: *Conservative Actuarial Assumptions. Normal Retirement Age. Normal Form of Benefit. Using Life Insurance.* Maximizing Defined-Contribution Plan Benefits: *Plan Coverage: Comparable Plans. Leased Employees. Combinations of Defined-Benefit and Defined-Contribution Plans.*

25 Nonqualified Executive Retirement Benefits   **288**

How Nonqualified Plans Are Used. Overview of Nonqualified Plan Design: *Overall Design. Contribution and Benefit Formulas. Funding and Informal Funding.* Designing the Plan: *Employer versus Employee Objectives. Defined-Contribution and Defined-Benefit Formulas. Form of Benefits. Termination Payments.* Funded and Unfunded Plans. Tax Issues in Plan Design: *Constructive Receipt. Economic Benefit. Reasonable Compensation. Taxation of Benefits and Contributions. Employer's Tax Treatment. Impact of ERISA and Other Regulatory Provisions.*

Appendix A	Pre-1989 Coverage, Vesting, and Integration Rules	299
Appendix B	Controlled Groups, Affiliated Service Groups, and Employee Leasing	312
Bibliography		321
Index		323

1
Retirement Needs of Employees

Objectives of This Chapter
- *Analyze potential sources of retirement income to evaluate the degree of need for private pension coverage.*
- *Discuss the factors involved in determining the needed level of retirement income.*

● Retirement plans, like health and accident plans, are a widespread employee benefit because they meet a fundamental economic need of employees. In an industrial society, the social and economic status of most individuals is directly related to work. Most people must support themselves and maintain their social status either through earnings from work or, after retirement, from earnings put aside during prior working periods. Because of the close linkage of retirement income sources with the employment relationship, it is natural that employers' compensation policies would tend toward helping employees meet this need.

Sources of Retirement Income

Information concerning the sources of income available to retirees is important in the design of both private plans and government programs, and in financial planning for individuals as well. Four sources of retirement income can be easily identified: earnings from employment, social security, private savings, and private (employer) retirement plans. The significant issues from the standpoint of this text are which retirees can count on income from these sources and how much income, if any, is available to them from such sources.

Earnings from Employment

Before the mid-20th century when private retirement plans were rare and government programs (in the United States, at least) were virtually nonexistent, the predominant source of income for persons past 65 was employment earnings. The importance of employment for retirees has declined since then, but, as Figure

FIGURE 1-1. Changing Composition of Family Income
(Family Head Age 65*; 1968-1980)

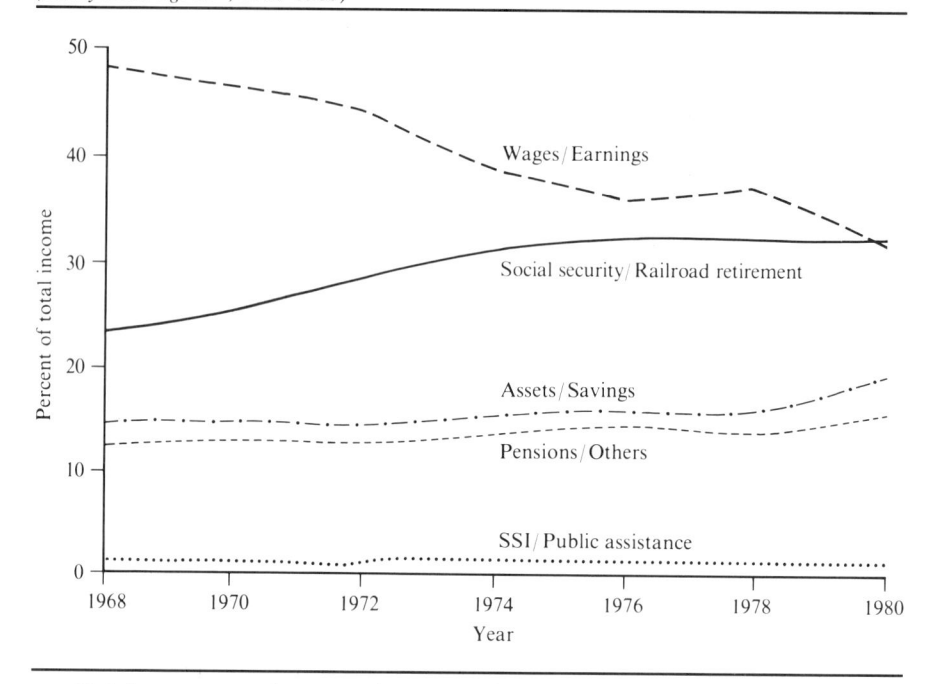

[Line chart showing percent of total income from 1968 to 1980 for: Wages/Earnings (declining from ~48% to ~32%), Social security/Railroad retirement (rising from ~23% to ~32%), Assets/Savings (~15%), Pensions/Others (~12-15%), SSI/Public assistance (~1-2%)]

*Includes veteran, unemployment, workers compensation, annuities, and alimony.

Source: Congressional Research Service. Special Tabulation from U.S. Bureau of the Census. Current Population Surveys, 1968-1980.

1-1 shows, as recently as 20 years ago earnings from work was considerably more significant than it is today.

The health of persons past 65 has improved in recent decades, which would tend to suggest that older people would be increasingly likely to work past 65.[1] Improvements in the federal age-discrimination law (see Chapter 8), particularly since 1978 with the general prohibition of mandatory retirement, also would seem to have created greater opportunities for older people to work. However, since such employment has actually declined, other factors apparently predominate.

First, nonemployment income for older people, particularly from social security, has risen and thus presumably created a corresponding disincentive to work. Also, the favorable factors for employment of older people probably have not been able to overcome the overall social trend favoring relatively early retirement. Employers generally encourage retirement to replace retirees with younger, lower-paid workers. And American society tends to be biased against older people

---

[1]See, for example, *Report of the Special Committee on Aging, United States Senate*, Rept. 98-360, 98th Cong. 2d. Sess. (hereafter cited as *Senate Aging Committee Report*) 1 (1983), pp. 353-54.

working, particularly in full-time jobs, and formal age-discrimination laws cannot prevent the manifold informal methods of forcing out older workers or failing to hire them.

Social Security

The retirement benefits of the federal OASDI program—which will be referred to generally in this text as social security benefits—are an extremely important factor in retirement planning from any standpoint. These benefits currently account for about 30 percent of the income of families headed by persons over 65 (see Figure 1–1). Social security benefits are covered in detail in Chapter 2 of this text.

Some significant points about the social security benefit should be noted here. First, the benefit was never designed to provide 100 percent of retirement income needs for all retirees. Furthermore, in light of the well-publicized problems of financing social security benefits, it is virtually certain that these benefits will not be increased to the point where they provide full retirement income for the majority of persons. Second, the social security system has only recently matured—that is, only recently have persons begun to retire who are life-long contributors to the system, which was originally installed in the late 1930s. Thus, it is reasonable to anticipate a flattening out of the relative contribution to retirement income attributable to social security. Finally, although many people may view social security as a kind of personal savings account to which they have contributed and anticipate withdrawals upon retirement, in fact the system is a political phenomenon. The political nature of social security has important implications; for example, it is reasonably likely that the benefits will not be drastically cut back in the foreseeable future, because they are very popular politically. On the other hand, since the social security tax is also politically determined, the benefits and costs of social security will always be in a state of tension that is continually subject to political debate and rebalancing by the political system. For example, the "baby-boom" generation born in 1946–1960 is a larger group than the succeeding generation; and when the baby-boomers retire, the ratio of workers to retirees will drop, resulting in pressures to reduce benefits to reduce the burden of the payroll tax.

Savings

Despite a relatively low historical and current rate of savings in the United States, compared with many other developed countries, income from savings, or asset income, is an important component of income for retirees.[2] As Table 1–1 indicates, asset income provides about one third of the total money income of elderly households earning $20,000 or more annually and even contributes somewhat (4 percent of income in Table 1–1) to the income of households with less than $5,000 of annual income.

---

[2]*Senate Aging Committee Report* 1 (1983), pp. 238–39.

TABLE 1–1. Asset Income Distribution among Aged Units, 1980

		Level of Total Money Income			
Item	All Units	Less than $5,000	$5,000- $9,999	$10,000- $19,999	$20,000 or More
Percent of units with asset income	66	38	72	89	97
Percent of all units relying on assets for 50 percent or more of total income	9	2	6	14	27
Percent of units with assets and relying on assets for 50 percent or more of total income	13	6	8	16	28
Share of aggregate income provided by assets	22	4	14	21	34

Source: *Social Security Bulletin*, January 1983.

Individual savings are particularly important for upper-income persons in maintaining a high standard of living after retirement, because there are upper limits on the potential income from both social security and private qualified employer retirement plans. The social security system provides no additional benefit credit for people who earn more than the social security taxable wage base in a given year. This wage base ($43,800 for 1987) is relatively high compared to historical levels, but is much lower than the salaries of top executives and professionals. Qualified retirement plans generally cannot pay out a pension greater than $90,000 annually (see Chapter 18). This $90,000 limit is subject to cost-of-living indexing for persons retiring in 1988 and thereafter.

Social trends and tax and other government policies generally provide a disincentive to savings in the United States. However, the impact of taxes on savings is somewhat mixed. Income from savings and investments is generally taxed, even though not withdrawn by the taxpayer for current consumption. On the other hand, income in the form of capital appreciation is not currently taxed. Another exception to the unfavorable taxation of investment earnings applies to qualified retirement plans and IRAs, as will be discussed at length in this book. Finally, ownership of a personal residence is subject to significant tax subsidy, which is almost unknown in other countries.

For a personal residence, interest on mortgage indebtedness used to finance the purchase of the dwelling is fully tax deductible. Local property taxes are also deductible as itemized deductions. In addition, the rental value of an owner-occupied dwelling is not treated as taxable income. Most people are not aware that this is a tax benefit, but its value can be recognized immediately by comparing the tax situation of a homeowner with that of a person who invests money equal to the cost of the home in other forms of investment and rents a dwelling unit. The latter, though identically situated objectively, pays substantially higher taxes. Home ownership is even further encouraged by a provision that allows a homeowner to sell a home and reinvest the proceeds within 18 months in a new personal residence without paying capital gain taxes. Finally, to cap it all off, the tax law completely exempts the first $125,000 of capital gain from taxation when a homeowner over the age of 55 sells the residence.

The tax subsidy of home ownership obviously draws money away from consumption or investment in other assets. The implications of this for retirement income adequacy are not entirely clear. To the extent that the subsidy encourages saving that would not otherwise take place, it is helpful after retirement. And, of course, home ownership reduces out-of-pocket housing costs if the owners continue to reside in the home after retirement. However, if the owners do not sell the residence after retirement, asset values in excess of those needed to cover housing costs cannot be withdrawn (although arrangements to do this, such as the "reverse mortgage," have been developed.)[3]

Home ownership even in recent years is limited to about two thirds of the U.S. elderly population, which is a high figure by world standards but nevertheless excludes a large number of people.[4] Also, many of these residences have a low asset value; a 1979 survey showed average equity in homes for those over 65 owning homes to be about $40,000.[5]

Private Retirement Plans

Retirement plans provided by private employers in the United States began developing in the late 19th century. This development coincided with the transition then taking place in the work force from agricultural to industrial. It is reasonable to draw a connection between these events; in an agricultural economy, workers do not retire until disabled, and then typically are cared for by the family, so there is no need for formal retirement programs. Industrial workers, however, must make provision out of their earnings at work to cover nonworking periods, and this need clearly has been a major factor in the expansion of employer plans.

By the 1920s, employer arrangements were common enough that it was deemed appropriate to include special provisions in the Revenue Acts of 1921 and 1926 to provide specific tax benefits for such plans. The original provision, like the present law, permitted employers a current deduction for contributions to pension trust funds set up to pay pension benefits to employees who retired in the future. As private retirement plans continued to grow, the tax benefits provided to them have continued. The growth of private plans and governmental policy in this area have been intertwined since then, as discussed in Chapter 3.

Private retirement plan coverage is substantial—56 percent of nonagricultural workers, according to a recent survey.[6] Lower-income persons are more likely to

---

[3]See K. Scholen and Y-P Chen, eds., *Unlocking Home Equity for the Elderly* (Cambridge, Mass.: Ballinger, 1980).

[4]Friedman and Sjogren, "Assets of the Elderly as They Retire," *Social Security Bulletin,* January 1981.

[5]*Senate Aging Committee Report* 1 (1983), p. 244.

[6]Employee Benefit Research Institute, *New Survey Findings on Pension Coverage and Benefit Entitlement,* August 1984.

be covered in an employer plan than to have substantial savings income.[7] Private plans thus have an important and continuing role in providing retirement income for a broad spectrum of employees. It is generally anticipated that this role will increase in the future; one study predicts that 77 percent of families will receive an employer pension benefit in 2004.[8] The same study predicts an increase in average private benefits up to about one third of retirement income (compared with the current level of about 15 percent of retirement income—see Figure 1–1).[9]

Income Needs after Retirement

Private plan designers, financial planners for individuals, and government policy specialists generally use the same standard of postretirement income adequacy—the maintenance after retirement of the retiree's preretirement standard of living, at least in the period immediately after retirement. In designing social insurance programs, some policy specialists amend this to assert that at least a minimum standard of living should be guaranteed the elderly, regardless of their preretirement living standard.

Retirees generally do not need 100 percent of their preretirement income to maintain their standard of living after retirement. Many postretirement expenses tend to be reduced from preretirement levels:

> Federal, state, and local taxes are generally lower for the retirees, either because of specific relief provisions in the tax law (such as the additional standard deduction for persons over 65 or the tax exemption for most social security benefits) or because the lifestyles of older people tend to attract less taxation—for example, reduced consumption reduces state sales taxes.
> Work-related expenses, such as commuting and specialized clothing, are lower (or nonexistent) for retirees.
> Savings needs are reduced, so more income is available for living expenses.

Table 1–2 shows the results of some recent calculations of income replacement needs for retirees of various income levels. The last column in Table 1–2 shows the desired ratio of private pension and social security benefits together to the preretirement income; this amount is sometimes referred to as the *replacement ratio*.

As Table 1–2 indicates, the calculated replacement ratios for purposes of designing private pension and social security coverage are lower for high-income retirees. The most significant reason for this is that income from savings is expected to be higher for high-income retirees. Table 1–3 shows the effect of this savings factor by itself. Another reason for the lower replacement ratio is the

---

[7]Sophie M. Korczyk, *Retirement Security and Tax Policy* 65–66, Washington, D.C.: Employee Benefit Research Institute, 1984.

[8]*Future Retirement Benefits under Employer Retirement Plans*, Prepared for the American Council of Life Insurance 40–45, Washington, D.C.: ICF Incorporated, 1984.

[9]Ibid., 45, Table IV–3.

TABLE 1-2. Retirement Income Equivalent to Preretirement Income for Married Couples Retiring in 1980
(Selected Income Levels)

Gross Preretirement Income	Preretirement Taxes Federal*	Preretirement Taxes State Local†	Disposable Income	Reduction in Expenses at Retirement Work-Related Expenses‡	Reduction in Expenses at Retirement Savings	Reduction in Expenses at Retirement Investments	Net Preretirement Income	Post-retirement Taxes§ Federal Income	Post-retirement Taxes§ State Local†	Equivalent Retirement Income Dollars	Equivalent Retirement Income Ratio
$ 6,500	$ 549	$ 29	$ 5,922	$ 355	0%	$ 0	$ 5,567	0	0	$ 5,567	.86
10,000	1,311	133	8,556	513	3	251	7,786	0	0	7,786	.78
15,000	2,550	310	12,140	728	6	728	10,684	0	0	10,684	.71
20,000	3,968	520	15,512	931	9	1,396	13,185	0	0	13,185	.66
30,000	6,986	1,061	21,950	1,317	12	2,634	17,999	53	10	18,062	.60
50,000	15,202	2,622	32,176	1,931	15	4,826	25,419	1,651	314	27,384	.55

*Federal income and social security (OASDHI) taxes.
†Based on state and local 1978 income tax receipts, which were 19 percent of federal income tax receipts. Does not include property taxes.
‡Estimated as 6 percent of disposable income.
§Postretirement taxes are on income in excess of social security benefits, which are nontaxable. Retirees without social security benefits would need higher replacement ratios.
Source: Preston C. Bassett, consulting actuary, President's Commission on Pension Policy, 1980.

TABLE 1–3. Target Replacement Ratios with and without Consideration of Preretirement Savings

Gross Income	With Savings	Without Savings
$ 7,500	73%	73%
10,000	70	70
12,500	65	68
15,000	60	68
17,500	55	69
20,000	51	70
25,000	51	71
30,000	50	71
40,000	51	71

Source: Howard Winklevoss and Dan McGill, *Public Pension Plans, Standards of Design, Funding, and Reporting* (Homewood, Ill.: Dow Jones-Irwin, 1979), Table 2–5, p. 40.

progressive tax rates, which make the proportionate tax savings after retirement greater for high-income persons. Finally, basic subsistence expenses for food and shelter are approximately the same for all retirees and, thus, are less as a proportion of preretirement income for higher-income retirees.

Effect of Inflation

The preceding discussion has essentially focused on retirement income in the period immediately after retirement. Without inflation, this amount would continue to have the same value indefinitely. However, inflation is a persistent worldwide feature of the post–World War II economy, though inflation rates vary widely in time and among various countries. Table 1–4 gives an idea of the seriousness of this problem; consider that people who retire at 65 can expect to survive for another 15 years or so, and that inflation rates of 10 percent have not been unheard of in recent years.

TABLE 1–4. Real Value of Retirement Income Based on Initial Replacement Rate of 100 Percent

Years in Retirement	No Inflation	3 Percent Annual Inflation	5 Percent Annual Inflation	10 Percent Annual Inflation
0	100	100	100	100
5	100	86	78	62
10	100	74	61	39
15	100	64	48	24
20	100	55	38	15
25	100	48	34	9

Source: Robert Clark, *The Role of Private Pensions in Maintaining Living Standards in Retirement* (Washington, D.C.: National Planning Association, October 1977), p. 42.

Private savings can generally be invested to reduce the impact of inflation. And social security benefits are currently indexed so they maintain their value. Also, any income from employment after retirement will generally be at current wage levels reflecting inflation. The inflation problem, thus, is most serious in the component of retirement income that comes from private retirement plans. Some of the methods used in designing benefit formulas to reflect this problem are discussed in Chapter 8.

Summary

Retirees can look for retirement income to one or more of: earnings from employment, social security, personal savings, and private employer-sponsored retirement plans. Employment earnings at older ages have declined in recent years. Social security is not designed to provide full retirement income, except for the poorest people. Personal savings are most important for the upper-income group. These factors define the role of the private employer-sponsored plan in providing retirement income.

An adequate retirement income generally means an income that allows the retiree to maintain preretirement living standards. Full replacement income is not required for a variety of reasons; the level of replacement income is an important factor in private plan design. Inflation must also be considered in this context.

2

Social Security Retirement Benefits

Objectives of This Chapter
- *Explain the extent of coverage under the social security program, and identify the categories of persons who are not covered.*
- *Explain how OASDI benefits are financed.*
- *Explain the eligibility requirements necessary for OASDI benefits.*
- *Describe the types of benefits available under the OASDI program.*
- *Describe the process by which OASDI benefits are calculated.*
- *Explain how OASDI benefits are taxed.*

● The proper design of any retirement plan takes into consideration the benefits that are provided by social security. When most people use the term *social security*, they are actually referring to the old-age, survivors', disability, and health insurance (OASDHI) program of the federal government. OASDHI is one of several programs resulting from the Social Security Act of 1935 and its frequent amendments over the years. The act established four programs aimed at providing economic security for the American society:

1. Old-age insurance.
2. Unemployment insurance.
3. Federal grants for assistance to certain needy groups: the aged, the blind, and children.
4. Federal grants for maternal and child welfare, public health work, and vocation rehabilitation.

This chapter was prepared by Burton T. Beam, Jr., CLU, CPCU, and is an adaptation of material that originally appeared in Beam and McFadden, *Employee Benefits* (Homewood, Ill.: Richard D. Irwin, 1985).

The old-age insurance program and the benefits that have been added to that program comprise what we now call "social security." These additional benefits include survivors' insurance (1939), disability insurance (1956), hospital insurance (1965), and supplementary medical insurance (1965). The latter two parts of social security comprise medicare and are often referred to as Part A and Part B, respectively.

The primary purpose of this chapter is to describe the retirement benefits available under social security. However, retirement plans may also provide death benefits and disability benefits. Therefore, the survivors' benefits and disability benefits available under social security are also discussed. All of these benefits comprise what is commonly referred to as old-age, survivors', and disability insurance, or OASDI. Medicare—the health insurance (HI) portion of the social security program—is beyond the scope of this chapter.

Extent of Coverage

Over 90 percent of the workers in the United States are in covered employment under the social security program and ultimately will be eligible for retirement benefits. This means that these workers have wages (if they are employees) or self-employment income (if they are self-employed) on which social security taxes must be paid. The following are the major categories of workers who are not covered under the program or who are covered only if they have met specific conditions:

> Civilian employees of the federal government who were employed by the government *prior to 1984* and who are covered under the Civil Service Retirement System or certain other federal retirement programs. These workers are covered by government plans that provide benefits similar to those available under social security. Coverage for new civilian federal employees under the entire program was one of the most significant changes resulting from the 1983 amendments to the Social Security Act. (It should be noted, however, that *all* federal employees have been covered under social security for purposes of medicare since 1983.)
> Railroad workers. Under the Railroad Retirement Act, employees of railroads have their own benefit system, which is similar to OASDI.
> Employees of state and local governments, unless the state has entered into a voluntary agreement with the Social Security Administration. Under such an agreement the state may either require that employees of local governments also be covered or allow the local governments to decide whether to include their employees. In addition, the state may elect to include all or only certain groups of its employees under the program. Prior to 1984, states and local government units were allowed to withdraw their employees from social security coverage. However, once employees are covered, this withdrawal privilege is no longer available.
> American citizens working abroad for foreign affiliates of U.S. employers, unless the employer owns at least a 10 percent interest in the foreign affil-

iate and has made arrangements with the Secretary of the Treasury for the payment of social security taxes.

Ministers who elect out of coverage because of conscience or religious principles.

Workers in certain jobs, such as student nurses, newspaper carriers under age 18, and students working for the school at which they are regularly enrolled or doing domestic work for a local college club, fraternity, or sorority.

Certain family employment. This includes the employment of a child under age 21 by a parent or employment of a married person by his or her spouse. This exclusion, however, does not apply if the employment is for a corporation owned by a family member.

Certain workers who must satisfy special earnings requirements. For example, self-employed persons are not covered unless they have net annual earnings of $400 or more.

Financing

The OASDI program is financed through a system of payroll and self-employment taxes paid by all persons covered under the program. In addition, employers of covered persons are also taxed.

In 1987, an employee and his or her employer pay a tax of 7.15 percent each on the first $43,800 of the employee's wages. Of this amount, 5.7 percent is for OASDI and 1.45 percent is for the hospital portion of medicare. The tax rate is scheduled by law to increase to 7.65 percent by 1990, but these scheduled changes can be adjusted if Congress so desires. In addition, the wage base is adjusted annually for changes in the national level of wages. Thus, if wage levels increase by 10 percent in a particular year, the wage base for the following year will also increase by 10 percent.

Over the years, both the tax rate and wage base have been dramatically increased to finance increased benefit levels under social security as well as new benefits that have been added to the program. Table 2–1 shows the magnitude of these increases for selected years.

Prior to 1984, the tax rate for self-employed persons was equal to approximately one and one-half times the tax rate for employed persons. Since there were no matching employer contributions, employed persons and their employers were in effect subsidizing the self-employed. Effective in 1984, the tax rate for the self-employed is now equal to the combined employee and employer rates. However, the self-employed are eligible for a decreasing federal income tax credit, so the full impact of the change will not be felt until 1990.

The social security program is essentially based on a system of pay-as-you-go financing with limited trust funds. This means that current payroll taxes and other contributions received by the program are put into trust funds, which are used to pay the current benefits of persons who are no longer paying social security taxes because of death, old age, or disability. This is in direct contrast to private insurance or retirement plans, which are based on advance funding, whereby assets are accumulated from current contributions to pay the future benefits of those making the contributions.

TABLE 2–1. Changes in Tax Rate and Wage Base under Social Security

Year	Wage Base	Tax Rate	Maximum Employee Tax
1950	$ 3,000	1.50%	$ 45.00
1955	4,200	2.00	84.00
1960	4,800	3.00	144.00
1965	4,800	3.65	174.00
1970	7,800	4.80	374.40
1975	14,100	5.85	824.85
1980	25,900	6.13	1,587.67
1981	29,700	6.65	1,975.05
1982	32,400	6.70	2,170.80
1983	35,700	6.70	2,391.90
1984	37,800	7.00	2,532.60
1985	39,600	7.05	2,791.80
1986	42,000	7.15	3,003.00
1987	43,800	7.15	3,131.70
1988–89	*	7.51	
1990 and after	*	7.65	

*Subject to automatic adjustment.

All OASDI payroll taxes are deposited into one of two trust funds: an old-age and survivors' fund and a disability fund. (There are two other trust funds for medicare.) Benefits and administrative expenses are paid out of the appropriate trust fund from contributions to that fund and any interest earnings on excess contributions. The social security program does have limited reserves to serve as emergency funds in periods when benefits exceed contributions, as in times of high unemployment. However, these reserves are relatively small and could pay benefits for only a limited time if contributions to a fund ceased.

In the early 1980s, considerable concern arose over the potential inability of payroll taxes to pay promised benefits in the future. Through a series of changes, the most significant being the 1983 amendments to the Social Security Act, these problems seem to have been solved for the OASDI portion of the program—at least in the short run. The changes approached the problem from two directions. On the one hand, payroll tax rates were increased; on the other hand, some benefits were eliminated and future increases in other benefits were scaled back. However, there is still concern about the medicare portion of the program. In the minds of many experts, some combination of increasing contributions or decreasing benefits will be needed to keep this program viable into the next century.

Eligibility

To be eligible for benefits under OASDI, an individual must have credit for a minimum amount of work under social security. This credit is based on *quarters of coverage*. For 1987, a worker receives credit for one quarter of coverage for each $460 in annual earnings on which social security taxes are paid. However, credit for no more than four quarters of coverage may be earned in any one calendar year. Thus, a worker paying social security taxes on as little as $1,840 (that is, $460 × 4) during the year will receive credit for the maximum four quarters. As in the case of the wage base, the amount of earnings necessary for a quarter of coverage is adjusted annually for changes in the national level of wages.

Quarters of coverage are the basis for establishing an insured status under OASDI. The three types of insured status are fully insured, currently insured, and disability insured.

Fully Insured

A person is fully insured under OASDI if either of two tests is met. The first test requires credit for 40 quarters of coverage. Once a person acquires such credit, he or she is fully insured for life even if covered employment under social security ceases.

Under the second test, a person who has credit for a minimum of six quarters of coverage is fully insured if he or she has credit for at least as many quarters of coverage as there are years elapsing *after* 1950 (or *after* the year in which age 21 is reached, if later) and *before* the year in which he or she dies, becomes disabled, or reaches age 62, whichever occurs first. Thus, a worker turning age 62 in 1987 would need credit for only 36 quarters of coverage to be fully insured for retirement purposes, even if retirement takes place at a later age. Similarly, a worker who reached age 21 in 1977 and who dies in 1987 would need credit for only nine quarters of coverage to be fully insured for purposes of survivors' benefits.

Currently Insured

If a worker is fully insured under OASDI, there is no additional significance to being currently insured. However, if a worker is not fully insured, certain survivors' benefits are still available if a currently insured status exists. To be currently insured, it is only necessary that a worker have credit for at least 6 quarters of coverage out of the 13-quarter period ending with the quarter in which death occurs.

Disability Insured

To receive disability benefits under OASDI, it is necessary to be disability-insured. At a minimum, a disability-insured status requires that a worker (1) be fully insured and (2) have a minimum amount of work under social security within a recent time period. In connection with the latter requirement, workers aged 31 or older must have credit for at least 20 of the 40 quarters ending with the quarter in which disability occurs; workers between the ages of 24 and 30, inclusively, must have credit for at least half the quarters of coverage from the time they turned 21 and the quarter in which disability begins; and workers under age 24 must have credit for 6 out of the last 12 quarters, ending with the quarter in which disability begins.

A special rule for the blind states that they are exempt from the recent-work rules and are considered disability insured as long as they are fully insured.

Types of Benefits

As its name implies, the OASDI portion of social security provides three principal types of benefits:

1. Retirement (old-age) benefits.
2. Survivors' benefits.
3. Disability benefits.

Retirement Benefits

A worker who is fully insured under OASDI is eligible to receive monthly retirement benefits as early as age 62. However, the election to receive benefits prior to age 65 results in a permanently reduced benefit.[1] In addition, the following dependents of persons receiving retirement benefits are also eligible for monthly benefits:

> A spouse aged 62 or older. However, benefits are reduced permanently if this benefit is elected prior to the spouse's reaching age 65. This benefit also is available to a divorced spouse under certain circumstances if the marriage lasted at least 10 years.
> A spouse of any age if the spouse is caring for at least one child of the retired worker who is (1) under age 16 or (2) disabled and entitled to a child's benefit as described below. This benefit is commonly referred to as a mother's or father's benefit.
> Dependent, unmarried children under 18. This child's benefit will continue until age 19 as long as a child is a full-time student in elementary or secondary school. In addition, disabled children of any age are eligible for benefits as long as they were disabled before reaching age 22.

It is important to note that retirement benefits, as well as all other benefits under social security, are not automatically paid upon eligibility but must be applied for.

Survivors' Benefits

All categories of survivors' benefits are payable if a worker is fully insured at the time of death. However, three types of benefits are also payable if a worker is only currently insured. The first is a lump-sum death benefit of $255, payable to a surviving spouse living with a deceased worker at the time of death, or, if there

---

[1]Beginning in 2003, the retirement age for nonreduced benefits will gradually be increased until it reaches age 67 in 2027.

is no such spouse, to children eligible for monthly benefits. If neither category exists, the benefit is not paid.

There are two other categories of persons who are eligible for survivors' benefits if a deceased worker was either fully or currently insured at the time of death:

1. Dependent, unmarried children under the same conditions as previously described for retirement benefits.
2. A spouse (including a divorced spouse) caring for a child or children under the same conditions as previously described for retirement benefits.

The following categories of persons are also eligible for benefits, but only if the deceased worker was fully insured:

A widow or widower at age 60. However, benefits are reduced if taken prior to age 65. This benefit is also payable to a divorced spouse if the marriage lasted at least 10 years. In addition, the widow's or widower's benefit is payable to a disabled spouse at age 50 as long as the disability commenced no more than seven years after (1) the worker's death or (2) the end of the year in which entitlement to a mother's or father's benefit ceased.

A parent aged 62 or over who was dependent on the deceased worker at the time of death.

Disability Benefits

A disabled worker under age 65 is eligible to receive benefits under OASDI as long as he or she is disability insured and meets the definition of disability under the law. The definition of disability is very rigid and requires a mental or physical impairment that prevents the worker from engaging in any substantial gainful employment. The disability must also have lasted (or be expected to last) at least 12 months or be expected to result in death. A more liberal definition of disability applies to blind workers who are aged 55 or older. They are considered disabled if they are unable to perform work that requires skills or abilities comparable to those required by the work they regularly performed before reaching age 55 or becoming blind, if later.

Disability benefits are subject to a waiting period and are payable beginning with the sixth full calendar month of disability. In addition to the benefit paid to a disabled worker, the other categories of benefits available are the same as those described under retirement benefits.

As previously mentioned, certain family members not otherwise eligible for OASDI benefits may be eligible if they are disabled. Disabled children are subject to the same definition of disability as workers. However, disabled widows or widowers must be unable to engage in any gainful (rather than substantial gainful) employment.

Eligibility for Dual Benefits

In many cases a person is eligible for more than one type of OASDI benefit. Probably the most common situation occurs when a person is eligible for both a spouse's benefit and a worker's retirement benefit based on his or her own social security record. In this case, and in any other case when a person is eligible for dual benefits, only an amount equal to the highest benefit is paid.

Termination of Benefits

Monthly benefits to any social security recipient cease upon death. When a retired or disabled worker dies, the family members' benefits that are based on the worker's retirement or disability benefits also cease, but the family members then are eligible for survivors' benefits.

Disability benefits for a worker technically terminate at age 65 but are then replaced by comparable retirement benefits. In addition, any benefits payable because of disability cease if the definition of disability is no longer satisfied. However, the disability benefits continue during a readjustment period that consists of the month of recovery and two additional months.

As long as children are not disabled, benefits will usually terminate at age 18 but may continue until age 19 if the child is a full-time student in elementary or secondary school.

The benefit of a surviving spouse terminates upon remarriage unless remarriage takes place at age 60 or later.

Benefit Amounts

With the exception of the $255 lump-sum death benefit, the amount of all OASDI benefits is based on a worker's primary insurance amount (PIA). The PIA, in turn, is a function of the worker's average indexed monthly earnings (AIME) on which social security taxes have been paid.

Calculation of AIME

Even though they may initially seem rather complex, the steps in calculating a worker's AIME are relatively simple. They are outlined below and will be best understood by referring to Table 2–2, which shows the computation of the AIME for a worker who attained age 65 in 1987 and retired.

1. First, list the earnings on which social security taxes were paid for each year beginning with 1951 (or the year in which age 22 was attained, if later) up to and including the year of death or the year prior to disability or retirement.
2. Second, index these earnings by multiplying them by an indexing factor that reflects changing wage levels. The only years that are indexed are those prior to the indexing year, which is the year a worker turned 60 for

retirement purposes or two years preceding the year of death or disability for purposes of survivors' or disability benefits. Therefore, the indexing factor for the indexing year and subsequent years is one. For years prior to the indexing year, the indexing factor for each year is equal to the *average annual covered wages* in the indexing year divided by the average annual covered wages in the year in which earnings are to be indexed. Average annual covered wages are the average wages on which social security taxes were paid. This figure is made available annually by the government for the previous year. In the example, the indexing year is 1982, since that is the year the worker turned age 60. Therefore, the indexing factor for 1981 is 1.05505—because average annual covered wages were $13,773.10 in 1981 and $14,531.34 in 1982.

3. Third, determine the number of years that are to be included in the calculation. For retirement and survivors' benefits the number of years is five less than the minimum number of quarters necessary to be fully insured. For disability benefits, a subtraction may also be made from the minimum number of quarters necessary for fully insured status. This subtraction is five for workers aged 47 or over, four for workers aged 42 through 46, three for workers aged 37 through 41, two for workers aged 32 through 36, one for workers aged 27 through 31, and none for workers under age 27. For survivors' or disability benefits, at least two years must remain. In the example, the worker needs a minimum of 33 quarters to be fully insured, since this is the number of years after 1950 and prior to 1984, which is the year the worker attained age 62. Subtracting 5 from 33 leaves 28 years to be included in the calculation.

4. Fourth, determine the years to be excluded from the calculation. This will be the years with the lowest indexed earnings. Of course, the number of years previously determined must remain. In the example, there are 36 years after 1950 and prior to the year of retirement. Therefore, 8 years can be excluded, leaving the required 28. The appropriately excluded years are 1951–1954 and 1962–1965.

5. Fifth, add the indexed earnings for the years to be included in the AIME calculation and divide the result by the number of months in these years. In the example, the divisor is 336 months, which represents the 28 years of earnings included in the calculation.

As mentioned earlier, the calculation of the AIME for retirement or disability benefits excludes the year in which retirement or disability takes place. However, the indexed earning for that year can be substituted for the lowest year in the calculation if the result will be a larger AIME. For simplicity's sake, it is assumed that the worker in the example retired in January 1987 and had insufficient earnings during the year for the substitution to be beneficial.

Determination of PIA and Monthly Benefits

Once a worker's AIME has been calculated, his or her PIA is determined by applying a formula to the AIME. The PIA is the amount the worker would receive

TABLE 2-2. Calculation of AIME

Year	Covered Earnings	×	Indexing Factor	=	Indexed Earnings	Earnings for Years to Be Included in Calculation
1951	$ 3,000	×	5.19132	=	$15,573.96	excluded
1952	3,200	×	4.88724	=	15,639.17	excluded
1953	3,400	×	4.62864	=	15,737.38	excluded
1954	3,600	×	4.60488	=	16,577.57	excluded
1955	3,800	×	4.40152	=	16,725.78	$16,725.78
1956	4,100	×	4.11378	=	16,866.50	16,866.50
1957	4,200	×	3.99024	=	16,759.01	16,759.01
1958	4,200	×	3.95540	=	16,612.68	16,612.68
1959	4,500	×	3.76870	=	16,959.15	16,959.15
1960	4,800	×	3.62638	=	17,406.62	17,406.62
1961	4,800	×	3.55571	=	17,067.41	17,067.41
1962	4,800	×	3.38615	=	16,253.52	excluded
1963	4,800	×	3.30510	=	15,864.48	excluded
1964	4,800	×	3.17533	=	15,241.58	excluded
1965	4,800	×	3.11917	=	14,972.02	excluded
1966	6,500	×	2.94254	=	19,126.51	19,126.51
1967	6,600	×	2.78728	=	18,396.05	18,396.05
1968	7,400	×	2.60803	=	19,299.42	19,299.42
1969	7,800	×	2.46555	=	19,231.29	19,231.29
1970	7,800	×	2.34899	=	18,322.12	18,322.12
1971	7,800	×	2.23660	=	17,445.48	17,445.48
1972	9,000	×	2.03697	=	18,332.73	18,332.73
1973	10,300	×	1.91702	=	19,745.31	19,745.31
1974	10,900	×	1.80946	=	19,723.11	19,723.11
1975	11,800	×	1.68364	=	19,866.95	19,866.95
1976	13,200	×	1.57496	=	20,789.47	20,789.47
1977	14,100	×	1.48591	=	20,951.33	20,951.33
1978	15,400	×	1.37659	=	21,199.49	21,199.49
1979	16,800	×	1.26586	=	21,266.45	21,266.45
1980	18,500	×	1.16126	=	21,483.31	21,483.31
1981	20,400	×	1.05505	=	21,523.02	21,523.02
1982	21,600	×	1.00000	=	21,600.00	21,600.00
1983	22,700	×	1.00000	=	22,700.00	22,700.00
1984	24,000	×	1.00000	=	24,000.00	24,000.00
1985	25,500	×	1.00000	=	25,500.00	25,500.00
1986	27,500	×	1.00000	=	27,500.00	27,500.00

$$\text{AIME} = \frac{\$556,399.19}{336} = \$1,655 \text{ (rounded to the next lowest dollar)}$$

if he or she retired at age 65 or became disabled in 1987, and it is the amount on which benefits for family members are based. In 1987, a worker who has had average earnings during his or her lifetime can expect a PIA of approximately $600. A worker who has continually earned the maximum income subject to social security taxes can expect a PIA of almost $800 for retirement purposes and a

PIA of between $750 and $950 for purposes of disability and survivors' benefits. The higher PIA occurs for workers who are disabled or die at younger ages.

The formula used for purposes of retirement benefits is the formula for the year in which the worker turned age 62. Therefore, the following 1984 formula would be used for a worker retiring at age 65 in 1986:

90 percent of the first $267 of AIME
plus 32 percent of the AIME in excess of $267 through $1,612
plus 15 percent of the AIME in excess of $1,612

Using this formula the worker in the example with an AIME of $1,665 would have a PIA of $641.30, calculated as follows:

90 percent of $267 = $240.30
plus 32 percent of $1,345 = 430.40
plus 15 percent of $53 = 7.95
$678.60 (rounded to next lowest $.10)

The dollar figures in the formula are adjusted annually for changes in the national level of wages. The formula used to determine survivors' and disability benefits is the formula in existence for the year in which death or disability occurs, even if application for benefits is made in a later year.

If a worker is retired or disabled, the following benefits are paid to family members:

Category	Percentage of Worker's PIA
Spouse aged 65	50
Spouse caring for disabled child or child under 16	50
Child under 18 or disabled	50 (each)

If the worker dies, survivors' benefits are as follows:

Category	Percentage of Worker's PIA
Spouse aged 65	100
Spouse caring for disabled child or child under 16	75
Child under 18 or disabled	75 (each)
Dependent parent	82½ (for one, 75 each for two)

However, the full benefits described above may not be payable, because of a limitation imposed on the total benefits that may be paid to a family. This family maximum will usually be reached if three or more family members (including a retired or disabled worker) are eligible for benefits. The family maximum for purposes of retirement and survivors' benefits can be determined with a formula, which, like the PIA formula, is adjusted annually based on changing wage levels. In the example, the following 1984 formula would be used:

150 percent of the first $342 of PIA
plus 272 percent of the PIA in excess of $342 through $495
plus 134 percent of the PIA in excess of $495 through $643
plus 175 percent of the PIA in excess of $643

The family maximum for purposes of disability benefits is limited to 85 percent of the worker's AIME or 150 percent of the worker's PIA, whichever is lower. However, in no case can the maximum be reduced below the worker's PIA.

If the total amount of benefits payable to family members exceeds the family maximum, the worker's benefit (in the case of retirement and disability) is not affected, but the benefits of other family members are reduced proportionately. For example, assume a worker dies, leaving a spouse under age 65 and three children who are each eligible for 75 percent of his or her PIA of $500. Ignoring the family maximum, the benefits would total $1,500 ($375 for each family member). However, the family maximum, using the above formula, is $923.20 (rounded to the next lowest $.10). Thus, each family member would have his or her benefit reduced to $230 (family benefits are rounded to the next lowest dollar). When the first child loses benefits at age 18, the other family members will have their benefits increased to $307 (ignoring any automatic increases in benefit amounts, including the family maximum). When a second family member loses eligibility, the remaining two family members will receive their full benefit of $375, because the total benefits received by the family will now be less than $923.20.

In addition to the family maximum, several other factors affect the level of monthly benefits.

Special Minimum PIA. There is a minimum PIA for workers who have been covered under OASDI for at least 10 years but at very low wages. This PIA is used only if it is higher than a worker's PIA based on actual wages, which is usually not the case. The benefit is first determined by multiplying $11.50 by the number of years of coverage less 10, subject to a maximum of 20. This figure is then adjusted for the cumulative change in the consumer price index (CPI) since 1979. In 1987, a worker with 30 or more years of coverage will have a minimum PIA at age 65 of approximately $400.

Benefits Taken Early. If a worker elects to receive retirement benefits prior to age 65, benefits are permanently reduced by 5/9 of 1 percent for every month that the early retirement precedes age 65. For example, for a worker who retires at age 62, the monthly benefit will be only 80 percent of that worker's PIA.[2] A spouse who elects retirement benefits prior to age 65 will have benefits reduced by 25/36 of 1 percent per month, and a widow or widower will have benefits reduced by 19/40 of 1 percent per month. In the latter case, benefits at age 60 will

---
[2]This reduction will gradually decrease from 80 percent to 70 percent when the retirement age starts increasing in 2003.

be 71.5 percent of the worker's PIA. If the widow or widower elects benefits at an earlier age because of disability, there is no further reduction.

Delayed Retirement. Workers who delay applying for retirement benefits until after age 65 are eligible for an increased benefit equal to ¼ of 1 percent for each month (or 3 percent per year) of delayed retirement beyond age 65 and up to age 70.[3]

Earnings Test. Benefits are reduced for social security beneficiaries under the age of 70 if they have wages from work that exceed a specified level. The rationale behind having such a reduction tied to wages, referred to as an earnings test, is that social security benefits are intended to replace lost wages but not other income, such as dividends or interest. In 1987, social security beneficiaries aged 65 through 69 are allowed annual wages of $8,160 without any reduction in their benefits. Beneficiaries under age 65 are allowed earnings of $6,000. These figures are also adjusted annually on the basis of national wage levels. If a beneficiary earns in excess of the allowable amount, his or her social security benefit is reduced by $1 for every $2 of excess earnings.[4]

The reduction in a retired worker's benefits resulting from excess earnings is charged against the entire benefits that are paid to a family and based on the worker's social security record. If large enough, this reduction may totally eliminate all benefits otherwise payable to the worker and family members. In contrast, excess earnings of family members are charged against their individual benefits only. For example, a widowed mother who holds a job outside the home may lose her mother's benefit, but any benefits received by her children will be unaffected.

Cost-of-Living Adjustments. OASDI benefits are increased automatically each January as long as there has been an increase in the CPI for the one-year period ending in the third quarter of the prior year. The increase is the same as the increase in the CPI since the last cost-of-living adjustment, rounded to the nearest 0.1 percent.

There is one exception to this adjustment. In any year that the combined reserves of the OASDI trust funds drop below 15 percent of expected benefits (20 percent after 1988), the cost-of-living adjustment will be limited to the lesser of the increase in the CPI or the increase in national wages used to adjust the wage base for social security taxes. When benefit increases have been based on wage levels, future cost-of-living increases can be larger than changes in the CPI to make up for the lower benefit increases in those years when the CPI was not used. However, this extra cost-of-living increase can be made only in years when the reserve is equal to at least 32 percent of expected benefits.

---

[3]Beginning in 1990, this percentage will gradually increase until 2009, when it will be 8 percent per year.

[4]Beginning in 1990, the reduction will be $1 for every $3 of excess earnings for beneficiaries aged 65 through 69 and will remain unchanged for beneficiaries under age 65.

Offset for Other Benefits. Disabled workers under age 65 who are also receiving workers' compensation benefits or disability benefits from certain other federal, state, or local disability programs will have their OASDI benefits reduced to the extent that the total benefits received (including family benefits) exceed 80 percent of their average current earnings at the time of disability. In addition, the monthly benefit of a spouse or surviving spouse is reduced by two thirds of any federal, state, or local government pension that is based on earnings not covered under OASDI.

Taxation of Social Insurance Benefits

Employer contributions to the social insurance programs described in this reading are tax deductible for federal income tax purposes. Any employee contributions must be paid with aftertax dollars.

Until 1984, all social security benefits were received tax-free. Effective in 1984, benefits received under OASDI (and railroad retirement benefits) are subject to taxation but only for recipients with moderately high incomes. The amount of the annual benefit that will be subject to taxation is equal to the *lesser* of (1) one half the social security benefit received or (2) one half the "excess" specified in the Internal Revenue Code. The excess is the amount by which one half of the annual social security benefit raises a recipient's "modified" adjusted gross income above a specified base amount, which is $25,000 for a single individual or $32,000 for a married person filing jointly. For purposes of the tax code, modified adjusted gross income is defined as including a taxpayer's adjusted gross income plus otherwise tax-free interest, such as interest on municipal bonds. For example, assume a single person had a modified adjusted gross income of $22,000 and received $8,000 in social security benefits. Adding one half of the social security benefit to the modified adjusted gross income yields a total amount of $26,000, or an excess of $1,000 over the base amount. One half of this excess is $500. Because it is less than one half of the annual social security benefit, the $500 is the amount subject to taxation.

Summary

The majority of workers are covered under the social security system and will receive benefits at retirement or disability. In addition, benefits will be paid to certain survivors is a worker should die.

Eligibility for benefits is based upon a worker having credit for a minimum number of quarters of coverage. Most benefits require a fully insured status, but some benefits will be paid if a worker is only currently insured. Special eligibility rules apply to disability benefits.

Full retirement benefits are payable at age 65, but reduced benefits are available as early as age 62. The retired worker receives a benefit for himself or herself, and additional benefits may be payable for a spouse and dependent, unmarried children. Benefits will be reduced for earned income above a specified level if a worker is under age 70.

Benefits are a function of the wages on which a retired worker paid social security taxes. Higher benefits generally are paid to persons who have had higher wages, but lower-paid workers receive relatively larger benefits as a percentage of earnings.

The OASDI portion of social security is financed by a wage tax paid equally by covered workers and their employers. Self-employed persons pay a tax equal to the combined employer and employee rates, but they will receive a decreasing tax credit until 1990. Social security taxes are paid into trusts from which benefits are paid. The system is not fully funded and can best be described as pay-as-you-go financing with limited reserves.

For lower-paid workers, social security benefits are free of income taxation. Higher-paid workers may be taxed on as much as one half of their benefit.

3

Introduction to Qualified Plans

Objectives of This Chapter
This chapter is an overview of the qualified plan area, designed to introduce some of the important terminology and put the entire complex area into some perspective. Objectives are:

- *Distinguish qualified plans from other types of deferred compensation.*
- *Describe in general the important characteristics of qualified plans.*
- *Explain the classification of qualified plans (defined-benefit/defined-contribution and pension/profit-sharing).*
- *Introduce the "menu" of specific plan types and their role in designing an employee benefit program.*

General Characteristics of Qualified Plans

As a result of the factors discussed in the first chapter, over the past half-century or so there has been a trend toward employer-sponsored retirement plans as an employee benefit. In effect, such a plan is a kind of forced saving. In an economic sense, the plan puts aside part of the employee's compensation over the employee's working life and defers payment of it until a later date, such as retirement—that is, it is a plan of *deferred compensation.*

To encourage employers to provide retirement plans for employees, the federal government offers tax benefits to a special class of employer-sponsored retirement plans that meet various complex requirements. These plans are known as *qualified* plans. The tax benefits, as discussed below, consist primarily of deferral of the employee's income taxes on the retirement savings until retirement, while allowing the employer a current tax deduction for amounts as they are put into the retirement plan over the employee's working career. Since these tax results cannot generally be achieved in a nonqualified retirement plan, most retirement plans are designed to be qualified. Nonqualified plans are used primarily for executives, as discussed in Chapter 25.

The term *qualified plan* is not susceptible to a simple definition; in a sense, it requires most of this text to provide an adequate definition. Nevertheless, it is helpful to take a brief overall look at the most significant requirements before getting into the details. These requirements are discussed in appropriate detail in subsequent chapters.

Eligibility and Plan Coverage

The plan can have almost any kind of initial eligibility provision, except for specific restrictions on eligibility provisions based on age or service. Generally, no minimum age greater than 21 can be required, nor can more than one year of service be required for eligibility. In addition, the plan *in operation* must generally cover at least 70 percent of all non-highly compensated employees. (These rules have many complex exceptions and limitations, as discussed in Chapter 6.) These rules generally require coverage of a cross section of employees; however employers often are able, within these rules, to exclude high-turnover employees, or design different plans for different groups of employees.

Nondiscrimination in Benefits and Contributions

Generally speaking, a qualified plan may not discriminate, either in plan benefits or employer contributions to the plan, in favor of employees who are *highly compensated*.[1] However, the plan contribution or benefit can be based on the employee's compensation or years of service, which often will provide a higher benefit for certain employees in the prohibited group. In addition, the qualified plan can be so integrated with social security that a greater contribution or benefit is available for higher-paid employees whose compensation is greater than an amount based on the social security taxable wage base. Because of the possibilities for abuse in this area, the rules for social security integration, discussed in Chapter 8, are complex.

Funding Requirements

Generally, a qualified plan must be funded in advance of the employee's retirement. This can be done either through contributions to an irrevocable trust fund for the employee's benefit or under an insurance contract. Although maximum tax benefits result from employer funding, employees also may contribute to the plan in certain plan designs. A plan in which all contributions are made by the employer is called a *noncontributory* plan. A plan permitting employees to contribute is called a *contributory* plan. There are strict limits on the extent to which the employer can exercise control over the plan fund. The fund must be under the control of a *fiduciary*—the legal designation for a person who holds the funds of another—and must be managed solely in the interests of the plan participants and their beneficiaries.

---

[1]There is a lengthy and highly specific statutory definition of highly compensated, Code Section 414(q), that is discussed in Chapter 6.

Vesting Requirements

Under the vesting rules, an employee must be given a nonforfeitable or *vested* benefit at the normal retirement date specified in the plan and, in case of termination of employment prior to retirement, after a specified period of service. For example, one common vesting provision grants a fully vested benefit after the employee has attained five years of service, with no vesting until then. If the plan has this vesting provision, an employee who leaves after, say, four years of service with the employer will receive no plan benefit, even though the employer has put money into the plan on his or her behalf over the four-year period. However, an employee who leaves after five or more years of service will receive the entire plan benefit earned up until that time.

The vesting rules are discussed more fully in Chapter 7. These rules are designed to make it more difficult for employers to deny benefits to employees by selectively discharging or "turning over" employees.

Limitations on Benefits and Contributions

To limit the use of a qualified plan as a tax shelter for highly compensated employees, the Internal Revenue Code (Section 415) contains a limitation on plan benefits or employer contributions, depending on the type of plan. Under these limitations, a plan cannot generally provide an annual pension of more than $90,000 or annual employer contributions of more than $30,000. The limitations are discussed in detail in Chapter 18. Practically speaking, these limits are high enough that only highly compensated participants are likely to encounter them. The dollar limits are scheduled to be adjusted to reflect inflation.

Payout Restrictions

To insure that the qualified plan benefits are used for their intended purposes, there are various restrictions on benefit payments. Certain plans (pension plans in particular) do not allow withdrawals of funds before termination of employment. There is a 10 percent penalty on withdrawal of funds from any qualified plan before early retirement, age 59½, death, or disability, with certain exceptions. Funds cannot be kept in the plan indefinitely; generally, the payout must begin by April 1 of the year after the participant's attainment of age 70½, in specified minimum annual amounts. Loans from the plan to participants are restricted. These rules are discussed further in Chapter 16.

Top-Heavy Rules

To reduce the possibility of excessive discrimination in favor of business owners covered under a qualified plan, special rules are provided for *top-heavy* plans. Basically, a top-heavy plan is one that provides more than 60 percent of its aggregate accumulated benefits or account balances to key employees. A plan that is top-heavy must meet three additional requirements to remain qualified: a special rapid vesting requirement, a requirement of minimum benefits for non-key employees, and a limitation on the compensation that is taken into account for benefit purposes ($200,000 annually, subject to cost-of-living adjustments). See Chapter 18 for further discussion.

Tax Benefits of Qualified Plans

The basic tax advantage of a qualified plan is best understood by comparison with the rules applicable to deferred compensation that is not paid under a qualified plan. As a general rule, the timing of the employer's income tax deduction for compensation of employees depends on when the compensation is included in the employee's income. If the employer puts no money aside in advance to fund the plan, there is no deduction to the employer until the retirement income is paid to the employee, at which time the employee also reports the compensation as taxable income.[2] If the employer puts money aside into an irrevocable trust fund, an insurance contract, or a similar fund for the benefit of the employee, the employer can get a tax deduction as soon as the employee's benefit is vested; but then the employee is also taxed at the same time—that is, there is no tax deferral for the employee.

These rules do *not* apply to a qualified plan. In a qualified plan, the employer obtains a tax deduction for contributions to the plan fund (with specified limits) for the year the contribution is made. Employees pay taxes on benefits when they are received. The combination of an immediate employer tax deduction plus tax deferral for the employee can be obtained only with a qualified plan.

Besides this basic advantage, there are other tax benefits for qualified plans. In total, four advantages are usually identified:

1. The employer gets an immediate deduction, with certain limits, for amounts paid into the plan fund to finance future retirement benefits for employees.
2. The employee is not taxed at the time the employer makes contributions for that employee to the plan fund.
3. The employee is taxed only when plan benefits are received. If the full benefit is received in a single year, it may be eligible for special favorable "lump-sum" income taxation.
4. Earnings on money put aside by the employer to fund the plan are not subject to federal income tax while in the plan fund; thus, the earnings accumulate tax-free.

Table 3–1 gives an example to quantify the value of these tax benefits.

Classification of Qualified Plans

There are two broad classifications of qualified plans. Plans are either pension plans or profit-sharing plans; they also are classified either as defined-benefit or

---

[2]Code Section 404(a)(5).

TABLE 3-1. What a Qualified Plan Can Do—Qualified Plan versus Personal Savings

The following example is an attempt to quantify the advantages of qualified plan coverage to a specific participant. The example involves a high-paid participant who might be, for example, the owner-employee of a closely-held business, and it uses a defined-benefit plan which for older employees, permits the highest possible annual deposits, as discussed in this chapter and Chapter 18.

Facts:
Professional, age 50, married
Wants to retire at 65
Total earnings after business expenses: $200,000
Personal deductions and exemptions: 30,000
Needs for living expenses: 110,000

	Without Plan	With Plan
Gross earnings	$200,000	$200,000
Pension contributions	—	46,275
Current compensation	$200,000	$153,725
Income taxes (federal only)	66,400	43,725
Net "take-home pay"	$133,600	$110,000
Living expenses	110,000	110,000
Personal savings	$ 23,600	$ -0-

At Age 65

	Without Plan	With Plan
Pension accumulation at 10 percent	$ -0-	$1,470,272
Savings accumulation at net 7 percent	593,045	—
Taxes on lump-sum distribution	—	625,986
Net cash after taxes	$593,045	$844,286

Gain for the Qualified Plan: $251,241

---

defined-contribution plans. These broad classifications are useful in identifying the broad overall goals of the employer. Once these have been determined, a specific qualified plan program can be developed for the employer, using one or more of the types of plans from a "menu" of specific plan types. The specific plan types contain a lot of flexibility in design to meet employer needs, and one or more different plans or plan types can be designed covering the same or overlapping groups of employees to provide the exact type of benefits that the employer desires.

Pension and Profit-Sharing Plans

One way of broadly classifying qualified plans is to distinguish between pension plans and profit-sharing plans. A *pension plan* is a plan designed primarily to provide income at retirement. Thus, benefits are generally not available from a pension plan until the employee reaches a specified age, referred to as the *normal retirement age*. Some plans also provide an optional benefit at an earlier age (the *early retirement age*). The design of a pension plan benefit formula must be such that an employee's retirement benefit is reasonably predictable in advance. Because the object of a pension plan is to provide retirement security, the employer must keep the fund at an adequate level. Pension plans are subject to the *minimum funding* rules of the Code, and these generally require the employer to make regular deposits to avoid a penalty, as discussed further in Chapter 11.

By contrast, a *profit-sharing plan* is designed to allow a relatively short-term deferral of income; and it is a somewhat more speculative benefit to the employee, because the employer's contribution can be based on the employer's profits. Furthermore, a profit-sharing plan can provide for a totally discretionary employer contribution; so, even if the employer has profits in a given year, the employer need not make a contribution for that year. The minimum funding rules do not apply. However, there must be substantial and recurring contributions or the plan will be deemed to have terminated.

In a profit-sharing plan, it is difficult to determine the employee's benefit in advance, and the plan is considered more an incentive to employees than a predictable source of retirement income. Because it is not exclusively designed for retirement income, employees may be permitted to withdraw funds from the plan before retirement. The plan may allow amounts to be withdrawn as early as two years after the employer has contributed them to the plan. However, as with any qualified plan, preretirement withdrawals may be subject to a 10 percent penalty. Finally, the deductible employer contribution generally is limited to 15 percent of payroll, an amount less than would usually be deductible under a pension plan.

Defined-Benefit and Defined-Contribution Plans

Qualified plans also are divided into defined-benefit and defined-contribution plans.

A *defined-contribution plan* has an *individual account* for each employee; defined-contribution plans, therefore, are sometimes referred to as individual-account plans. The plan document describes the amount the employer will contribute to the plan, but it does not promise any particular benefit. When the plan participant retires or otherwise becomes eligible for benefits under the plan, the benefit will be the total amount in the participant's account, including past investment earnings on the amounts put into the account. The participant can look only to his or her own account to recover benefits; the participant is not entitled to amounts in any other participant's account. Thus, the participant bears the risk of bad plan investments.

In a *defined-benefit plan,* the plan document specifies the amount of the benefit promised to the employee at normal retirement age. The plan itself does not specify the amount the employer must contribute annually to the plan. The plan's actuary will determine the annual contribution required so the plan fund will be sufficient to pay the promised benefit as each participant retires. If the fund is inadequate, the employer is responsible for making additional contributions. There are no individual participant accounts, and each participant has a claim on the entire fund for the defined benefit. Because of the actuarial aspects, defined-benefit plans tend to be a good deal more complicated and expensive to administer than defined-contribution plans.

Specific Types of Qualified Plans

As Figure 3–1 indicates, within the broad categories (pension, profit-sharing, defined-benefit, defined-contribution) a number of specific types of plans are available to meet various retirement-planning objectives.

Defined-Benefit Pension Plan. All defined-benefit plans are pension plans—that is, they are designed primarily to provide income at retirement. A defined-benefit plan specifies the benefit in terms of a formula, of which there are many different types. Such formulas may state the benefit in terms of a percentage of earnings measured over a specific time, and they also might be based on years of service. For example, a defined-benefit plan might promise a monthly retirement benefit equal to 50 percent of the employee's average monthly earnings over

FIGURE 3–1. Types of Qualified Plans

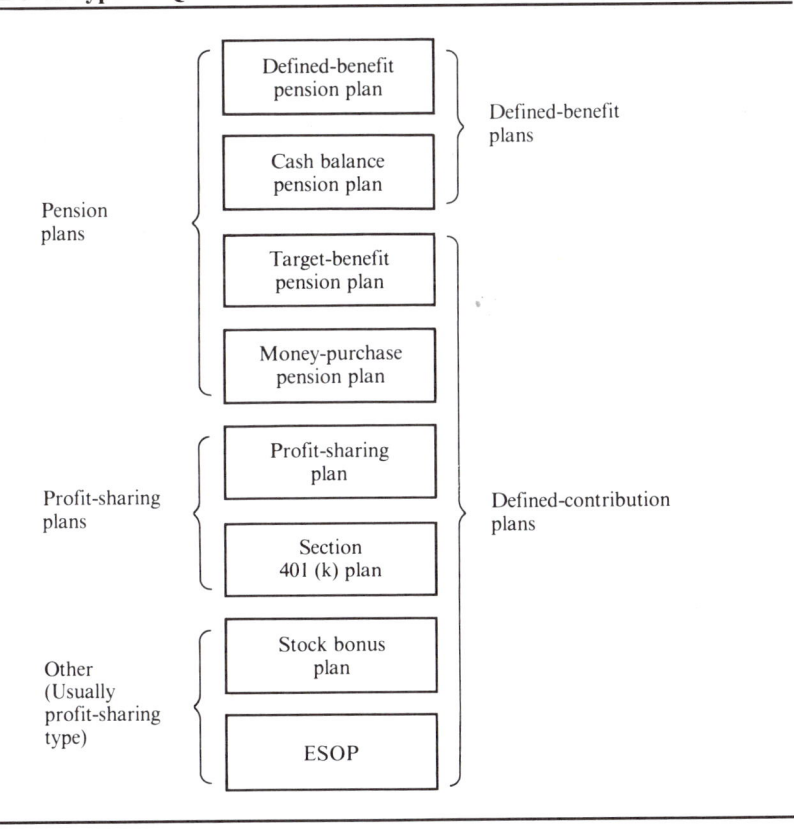

Category	Specific Plan	Grouping
Pension plans	Defined-benefit pension plan	Defined-benefit plans
	Cash balance pension plan	
	Target-benefit pension plan	Defined-contribution plans
	Money-purchase pension plan	
Profit-sharing plans	Profit-sharing plan	
	Section 401(k) plan	
Other (Usually profit-sharing type)	Stock bonus plan	
	ESOP	

the five years prior to retirement. Or, instead of a flat 50 percent, the plan might provide something like 1.5 percent for each of the employee's years of service, with the resulting percentage applied to the employee's earnings averaged over a stated period. Employer contributions to the plan are determined actuarially. Thus, for a given benefit, a defined-benefit plan will tend to result in a larger employer contribution on behalf of employees who enter the plan at older ages, since there is less time to fund the benefit for them.

Cash Balance Pension Plan. In a cash balance plan (also called a guaranteed account plan and various other titles), each participant has an "account" that increases annually as a result of two types of credits: a compensation credit based on the participant's compensation and an interest credit equal to a guaranteed rate of interest. As a result, the participant does not bear the investment risk. Unlike defined-benefit formulas, the plan deposits are not based on age, and younger employees receive the same benefit accrual as those hired at older ages. The plan is funded by the employer on an actuarial basis; the plan fund's actual rate of investment return may be more or less than the guaranteed rate, and employer deposits are adjusted accordingly. Technically, because of the guaranteed minimum benefit, the plan is treated as a defined-benefit plan. From the participant's viewpoint, however, the plan appears very similar to a money-purchase plan, described below.

Target-Benefit Pension Plan. A target plan uses a benefit formula (the "target") like that of a defined-benefit plan. However, a target plan is a defined-contribution plan and, therefore, the benefit consists solely of the amount in each employee's individual account at retirement. Initial contributions to a target plan are determined actuarially, but the employer does not guarantee that the benefit will meet the target level, so the initial contribution level is not adjusted to reflect actuarial experience. Like a defined-benefit plan, a target-benefit plan provides a relatively higher contribution on behalf of employees entering the plan at older ages.

Money-Purchase Pension Plan. A money-purchase pension plan is a defined-contribution plan that is in some ways the simplest form of qualified plan. The plan simply specifies a level of contribution to each participant's individual account. For example, the plan might specify that the employer will contribute each year to each participant's account an amount equal to 10 percent of that participant's compensation for the year. The participant's retirement benefit is equal to the amount in the account at retirement. Thus, the account reflects not only the initial contribution level but also any subsequent favorable or unfavorable investment results obtained by the plan fund. The term *money purchase* arose because, in many such plans, the amount in the participant's account at retirement is not distributed in a lump sum but, rather, is used to purchase a single or joint life annuity for the participant.

Profit-Sharing Plan. As described earlier, the significant features of a profit-sharing plan are that the employer contributions, within limits, are discretionary on the part of the employer and that employee withdrawals before retirement may be permitted. Profit-sharing plans designed to allow employee contributions are sometimes referred to as *savings* or *thrift* plans.

Section 401(k) Plan. A Section 401(k) plan, also termed a *cash or deferred plan,* is a plan allowing employees to choose (within limits) to receive compensation either as current cash or as a contribution to a qualified profit-sharing plan. The amount contributed to the plan is not currently taxable to the employee. Such plans have become popular because of their flexibility and tax advantages. However, such plans must include a number of restrictions that may be burdensome to employer or employees. The most significant restrictions are a requirement of immediate vesting for amounts contributed under the employee election, and restrictions on distribution of these amounts to employees prior to age 59½.

Stock-Bonus Plan. The stock-bonus plan resembles a profit-sharing plan except that employer contributions are in the form of employer stock, rather than cash, and the plan fund consists largely of employer stock.

The fiduciary requirements of the pension law generally forbid an employer from maintaining more than 10 percent of a pension plan fund in the stock of the employer company.[3] This is to prevent the employer from utilizing the plan funds primarily as a means of financing the business, rather than providing retirement security for employees. However, the 10 percent restriction does not apply to profit-sharing or stock-bonus plans. Stock-bonus plans are specifically intended to give employees an ownership interest in the company at relatively low cost to the company. Another tax incentive for this type of plan is that distributions of stock from the plan are taxed favorably; in addition to the regular benefits applicable to distributions from a qualified plan, the net unrealized appreciation of shares of stock in the stock-bonus plan is not taxed at the time of the distribution. Stock-bonus plans are used not only by small employers but also by some relatively large employers.

ESOPs. Employee stock-ownership plans (ESOPs) are similar to stock-bonus plans in that most or all of the plan fund consists of employer stock, and employee accounts are stated in shares of employer stock. However, ESOPs are designed to offer certain special benefits; the employer can use an ESOP as a mechanism for financing the business through borrowing. These plans must meet specific requirements of the Internal Revenue Code.

Plans for Special Types of Organizations

Plans Covering Partners and Proprietors

Under federal tax law, partners and proprietors (sole owners) are not considered to be employees of their unincorporated business, even if they perform substantial

---

[3] ERISA Section 407.

services for the business. (By comparison, shareholders of a corporate business who are employed by the business are considered to be employees for retirement planning and other employee-benefit purposes.) For many years, there were restrictions on the benefits available from a qualified plan to partners or proprietors. Special plans called *Keogh* or *HR–10* plans were used if partners or proprietors were covered. Since 1983, most of these restrictions no longer apply, and qualified plans can cover partners and proprietors on virtually the same terms as regular employees of the business.

S Corporations

An S corporation is a corporation that has made an election to be treated substantially like a partnership for federal income tax purposes. Certain shareholder-employees of S corporations were once subject to qualified plan restrictions similar to those for partners and proprietors; however, after 1983, most of these restrictions do not apply. Thus, S corporation shareholder-employees are now treated basically like regular employees for qualified plan purposes. However, an S corporation employee who owns more than 2 percent of the corporation's stock is treated as a partner for *other* employee-benefit purposes.

Multiple-Employer, Collectively Bargained, and Multiemployer Plans

In this text, if not stated otherwise, it will be assumed that any qualified plan or plans referred to are maintained by a single employer or by a group of related employers. It is possible, however, for more than one employer or related group to participate in a single qualified plan. If such a plan is established under a collective bargaining agreement (as is usually the case), it is referred to as a *collectively bargained plan*. With a collectively bargained plan, the plan is usually designed and maintained by a labor union, and employers who recognize the union as bargaining agent for their employees agree to contribute to the plan on a basis specified in the collective bargaining agreement. If the plan is not the result of a collective bargaining agreement, it is referred to as a *multiple-employer plan*. Such plans might, for example, be maintained by trade associations of employers in a certain line of business. There are special rules for applying the participation and other requirements to these plans.

There are also provisions for a special type of collectively bargained plan, known as a *multiemployer plan* (Section 414(f) of the Code). A multiemployer plan is a plan to which more than one employer is required to contribute and which is maintained under a collective bargaining agreement covering more than one employer; the Department of Labor can also impose other requirements by regulation. Presumably, most large collectively bargained plans will qualify as multiemployer plans. Because of the nature of the multiemployer plan, the funding requirements are somewhat more favorable than for other plans. However, the employer may incur a special liability on withdrawing from the plan, as discussed in Chapter 20.

4

Government Policy and Regulation of Qualified Plans

Objectives of This Chapter
- *Discuss the background to current government regulation of qualified plans.*
- *Describe the policy issues underlying ERISA and ERISA's responses.*
- *Discuss ongoing post-ERISA issues in retirement policy.*
- *Explain the technical mechanisms by which the IRS, the Labor Department, and other governmental entities carry out the regulation of qualified plans.*

Policy Issues and Their Resolution

Throughout history, many governments have had, to one extent or another, policies of maintaining incomes of individuals. In the United States, the federal government had little direct involvement in this area, apart from military pensions, until the 20th century. However, states and localities maintained various relief programs beginning long before that. It has also been a traditional practice to grant exemption from federal and state taxation to charitable private organizations, including those providing retirement or similar benefits. For example, there has long been a federal tax exemption for workmen's benevolent associations that provide health, disability, and similar benefits out of dues voluntarily paid by worker-members; such organizations were important sources of income security before the advent of widespread government and employer programs. Today's federal governmental policy encouraging qualified private pension plans has its origins in that tradition, since the current rules are, in effect, an elaborate type of federal tax exemption.

Federal government support for retirement income currently has two principal aspects: the social security system, and the tax incentives and regulatory measures aimed at private qualified employer plans and individual retirement accounts (IRAs). Social security retirement benefits are discussed in Chapter 2. This chapter and most of this book are devoted to the second aspect of government policy—that related to qualified plans and similar arrangements.

Federal tax benefits to private pension, profit-sharing, and stock-bonus plans began by granting a tax exemption on income from investments of such plans; this was done in the Revenue Acts of 1921 and 1926. Shortly thereafter, in the Revenue Act of 1928, the foundations of the current tax treatment were completed by allowing employers a current tax deduction for contributions to a pension plan to cover future as well as current pension liabilities.[1]

Private retirement plans were in their infancy in the 1920s, involving only about 10 percent of the work force. There were few legal restrictions on early plans, either directly or indirectly through the federal tax laws, and many early plans discriminated in favor of higher-paid employees or were financially unsound. However, in the depression of the 1930s, many plans failed financially and few new plans were started; consequently, interest in corrective pension legislation was then minimal.

The economic recovery beginning with World War II saw a great increase in private employer retirement plans. This was fueled not only by the rising economy but also by wartime wage controls that encouraged noncash compensation arrangements. The step-up in retirement plan activity renewed Congressional interest in these plans and, in the Revenue Act of 1942, various provisions to prevent discrimination—essentially the basic rules as we know them today—were enacted into the tax law.

In the postwar period, retirement plan coverage and plan assets in particular grew to a marked degree. Probably the most important factor was the increase in collective bargaining in those years and the interest by unions in negotiating retirement plans for bargaining units. After a long dispute, the federal courts, in the *Inland Steel* case, finally held in 1949 that employers were obligated to bargain on the issue of retirement benefits.[2] This holding, along with the development of the pooled multiemployer plan fund, vastly increased the growth of collectively bargained plans.[3]

ERISA

By the late 1950s, the magnitude of the private retirement plan system had begun to attract attention to various shortcomings not dealt with adequately by the 1942 tax legislation and by IRS regulatory activity based on that legislation. The most obvious problem apparent at the time was the potential for abuse, mismanagement, and corrupt activities relating to plan funds. The Welfare and Pension Plans Disclosure Act (WPPDA) was enacted in 1958 to require certain financial disclosure by plans to participants and the Department of Labor. The WPPDA was a

---

[1] For a more complete discussion of the legislative history, see Sophie M. Korczyk, *Retirement Security and Tax Policy* (Washington, D.C.: Employee Benefit Research Institute, 1984), pp. 15–18.

[2] *Inland Steel Co. v. NLRB*, 170 F.2d 251 (7th Cir. 1949), cert. denied, 366 U.S. 960 (1949).

[3] A useful brief history of pre-ERISA private pension plan growth is found in U.S. Congress, Senate, Special Committee on Aging, *The Employee Retirement Income Security Act of 1974: The First Decade*, Information Paper pp. 2–25, S. Rep. 98–221, 98th Cong. 2d Sess, 1984.

relatively weak law, however, and did not cover many problem areas unrelated to financial disclosure.

After a long gestation period, during which the problems of the private retirement plan system were debated at length among plan designers and administrators, academics, and legislators, the Employee Retirement Income Security Act of 1974 (ERISA) was enacted by Congress. The fundamental policy issues addressed by ERISA, and ERISA's responses, can be summarized as follows:

Vesting. Under pre-ERISA law, employees who terminated employment before retirement often forfeited all their retirement plan benefits; some studies showed that, because of the mobility of the labor force, only a small percentage of employees who were then covered under a plan would actually receive benefits from that plan. This was deemed both an injustice and an obstacle to desirable work force mobility. ERISA requires the minimum vesting standards, which are discussed in detail in Chapter 7.

Funding. Under pre-ERISA law, there was no requirement that plans be funded in advance. Potentially—and actually in many cases, such as the Studebaker bankruptcy in 1962—employees could be left with no pension benefit if an underfunded plan terminated. ERISA imposed specific minimum funding requirements for pension plans, as discussed further in Chapter 11. ERISA also established a system for federal insurance of pension benefits, to be administered by a new government corporation, the Pension Benefit Guaranty Corporation (PBGC); this is discussed in Chapter 21.

Fiduciary Standards. Despite WPPDA, many abuses in the handling of plan assets occurred in the pre-ERISA era. ERISA attempted to cut back on these by imposing specific federal fiduciary standards on persons handling plan assets; these would be enforceable in federal courts to replace the uncertain state-law remedies formerly available.

Reporting and Disclosure. ERISA greatly expanded the disclosure concept used by WPPDA; various reports both to participants and the government are now required, as described in Chapter 20.

Limitations on Benefits and Contributions. Even prior to ERISA, qualified plan formulas could not discriminate in favor of highly compensated employees. However, formulas that provide benefits or contributions as a uniform percentage of compensation for all employees are not deemed to be discriminatory, and these potentially can provide unlimited amounts for very highly compensated employees. ERISA introduced a set of limits, discussed in Chapter 18, that prevent this.

Post-ERISA Policy Issues

The qualified plan rules have been revised by Congress many times since 1974, though never so comprehensively as in ERISA. These revisions have involved a number of continuing policy issues, which are still subjects of controversy. Because of these issues, the pension rules are frequently changed in major and minor details.

Tax Revenue Loss. At times, revenue-raising needs outweigh retirement policy issues in Congress. The tax benefits for qualified plans cause a substantial apparent decrease in tax revenues. The criticism is also frequently made that too much of the tax benefit goes to high-income individuals who don't need government help.

The 1986 Congressional Special Analysis of the Budget of the U.S. Government indicated a "tax expenditure" of $81 billion for employer plans in 1986. However, only about $20 billion of this is directly attributable to tax deferral for plan contributions by private employers, and the entire Congressional analysis is subject to criticism on accounting and tax policy grounds.[4]

The need to raise revenue has motivated a number of recent changes in the qualified plan law, and it probably will be a factor in future legislation. Revenue-motivated changes are often criticized as resulting in bad retirement policy.

Discrimination in Favor of Highly Compensated Employees. Although a major thrust of virtually all qualified plan legislation since the 1940s has been to discourage employers from discriminating in their plans in favor of highly compensated employees, a considerable amount of such discrimination is still possible, as will be discussed throughout this text. Because of this, much qualified plan legislation has been designed to reduce the "tax shelter" aspects of qualified plans, particularly those for smaller businesses where owner-employees receive substantial benefits. Many of the most complex and awkward provisions of the law, such as the top-heavy rules discussed in Chapter 18, were designed in this vein.

Seemingly, it would be easy to eliminate the discrimination problem by simple, appropriate benefit or contribution limits. However, there is a countervailing policy consideration. Small businesses, collectively, employ a large and increasing segment of the work force. Owners of these businesses may not be interested in maintaining a qualified plan for their employees unless the plan provides substantial, and possibly disproportionate, benefits for the owners themselves. This policy issue, therefore, involves tension between tax-benefit equity and efficiency, on the one hand, and the need to encourage small business retirement plans, on the other. No simple resolution of this is likely in the near future, and complex legislative compromises on this issue will probably continue to emerge from Congress.

Encouraging Private Saving. Private pension funds amount to about $1.3 trillion.[5] Surprisingly, in view of the size of this figure, relatively little policy

---

[4]See Paul H. Jackson, "Pensions as Tax Expenditures: How the Figures Mislead," *Journal of Compensation and Benefits*, January–February 1986.

[5]*EBRI News*, November 13, 1986 (Washington, D.C.: Employee Benefit Research Institute).

emphasis has been given to the role of the qualified plan rules in encouraging private savings, as they very likely do. One problem is that policymakers do not agree on the appropriate level for private savings, nor whether government policy should encourage savings, rather than allowing the free market to set the level. This issue, however, is an ongoing factor in the policy debate.

Interest-Group Pressures. As the foregoing discussion indicates, retirement policy poses difficult problems even if viewed from a neutral intellectual viewpoint. The actual political climate, of course, is not neutral. The qualified plan business is large and involves many firms and individuals. Most of these organizations eagerly and frequently convey their views to Congress in great technical detail. This complicates the resolution of issues and makes change more difficult.

Mandatory Retirement Plan Coverage. A Presidential commission, formed in the late 1970s to study pension policy, recommended the establishment of a Minimum Universal Pension System (MUPS) for all workers, to be funded by employers at an initial rate of at least 3 percent of payroll.[6] The MUPS benefit would be completely portable from job to job. In general, the MUPS approach is not popular with employers and benefit plan designers, who prefer the flexibility of current rules, and Congress is not currently considering it seriously.

Age and Sex Discrimination. Age and sex discrimination have not been addressed by Congress specifically as retirement plan issues. However, recent federal legislative and regulatory activity related to employment discrimination in general has affected retirement plans, as discussed further in Chapter 8.

Application of the Law

The next section of this chapter will discuss how the federal government imposes its policies on qualified plans. The federal rules are the most important, because federal law generally preempts state and local laws in the qualified plan area.

It is important in retirement planning to have a basic understanding of the federal regulatory scheme. There are many stages of planning at which the planner must interpret the significance of various official rules and must interact with governmental organizations. The roles of these governmental rules and organizations must be understood to carry out the planning process.

Federal Tax Law

The most important body of statutory law affecting qualified retirement plans is found in the Internal Revenue Code. The Code is a compilation of the federal tax

---

[6]*Coming of Age: Toward a National Retirement Income Policy*, President's Commission on Pension Policy, 1981.

legislation enacted by Congress over the years. Code sections with numbers in the 400s, as well as certain other sections, relate directly to qualified plans and similar arrangements, such as individual retirement accounts.

The Code provisions dealing with qualified plans are very complex and detailed. However, the code provisions are far outdone in bulk by the official rulings and regulations interpreting these Code sections and issued by the Internal Revenue Service and the Treasury Department. Important points of law are also found in court decisions. A brief discussion of the process of administering tax laws is necessary to explain the significance of these rulings, regulations, and cases.

Congress has long recognized that the Internal Revenue Code itself cannot cover all the infinitely variable situations that occur among real-life taxpayers. Consequently, the Treasury Department and its suborganization, the Internal Revenue Service, have been given considerable authority to interpret Code provisions and to issue regulations and rulings involving these Code provisions.

Regulations are formal, published interpretations of the Code. They are structured as abstract rules, like the Code itself, and are not related only to a particular set of facts. However, the regulations often contain examples that are extremely helpful in interpreting the regulations. Regulations are promulgated within the Internal Revenue Service and issued by the Treasury Department after a prescribed procedure involving hearings and public comment. Treasury regulations are initially published in the periodical *Federal Register* and are then compiled with all other federal regulations in the multivolume Code of Federal Regulations, or CFR. In addition, the regulations relating to income taxes are published commercially by various private publishers for the convenience of tax and pension practitioners.

The IRS also issues *rulings* relating to issues of tax law. IRS rulings are responses by the IRS to requests by taxpayers to interpret the law in light of their particular fact situations. IRS rulings are of two types—*Revenue Rulings,* which are published, and *Letter Rulings,* which are addressed only to specific taxpayers. The IRS publishes Revenue Rulings in periodic Internal Revenue *Bulletins,* which are then collected each year into a *Cumulative Bulletin* for that year. IRS personnel are bound by published Revenue Rulings when they are dealing with taxpayers involved in the same factual situation as that described in the ruling. However, in many cases, a taxpayer's factual situation can be distinguished from that in the ruling, and, therefore, the ruling will not be considered applicable.

Letter Rulings are not published officially by the IRS, but, under recent legislation, they are available to the public for inspection and copying, with the taxpayer's name and other identifying information deleted. A number of commercial services publish texts of Letter Rulings to assist practitioners in determining IRS positions on various issues. The IRS asserts that Letter Rulings are not binding on its personnel because they are aimed only at specific taxpayers. However, a thorough job of legal research on a particular issue will always involve a search for applicable Letter Rulings, because they may be the only indication of the IRS position on certain issues.

Tax Cases in the Federal Courts

The courts are another source of authority in the tax law. The courts enter the picture when a specific taxpayer decides to appeal a tax assessment made by the IRS. In the pension area, it is also possible to appeal to the United States Tax Court if the IRS refuses to issue an advance determination letter (see Chapter 19). Tax cases can be heard in the Federal District Court in the taxpayer's district, the United States Tax Court, or the United States Claims Court. Decisions of these courts can be appealed to the Federal Court of Appeals for the applicable federal judicial circuit. These circuit courts sometimes differ in interpreting points of the tax law. When this is the situation, tax and pension planning may depend on what judicial circuit the taxpayer is located in. Eventually, one or more taxpayers will appeal a decision by the Courts of Appeals to the United States Supreme Court to resolve differences of interpretation among the various judicial circuits, but this process often takes many years.

Tax cases often involve an interpretation of the Internal Revenue Code, Regulations, and IRS rulings. Sometimes, courts invalidate rulings or regulations. In other situations, courts interpret Code provisions in areas in which there are no regulations or rulings. Courts also interpret nontax statutes and regulations relating to qualified plans. Thus, court decisions form an important part of the pension law. Court decisions are published in official reporters by each of the courts involved. In addition, commercial reporting services collect tax and pension cases and publish them.

Federal Labor Law

The federal labor laws are another substantial body of federal law affecting qualified plans. Labor laws affect wages, hours, and conditions of employment, generally, and therefore apply to all types of employee benefits. In addition, ERISA included a number of labor law provisions relating to employee-benefit plans specifically, including pension plans and other types of plans (referred to as "welfare plans"), such as group insurance and medical-benefit plans. Some of the ERISA labor provisions overlap with Internal Revenue Code provisions, and the regulation of employee-benefit plans has consequently been divided between the Labor Department and the Internal Revenue Service. In the area of qualified retirement plans, the Internal Revenue Service is involved in the areas that will be encountered most frequently by the planner. However, Labor Department regulations and administrative jurisdiction affect such areas as fiduciary responsibility (plan investments) and information reporting and disclosure to plan participants and the government.

Pension Benefit Guaranty Corporation

Another area of government regulation involves the Pension Benefit Guaranty Corporation (PBGC), the government corporation set up by ERISA to provide termination insurance to qualified defined-benefit plans to protect participants from losing pension benefits if a plan terminates or an employer goes bankrupt. In connection with this responsibility, the PBGC imposes a number of reporting requirements and regulates certain plan terminations (see Chapter 21).

Other Regulations

The complexity of qualified plans is such that they are affected by much federal legislation not aimed specifically at them. Three significant areas should be noted: the federal securities laws, civil rights, and age discrimination.

Securities Laws. The federal securities law is a body of statutes, regulations, and cases designed to protect investors from being deceived by investment advisers and promoters. A qualified plan is, in effect, a means by which a portion of an employee's compensation is invested until the employee's retirement. Most qualified plans are exempted from coverage under the federal securities laws, because the Internal Revenue Code and appropriate labor laws have specific investment provisions for qualified plans. However, some types of plans, such as those involving employer stock, may be affected by securities laws and this must be kept in mind by the plan designer.

Civil Rights. Federal civil rights legislation prohibiting employment discrimination would generally prevent a qualified plan from discriminating on the basis of race, religion, or national origin, even though this is not prohibited in the Internal Revenue Code itself.[7] The area of sex discrimination, discussed in Chapter 8, is currently in controversy.

Age Discrimination. The age-discrimination legislation prohibits a variety of employment practices discriminating against the aged, including, in particular, a prohibition against forced retirement. Since the specification of a normal retirement age is an important part of qualified plan design, the age-discrimination law has an effect—but currently the effect is rather complex. This is discussed further in Chapter 8.

Summary

Federal government regulation and encouragement of qualified plans, primarily through the tax and labor laws, dates to the 1920s when the current tax-exemption and tax-deduction provisions were first enacted. This favorable treatment is essentially part of a long tradition of governmental income-support activity.

Growth in private retirement plans in the post-World War II era exposed a number of basic policy problems that led to the enactment of ERISA. The ERISA reforms increased participant benefit security but also the cost and complexity of

---

[7]Civil Rights Act of 1964, Section 2000e-2.

plan administration. In the post-ERISA era, many changes in the law have resulted from continuing concern about the revenue cost of qualified plans and their potential for discriminating in favor of highly compensated employees.

Government regulation of plans is carried out primarily through federal statutes administered by the Labor Department and the Treasury Department (Internal Revenue Service). The Internal Revenue Service has developed a particularly detailed body of regulations, rulings, and procedures. Qualified plan issues are also sometimes decided by the federal courts.

5

Designing a Plan to Meet Employer Needs

Objectives of This Chapter
- Because of the complexity of qualified retirement plans, it is not possible to fully discuss all the issues in plan design until substantive plan design features are understood. Nevertheless, it is useful to take an initial overview of the subject, aimed at the following:
- What is the overall role of the plan for the employer?
- Within this overall role, what problems can be solved by qualified plan design?
- What specific plan design features are available to address these problems?

● With these considerations in mind, the complexities to be discussed in subsequent chapters may be seen in some perspective. The purpose for plan design features then can be used as guidelines for organizing and analyzing the substantive issues.

Design Orientation

Much of the variation in plans used by different employers results from the fact that there are two overall approaches in designing a plan that are fundamentally different in certain ways. Some employers view plan design primarily as part of their overall approach to compensation planning, while others (particularly smaller employers) aim primarily at maximizing tax benefits under the plan.

Compensation Policy Approach

Because a qualified plan is fundamentally a form of compensation, many larger employers view plan design as part of overall compensation policy. For a larger employer, providing special benefits for key executives or owners of the business may not be a major factor in plan design. Such employers might, of course, adopt special compensation policies for executives, but would not view the qualified retirement plan as the primary method of doing this.

Retirement Plans versus Cash

An initial question is why to provide retirement benefits, rather than cash compensation. First, it should be noted that the tax advantages of qualified plans automatically increase the compensation value (at least to some employees) of dollars spent on plan benefits, as compared with cash. An employer gets a current tax deduction for the cost of the plan, while the employee's tax on the benefit is deferred until the benefit is distributed. Because of the time value of money, this tax deferral is a cost to the U.S. Treasury and a corresponding benefit to the employee. In other words, a qualified plan represents a form of compensation, part of which is paid by the federal government (actually, the taxpaying public), rather than by the employer.

Because of this tax benefit, it might seem advantageous for an employer to maximize this type of compensation. However, the practical limits on maximizing qualified plan benefits are determined by the willingness of employees to accept this form of benefit. Although a retirement plan is highly attractive to employees, all employees do not automatically prefer retirement benefits over cash just because the retirement benefits are somewhat more valuable as a result of the contribution by the Treasury. Some employees may not be interested in a qualified plan from a given employer, because they do not expect to stay with the employer long enough to receive a substantial benefit. Also, for lower-paid employees, current consumption needs represent a high percentage of their compensation, and they must assign a low priority to retirement saving. The other side of this argument, however, is that qualified plans are almost always advantageous to higher-paid employees, because they intend to save, anyway. Thus, despite the existence of tax benefits that are lost unless the employer adopts a qualified plan, it is not necessarily true that every employer ought to adopt one for all employees.

Compensation Policy Objectives. In addition to the dollar leverage from tax benefits, however, specific compensation policy objectives can be addressed with a qualified plan:

- Every employer wishes to minimize the cost of turnover in the work force. Certain plan designs can encourage employees to keep working for the employer by tying benefits to long service.
- Employers typically want to encourage employees to retire when it is appropriate—when their productivity has begun to decline, when the organization needs new blood, and the like. Qualified plans can be designed to facilitate this while maintaining the employee's dignity.
- A qualified plan can act as an incentive to better productivity.
- A qualified plan can help employees to identify with the organization.
- Retirement saving is difficult for most people; a qualified plan can help with this goal and, for this reason alone, may be more valuable than cash compensation.

Turnover. Traditionally, it has been thought that the defined-benefit plan encourages long service for a number of reasons. First, the plan's benefit formula often is based on years of service. Full retirement benefits are then usually not available unless the participant has some required length of service, often 25 or 30 years. In addition, benefits are sometimes based on the employee's highest compensation, and this is usually maximized by staying with the employer until retirement.

However, it is not always possible for the employer to follow this rationale fully. For example, the employer may wish to recruit executives, middle managers, or engineers in their 30s or 40s; a 30-year requirement for full benefits would not be attractive to them, so the plan may be compromised in this respect.

In addition, some employers are rethinking the effect of a traditional defined-benefit plan on employee turnover decisions. Some employees may be better encouraged to stay with the employer by a type of plan that provides a more immediate and perceptible benefit than the defined-benefit plan. A money-purchase or cash-balance plan provides employees with a benefit that begins growing shortly after being hired, and the benefit can increase to a substantial amount by retirement age if the employee continues in the plan.

Another plan feature that theoretically discourages turnover is a graduated vesting schedule.[1] Up to a five-year wait for full vesting may be permitted unless the plan is top-heavy. However, it is questionable how much effect a vesting schedule actually has on employee turnover decisions because typically, when an employee is not fully vested, the employee's accrued benefit is still small. Thus, in only rare cases does it make sense for an employee to continue working just to advance on the vesting schedule. Vesting is probably better viewed as a cost-saving aspect of a qualified plan; it allows the employer to recover part or all of the cost of plan contributions made for short-service employees.

Encouraging Retirement. A defined-benefit plan can encourage retirement or early retirement by a provision under which accrued benefits do not increase after a specified period of service. Thus, after the full benefit has accrued, the employee has no incentive to stay on. (However, the benefit at later retirement may be greater if it is based on final compensation and the employee's compensation is increasing.) Early retirement, say at age 62, rather than 65, can be encouraged by "subsidizing" the early retirement benefit—that is, providing a benefit at age 62 which is reduced by less than the full reduction that would be required under actuarial principles.

Defined-contribution plans typically provide no incentive to retire before age 65, because the participant's account balance continues to increase as long as the participant is employed.

Finally, it should be noted that any employer retirement plan acts as a retirement incentive to some degree, since it allows the participant to maintain himself

---

[1]Section 401(k) and Section 403(b) plans do not permit graduated vesting. See Chapters 14 and 23.

and his dependents after retirement. The importance of this should not be underestimated, as indicated by the statistics given in Chapter 1 showing the marked recent decline in employment by persons past retirement age.

Incentive. Almost any retirement plan has some positive impact on employee morale—that is, positive feelings toward the organization and a desire to do good work for it. A retirement plan indicates some thought on the part of the employer regarding employees' needs, and this generates positive feelings. However, a qualified plan can be designed specifically to maximize its incentive aspects.

A profit-sharing plan is viewed as having substantial incentive features. Contributions to the plan generally come out of current or accumulated profits, so contributions are tied to the performance of the organization and (theoretically) the work force. However, to individual employees this collective responsibility for plan contributions may appear to be only a remote incentive. Also, many profit-sharing plans are designed to provide maximum contribution flexibility to the employer, and the resulting discretion may be exercised by the employer in such a way as to destroy or minimize the connection between performance and plan contributions.

Plans using employer stock (stock-bonus plans and ESOPs) have even more direct incentive features than regular profit-sharing plans, since the participant's account increases or decreases with the value of the employer stock and, therefore, is related almost entirely to organizational performance. Employer stock can also be used as an investment in a regular profit-sharing plan to enhance the plan's incentive aspects.

All defined-contribution plans, including profit-sharing plans, can be viewed as having better incentive aspects than defined-benefit plans, because the defined-contribution plan benefit is expressed as an easily understood account balance that begins growing as soon as the participant enters the plan. This aspect of defined-contribution plans also can be achieved with the cash-balance plan, which has the additional attraction of providing a guaranteed minimum benefit.

Retirement Savings. The objective of providing an attractive retirement savings medium to employees is closely related to the incentive motive. It helps to maintain employee morale and identification with the organization. Retirement saving is perceived as an important need by employees, and they appreciate their employer's help. In fact, if employees really understand the tax benefits available only from qualified plans, they are likely to resent an employer who does not adopt such a plan.

Since all plans help employees plan for retirement, if furnishing an attractive savings medium is the focus of plan design, it is important for employers to determine employees' needs. While there is no valid argument against educating employees about their actual retirement planning needs, the fact remains that perceived needs by employees are more important than actual needs in benefit design. Of course, it can be argued that "actual" needs can never be determined and that such a concept is unacceptably paternalistic. At any rate, many benefit consultants have developed employee surveys that determine employees' views including, if appropriate, any dissatisfaction with existing plan designs.

One problem that almost always crops up in this type of planning is differences in employee preferences based on age. These result from a number of factors. Retirement is a remote contingency to younger employees; they tend not to give it serious thought and often make unrealistic assumptions about their future careers when doing so. Table 5–1 shows the result of a recent survey of employees' views about future sources of retirement income. Notice that the younger employees in this survey were optimistic about their private savings and investments as a source of retirement income. Older employees, in contrast, generally know where their careers and incomes are going and realistically recognize their need for an employer-sponsored plan. Another factor accounting for differences based on age is that younger employees are less likely to expect a long-term or lifetime career with their present employer and, therefore, will want more money up front, perhaps even preferring cash compensation.

As a result of these differences, defined-contribution plans with their "savings account" aspect are often popular with younger employees, while older employees might prefer defined-benefit plans. However, some employers have found that defined-benefit plans are so much more difficult to explain that even older employees like defined-contribution plans better, as long as the plan provides them with a good retirement benefit. A plan like the cash-balance plan, with its guarantee feature, often will help to resolve conflicting interests based on age. The employer can also use a combination of plans to help satisfy both groups; most typical is a combination of defined-benefit and profit-sharing plans, with the profit-sharing plan typically of the 401(k) type.

The issue of employee contributions often arises in connection with plan design issues of the type discussed here, where providing a retirement savings medium is an important goal. Some employers believe that retirement plan bene-

TABLE 5–1. Main Source of Expected Income in Retirement *(Nonretired Only)*

	Years		
	25–34	35–44	45–61
Pension payments from a company pension plan of your own or your spouse*	27%	29%	30%
Payments from social security	15	24	29
Money accumulated through savings or investments	26	19	14
Money from an IRA or Keogh plan	15	9	6
Money you can get from selling your house or property	5	6	6
Pension payments from a union pension plan of your own or your spouse	3	3	6
Money from an annuity policy with an insurance company	4	3	†
Something else	1	1	1
Not sure/no answer	4	6	8

*Respondents reporting they are now covered by a company pension plan: Nonretired respondents, 61%; 25–34 years, 60%; 35–44 years, 64%; 45–61 years, 62%.

†Less than 0.5%

Source: "The Attitudes of the American Public on Social Security," Yankelovich, Skelly, and White, Inc., August 1985.

fits are appreciated more by employees if the employees themselves contribute (or feel that they are contributing) toward their cost. Of course, all compensation dollars come from the employer (except for the tax benefits contributed by the Treasury), and compensation represents virtually all income for most employees, so there is something of an illusion in such thinking. For the same reason, employee contributions do not really lower employer costs for the plan, except to the extent that employees choose not to participate and lose an employer matching contribution or contribute to the plan from funds not originally supplied by the employer. Nevertheless, contributory approaches have proved popular with both employers and employees.

Employee contributions can be structured two ways: as aftertax (i.e., nondeductible) contributions to a traditional thrift or savings plan, or as nontaxable salary reductions.[2] Since the salary reduction approach provides full tax benefits from the plan, just as if the employer had made the entire plan contribution, it is increasingly popular and the older thrift plan approach is declining.

Employee contributions can also be used in other ways; for example, even a defined-benefit plan can use employee contributions to increase benefits at the employee's option. This feature in a defined-benefit plan, however, involves administrative complications and is rarely used.

Tax-Sheltering Orientation

Many smaller employers view qualified plans not primarily as part of compensation planning but rather as tax planning. Smaller employers may be reluctant to adopt a qualified plan, because it imposes a long-term burden on the business. However, as discussed often in this text, qualified plans provide significant tax benefits for covered employees. If these benefits can be provided to a significant degree to owner-employees and key employees in a small, closely held business, the business may be induced to adopt a qualified plan.

Plans designed for smaller businesses to maximize tax shelter benefits for owners are often more complex than larger plans. The owners frequently want to provide maximum benefits for themselves while minimizing benefits for rank-and-file employees. Therefore, the nondiscrimination rules must be pushed to their limits in designing such plans.

In designs of this type, the plan contribution for the benefit of non-key employees is treated as the "cost" of the tax-sheltering objective, and various plan alternatives are compared in terms of minimizing this cost within a certain contribution goal. An analysis such as this might be made:

	Alternative A	Alternative B
Annual cost for key employees	$60,000	$55,000
Annual cost for other employees	5,000	10,000
Percent for key employees	92%	85%

---

[2]Salary reductions are permitted only in a Section 401(k) plan, Section 403(b) plan, Section 457 plan, or a SEP. See Chapters 14, 22, and 23.

There is no specific planning rule indicating how high the cost percentage for key employees must be for the plan to work as a pure tax shelter; this can be done only on an individual basis by comparing the present value of the tax savings to the key employees with the outlay required for the plan. This depends on key employees' ages, tax brackets, and income projections. Planners do not always perform the complete calculations required, although such calculations have become easier with the computerization of the plan design business. As a rough indication, a plan might typically work as a pure tax shelter if about 60 percent of its benefits or contributions go to key employees.

Some smaller employers will adopt a plan even if it does not function purely as a tax shelter. Their motives are often mixed; they see advantages in providing substantial retirement benefits for regular employees as well as for key employees, with the compensation planning objectives discussed in the first part of the chapter. Most smaller employers, however, are interested to some degree in maximizing tax-sheltering benefits for key employees.

Some common approaches to maximizing key employee benefits will be discussed here in summary form. This type of planning is complex and aspects of it will be discussed in detail throughout this text.

Maximizing Contributions for Older Entrants. In a common planning situation for a small business, the plan will be considered after the business has been established and achieved some success. At that point, key and controlling employees typically are older than regular employees.

The defined-benefit plan provides actuarial funding and, thus, requires a higher contribution at any benefit level for employees who enter the plan at older ages. For key employees near retirement age when the plan is established, this permits very high deductible annual contributions to the plan, sometimes more than 100 percent of the employee's compensation. For example, note the following contribution level at older ages to provide the maximum benefit of $90,000 annually at age 65:

Age at Entry	Annual Contribution
50	$ 37,712
55	64,698
57	85,219
60	147,272
63	396,961

In this type of situation, the defined-benefit plan's advantages can sometimes be improved further; a defined-benefit plan can take account of service for the employer before the plan is adopted. Such prior service credit must be given to all plan participants, but typically most of the prior service has been accrued by key employees.

A target-benefit plan also provides a higher contribution level for older entrants. However, since it is a defined-contribution plan, contributions are limited to 25 percent of compensation/$30,000 annually, so it would be used for this type of tax sheltering only if the expense of setting up and administering a defined-benefit plan is excessive, or if the employer is satisfied with an annual contribution for key employees limited to $30,000 annually.

Defined-benefit and target plans operate as tax shelters in this manner when key employees are at least 45 to 50 years old when the plan is established. If they are younger, a defined-contribution plan may be more favorable. The exact point at which this occurs can only be determined individually for each employee group, plan design, and set of actuarial assumptions.

Minimizing Plan Cost for Lower-Paid Employees. Integrating a plan's contribution or benefit formula with social security produces a lower relative employer cost for lower-paid employees. The qualified plan rules permit this on the theory that social security retirement benefits are paid for by the employer already and, therefore, these costs can be reflected in designing the private qualified plan. In practice, considerable discrimination in favor of the higher paid is possible.

The detailed rules (Chapter 9) are complicated. Some examples will provide an idea of the planning possibilities. An integrated defined-benefit formula might provide a retirement benefit for a participant of 30 percent of compensation if the participant's compensation is less than $21,000, while for a participant with compensation above $21,000 the formula would be 30 percent of all compensation, plus 25 percent of compensation over $21,000. An integrated defined-contribution formula might provide, for example, an annual employer contribution of 10 percent of compensation, plus an additional 5.7 percent of compensation over a specified level, such as $20,000.

Flexibility of Contributions. All employers, and smaller employers in particular, must consider the long-term financial impact of adopting a qualified plan. Pension plans (defined-benefit, money-purchase, and target) are subject to the Code's minimum funding requirements, which generally require minimum annual contributions. Defined-benefit plans allow some choice of actuarial methods and assumptions, and this permits some flexibility in funding. Defined-contribution pension plans, however, require an annual contribution in accordance with the plan's formula. Plans can be amended to reduce future benefit accruals or contributions if costs become burdensome; but this usually is not attractive, because of its unpopularity with employees and the legal and administrative costs involved.

The traditional thrift or savings plan involves matching employer contributions that the employer must make if the plan calls for them. The 401(k) approach, however, can be funded entirely through salary reduction and, thus, does not appear to represent additional costs beyond the regular payroll.

A profit-sharing plan can leave to employer discretion whether to contribute in a given year. However, contributions must be "substantial and recurring" or the IRS may deem the plan to have terminated. The IRS has not further defined substantial and recurring, so it is unclear how many years can be skipped.

A stock-bonus plan can be operated in a way (seemingly) to cost the employer almost nothing, since contributions may be made directly in employer stock.

However, if the stock has a market value, the employer could sell it and realize that value, so the stock contribution is not actually cost-free.

Summary

Plan design approaches will depend initially on whether the employer views the plan primarily as a compensation-planning tool or, as in the case of many smaller employers, primarily as a tax-planning technique. For smaller employers both motivations are often present.

As a compensation-planning tool, qualified plans can be designed to minimize turnover, encourage retirement, provide performance incentives, and provide a retirement savings medium of perceived value to employees.

As a tax-planning device, the cost of the plan is viewed as basically the cost of covering non-key employees. Design goals, therefore, include reducing this cost through social security integration and minimum plan coverage for non-key employees, while maximizing benefits for key employees, often by using a defined-benefit plan. Also, flexibility of plan contributions is often an important goal for smaller employers to avoid financial burdens.

6

Qualified Plan Eligibility and Participation

Objectives of This Chapter
- *Give some reasons why plan eligibility is often restricted to a specific group of employees.*
- *Distinguish between eligibility requirements written into a plan and coverage of a plan in actual operation.*
- *Describe the extent to which a plan can restrict eligibility based on age or service.*
- *Explain the three alternative coverage tests, including the rules for interpreting them, and give some examples of their application.*
- *Explain how an employer can meet the coverage tests by using one or more plans for different groups of employees.*
- *Describe the situations in which an employer must give credit for service with other employers.*
- *Describe in general terms the types of employers that must be aggregated under the common control rules, the affiliated service group rules, and the leased employee rules.*

● One of the first specific plan design decisions the employer must make is the group to be covered by the qualified plan. In a closely held business, the employer will often want to provide a large portion of the plan's benefits to controlling and to key employees, and to minimize benefits for rank-and-file employees. In larger plans, employers will often want to provide a different qualified plan (or no plan) for different groups of employees for various reasons; for example, the existence of collective bargaining units with separate plans, a desire for different benefit structures for hourly and salaried employees, or differences in benefit policy for employees at different geographical locations.

In reviewing the many limitations imposed on the plan designer by the qualified plan rules, note that the overriding purpose for most of these rules is to prevent discrimination by the employer in favor of highly compensated employees. A secondary purpose, related to the first, is to provide and maintain some security of benefits for participants, particularly participants who are not highly compensated. Most of the qualified plan rules can be explained by these rationales, and most questions about the meaning of particular rules and how they apply in a particular situation can be resolved by referring to these basic purposes of the law.

The Code imposes two types of limitations on the employer's freedom to designate the group of employees to be covered under the plan. The first limitation applies to the plan as it exists on paper—that is, the eligibility provisions written into the plan. The second type of limitation applies to the plan in operation and provides minimum coverage requirements in the form of three alternative coverage tests. Both limitations are contained in Section 410 of the Code and its accompanying regulations and rulings.

First of all, concerning plan coverage in the document itself, the designer has a good deal of freedom. The plan may cover only employees at a certain geographical location, employees in a certain work unit, salaried employees only, hourly employees only, or almost any other variation. However, when eligibility is restricted on the basis of age or service with the employer, there are specific limits.

Age and Service Requirements

Although not all plans have age or service conditions for entry, many employers prefer such conditions, because they help to avoid the cost of carrying an employee on the records as a plan participant when the employee quits after a short period of service. Generally, a plan cannot require more than one year of service before eligibility, and an employee who has attained the age of 21 must be permitted to participate in the plan if the employee has met the other participation requirements of the plan. Both age and service requirements can be imposed. For example, for an employee hired at age 19, the plan can require that employee to wait until age 21 to participate in the plan. However, an employee hired at age 27 cannot be required to wait more than one year before participating in the plan.

As an alternative to the one-year waiting period, a plan may provide for a waiting period of up to two years if the plan provides immediate 100 percent vesting upon entry. (In most other cases, graduated vesting is allowed—see the discussion in Chapter 7). The two-year provision is often used by employers with very few employees and a high turnover rate—for example, a self-employed physician with one or two clerical or technical employees who have high mobility in their labor market. With a two-year eligibility provision, few of the doctor's employees may ever be covered under the plan.

One problem with these age and service requirements is that it is often desirable for a plan to have *entry dates*—that is, specific dates during the year in which plan participation is deemed to begin, in order to simplify recordkeeping. The Regulations provide that no employee may be required to wait for participation more than six months after the plan's age and service requirements are met.[1] Thus, a plan having entry dates must adjust its eligibility provisions accordingly.

Example

The Blarp, Inc. pension plan wishes to have a one-year, age-21 entry requirement and to use an entry date or dates. Any of the following options will meet the requirement in the Regulations:

> Two entry dates in the year, six months apart, with participants entering on the next entry date after they satisfy the one-year, age-21 condition;
>
> One entry date, but a minimum entry age of no more than 20½ and a maximum waiting period of six months;
>
> One entry date, with participants entering the plan on the date *nearest* (before or after) the date on which the one-year, age-21 requirement is satisfied.

All qualified plans are subject to the age-21 requirement, except for a plan maintained exclusively by a tax-exempt educational institution as defined in Code Section 170(b)(1)(a)(ii). To avoid coverage of such temporary employees as graduate teaching assistants, such a plan may provide a minimum age of 26, but the plan must have 100 percent vesting after one year of service.

Maximum Age Limits and Coverage of Older Employees

Coverage of employees who enter a defined-benefit or target plan when they are close to the plan's retirement age can present a funding problem, since relatively few years are available to fund the benefit. If the participant enters the plan within a few years of retirement, the employer contribution may be burdensome. For example, using a given set of actuarial assumptions, the annual cost to fund the same benefit of $1,000 per month at age 65 varies with age at entry as follows:

Age at Plan Entry	Annual Cost
30	$ 537
50	3,410
55	6,391
60	15,783
62	28,521
64	92,592

---

[1] Reg. Sec. 1.410(a)-4(b)(1)

The age-discrimination law prohibits exclusion of employees who enter at later ages. However, as discussed further in Chapter 8 under "Retirement Age," a plan can define normal retirement age as the fifth anniversary of plan entry for a participant entering within five years of normal retirement age. This provides at least five years for funding. Alternatively, the time for funding the benefit can be extended simply by having the plan delay the beginning of benefit payments beyond retirement age; but payments cannot be delayed beyond the 10th anniversary of plan participation, and benefit payments must begin no later than April 1 of the year after attainment of age 70½; see Chapter 16.

Definition of Year of Service

The term *year of service* is used in different ways in the qualified plan rules. It is used to define the age and service rules for eligibility that were just discussed, and it is also used in connection with the vesting and benefit accrual rules discussed in the next chapter. Since it plays such an important part in these rules, it has a specific definition under the law.

Generally, a year of service is a 12-month period during which the employee has at least 1,000 hours of service.[2] For purposes of determining eligibility, the *initial* 12-month period must be measured beginning with the date the employee begins work for the employer. For other purposes, the 12-month accounting period used by the plan (the *plan year*) can generally be used. For example, suppose the plan uses the calendar year as the plan year. If an employee began work on June 1, 1987, the initial 12-month period for determining whether the 1,000-hour requirement had been met would be June 1, 1987, through May 31, 1988. If the employee did not perform 1,000 hours of service during that period, the plan could begin the next measuring period on January 1, 1988, with subsequent years being determined similarly on the basis of the plan year.

The employer may determine hours of service using payroll records or any other type of records that accurately reflect the hours worked. Alternatively, the regulations allow a plan to use "equivalency" methods for computing hours of service. These equivalencies allow employees to be credited with hours worked that are based on completion of some other unit of service, such as a shift, week, or month of service, without actual counting of hours worked.

Breaks in Service

A larger employer may reduce the cost of a plan somewhat by including a "break in service" provision in the plan's eligibility requirements. Under such a provision, an employee whose continuous service for the same employer is interrupted loses credit (upon returning to work) for service prior to the break and again must meet the plan's waiting period for eligibility. For a smaller employer, breaks in service followed by reemployment are relatively rare and such a provision may have no substantial cost impact.

---

[2] See Code Sections 410(a)(3) [eligibility] and 411(a)(5) [vesting], and regulations thereunder.

The rules under which a plan may interrupt service credits for breaks in service are somewhat complicated.[3] A one-year break in service for this purpose is defined as a 12-month period during which the participant has 500 or fewer hours of service. Service prior to a break cannot be disregarded until there is a one-year break in service. In that case, prebreak service may be disregarded (and the participant regarded as a new employee for participation purposes) in three situations only:

1. Service prior to the one-year break in service does not have to be counted unless the returned employee completes a year of service. Participation then is effective as of the first day of the plan year in which eligibility was reestablished.

2. If the plan has a two-year/100 percent vesting eligibility provision, prebreak service need not be counted if the employee did not complete two years of service before the break.

3. If the participant had no vested benefits at the time of the break, prebreak service need not be counted if the number of consecutive one-year breaks in service equals or exceeds the greater of five or the participant's years of service before the break. For example, suppose that participant Arlen works for Maple Corporation for eight months, quits, and then returns seven years later. For purposes of determining eligibility in the Maple Corporation plan, Arlen's eight months of prebreak service do not have to be counted.

Other Eligibility Criteria Related to Age and Service

Since the age and service limitations must be met by the plan document as drafted, the IRS will scrutinize the plan carefully to ascertain whether there are eligibility criteria that indirectly base eligibility on age and service.[4] For example, the employer may wish to exclude part-time employees. The IRS views an exclusion of part-timers as a service-based eligibility provision. If the plan has a one-year service requirement for entry, it will exclude all employees who never work more than 1,000 hours in any year. However, the plan cannot exclude part-timers who work more than 1,000 hours in a year, but less than a full year, because such a requirement would be seen as a service requirement that violated the one-year/1,000-hour criteria. Even if some part-timers must be included, the plan is allowed to have a benefit formula that provides smaller benefits for them, because of their lesser compensation, or because part-time service is given less credit for benefit purposes than full-time service.

The IRS will also look carefully at how a plan is actually operated to make sure that the age and service limitations are not violated. For example, suppose an employer has a plan for Division B of the business, and employment in Division B requires five years of service in Division A. Division B has a qualified plan and Division A does not. This service requirement, although outside the plan

---

[3]The rules are set out in Code Section 410(a)(5) and regulations thereunder, as well as Labor Regs. Section 2530.200b.

[4]Reg. Sec. 1.410(a)-3(e).

itself, could be seen as an attempt to circumvent the service limitation for the plan maintained by Division B.

Overall Coverage Tests

In addition to the specific rules relating to age and service eligibility provisions, the second major limitation on the employer's freedom to exclude employees from a qualified plan is a set of three alternative statutory tests (Code Section 410) to be applied to the plan in actual operation to determine if coverage is discriminatory. A qualified plan must satisfy one of three coverage tests:

1. The plan must cover at least 70 percent of employees who are not highly compensated—the *percentage test*, or
2. the plan must cover a percentage of non-highly compensated employees that is at least 70 percent of the percentage of highly compensated employees covered—the *ratio test*, or
3. the plan must meet the *average-benefit test*. Under the average-benefit test, the plan must benefit a nondiscriminatory classification of employees, and the average benefit, as a percentage of compensation, for non-highly compensated employees must be at least 70 percent of that for highly compensated employees.

Employees Excluded. In applying these tests, certain employees are not taken into account:

Employees who have not satisfied the plan's minimum age and service requirements, if any.

Employees included in a collective bargaining unit, if there is evidence that retirement benefits were the subject of good-faith bargaining under a collective bargaining agreement.

Employees excluded under a collective bargaining agreement between air pilots and employers under Title II of the Railway Labor Act.

Employees who are nonresident aliens and who receive no earned income from sources within the United States.

The coverage tests apply not only at the plan's inception, but on an ongoing basis. Generally, all of the nondiscrimination requirements must be met by a plan on at least one day of each quarter of the plan's taxable year (Section 401(a)(6) of the Code). Although the IRS does not perpetually monitor a plan's compliance with the percentage coverage requirements, these requirements give the IRS an ongoing weapon to challenge a plan that may have become discriminatory.

Highly Compensated. For purposes of the coverage tests just described (and for many other employee-benefit purposes, as well), Section 414(q) of the Code provides a very specific definition of *highly compensated employee*. A highly compensated employee means any employee who, during the year or the preceding year:

1. Was at any time an owner of a more than 5 percent interest in the employer, or
2. received compensation from the employer in excess of $75,000, or
3. received compensation from the employer in excess of $50,000 and was in the top-paid 20 percent of employees for such year, or
4. was at any time an officer and received compensation greater than 150 percent of the Section 415 annual additions limit. Currently, the annual additions limit is $30,000, so this limit is $45,000.

Features of the Average-Benefit Test

In some respects, the average-benefit test is the least stringent of the three coverage tests, and many types of plan design will be able to qualify only under this test. For example, a common plan design provides separate plans for salaried and for nonsalaried employees. In many cases, neither plan individually—the salaried plan in particular—can meet either of the first two tests and, thus, must meet the average-benefit test.

The average-benefit test is two-pronged. First, the plan must cover a *nondiscriminatory classification* of employees. Because of this aspect of the test, the IRS has a degree of discretion in the determination of whether a classification is nondiscriminatory. The other two tests are strictly mathematical and do not involve IRS discretion. Although the determination of a nondiscriminatory classification is discretionary, the IRS is expected to develop some guidelines for it. Under a prior version of this test (see Appendix A), the pre-1988 discretionary coverage test, there were a variety of regulations and other pronouncements of the IRS that provided some guidance. In general, the IRS would approve a plan under the old test if it covered a "fair cross section" of employees at all wage levels. Thus, if the plan covered some employees with low wages or salaries, it could be approved even if the plan as a whole covered primarily higher-paid employees. However, if very few or no low-paid employees were covered, the plan generally did not meet the pre-1988 discretionary coverage test. It is expected that the nondiscriminatory classification test will be applied in much the same manner.

The second requirement of the average-benefit test is that the *average benefit*, as a percentage of compensation for non-highly compensated employees must be at least 70 percent of that for highly compensated employees. In making this determination, all employees, whether or not covered under the plan in question are counted, and benefits from all qualified plans are taken into account.

Examples

Plan Coverage Meeting Various Tests

Acme Trucking Company has 10 employees, 3 of whom are highly compensated. A qualified plan covers the three highly compensated employees and five of the seven non-highly compensated employees. This plan meets the percentage test, since it covers at least 70 percent of non-highly compensated employees.

Barpt Products, Inc., has 20 employees, 5 of whom are highly compensated. If a qualified plan covers four of the highly compensated employees—that is, 80 percent—then the plan must cover at least 56 percent of non-highly compensated employees—70 percent of 80 percent—or, in this case, nine non-highly compensated employees.

Flim Company, Inc., has 100 employees, 20 of whom are salaried. Flim has a plan for salaried employees covering 10 salaried employees. Flim has received a determination from the IRS that the 10 salaried employees covered do not form a discriminatory classification, presumably because some low-paid salaried employees are covered as well as the highly paid. The Flim Company plan will qualify, as long as benefits are provided for non-highly compensated employees as a group that are at least 70 percent of that for highly compensated employees as a group. Thus, some kind of retirement plan coverage for the nonsalaried employees would be necessary.

Plans for Separate Lines of Business

If an employer has separate lines of business, the participation tests can be applied separately to employees in each line of business (Code Section 414(r)). A separate line of business must be operated for bona fide business reasons and must have at least 50 employees. If highly compensated employees constitute more than a specified percentage of the employees of the separate line of business, special guidelines apply or specific IRS approval may be required to use the separate line of business provision.

The separate line of business provision may allow a larger employer, or a controlled group of employers, to design separate plans—with separate coverage provisions—for its various operations. This increases the flexibility available in plan design, to some extent.

Coverage of Employees in Comparable Plans

The coverage rules discussed so far have applied the nondiscrimination coverage standards as if the employer had only a single plan. This raises the question whether a plan covering a subgroup of employees can be considered nondiscriminatory on the ground that the excluded employees are covered under other qualified plans of the employer. As the rules discussed so far indicate, this is possible if the excluded group of employees is in a collective bargaining unit, because they then are excluded from application of the percentage test. However, if this is not the case, an employer also is permitted to designate two or more plans as a single plan for purposes of satisfying the coverage requirements, as long as the plans so combined are "comparable" in contributions or benefits. Revenue Ruling 81–202 provides guidelines for determining whether plans are comparable for this purpose. The ruling imposes a series of complicated actuarial standards for benefits and contribution rates.

In addition, no plan can be qualified unless it covers, on each day of the plan year, the lesser of (1) 50 employees of the employer or (2) 40 percent or more of all employees of the employer (Code Section 401(a)(26)). In applying this test, the same employees can be excluded as for the coverage test described earlier. The purpose of the 50/40 percent requirement is primarily to prevent abuses in the use of the comparable plan technique.

To summarize the criteria for comparability in Revenue Ruling 81–202, plans can be considered comparable if either the benefits provided by the plans (projected to retirement dates), or the contributions under the plans, do not constitute a greater percentage of compensation for employees in the prohibited group than for regular employees. Benefits provided by social security may be taken into account in making the computation. These tests are often relatively easy to meet, with only a minimal plan for rank-and-file employees (compared with the plan for prohibited group employees) because of two common factors encountered in this type of planning. First, rank-and-file employers often are relatively younger than prohibited group employees. This means that their benefits at age 65 are projected so far into the future that even a small defined-contribution plan will build up to a substantial percentage of their current salaries (the Rev. Rul. 81–202 tests do not require salaries to be adjusted to reflect probable pay increases in the future). Second, social security benefits are usually a greater percentage of pay for lower-paid rank-and-file employees than for prohibited group employees; this helps in meeting the comparability tests.

Service for Predecessors and Other Employers

A plan of one employer generally does not need to give an employee credit for service with another employer. Some situations, however, require this. Under collectively bargained, multiemployer, or multiple-employer plans, service with more than one employer may have to be taken into consideration. Also, if the employer has chosen to take over or maintain the plan of a predecessor employer, service for the predecessor must be given credit. The IRS has not yet made clear what is meant by "predecessor employer," leaving some doubt about the rules in this area. A common situation is the incorporation of a partnership and the continuation of the qualified plan of that partnership by the new corporation. The IRS once took the position that corporate employees who were partners in the prior partnership may not be given credit for prior service as partners. However, the IRS currently will probably permit this as long as regular employees receive full credit for service under the partnership.

Finally, service credit must be given for service with all employers under "common control." The definition of common control, an important concept in the qualified plan area, is discussed next, in general terms, with a detailed discussion provided in Appendix A.

Commonly Controlled Employers

Often an employer organization (incorporated or unincorporated) is owned or controlled in common with other such organizations. The qualified plan designer must then in many cases coordinate plan coverage for the first employer with plan coverage for employees of other members of the commonly controlled group of employers.

The Code has a number of provisions relating to this issue; their basic objective is to prevent a business owner from getting around the coverage and nondiscrimination requirements for qualified plans by artificially segregating employees to be benefited from the plan into one organization, with the remainder being employed by subsidiaries or organizations with lesser plan benefits or no plan at all. While this is still technically possible, the controlled group rules restrict this practice considerably.

Controlled Group Rules in General

Because the forms of business ownership can be tangled and complex, the common control rules for qualified plans are appropriately complicated. There are four sets of these rules:

1. Under Code Section 414(b), all employees of all corporations in a *controlled group* of corporations are treated as employed by a single employer for purposes of Sections 401, 408(k), 410, 411, 415, and 416. The major impact of this comes from the participation rules of Section 410, which, in effect, require the participation and coverage tests to be applied to the entire controlled group, rather than to any single corporation in the group. Code Section 414(c) provides similar rules for commonly controlled partnerships and proprietorships.

2. Code Section 414(m) provides that employees of an *affiliated service group* are treated as employed by a single employer. This requirement similarly has its major impact in determining participation in a qualified plan, but it applies to other employee benefit requirements as well.

3. A *leased employee* is treated as an employee of the lessor corporation under certain circumstances, under Code Section 414(n).

4. If a qualified plan covers a partner or proprietor who owns more than 50 percent of another business, then the plan or comparable plan must provide for employees of the controlled business (Code Section 401(d)).

Some examples will give a general idea of the impact of these provisions on plan design; these are discussed in detail in Appendix B and in later chapters. *Note:* the common thread of these examples is that the related organization's employees must be *taken into account* in applying the participation rules. This does not mean that these employees must necessarily be covered.

> Alpha Corporation owns 80 percent of the stock of Beta Corporation. Alpha and Beta are members of a parent subsidiary-controlled group of corporations. In applying the participation and coverage rules of Section 410 of the Code, Alpha and Beta must be considered as a single employer.
> Bert and Harry own stock as follows:

Owner	Corporation A	Corporation B
Bert	60%	60%
Harry	30	30
	90%	90%

- Corporations A and B are a brother-sister controlled group. Thus, A and B must be considered as a single employer for purposes of Code Section 410 and most other qualified plan rules.
- Medical Services, Inc., provides administrative and laboratory services for Dr. Sam and Dr. Joe, each of whom is an incorporated sole practitioner. Dr. Sam and Dr. Joe each own 50 percent of Medical Services, Inc. If either Dr. Sam or Dr. Joe adopts a qualified plan, employees of Medical Services, Inc., will have to be taken into account in determining if plan coverage is nondiscriminatory.
- Calculators Incorporated, an actuarial firm, contracts with Temporary Services, Inc., an employee-leasing firm, to lease employees on a substantially full-time basis. The leased employees will have to be taken into account in determining nondiscrimination in any qualified plan of Calculators, unless Temporary maintains a minimum (10 percent nonintegrated) money-purchase pension plan for the leased employees.
- Stan and Fran are partners in a construction business. Fran is also a 60 percent partner in a road paving business that has 50 employees. If the Stan and Fran partnership adopts a qualified plan covering Stan and Fran, then the plan must either cover the 50 employees of the road paving business or the road paving business must provide a plan with coverage comparable to that provided for Stan and Fran.

Summary

Qualified plan eligibility is often restricted to a specific group to obtain specific compensation planning objectives. If eligibility criteria are based on age or service, eligibility must begin no later than attainment of age 21 and one year of service, with some flexibility to accommodate plan entry dates.

Whatever eligibility criteria are used, actual plan coverage must meet one of three alternative coverage tests: the percentage test, the ratio test, or the average-benefit test. These tests are designed to prevent disproportionate coverage of highly compensated employees, as specifically defined in the rules. Certain employees, such as collective bargaining unit employees, are not counted in applying these tests, thus making it easier to have separate plans for such employees. Also, the tests can be applied separately for separate lines of business meeting certain criteria. Comparable plans for different employee groups can be aggregated to meet the tests, if each plan meets appropriate standards. To prevent evasion of the coverage rules by separating a single business into multiple entities, all commonly controlled employers are treated as a single employer. Similarly, employees of affiliated service groups and leased employees are under certain conditions treated as employees of the employer sponsoring the plan.

7

Vesting and Benefit Accrual

Objectives of This Chapter
- *Describe the minimum vesting requirements for qualified plans.*
- *Discuss the considerations involved in choosing a vesting schedule.*
- *Describe how a participant's plan benefits at termination of employment are computed and how they are paid.*
- *Explain the concept of benefit accrual and the restrictions on benefit accrual imposed by the qualified plan law.*

Vesting Rules

At one time, a qualified plan could be designed so that a long-term employee who terminated employment before the plan's normal retirement date, even one day before, would receive no plan benefit. Since this type of design does not serve the public interest in having the widest possible coverage in the private pension system, and since it is open to abuse and discrimination on the part of the employer, ERISA (1974) added specific graduated vesting requirements for qualified plans, as well as for certain funded nonqualified plans, which are discussed in Chapter 25.

A qualified plan must provide a nonforfeitable or vested benefit for participants who attain certain service requirements. Once vested, this benefit cannot be forfeited by the participant. Therefore, the plan cannot contain a clause that, for example, requires an employee to forfeit part or all of the vested benefit required by the Code if the employee commits an act of misconduct, such as embezzlement or going to work for a competitor. The strictness of the vesting rules was designed to provide additional benefit security and to protect employees against arbitrary acts of the employer.

Vesting at Normal Retirement Age and Termination of Employment

First of all, the plan must provide a fully vested benefit at the normal retirement age; this rule applied even before ERISA. Under ERISA, the plan must also provide that benefits are vested under a specified *vesting schedule* during the participant's employment, so that if the participant terminates employment prior to retirement age, the participant is entitled to a vested benefit with some stated minimum amount of service.

If the plan provides for employee contributions, the participant's accrued benefit is divided between the part attributable to employee contributions and the part attributable to employer contributions. The part attributable to employee contributions must at all times be 100 percent vested. The part attributable to employer contributions must be vested in accordance with a vesting schedule set out in the plan.

There is some flexibility in designing a vesting schedule to meet various employer objectives. However, the vesting schedule must be at least as favorable as one of two alternative minimum standards. These are:

Five-Year Vesting. The vesting schedule satisfies this minimum requirement if an employee with at least 10 years of service is 100 percent vested in the employer-provided portion of the accrued benefit. This rule is satisfied even if there is no vesting at all before five years of service. This rule, therefore, is sometimes referred to as "cliff" vesting.

Three- to Seven-Year Vesting. A vesting schedule satisfies this minimum standard if the vesting is at least as fast as under the following table:

Years of Service	Vested Percentage
3	20%
4	40
5	60
6	80
7 or more	100

In applying the vesting rules, all of a participant's years of service for the employer must be taken into account, even years prior to plan participation, except that years of service prior to age 18 may be excluded. The plan's vesting schedule may also ignore service prior to a break in continuous service with the employer; however, the Code has elaborate restrictions on how this may be done (Code Section 411(a)(6)).

Probably the most common vesting provision in defined-benefit plans is the five-year provision, because of its simplicity and because it is generally the most favorable to the employer. Defined-contribution plans are often designed with a more generous (to the employee) vesting schedule using the three- to seven-year schedule or one that is even faster.

Top-Heavy Vesting. To complete this discussion, it should be mentioned that top-heavy plans as defined in the Code are required to provide faster vesting than under most of the schedules previously mentioned. The top-heavy minimum vesting schedule is:

Years of Service	Vested Percentage
2	20%
3	40
4	60
5	80
6 or more	100

A 100 percent vesting provision with two years' eligibility also meets the top-heavy minimum vesting requirement. Top-heavy plans are discussed in detail in Chapter 18. As discussed below, the top-heavy requirements have a significant impact in designing a vesting schedule for plans of smaller employers.

Choosing a Vesting Schedule

Choosing an appropriate vesting schedule is an important plan design decision. When a defined benefit plan participant terminates employment, unvested funds contributed to the plan for that participant *(forfeitures)* are used to reduce future employer costs for the pension plan. Liberal vesting, therefore, increases the plan's cost to the employer. In a defined-contribution plan, forfeitures can be reallocated to remaining participants' accounts. Thus, there should be a reason for adopting more than a minimum vesting schedule. Some reasons for using liberal vesting include the need to provide employee incentive and involvement in situations where a five-year vesting schedule might appear too remote and, therefore, of no value to employees.

The vesting schedule should be chosen carefully, because, if a plan is amended to make vesting less liberal, the less liberal vesting provision applies only to new employees—existing employees must be given an option to retain vesting under the old rule.[1]

Vesting on Plan Termination

The final vesting rule relates to a plan that has terminated. The IRS will regard a plan as having terminated if it is either formally terminated or if the employer permanently ceases to make contributions to the plan. When a plan is terminated, all benefits must be fully vested to the extent funded. Therefore, when a defined-contribution plan terminates, all participants are immediately 100 percent vested in their account balances. When a defined-benefit plan terminates, participants are 100 percent vested in their accrued benefits; however, if the plan funds are insufficient, they are vested only to the extent that the plan is funded. Many terminated qualified defined-benefit plans are insured by the Pension Benefit Guarantee Corporation (PBGC). The procedures that come into operation on plan termination under the PBGC rules are discussed in Chapter 21.

---

[1] Reg. Sec. 1.411(a)-8.

Benefits at Termination of Employment

The vesting provisions of a plan basically determine the amount of benefit that a participant is entitled to upon terminating employment prior to retirement.

In a defined-contribution plan, the termination benefit is the vested portion of the participant's account balance. In defined-contribution plans, particularly profit-sharing plans, the account balance usually is distributed to the participant in full at termination of employment. It is technically possible to defer the distribution to the participant's normal retirement date, but this is rarely done in defined-contribution plans, because it causes additional expense to the plan with little or no corresponding benefit to the employer or the plan.[2] However, the plan may give the participant the option to leave the funds on deposit in the plan for withdrawal at a later date; this allows the participant to take advantage of the tax-deferred investment medium afforded by the plan (with a possible loss of favorable income tax treatment on the later plan distribution—see Chapter 16).

For a defined-benefit plan, the benefit on termination of employment is more complicated. The benefit basically will be the vested accrued benefit as of the date of termination, determined under the vesting and accrual rules described in this chapter. Thus, suppose that an employee terminates employment at age 55 after 20 years of service and the plan's normal retirement age is 65. If the participant is fully vested and the accrued benefit is $8,000 per year, an annuity of $8,000 per year will be payable beginning at age 65.

To make sure that terminated participants actually do receive deferred vested benefits at retirement (which may be many years after termination) the employer must report all deferred vested benefits of terminated participants to the Social Security Administration, which then can inform retirees of their rights to benefits from plans of former employers.

In some cases, the deferred vested benefit may be such a small amount that keeping track of it until the participant's retirement is merely a nuisance for both employer and employee. The employer can *cashout* a distribution (pay cash to the employee in lieu of the deferred vested benefit) without the employee's consent, so long as the entire benefit is distributed and the employer portion of the benefit so distributed does not exceed $3,500. The involuntary cashout must be within one year of termination of participation in the plan, and the plan must have a provision permitting the employee to repay the cashout to the plan if the employee was not fully vested at the time of termination, in case the employee should resume participation in the plan. A cashout of a benefit that exceeds the $3,500 limit can be made, but only with the consent of the employee.

The Accrued Benefit

Under the vesting rules discussed in this chapter, many employees will be entitled to a benefit from their qualified plan if they terminate employment before retire-

---

[2] For an ESOP, deferral of a distribution is restricted by specific rules. See Chapter 15.

ment. Therefore, the plan must provide a means of determining the amount of benefit payable to employees with a given termination date. To do this, the qualified plan benefit is treated as having been earned over the employee's entire period of employment. The amount of benefit earned as of a given date is referred to as the *accrued benefit* at that date. The concept of the accrued benefit is also important in certain actuarial methods for determining annual plan costs.

Every qualified plan must include a means for determining the participant's accrued benefit. Furthermore, to prevent discrimination, Section 411(b) of the Code requires benefits to accrue at a minimum specified rate. The purpose of the benefit accrual rules is to prevent the plan from having an excessive amount of what is known as *backloading*. An extreme example of a backloaded plan would be one that had a normal retirement age of 65 with a provision that no employee who terminated employment prior to age 63 would receive any benefit under the plan. In effect, all of the benefits under this plan would accrue during the two years between the ages 63 and 65. This much backloading is not permitted under current rules. Obviously, the purpose of the accrual rules is to prevent employers from favoring highly compensated employees who are the ones most likely to continue employment to later ages. Incidentally, the benefit accrual rules do not prevent "frontloading"—that is, rapid benefit accrual during a participant's earlier years of employment. However, few employers would have any reason for designing a frontloaded plan.

Benefit Accrual Rules

In a defined-contribution plan, a participant's accrued benefit is simply equal to the balance in that participant's account under the plan. The account balance includes employer and employee contributions, forfeitures from accounts of other employees in the case of profit-sharing plans, and investment earnings on the account, less any distributions from the account. If a defined-contribution plan has a nondiscriminatory contribution formula, normally there is no problem of backloading. Consequently, no specific rates of accrual are required for defined-contribution plans.

For defined-benefit plans, however, benefits must accrue at a rate specified in Section 411(b) of the Code. Basically, the plan's accrual rate must be at least as fast as one of three alternative minimum rules:

1. *Three Percent Rule.* Under this rule, the benefit accrued by a participant during each year of participation must be at least 3 percent of the maximum benefit that a hypothetical participant can accrue by entering at the plan's earliest entry age and participating until normal retirement.

2. *133 1/3 Percent Rule.* Under this rule, the rate of benefits accrued in any given plan year cannot be more than 133 1/3 percent of the rate of benefit accrual during any prior year.

3. *Fractional Rule.* Under this rule, the benefit the employee has accrued at the date of termination of service must be proportionate to the normal retirement benefit; the following requirement must be satisfied.

$$\text{Benefit on termination} = \text{Normal retirement benefit if participant continued to normal retirement age} \times \frac{\text{Years of actual participation}}{\text{Years of participation if terminated at normal retirement}}$$

As an example of the fractional rule, suppose that an employee has participated in the plan for 20 years and terminates at age 55. The plan's normal retirement age is 65. If the employee had continued working to age 65, the plan would have provided an annuity of $12,000 per year beginning at age 65. The fractional rule would require a termination benefit of at least 20/30 (or two thirds) of $12,000, or $8,000 annually beginning at age 65. If the plan does not provide at least this amount, it must meet one of the other two accrued benefit rules or it will be disqualified.

The tendency is for most plans to provide a termination benefit based on the fractional rule, since it is simpler to design and explain to participants.

Plans that are funded exclusively by the purchase of insurance contracts providing level annual premium payments to retirement and providing benefits guaranteed by an insurance company are not specifically subject to the three accrual rules above, if the accrued benefit meets the following tests: (1) the accrued benefit is not less than the cash surrender value of the participant's insurance contracts at any time and (2) the insurance premiums are paid up, the insurance contracts are not subject to a security interest, and no policy loans are outstanding. The assumption is that, if all these conditions are satisfied, plans funded with insurance contracts will automatically meet or exceed the benefit accrual test. *Note:* this exception applies only to what are known as "fully insured" plans, not to all plans that use an insurance contract or contracts for funding. The use of insurance contracts in plan funding is discussed in Chapter 11.

Summary

A qualified plan must provide vesting at least as fast as that provided under two standards: the five-year rule and the three- to seven-year rule. The plan designer should choose a vesting schedule that meets these rules and also meets the employer's cost and incentive standards.

The vesting rules determine the amount of benefit payable to a participant upon termination of employment. Payment of such benefits is usually deferred to retirement age for a defined-benefit plan, but may begin earlier in a defined-contribution plan.

A qualified plan must specify the amount of benefit accrued each year by a plan participant. The rate of benefit accrual is subject to legal limits designed to prevent excessive backloading of plan accruals.

8

Pension Plan Design: Benefit Formulas

Objectives of This Chapter

So far, the discussion in this text has been relatively general; Chapters 8–12 will now focus on the design of pension *plans—that is, those designed primarily for retirement benefits. The objectives of Chapter 8 are:*

- Outline the decisions to be made in the process of designing a pension plan.
- Explain the significance of a plan's normal retirement age, how it is determined, and its relation to early and late retirement.
- Describe the money-purchase plan formula and its uses.
- Describe the target formula and its uses.
- Discuss how defined-benefit formulas differ from defined-contribution formulas and the planning significance of these differences.
- Describe flat-benefit formulas and unit-benefit formulas, and when it is appropriate to use one or the other.
- Discuss cash-balance formulas and their uses.
- Discuss the definition of compensation, distinguishing career-average and final-average formulas.
- Explain the rules restricting plan discrimination based on sex.
- Discuss the ways in which a pension plan can deal with inflation as it affects benefit adequacy.

Structure and Design of a Pension Plan

A qualified pension plan is a labyrinth of concepts and terminology. One way to thread the labyrinth is to follow an employee covered under a typical plan. This may help to illustrate the process of qualified pension plan design discussed here.

Suppose Clutch Company has a qualified defined-benefit plan. When employee Bill is hired, he does not automatically become a participant, because he must meet the plan's eligibility requirements, basically consisting of a definition of the covered group and a waiting period. When Bill enters the plan and becomes a plan *participant*, Clutch Company must begin to put money into a fund designed to accept, invest, accumulate, and pay out money belonging to the plan. Also, when Bill enters, he begins to *accrue benefits* under the plan. In the Clutch plan, as in many plans, the amount of benefit accrued each year is determined by estimating the benefit Bill will receive at retirement and allocating that amount in a specified manner over each of Bill's anticipated years of employment prior to his expected retirement date.

Since the Clutch plan does not allow loans to participants or provide incidental insurance coverage (although it could do these things), Bill will receive no benefit from the plan until he terminates employment with Clutch. If he terminates before retirement and before he has served Clutch long enough to be *vested*, he will receive nothing, even though he has accrued a benefit under the plan. If he terminates after vesting, he will receive all or a portion of his benefit accrued to that date. This benefit will begin immediately if he has reached the plan's specified early retirement age or normal retirement age. These ages are 62 and 65 in the Clutch plan, a typical choice of ages that is within the limits of the qualified plan law. If Bill has not reached either of these ages, the Clutch plan (a typical plan) will not pay benefits until Bill reaches age 65, unless the benefit is very small, in which case Bill will be paid his benefit immediately in a cash lump sum. Except for this, the plan gives Bill a choice of various forms of benefit (all of equal value to the plan) at retirement—a life annuity, an annuity for the joint lives of Bill and his wife, and several others.

This little scenario illustrates major planning decisions:

> The initial question in designing any qualified plan—What group of employees should be covered under the plan? (Chapter 6.)
> Should there be a waiting period for plan entry by new emloyees? (Chapter 6.)
> Should the plan be funded solely by the employer or should employees contribute? (Chapter 5.)
> What is the plan's normal retirement age (and how are earlier and later retirement treated)? (Chapter 8.)
> What is the plan benefit at retirement? (Chapters 8 and 9.)
> How fast do benefits accrue to employees? (Chapters 7 and 8.)
> What do employees receive upon termination of employment before retirement (i.e., what vesting schedule)? (Chapter 7.)
> What provisions should the plan have for employees who terminate employment because of death or disability? (Chapter 10.)
> Who should hold the plan funds, and on what terms? (Chapter 12.)
> What will the plan cost the employer each year? (Chapter 11.)
> In what form are benefits paid? (Chapter 16.)

Retirement Age

A plan's *normal retirement age* is the age at which a participant can retire and receive the full specified retirement benefit. A defined-benefit plan must specify a normal retirement age to fully define the benefit. Defined-contribution plans do not need a normal retirement age for this purpose, but they may have a normal retirement age to specify an age at which participants can retire and begin to receive benefits.

A plan's normal retirement age can be no greater than the latest of:

Age 65.

If a participant entered within five years of normal retirement age, the fifth anniversary of plan entry.

For a participant not covered by the preceding five-year rule, the 10th anniversary of plan entry.[1]

Thus, for example, a plan having a normal retirement age of 65 could provide normal retirement at age 67 for a participant entering at age 62, or age 68 for a participant entering at age 58.

Although most plans use 65 as the normal retirement age, the plan may specify an earlier normal retirement age. The use of an earlier normal retirement age in a defined-benefit plan requires that funding be accelerated—that is, larger amounts must be contributed to the plan each year to fund each employee's benefit, because the benefit will become payable at an earlier date. For plans in which tax sheltering is a primary consideration, such as plans oriented toward key employees in a closely held business, the use of the earliest possible normal retirement age can provide significant additional tax benefits by increasing the deductible plan contributions each year. However, if the normal retirement age is less than the social security retirement age, the Section 415 limitations are reduced, as discussed in Chapter 18. This tends to provide some limit on the use of unrealistically low normal retirement ages.

The IRS considers a plan's retirement age to be an actuarial assumption.[2] Therefore, the requirement of "reasonableness" for actuarial assumption, as discussed in Chapter 11, also puts some limit on the use of unrealistically low normal retirement ages.

Early Retirement

A qualified plan may designate an *early retirement age* at which an employee may retire and receive an immediate benefit. The early retirement benefit is usually reduced below that payable at normal retirement. The plan may have some specific

---

[1] Code Section 411(a)(8)

[2] IRS 7(10)5(10), *Actuarial Guidelines Handbook*, (Department of the Treasury, Internal Revenue Service, December 12, 1984).

service retirement for early retirement, such as 10 years of service, or it may permit early retirement simply upon attainment of the early retirement age.

Under most defined-benefit plans, the monthly early retirement benefit is reduced below the monthly normal retirement benefit payable at age 65, because of two factors. First, the early retirement benefit will usually be limited to the participant's accrued benefit, and, in many cases, the participant will not have accrued the full benefit at early retirement. Second, most plans require an actuarial reduction. The actuarial reduction is a mathematical adjustment based on (1) longer life expectancy at early retirement, (2) loss of investment earnings to the plan fund due to payments beginning earlier, and (3) mortality—the fact that the plan has lost the possibility that the participant might die before payments begin. It is possible for the plan to provide a reduction less than the full amount dictated by these two factors, perhaps as an incentive to encourage older employees to retire. However, if the plan formula is integrated with social security, specific early retirement reductions are required, as discussed in Chapter 9.

Most plans do not require employer consent for early retirement. If employer consent is required, the IRS limits the early retirement benefit to the vested accrued benefit that would be payable if the employee terminated employment unilaterally—to avoid the possibility that the employer will favor highly compensated employees in granting early retirement benefits.

For defined-contribution plans, early retirement is usually treated the same as a termination of employment, and the benefit payable at early retirement is simply the amount of the participant's account balance as of that date. Thus, many defined-contribution plans do not specify an early retirement age.

Late Retirement

A qualified plan design should also cover the possibility of late retirement—that is, retirement after the normal retirement age. Under the age-discrimination rules discussed below, the plan must continue benefit accruals for employees who continue working after the normal retirement age, unless the plan's benefit formula stops benefit accruals after a specified number of years and the employee has enough years of service to cease accruals for that reason. Benefit formulas must be designed carefully to insure appropriate treatment of older employees. Often in smaller businesses, older participants are owners or key employees who will want the plan to provide substantial benefits. On the other hand, many larger employers want to encourage earlier retirement and will want to provide only the minimum late retirement benefit required under the law.

Age Discrimination

The Federal Age Discrimination Act, as amended in 1978 and 1986, has an impact on qualified plans. The Age Discrimination Act applies to workers and managers of any business that engages in interstate transactions (a very broad category) and employs at least 20 persons during the year. Certain hazardous occupations are excluded, as well as executive employees who would be entitled, upon retirement, to an annual pension of $44,000 or more over and above social security benefits.

The main provision of the age-discrimination law that affects qualified plans prohibits involuntary retirement at any age.[3] A qualified plan must not in any way require mandatory retirement.

In addition, the 1986 age-discrimination provisions added specific Code provisions (Sections 411(b)(1)(H) and 411(b)(2)) dealing with benefits for older workers. In general, older workers must be treated the same as younger workers with regard to plan contributions (for a defined-contribution plan) and benefit accruals (for a defined-benefit plan). However, for a defined-benefit plan, the benefit formula can provide that benefits are fully accrued not at a specified age but after a specified number of years of service, such as 25. This will cut off further benefit accrual for many older employees, but it is permitted. If a plan provides for normal retirement at 65, with actuarial increases for later retirement, the actuarial increases are credited toward any requirement of benefit accrual that applies. For example, if a plan provides a benefit of $1,000 per month beginning at age 65 or an actuarially adjusted $1,100 per month beginning at age 66, the extra $100 is counted as an additional benefit accrual.

Benefit Formulas

A pension plan's benefit formula is obviously the central issue in plan design. Great variety is possible, within the restrictions to be discussed here. Some simple rules can be set forth at the outset. First, the plan formula cannot, on its face, discriminate in favor of highly compensated employees. Also, civil rights laws prevent discrimination with respect to race, religion, or national origin. Age-discrimination issues were discussed earlier in this chapter.

Another basic rule for pension formulas is that a pension plan must provide *definitely determinable* benefits.[4] The plan must permit a determination of each participant's benefit at retirement. For a defined-benefit plan this is inherent in the formula; for a defined-contribution plan the benefit will vary according to the investment results of the plan fund, but this does not violate the definitely determinable requirement as long as the employer is obligated to make a definite contribution each year. The definitely determinable rule prohibits a defined-benefit pension plan from using forfeitures from terminating employees to increase plan benefits. Forfeitures are amounts left behind in the plan fund when participants terminate employment without a fully vested benefit. In a defined-benefit plan, these forfeitures must be used to reduce future employer contributions. However, forfeitures in a defined-contribution plan (pension or other) may be reallocated to the remaining participants' accounts. The impact of this is discussed further in Chapter 13 in connection with profit-sharing plans.

---

[3]29 USC §623(f)(2).
[4]Reg. Sec. 1.401-1(b)(1)(i).

Defined-Contribution Formulas

A defined-contribution plan is much simpler than a defined-benefit plan. In a defined-contribution plan, the plan simply specifies the amount that the employer will contribute to the plan. Basically, there are two types of contribution formulas for defined-contribution pension plans—the *money-purchase* formula and the *target-benefit* formula.

In terms of the number of plans, defined-contribution plans (including profit-sharing as well as pension plans) constitute about 70 percent of all qualified plans.[5] However, if a comparison is made on the basis of employees covered under qualified plans, the result is the opposite—about 60 percent of such employees are in defined-benefit plans. This indicates, not surprisingly, that defined-benefit plans tend to cover larger groups. However, defined-benefit plans are often used for smaller groups as well.

Money-Purchase Formulas. For a *money-purchase* formula, the annual employer contribution is usually a stated percentage of each employee's compensation—for example, 6 percent of compensation.

In a money-purchase plan, as in all defined-contribution plans, there is an individual account for each employee. The amount of the benefit at retirement is equal to the employee's account balance at the retirement date or at a valuation date near the time of the retirement date. The plan may provide for payment of the benefit in a lump sum, or a variety of payment options including annuity benefits may be made available. The accounts of all employees are usually commingled for investment purposes, but each account is kept separate administratively, so the account increases and decreases in accordance with the investment performance of the fund. Thus, the benefit available at retirement cannot be predicted exactly. Investment risk lies with the employee. If the employee's account is less than anticipated, the employer is not required to make additional contributions.

As Table 8–1 shows, money-purchase plans tend to provide a better benefit for employees who enter the plan at younger ages, because a longer time is available to accumulate plan contributions and compound these contributions with investment earnings. If the employer has employees with a wide range of ages at the inception of the plan, this feature of a money-purchase plan makes it impossible to provide older employees with retirement income that is comparable, as a percentage of their preretirement income (the *replacement ratio*), to that of the younger employees. As discussed below, comparable replacement ratios for older and younger employees can be better achieved with a target plan or defined-benefit plan.

The great advantage of a money-purchase plan is simplicity. The benefit formula is readily understandable by employees and employer, actuarial services are not required, and plan installation and drafting are simpler. Also, the PBGC in-

---

[5]*Employee Benefit Notes*, September 1986 (estimate based on Labor Department data and IRS determination letter statistics) (Washington, D.C.: Employee Benefit Research Institute).

TABLE 8–1. Defined-Contribution Plan Accumulations *(Annual Employer Contributions $1,000 per Employee; Retirement Age 65; Average Investment Return 7 Percent)*

Age at Plan Entry	Account Balance at Retirement
25	$213,609
30	147,913
40	67,676
50	26,888
55	14,783
60	6,153

surance and reporting requirements do not apply to defined-contribution plans, including money-purchase plans.

Target Plans

From a planning point of view, the target-benefit plan is a hybrid of the defined-contribution and defined-benefit approaches. Under a target plan, the employer chooses a target level of retirement benefit using a benefit-formula approach similar to that used in designing a defined-benefit plan.

For example, the target-benefit level might be some percentage of final-average compensation. An actuarial calculation is made at the plan's inception of the level annual contribution amount (for each participant) that would be required to fully fund this benefit at the participant's normal retirement date. These level amounts are then actually contributed by the employer to the plan each year. Unlike a defined-benefit plan, however, there is no change in the level contribution amount if actual investment return or mortality varies from the assumptions used in determining the initial contribution level. Therefore, at retirement, the amount actually available may be more or less than anticipated. The plan has individual accounts for each participant and, unlike a defined-benefit plan, each employee's benefit is limited to the amount actually in his or her individual account. The plan, therefore, meets the definition of a defined-contribution plan, because it is an individual account plan.

A variation of this planning approach might be for the employer to guarantee a floor amount to each participant to prevent devastating losses. From the point of view of the tax law, a plan with such a floor would actually constitute two plans: one a defined-benefit plan with a benefit equal to the floor amount, and the other a defined-contribution target plan superimposed on top of the floor plan.

The best way to understand how a target plan works is to examine Table 8–2.

This example uses a somewhat unrealistic employee census for illustrative purposes—the employees vary in age but the same annual compensation of $30,000 is assumed for each. The target benefit is 50 percent of the final-average

TABLE 8–2.* Target-Benefit Plan (Nonintegrated)

Employee's Age	Compensation Pay	50 Percent "Target" Benefit	Annual Contribution	5½ Percent "Target" Maturity Value†	4 Percent Return Maturity Value	8 Percent Average Return Maturity Value	10 Percent Average Return Maturity Value
20	$30,000	$15,000	$ 901	$175,000	$113,398	$376,067	$712,506
30	30,000	15,000	1,655	175,000	126,739	307,998	493,400
40	30,000	15,000	3,243	175,000	140,451	256,030	350,833
45	30,000	15,000	4,757	175,000	147,327	235,117	299,703
50	30,000	15,000	7,402	175,000	154,146	217,056	273,502
55	30,000	15,000	12,883‡	175,000	160,866	201,554	225,854
60	30,000	15,000	29,721‡	175,000	167,418	188,312	199,594

*This table is adopted from an illustration used in The American College's Advanced Pension Planning course.
†Based on a 5½ percent interest rate and an annuity purchase rate of $1,400 for $10 per month.
‡Since a target plan is subject to the defined-contribution maximum annual-additions limitation of 25 percent or $30,000, the contribution for these two employees would have to be limited to $7,500 ($30,000 x 25%).

compensation and, for purposes of funding the plan initially, the current compensation is used. This is the usual approach, even though it theoretically might be possible to use an assumption of salary increases (salary scale). However, this ordinarily would not be feasible, because the projected compensation levels, particularly for younger employees, would tend to reach very high levels. In this illustrative plan the 50 percent target benefit would provide a pension of $15,000 annually for each employee.

The column of Table 8–2 headed "Annual Contribution" represents the annual level employer contribution determined by the actuary in order to fund this pension beginning at age 65. Actuarial methods and assumptions are discussed in Chapter 11. For reference, the assumptions here are 5½ percent interest rate and an annuity purchase rate at age 65 of $1,400 for $10 per month. At that annuity purchase rate, it would be necessary to have $175,000 in the fund for each participant at age 65 to provide a pension of $15,000 annually. The annual contribution is the amount determined by the actuary as the level-funding amount that will provide a fund equal to $175,000 for each employee as that employee reaches age 65. The calculation does not use a mortality assumption. This will be appropriate for a small employee group and a plan that provides a death benefit equal only to the participant's account balance. If this is not the case, the funding calculation should consider taking mortality into account.

Note: first, the annual contribution on behalf of the employees of varying ages is radically different. The contribution for older employees is much greater, relatively speaking, because less time is available to fund the benefit. In this respect, a target plan is similar to a defined-benefit plan. In some cases, this may allow the plan to discriminate significantly in favor of employees who are older when the plan is initiated—typically, the owners of the company or other members of the prohibited group. The extent to which such discrimination is possible is somewhat limited, however, as will be discussed below.

Second, a target plan is a defined-contribution plan for purposes of the Section 415 limits (see Chapter 18). Thus, the annual addition to each participant's account cannot exceed the lesser of 25 percent of compensation or the applicable dollar figure for the year in which the annual addition is made ($30,000, to be indexed after 1987). In this example, it means that the contribution determined by the actuary for the employees aged 55 and 60 is too much. For those employees, only $7,500 (25 percent of $30,000) can be contributed because of the annual-additions limit. Thus, because the annual-additions limit applies to a target plan, it restricts to some degree the amount of discrimination in favor of older employees that is possible in a target plan, compared with a defined-benefit plan. If the plan in this example were a defined-benefit plan, the corporation could contribute the actuarially determined amount for the two employees aged 55 and 60 ($12,883 and $29,721, respectively) because the annual-additions limit would not apply, and the benefit of 50 percent of final-average compensation would be well within the Section 415 limit for defined-benefit plans.

A third important feature of the target plan illustrated here is that, even though the actuarially determined contribution level is designed to provide the same pension benefit for all participants (50 percent of compensation or $15,000), if the actual rates of return vary from the actuarial assumptions, the benefits will differ. A lower rate of return will produce a lower benefit for everyone (refer to the column headed "4 percent Average Return Maturity Value"), but the older employees will do better at retirement than the younger employees. Conversely, a return higher than the assumed rate will provide everyone with a better pension than expected, but the higher rate will tend to favor the younger employees (refer to the column headed "8 percent" or "10 percent Average Return Maturity Value").

This feature of the target plan provides a possibility for manipulating the initial interest assumption to discriminate in favor of older or younger employees, depending on which group the planner desires to favor. Because of this, the IRS imposes a restriction on assumed investment rates in Rev. Rul. 76-464; the assumed rate essentially must be between 5 and 6 percent to avoid special IRS scrutiny. If a different assumed rate is used, the employer will have to prove that the plan does not discriminate in favor of the prohibited group. *Note:* these restricted rates are rather low in terms of current investment returns, and, consequently, a plan complying with Rev. Rul. 76-464 would currently tend to be relatively favorable to younger employees.

The contributions to a target-benefit plan may be invested in a variety of ways. Generally, the approach is to invest in a separate equity portfolio to obtain the benefits of equity growth and provide a hedge against inflation. At retirement, the existing account may be used to provide a benefit in whatever form is appropriate. A lump sum or an annuity are the usual forms of benefit.

It is possible to integrate a target-benefit plan with social security. The detailed rules for this are somewhat complex and will not be given in detail here.[6]

---

[6]The rules are given in Section 18 of Rev. Rul. 71-446, but must be interpreted in light of subsequent changes in the law which reduced the maximum integration percentage for defined-

In general, the integration rules are not those for a defined-contribution plan, but are similar to those applicable to a defined-benefit plan, with modifications reflecting the fact that the actual benefit may be in excess of the initial target level.

Defined-Benefit Formulas

The basic difference between a defined-benefit plan and a defined-contribution plan is that, in a defined-benefit plan, the plan formula specifies the benefit that will be paid to the employee. There are no individual accounts for employees, and, consequently, the employee does not bear the risk of bad investment results. Payment of the promised benefit is an obligation of the employer, and the employer is required to fund the plan in advance so that sufficient funds will be available.

Defined-benefit plans are the most complex of all qualified plans. The benefit formulas themselves tend to be complex because of the complex employer objectives sought. The actuarial funding approach requires additional administrative costs for the plan. Also, the law dealing with defined-benefit plans is appropriately complex.

General Characteristics of Defined-Benefit Formulas

Defined-benefit formulas have two basic characteristics that determine their use in pension plan design. First, the amount of an employee's benefit is not necessarily directly related to total compensation from the employer during the period the employee is covered under the plan, as with a defined-contribution plan (except for a target-benefit plan). This means that the employer can design the plan with reference to a desired retirement income level for an employee, even if the employee had relatively low compensation in certain years or participated in the plan for a relatively short time.

The second basic characteristic is that defined-benefit formulas can favor those employees who enter the plan at later ages. This is because the benefit for such employees is a stated amount—often the same amount payable to employees who entered the plan at earlier ages—even though the employer's annual cost for funding the benefit is greater for employees entering the plan at later ages. As an example, consider three employees having the same compensation of $50,000 annually, and a plan providing a benefit of 50 percent of this compensation at age 65. If these employees entered the plan at ages 30, 40, and 50, respectively, the employer's level annual cost to provide the same retirement benefit for each is illustrated in Table 8–3.

These basic characteristics relate to the two principal types of employer objectives that can be met with a defined-benefit plan. One objective is to provide a reasonable income replacement ratio for all covered employees; the flexibility of defined-benefit formulas permits this. The other type of objective is philosophi-

---

contribution plans from 7 percent to 5.7 percent (see Chapter 9). Thus, the actual allowable integration levels may only be $5.7/7$ of the levels prescribed in Rev. Rul. 71–446.

TABLE 8–3

Age at Entry	Employer Contribution Each Year to Retirement
30	$ 1,971
40	4,309
50	10,847

Assumptions: 7 percent investment return, no mortality, unisex annuity purchase rate $1,400 per $10 monthly at age 65.

cally quite different—the objective of providing the maximum tax shelter under the plan for key employees. In a closely held business, where this objective is often dominant, the key employees are typically older at the plan's inception. Thus, the second basic defined-benefit plan characteristic illustrated in Table 8–3 is significant, as is the flexibility of defined-benefit formula design.

Replacement Ratio Approach. In adopting an income replacement ratio approach to benefit formula design, the starting point is to examine the employee census of the employees to be covered and determine an appropriate level of retirement income. As discussed in Chapter 1, for all but the lowest-paid employees, a retiree's standard of living usually can be maintained with less than 100 percent of preretirement income. Qualified plans that use this approach typically aim at providing (from the plan, plus social security retirement benefits) about 50 to 75 percent of preretirement gross (before-tax) income.

An appropriate benefit formula is designed to provide the desired replacement ratio, using the design rules discussed in the rest of this chapter. The annual cost of the plan is then determined. If this exceeds the employer's cost objectives, the plan must be redesigned until the cost comes within the appropriate range. It is also possible to vary the annual cost by varying the actuarial methods and assumptions used, as discussed in Chapter 11.

Types of Formulas

Many different benefit formulas have been developed to meet various plan design objectives. A very large degree of variation is possible, within the limits of the rules for integration with social security, discussed below, the benefit accrual rules discussed in Chapter 7, and the general nondiscrimination requirements for qualified plans. The possible benefit formulas can be divided into a number of specific types. The IRS distinguishes two different types of benefit formulas: the flat-benefit formula and the unit-benefit formula.

Flat-Benefit Formula. This type of formula does not take an employee's service into account. Such a benefit formula might be either a *flat-amount* formula, such as a formula providing a benefit of $100 per month at retirement for each employee, or a *flat-percentage* formula—for example, a benefit of 40 percent of compensation at retirement.

The flat-amount approach is usually suitable only for a group of employees having almost the same compensation levels, because most pension planners would want to take differing compensation levels into account in determining the retirement income level. However, the flat-amount formula has the advantage of simplicity. The flat-percentage approach takes differing compensation into account, and is frequently used. The plan's definition of compensation, as discussed below, is an important element of this formula.

All flat-benefit formulas raise the problem of fairness among employees with differing amounts of service with the employer. Many employers would prefer not to give the same benefit to short- and long-service employees, even though they have the same compensation levels. This objective can often be resolved by having a minimum period of service required to receive the full stated dollar amount or percentage, with reductions for lesser amounts of service. A more definite solution is to use a unit-benefit formula, discussed next.

Unit-Benefit Formula. A unit-benefit formula is a formula based on the employee's service. Some unit-benefit formulas take only service into account, with no compensation factor—for example, a benefit providing $10 per month for each year of service. As with the flat-amount formula, such a formula is usually only suitable for a group having a fairly narrow range of compensation. Such formulas are sometimes used in collectively bargained plans, for example. A unit-benefit formula may also take account of compensation—for example, a formula providing a benefit of 1 percent of compensation for each year of service (or to state it another way, 1 percent of compensation times the employee's years of service).

Past Service. When a unit-benefit plan is installed for an existing, rather than a new, employee group, the employer must decide whether to give service credit only for prospective or future service or to give some credit for existing employees' prior service for the employer. In the case of small closely held businesses, the owners and key employees often have considerable past service, compared with other employees, and it is particularly common to have past-service provisions in such plans. Past-service credit can be provided in many ways, as long as there is no discrimination in favor of highly compensated employees. Past service can be treated the same as future service, or the formula can provide somewhat lesser credit for past service.

The ability to utilize past service is one of the major advantages of a defined-benefit plan over a defined-contribution plan. For example, suppose a plan is adopted by an employer with two employees, one aged 30 with 5 years of prior service and the other aged 50 with 25 years of prior service. If a defined-contribution plan is adopted, the younger employee will have at age 65 a plan account representing 35 years of employer contributions, while the older employee will have only 15 years of contributions at retirement. However, a unit-benefit plan providing an annual benefit of 1 percent of compensation for each year of past and future service would allow each employee to retire at age 65 with an annual benefit of 40 percent of compensation.

The Cash-Balance Formula

The cash-balance formula—sometimes referred to as a guaranteed-account formula, as well as other names—is a type of hybrid between defined-benefit and defined-contribution approaches that is, in a sense, the opposite of the other hybrid, the target-benefit formula. In the target formula, employer contributions are based on age at entry, but ultimate benefits are not guaranteed. With a cash-balance formula, employer contributions are based on compensation, not on age at entry, but the ultimate benefit (account balance) is subject to a guaranteed rate of return.

In a cash-balance plan, "accounts" for each participant are set up. Unlike the accounts in a defined-contribution plan, there is no investment risk—the accounts are merely a computational formality. The accounts are credited at least annually with two types of credits—a pay credit and an interest credit. The pay credit is generally a percentage of compensation. The pay credit formula may be integrated with social security; for example, the plan might provide a pay credit each year of 2 percent of each participant's total earnings plus 3 percent of the participant's earnings above an integration level related to the social security taxable wage base.[7] The interest credit is an amount representing earnings on the participant's account balance. To meet the definitely determinable rule applicable to pension formulas, the interest credit must be an amount that is defined in the plan and not subject to the employer's discretion. For example, the interest credit each year might be defined as the lesser of the change in the consumer price index (CPI) for the preceding year or the one-year rate for Treasury securities. However, the employer can have the option of crediting actual plan earnings, if these are higher.

Because there are no true individual accounts—participants have a guaranteed minimum benefit that can be legally satisfied out of the entire plan fund—the plan does not meet the definition of a defined-contribution plan and is, thus, technically a defined-benefit plan. Consequently, the plan is subject to a more complex legal environment; it is subject to PBGC reporting and termination requirements (Chapter 21) and the requirement of actuarial certifications.

The employer's cost for the plan is determined actuarially, because of the guarantee features. Costs can be controlled to some extent by choosing appropriate factors for the interest credits. However, if interest credits do not generally keep pace with actual plan earnings, participants are likely to be dissatisfied with the plan.

---

[7]A cash-balance formula must meet the rules for integrating a defined-benefit plan—see the following chapter. The actuary typically will do this by showing that the "worst case"—the most discriminated-against participant—will receive at least as much as under the defined-benefit integration rules.

Despite the plan's technical status as a defined-benefit plan, a cash-balance plan looks to employees very much like a money-purchase plan and serves some of the same objectives. Typically, the cash-balance plan will be attractive to younger employees, for the reasons already discussed. Thus, it is attractive to employers wishing to retain younger employees or to allocate pension costs in a way that does not discriminate against younger employees. At the same time, the guarantee features help to meet some of the retirement-security objectives of the traditional defined-benefit plan.

Definition of Compensation

For formulas that are based on compensation, the definition of compensation provides some flexibility in planning. Definitions of compensation can be classified into two categories: *career average* and *final average*. With a career-average formula, the employee's compensation over the entire working period is averaged. Another way of putting this is that the benefit earned in a given year of service is based on the compensation for that year. Any defined-contribution formula is effectively a career-average formula, but defined-benefit plans can also use the career-average approach. In a final-average formula, the compensation used is averaged over a specified period of years, usually chosen to produce a relatively high benefit. For example, the compensation used in the benefit formula could be defined as compensation over the employee's five final years of service. To guard against the possibility of a salary decrease in the final years of service, due to partial disability or other cause, many plans define compensation as the compensation over a specified consecutive period during which the average compensation is the highest. There is some flexibility in the number of years that can be used for the averaging, but at least three years must be used in a plan integrated with social security (discussed in the next chapter).

In defining compensation for plan purposes, a decision must be made whether to use total compensation (salary or wages plus bonuses, overtime, and the like) or some lesser amount, such as base salary only. Flexibility is permitted here, but, if anything other than total compensation is used, the method chosen must not produce discrimination. For example, excluding overtime pay in the benefit formula might be discriminatory if lower-paid workers typically receive substantial overtime pay while highly compensated employees do not.

Sex Discrimination

Sex discrimination as it relates to qualified plans, annuities, and life insurance is a subject that, at this writing, is not completely resolved, but some clear rules for qualified plan design have emerged. The issue arises from the statistical fact that women, as a group, live longer than men. This means that, if actuaries make separate calculations for men and women, the same periodic annuity costs more for women than for men of the same age. Or, for a given annuity premium, the periodic annuity amount is lower for women than for men.

The Civil Rights Act of 1964, like its predecessor, the Equal Pay Act of 1963, provides that it is an unlawful employment practice for an employer

> to discriminate against any individual with respect to his compensation, terms, conditions, or privileges of employment, because of such individual's race, color, religion, sex, or national origin . . . [Sec. 2000e-2(a), Civil Rights Act of 1964].

It is clear that qualified plan benefits are part of an employee's "compensation"; it was not originally clear, however, what constituted discrimination because of sex in a qualified plan. Must the plan provide the same periodic *benefit* for men and women employees, or must the plan provide only the same employer *contribution* to the plan? Early federal administrative guidelines under the Equal Pay Act of 1963 indicated that an employer satisfied the nondiscrimination requirement if it provided *either* equal periodic benefits or equal contributions. However, in 1972 the Equal Employment Opportunities Commission (EEOC) issued a revised sex discrimination guideline under the Civil Rights Act of 1964, stating that to avoid sex discrimination in retirement plans the employer must provide equal periodic benefits to men and women employees in all circumstances. Employers originally resisted this, but recent court cases clearly point in this direction. The most significant case so far is one that went to the United States Supreme Court, *Los Angeles Department of Water and Power* v. *Manhart*, 435 US 702 (1978). That case involved a contributory pension plan of a municipality. The Supreme Court held that the plan could not require women to pay higher contributions than men to receive equal periodic benefits upon retirement. More recently, the Supreme Court held in *Arizona Governing Committee* v. *Norris*, No. 82–52 (1983), that a municipal retirement plan could not provide sex-based annuity choices at retirement. No employer contributions were involved, only employee contributions.

Neither the *Manhart* nor *Norris* case nor any of the other cases has yet actually clearly settled the question whether the Civil Rights Act requires equal periodic benefits for men and women in an employer-provided retirement plan under all circumstances. Each case depends on specialized facts. However, the trend favors an equal-benefit approach, and virtually all planners assume this to be the law.

Most qualified plans already avoid obvious sex-discrimination problems. Most defined-benefit plans provide the same normal retirement benefit for men and women employees, and most defined-contribution plans provide the same employer contribution for men and women employees. Discrimination problems arise where a qualified plan (either defined-benefit or defined-contribution) offers participants a choice of benefits, including a retirement annuity. Most plan designers advise using only "unisex" annuities (those providing the same annuity rate for both men and women) for this purpose. Similarly, if a qualified plan offers life insurance as an incidental benefit (see Chapter 10), the life insurance cost to the employee must be determined on a unisex basis. However, in determining the annual deposit to a defined-benefit plan, the sex of covered employees may be taken into account, since it affects only the employer's costs and not the ultimate benefit that the employee will receive.

The sex-discrimination issue is complicated by the fact that the Civil Rights Act does not govern the pricing of insurance products, and private insurance companies, therefore, currently are allowed to use sex as a factor in determining life insurance and annuity rates. Where a qualified plan uses a group pension contract for funding (see Chapter 12), the argument has been made that this allows the use of sex-based annuity options under the group contract. However, it is the employer, not the insurance company, that provides the pension as part of an employee's compensation. In view of this and the trend of the court cases, insurance companies no longer offer sex-based annuities as part of a group pension contract.

Even if employers remove any conceivable sex discrimination from qualified plan documents as such, effective sex discrimination will still be possible as long as sex-based annuities are available from insurance companies, if the plan is designed so that participants can withdraw their benefits at retirement. In that situation, men can withdraw their benefits and purchase an annuity from an insurance company providing greater periodic payments than women would be able to purchase for the same amount (or payments greater than those available under the plan if the plan provides a unisex annuity). Because of this and other related problems, Congress is currently reconsidering the question whether insurance companies should be allowed to determine annuity and life insurance premiums on the basis of sex.

There is no doubt that sex is a relevant actuarial classification, as is any ascertainable factor affecting life expectancy, which could conceivably include such things as race, religion, or national origin. Insurance companies do not commonly use race or other potentially offensive actuarial factors, regardless of their relevance as predictors of life expectancy. However, they are strongly attached to the use of sex classifications and have vigorously opposed restrictions proposed in Congress.

Both sides of the controversy view the issue as one of fairness. Advocates of sex classification argue that unisex annuity rates are unfair to men, who should be allowed to purchase annuities reflecting their group's life expectancy. Opponents argue that it is unfair to attribute to an individual the characteristics of a group to which that individual belongs, regardless of whether the individual actually possesses those characteristics. Ultimately, Congress will probably have to determine the appropriate social policy in connection with insurance company practices.

Inflation and Pension Planning

Inflation has been a persistent feature of the U.S. economy since World War II. Although the rate of inflation has gone up and down during that period, many economists believe that some degree of inflation is a permanent structural feature of our economy. A qualified plan, particularly a defined-benefit pension plan, is at least theoretically a long-range program; benefit levels are often determined for a 25-year-old employee that will not be paid until 50 years later. Thus, inflation is a serious problem in the design of pension plans.

Although no really satisfactory solution to the problem of inflation in private pension plans has yet been devised, some planning approaches can help with this problem. A distinction can be made between approaches that are applied in the preretirement period, while the employee is still at work, and in the postretirement period, when the employee is least able to protect against inflation.

Preretirement Inflation

Some types of benefit design are inherently better able to cope with preretirement inflation than others. If the plan benefit depends upon employee compensation, the final-average definition of compensation usually does a better job in protecting the employee against inflation than the career-average definition, because the final-average definition bases benefits on the employee's highest compensation level. Much of the increase in an employee's compensation level over a working career merely reflects inflation. Other reasons for compensation increases are increases in general employee productivity and increases in the individual employee's merit, and both are also appropriately reflected in the retirement benefit. If the plan does not use a final average formula, the employer should consider reviewing periodically the plan's benefit level in light of inflation and amending the plan to increase benefits as appropriate. Also, it is possible to include an automatic mechanism in the plan, under which future benefit levels for current employees are increased in accordance with some kind of formula based on the inflation rate; however, this is rarely done.

Defined-contribution plans provide some inflation protection not available under defined-benefit plans, because the benefit in the defined-contribution plan depends upon the value of the investments in each participant's account. In the long run, a reasonably diversified investment portfolio tends to increase in value to keep pace with inflation. This is not necessarily true for short periods, however; in the 1970s, for example, common stocks often declined even as inflation reached new heights. However, most economists believe that the long-range linkage between asset values and inflation will continue, so defined-contribution plans can be useful in dealing with inflation. Naturally, for this to occur the investment portfolio has to be chosen to emphasize the types of assets—common stocks, for example—that typically show inflation-related growth.

A defined-contribution plan, however, has a disadvantage similar to that of a career-average benefit formula; contributions to the participant's account in the early years are based on then-current compensation, which typically is at a low level, compared with later years. This disadvantage tends to mitigate the advantage of possible investment-related growth.

Postretirement Inflation

In the postretirement period, one approach to inflation protection in defined-benefit plans is *indexation* of retirement benefits. With an indexed formula, the plan provides that the benefit is to be increased after retirement in accordance with some formula contained in the plan. The design problem here is the choice of a formula that accurately reflects the impact of inflation on retirees.

One approach is to use the consumer price index, a government-provided price index. The CPI is a measure of the relative rise from month to month of a "market basket" of consumer products purchased by a hypothetical average consumer. There is some debate about whether the CPI accurately reflects the impact of inflation on retired persons, since it may emphasize rising prices of items not normally purchased by retirees or, conversely, may understate the impact of rising prices for items particularly important to retirees. At one time, for example, the CPI had a large component reflecting the cost of new housing, which typically is not a significant item in retirees' budgets.

The government also provides various types of wage indexes indicating the increase in wages in specific portions of the work force. Theoretically, it is possible to index retirement benefits in accordance with a wage index. Based on past experience, in the long run this would produce a larger degree of increase in retirement benefits than the use of a price index, because wage indexes reflect increases in productivity, which have historically outdistanced inflationary price increases. However, in short-term periods, wage indexes can fall behind such cost indexes as the CPI. A theoretical advantage of wage indexing is that retirees will obtain the same (but no better) protection against inflation than people currently in the work force. Whatever the merits of this argument, however, wage indexes currently are rarely used.

A third approach to indexation is to use a formula for increasing benefits that is included in the plan itself and is not dependent on external price or wage indexes. Such a formula makes it easier for the employer to anticipate the cost of the benefit increases. The risk of possibly running ahead of the CPI can be minimized by providing that the formula increase will not exceed an amount determined by reference to the CPI or to other chosen economic indexes.

Indexed pension benefits are obviously attractive to participants, but currently they are not extensively used in the private pension system. This is because even a small annual or periodic percentage increase in pension benefits can result in a very large increase in the ultimate cost of the benefit. Private employers, therefore, often avoid indexation because of the possibility of incurring an uncontrollable future liability. However, indexation is quite common in pension programs of federal, state, and local government units. There, elected officials often grant indexed pensions to government employees, with the implicit expectation that taxpayers in the future (after current officials' terms have expired) will accept tax increases to fund the increased pension costs.

In the private sector, probably the most common mechanism for dealing with postretirement inflation is to increase pension benefits through ad hoc "supplemental payments" to retirees. At one time, there was some concern that a program of supplemental payments might be deemed a separate pension plan involving various federal regulatory complexities. However, to encourage employers to make such supplemental payments, the Labor Department recently issued relatively permissive new regulations concerning these payments. Under these regulations (Labor Regulations Sec. 2510.3-2(g)) a supplemental payment plan will not be treated as a separate pension plan but rather as a "welfare plan," which is subject to much simpler regulatory requirements, if the amount paid is limited by a formula that effectively restricts it to the cost-of-living increases that have occurred since the retirees' pension payments commenced. The supplemental payments can be made out of the employer's general assets or a separate trust fund can be established for them. In addition, there are special Code provisions (Section 415(k)(2)) allowing employees to contribute additional amounts to a defined-benefit plan to provide cost-of-living adjustments to benefits.

Summary

A plan's normal retirement age defines the age at which full plan benefits are available. The normal retirement age can be no greater than age 65 or 10 years after plan entry. However, federal age discrimination law prohibits mandatory retirement. A plan can have special provisions for early or late retirement.

Plan benefit formulas can be either defined contribution or defined benefit. Defined-contribution formulas provide a separate account for each employee, and the employee bears the investment risk. Defined-contribution pension plans are of the money-purchase or target type. The money-purchase plan provides a fixed percentage of compensation as a plan contribution, while in the target plan the contribution is based on both age and compensation, with higher contributions for older plan entrants.

Defined-benefit formulas can provide good replacement ratios, even for participants with relatively short service or low compensation in early years, and tend to favor older plan entrants. Flat-benefit formulas and unit-benefit (service-based) formulas can be used. Compensation as used in the formula can be career-average or final-average. The formula can also reflect past service in various ways. A cash-balance formula is a defined-benefit plan that works much like a money-purchase plan, with guarantee features shifting investment risk to the employer.

Qualified plans, as a form of compensation, are subject to the Civil Rights Act and, therefore, may not discriminate on the basis of sex. This has been interpreted to mean that no plan benefit can reflect the participant's sex. However, employer contributions to provide benefits can reflect cost differences based on sex.

Maintaining benefit adequacy to retirees in inflationary periods is a serious problem in designing private pensions. Full indexing is rarely used because of potentially uncontrollable costs. However, various approaches can be used to ease the burden of inflation.

9

Integration of Qualified Plans with Social Security

Objectives of This Chapter
- *Describe how social security integration is used in qualified plan design.*
- *Explain the theoretical rationale for social security integration.*
- *Discuss the rules for integrating defined-benefit plans under the offset and integration level methods.*
- *Discuss the rules for integrating defined-contribution plans.*

Purpose and Effect of Social Security Integration

Integration of a plan with social security further complicates the design of the benefit formula. More than half of all private qualified plans are integrated with social security, and the percentage is even higher among defined-benefit plans considered separately. The reason for this is the obvious overlap between private retirement benefits and the social security benefit. Although this is a complication, it also provides advantages in private plan design.

The existence of social security benefits is relevant to a number of objectives in designing a qualified plan.

1. The objective of providing an appropriate income replacement ratio must take into account the fact that the employee will receive social security benefits as well as benefits from the plan. If plan benefits alone are considered for this purpose, the actual replacement ratio will often be very different from what was intended.

2. The objective of plan efficiency can be met only if retirement benefits from social security are considered in designing the plan. Otherwise, private plan benefits for some employees may duplicate benefits they already receive from social security.

3. For the owner of a small business who is interested in maximizing the tax-sheltering benefits from the qualified plan, an integrated plan, as will be discussed below, provides a method by which the plan itself can, to a considerable

extent, discriminate in favor of higher-paid employees. Therefore, the objective of maximizing the tax-sheltering benefits of the qualified plan may lead to a consideration of integrating the plan with social security.

4. Finally, with regard to the employer's cost objectives, an integrated plan may provide a satisfactory level of retirement benefits to all employees at the lowest possible employer cost.

The principles of the integration rules are based on the way the OASDI social security benefit is calculated. For simplicity, this benefit will be referred to in this chapter as the social security benefit.

The social security benefit basically uses a unit-benefit type of formula based on the number of the employee's past years of work experience and the employee's compensation income in each of those years. More benefit credit is given for the "first dollars" of compensation than for larger amounts; and for compensation in a given year that exceeds the taxable wage base for that year, there is essentially no benefit credit.

The integration rules are designed to allow a private qualified plan to provide a benefit that is a mirror image of the social security benefit, so the two sources of retirement income together form a retirement program that is nondiscriminatory. Because of the nature of the social security benefit calculation, social security alone provides a higher percentage of income replacement for lower-paid employees than for higher-paid employees. Thus, the private plan correspondingly may provide a proportionately greater benefit for the *higher*-paid. Figures 9–1 and

FIGURE 9–1. Integrated Plan: Portion of Replacement Income—50% of Final-Average Compensation—Provided by Social Security and Private Plan

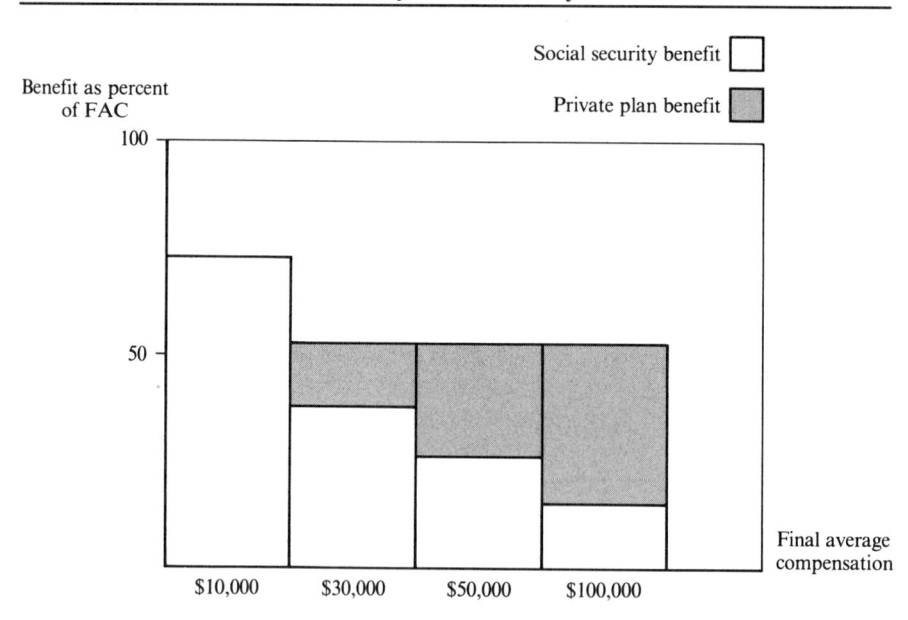

FIGURE 9–2. Integrated Plan—Sources of Total Retirement Benefit *(Qualitative Diagram for Illustration, Not for Calculation)*

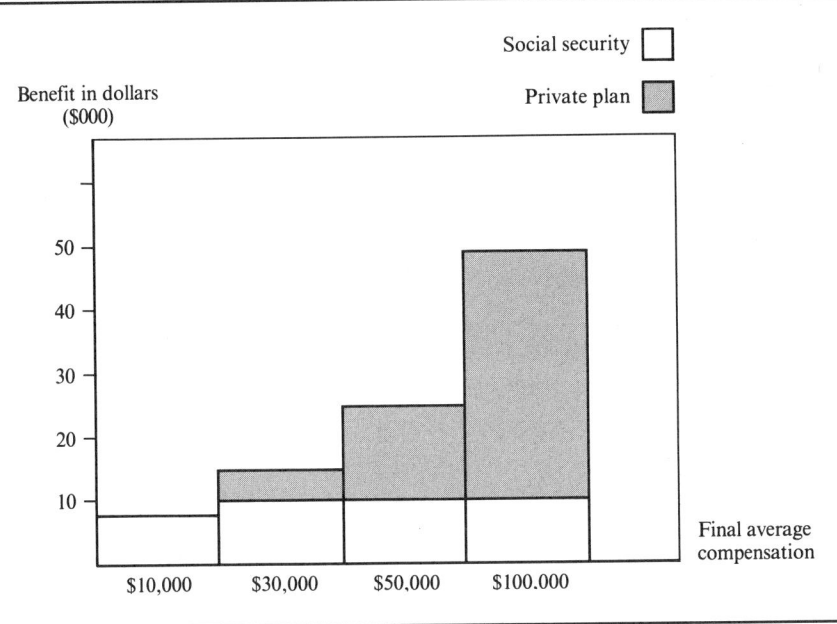

9–2 illustrate this qualitatively, while Table 9–1 gives some specific numerical examples. In all cases, note how social security integration allows the private plan (considered alone) to discriminate substantially in favor of the highly compensated, both in terms of benefit amounts and percentages of compensation.

An employer has much less freedom in integrating a qualified plan with social security than in integrating other types of benefit plans, such as disability income plans. Because of the potential for discrimination, the Code and associated regulations and IRS rulings impose very detailed limitations on integrating qualified plans. The law in effect before plan years beginning in 1989 was based almost exclusively on IRS rulings, particularly Rev. Rul. 71–446. The pre–1989 rules are discussed in some detail in Appendix A. The rules for 1989 and later are statutory (Code Sections 401(a)(5) and 401(l)), although IRS rulings and regulations will also be required to clarify certain points. The discussion in this chapter is based on the law applicable to 1989 and later plan years.

Under the principles of Rev. Rul. 71–446 as well as current Code Section 401(l), there are two basic approaches by which a qualified plan can be integrated with social security—the *offset* approach and the *integration level* approach (sometimes called the "excess" approach). Under the offset approach, a specified fraction of the primary social security benefit is subtracted from the benefit otherwise payable under the plan. The offset approach can be used only with a defined-benefit plan. Under the integration level approach, the plan specifies a level of compensation called the integration level. Benefits or contributions below this

TABLE 9–1. Effect of Integration on Replacement Percentage

Final-Average Pay in 1982	Replacement Percent—Social Security Only*	Replacement Percent—Integrated Plan A plus Social Security	Replacement Percent—Integrated Plan B plus Social Security
$ 5,000	54%	54%	59%
15,000	36	46	56
30,000	19	42	53
50,000	11	39	52
75,000	8	39	52
100,000	6	38	51

Integrated Plan A—flat-percentage plan: 0 percent of final-average pay up to $11,004; 36 percent over $11,004.

Integrated Plan B—offset plan: 50 percent of final-average pay, offset by 83⅓ percent of primary insurance amount.

*The examples reflect pre–1989 law, discussed in detail in Appendix A. The following assumptions are made: Employee retires at age 65 in 1982 with 35 years of service with employer. Final-average pay is the average over the last five years. Earnings assumed to increase at 6 percent per year from 1978 to 1982. For more details and illustrations see the President's 1978 Tax Program, U.S. Treasury Department Publication, 1978, the source from which the above chart was prepared.

integration level are provided at a lower rate than the benefits or contributions for compensation above the integration level. An integration level approach can be used with both defined-benefit and defined-contribution plans. The rules will next be discussed in detail, beginning with the integration of defined-benefit plans.

Integration of Defined-Benefit Plans

Offset Approach

As indicated above, a defined-benefit plan can be integrated with social security using either the offset approach or the integration level approach. Since the offset approach is simpler, it will be discussed first.

With the offset method, the private plan benefit is initially structured to provide the replacement ratio desired, without taking social security into account. Then the benefit formula is modified to subtract a specified amount to reflect the employee's social security benefit. For example, an offset formula might read as follows:

> Upon retirement, the participant shall be entitled to a monthly retirement benefit equal to 60 percent of the participant's final average monthly compensation, less 0.5 percent of the participant's monthly final average compensation for each year of service.

An offset cannot result in a complete elimination of the private plan benefit. The plan benefit may not be reduced by more than the *maximum offset allowance*, which is:

> For any year of service, 0.75 percent of the participant's final-average compensation, or,

for total benefits, 0.75 percent of the participant's final-average compensation multiplied by the participant's years of service with the employer, not in excess of 35.

Furthermore, in no event can the maximum offset allowance be more than 50 percent of the plan benefit that would have accrued without the offset.

The 0.75 percent fraction is reduced if the participant's final-average compensation exceeds covered compensation (see Table 9–2 and the explanation below). The IRS is scheduled to publish annually a table with the appropriate offset factors for brackets of final-average compensation that exceed covered compensation.

An offset plan must base benefits on average annual compensation for at least a three-year period, or the total number of the participant's years of service, if less. The 0.75 percent factor in the maximum excess allowance is reduced actuarially for early retirement benefits. For this purpose, an early retirement benefit is any unreduced benefit other than a disability benefit beginning before the social security retirement age. The 0.75 factor is to be reduced by one 15th for each of the first five years that the benefit's commencement date precedes social security retirement age, and by an additional one 30th for each of the next five years that the benefit commencement date precedes the social security retirement age, with actuarial reductions for additional years (more than 10) of commencement prior to the social security retirement date.

Social security benefits currently are subject to indexing to reflect increases in the cost of living. However, the benefit paid by a private integrated plan cannot be reduced to reflect postretirement increases in social security benefits, even if an offset formula is used. In other words, the amount of benefit payable to a participant from the plan itself generally will be fixed when the participant retires, regardless of changes in social security benefits paid thereafter to the participant.

As will be evident after reviewing the rules for social security integration using integration levels (discussed next), the principal advantage of a social security offset formula is its simplicity, both in designing the plan and in communicating the plan effectively to employees.

Integration Level Approach

Using the integration level approach in a defined-benefit plan, a specified level of compensation, called the "integration level," is defined by the plan. The plan then provides the participant a higher rate of benefits for compensation above the integration level than for compensation for below the integration level. This clearly is a mirror image to the social security benefit structure, which provides a *lower* (zero) rate of benefits above a specified compensation level (the taxable wage base) than it does for compensation below the taxable wage base.

An example of a formula using an integration level approach is:

> Upon retirement, a participant will be entitled to an annual retirement benefit equal to 30 percent of the participant's final-average annual compensation up to $7,000, plus 56 percent of the participant's final-average annual compensation in excess of $7,000.

Another way of drafting the same formula is:

Upon retirement, a participant will be entitled to an annual retirement benefit equal to 30 percent of the participant's full final-average annual compensation, plus 26 percent of the participant's final-average compensation in excess of $7,000.

In both of these examples, the integration level is $7,000.

Under the Code, two percentages are defined: the *excess-benefit percentage* is the benefit as a percentage of compensation above the integration level. The *base-*

TABLE 9–2. Official 1985 IRS Tables of Covered Compensation

Calendar Year of 65th Birthday	Table I	Table II
1985	$13,800	$13,800
1986	15,000	14,760
1987	15,600	15,648
1988	16,200	16,464
1989	17,400	17,244
1990	18,000	17,964
1991	18,600	18,636
1992	19,200	19,272
1993	19,800	19,872
1994	20,400	20,436
1995	21,600	21,432
1996	22,200	22,428
1997	23,400	23,412
1998	24,600	24,408
1999	25,200	25,404
2000	26,400	26,408
2001	27,600	27,396
2002	28,200	28,332
2003	29,400	29,280
2004	30,000	30,192
2005	31,200	31,092
2006	31,800	32,004
2007	33,000	32,916
2008	33,600	33,792
2009	34,800	34,608
2010	35,400	35,364
2011	36,000	36,096
2012	36,600	36,792
2013	37,200	37,452
2014	37,800	38,076
2015	38,400	38,556
2016	39,000	38,940
2017	39,000	39,228
2018	39,600	39,432
2019	39,600	39,540
2020 and later	39,600	39,600

benefit percentage is the percentage of compensation provided for compensation up to and including the integration level. Under the Code, the difference between these two percentages cannot exceed the *maximum excess allowance*. The maximum excess allowance is 0.75 percent for any year of service or, in total, 0.75 percent multiplied by the participant's years of service up to 35.

For example, if the plan provides a benefit of 1.0 percent of compensation below the integration level for each year of service, then it can provide no more than 1.75 percent of compensation above the integration level for each year of service. Or, for a participant with 35 years of service, if the plan provides a benefit of 30.0 percent of final-average compensation below the integration level, it cannot provide more than 56.25 percent of compensation above the integration level. (The spread of 26.25 percent is three fourths of one percentage point multiplied by 35 years of service.)

Furthermore, the maximum excess allowance can be no greater than the base percentage. Thus, if a plan provides 10 percent of final-average compensation below the integration level, it can provide no more than 20 percent of compensation above the integration level.

The maximum permitted integration level is the appropriate amount from the IRS table of *covered compensation* (Table 9–2). The table essentially gives the average of the taxable wage base over the 35-year period prior to an employee's retirement, as explained further below. Covered compensation can be taken from either the "table I" or "table II" columns of Table 9–2. Since this amount varies with each participant's age, some planners may prefer to use a uniform dollar amount as the integration level for all participants—to make the plan simpler and easier to communicate to participants. It should be permissible to use any uniform dollar amount that does not exceed the covered compensation from "tables I" or "II" for the oldest possible prospective employee of the employer.

The Covered Compensation Table

In specifying the maximum integration levels and the maximum percentages that may be used in integration level plans, IRS actuaries have made a computation based on the value of social security benefits. Since the integrated private plan is designed to be a mirror image of the social security benefit, the maximum integration level in private plans should correspond generally to the maximum compensation taken into account in determining the social security benefit. For this purpose, the IRS has promulgated the *covered compensation* table. Basically, covered compensation represents an averaging of the taxable wage base that has been in effect over each employee's working career. The covered compensation figure, therefore, will vary depending upon the year in which the employee reaches age 65 and becomes eligible for full social security retirement benefits. The current IRS table of covered compensation is given in Table 9–2. The "table II" column gives the exact covered compensation level. The IRS has also provided "table I," containing the covered compensation level rounded to the nearest multiple of $600 (i.e., $50 per month). The IRS does not always update its covered compensation table as rapidly as the taxable wage base changes, and when this is the case it is permissible to use a covered compensation table computed by a private actuary in lieu of the official IRS table.

The relevance of the table of covered compensation is that, as described above, the covered compensation specifies the maximum integration level permitted for most types of defined-benefit plan.

Integration of Defined-Contribution Plans

Since the benefits in a defined-contribution plan are based on the participant's account balance, the integration rules for defined-contribution plans apply to the amounts allocated to participant's accounts, rather than to the benefits. Only an integration-level approach (not an offset) can be used.

The integration level for a defined-contribution plan can be any amount up to the taxable wage base for the year. Table 9–3 gives the taxable wage base for a number of recent years. The integration rules for defined-contribution plans are further stated in terms of two defined quantities: The *base-contribution percentage* is the plan's contribution level for compensation below the integration level, while the *excess-contribution percentage* is the contribution level for compensation above the integration level. The difference between excess-contribution percentage and the base-contribution percentage cannot be more than the lesser of

The base-contribution percentage, or
the nonmedicare social security tax rate, currently (1986) 5.7 percent.

Under this rule, a plan having a zero base-contribution percentage would also have to have a zero excess-contribution percentage; therefore, it is not possible to have

TABLE 9–3. Social Security Taxable Wage Base

Year	Taxable Wage Base (Annual)
1972	$ 9,600
1973	10,800
1974	13,200
1975	14,100
1976	15,300
1977	16,500
1978	17,700
1979	22,900
1980	25,900
1981	29,700
1982	32,400
1983	35,700
1984	37,800
1985	39,600
1986	42,000
1987	43,800

a plan that provides no contribution at all for participants at compensation levels below the integration level.

Some examples of the application of the rules are:

1. A plan providing a 4 percent base-contribution percentage could provide no more than 8 percent excess-contribution percentage.
2. A plan providing a 6 percent base-contribution percentage could provide no more than an 11.7 percent excess-contribution percentage.

Multiple Plans

If the employer has more than one plan covering the same employee, both plans cannot be fully integrated. The degree of integration must be cut back in one or both. The most common approach is to fully integrate one plan (typically, a defined-benefit plan) and not to integrate the other (typically, a defined-contribution plan).

Adjustments for Additional Benefits and Benefit Forms

The rules discussed up to this point have referred only to the basic percentages and other limits. These basic rules apply to a plan providing a straight-life annuity as the basic form of benefit, with no integrated death or disability benefits, and satisfying certain other restrictions. Also, the basic rules apply only if the normal retirement age is at least age 65, although earlier retirement is permitted if the benefit is adjusted in accordance with the limits described below.

As of early 1987, the IRS had not issued any guidelines for making adjustments for varying forms of benefit. However, such guidelines are expected to follow generally the form of those issued under pre–1989 law. These are discussed in detail in Appendix A.

Summary

Qualified plan benefit or contribution formulas can be integrated with social security to reflect the value of the employer's social security contribution for the employee. This reduces plan costs by avoiding duplication of benefits provided by social security. It also tends to provide relatively higher plan benefits for highly compensated employees.

A *defined-benefit* plan can be integrated using either the offset or the integration level method.

Offset method. The maximum offset allowance is 0.75 percent of final-average compensation for any year of service, or a total of 0.75 percent multiplied by years of service up to 35; total offset can't exceed 50.0 percent of benefit otherwise payable.

Integration level method. The maximum integration level is covered compensation. Maximum excess allowance is 0.75 percent for any year of service or, in total, 0.75 percent multiplied by years of service up to 35.

A *defined-contribution* plan may use only the integration level approach. The maximum integration level is the taxable wage base for the year. The difference between the base-contribution percentage and the excess-contribution percentage can't exceed the lesser of the base-contribution percentage or the nonmedicare social security tax rate.

The above rules are subject to adjustment for varying forms of benefit and incidental benefits.

10

Death Benefits and Other Incidental Benefits

Objectives of This Chapter
- *Describe the mandatory death benefit provisions of qualified plans—the qualified joint-and-survivor annuity and the preretirement survivor annuity.*
- *Discuss the factors involved in designing incidental death benefits in qualified plans, including the use of insurance, the limits on the amount of benefit, and the tax treatment of this benefit.*
- *Discuss how medical and disability benefits can be used as incidental benefits in a qualified plan.*

● Qualified plans are intended primarily to provide deferred compensation or retirement benefits. However, most qualified plans must provide some form of death benefit to the participant's spouse. In addition, a plan may provide, as an option, death benefits to nonspouse beneficiaries, or disability benefits to the participant. These death and other benefits are referred to as incidental benefits. The Regulations have long provided that such benefits may be included in the plan, as long as they are within limits to be discussed here.

Required Spousal Death Benefits

Prior to ERISA, qualified plans were not required to provide any benefits to participants' spouses, although it was not uncommon to do so. ERISA required most pension plans to provide a qualified joint-and-survivor annuity (joint and at least 50 percent survivorship benefit for the spouse) as the plan's automatic benefit option, unless the participant elected otherwise. ERISA also required most pension plans to provide a spousal survivorship benefit at the election of the participant who reached early retirement age but continued working. As part of a reform aimed at improving qualified plan rights of women workers and participants' spouses (the Retirement Equity Act of 1984), Congress greatly expanded these spousal benefits.

Currently, two types of spousal survivorship benefits are required: the *qualified joint-and-survivor annuity* and the *qualified preretirement survivor annuity*. All pension plans must provide these, but stock-bonus or profit-sharing plans need not provide them if the participant's vested account balance is payable as a death benefit to the spouse.[1] ESOPs generally are not required to provide survivorship benefits.

Qualified Joint-and-Survivor Annuity

The qualified joint-and-survivor annuity is a postretirement death benefit for the spouse. Plans subject to this requirement must provide, as an automatic form of benefit, an annuity for the life of the participant with a survivor annuity for the life of the participant's spouse. The survivor annuity must be not less than 50 percent of, nor greater than, the annuity payable during the joint lives of participant and spouse.[2] The spouse annuity must be continued even if the spouse remarries. The joint-and-survivor annuity must be at least the actuarial equivalent of the plan's normal form of benefit or any optional form of benefit offered under the plan. Optional benefit forms are discussed further in Chapter 16.

The qualified joint-and-survivor form must be offered automatically to a married participant at retirement. The participant may elect to receive another form of benefit if the plan so provides; however, the spouse must consent in writing to the election, and the consent form must be notarized or witnessed by a plan representative. An election to waive the joint-and-survivor form must be made during a 90-day period ending on the annuity starting date. A waiver of the joint-and-survivor annuity can be revoked—the participant can change the election during the 90-day period. The plan administrator must provide the participant with a notice of the election period and an explanation of the consequences of the election within a reasonable period before the annuity starting date.

Preretirement Survivor Annuity

Code Section 401(a)(11) mandates a preretirement death benefit for the spouse of a vested plan participant. The survivor annuity payable if the participant dies before retirement is the amount that would have been paid under a qualified joint-and-survivor annuity if the participant had either (1) retired on the day before his or her death or (2) separated from service on the date of death and survived to the plan's earliest retirement age, then retired with an immediate joint-and-survivor annuity. For a defined-contribution plan, a qualified preretirement survivor annuity is an annuity for the life of the surviving spouse that is the actuarial equivalent of at least 50 percent of the participant's vested account balance as of the date of death.

---

[1] Code Section 401(a)(11).

[2] Code Section 417 (definition of joint-and-survivor annuity and preretirement survivor annuity).

As with the qualified joint-and-survivor annuity, a participant can elect to receive an alternative form of preretirement survivorship benefit, including a benefit that does not provide for the spouse. However, written consent by the spouse is required for such an election. The right to make such an election must be communicated to all participants with a vested benefit who have attained age 32, and the participant can elect to waive the preretirement survivor annuity at any time after age 35.

Subsidizing Survivor Annuities

A plan can provide that, when a participant receives either the qualified joint-and-survivor annuity or the preretirement survivor annuity, the annuity payment is reduced from the amount that would be paid under a straight-life annuity; the reduction reflects the extra cost to the plan for the survivorship feature. For example, the normal form of benefit might be a straight-life annuity of $1,000 per month, but the joint-and-survivor annuity might pay only $800 per month while both spouses survived, then $400 per month to the survivor. However, a plan is permitted to subsidize all or part of the cost of the survivorship feature. If the survivorship feature is fully subsidized, the plan does not have to allow the participant to elect an alternative form of benefit.

Employee Death Benefit Planning

Although the survivorship benefit applies to all vested participants, regardless of how young, a plan need not begin making payments under the preretirement survivor annuity until the year in which the deceased participant would have attained the plan's earliest retirement age, which is typically at least 55. Also, the amount payable need not be more than the participant's vested accrued benefit at the date of death. Thus, this provision may not have much value as a death benefit for the spouse or family of a young plan participant. However, as the participant nears retirement age, this benefit is of increasing significance and must be taken into account in personal financial planning.

Since this benefit results in increased costs to the employer for the qualified plan, it must be properly integrated with other employee-benefit programs providing life insurance or other death benefits so there is no unnecessary duplication. Life insurance or employer-provided death benefits are often more significant to younger employees, because of family responsibilities, and the preretirement survivor annuity is not often very significant in this area.

Incidental Death Benefits

A qualified plan may provide a death benefit over and above the survivorship benefits required by law. In a defined-contribution plan, probably the most common form of death benefit is a provision that the participant's vested account balance will be paid to the participant's designated beneficiary in the event of the participant's death before retirement or termination of employment. Defined-benefit plans, unless they use insurance as discussed below, usually do not provide an incidental death benefit; in such cases, the survivors receive no death benefit, except for whatever survivor annuity provision the plan provides.

To provide any substantial preretirement death benefit, it is usually necessary for a plan to purchase life insurance. This provides the plan with significant funds at a participant's death; and this is particularly important in the early years of a participant's employment, when the amount contributed on behalf of the participant is still relatively small. An insured preretirement death benefit can be provided in either a defined-benefit or defined-contribution plan. Contributions to the plan by the employer may be used to pay life insurance premiums, as long as the amount qualifies under the tests for incidental benefits.

In general, the IRS considers that nonretirement benefits—such as life, medical, or disability insurance—in a qualified plan will be incidental and, therefore, permissible, as long as the cost of providing these benefits is less than 25 percent of the cost of providing all the benefits under the plan. In applying this approach to life insurance benefits, the 25 percent rule is applied to the portion of any life insurance premium that is used to provide current life insurance protection. Any portion of the premium used to increase the cash value of the policy is considered a contribution to the plan fund available to pay retirement benefits and is not considered in the 25 percent limitation.

The IRS has ruled, using its general 25 percent test, that, if a qualified plan provides death benefits using ordinary life insurance (life insurance with a cash value), the death benefit will be considered incidental if either (1) less than 50 percent of the total cumulative employer contribution credited to each participant's account has been used to purchase ordinary life insurance or (2) the face amount of the policy does not exceed 100 times the anticipated monthly normal retirement benefit, or the accumulated reserve under the life insurance policy, whichever is greater. In practice, defined-benefit plans using ordinary life insurance are usually designed to take advantage of the 100-times rule, while defined-contribution plans, including profit-sharing plans, that use ordinary life contracts generally make use of the 50 percent test.

If term insurance contracts are used to provide the death benefit, then, because the 25 percent test will be applied to the entire premium, the aggregate premiums paid for insurance on each participant should be less than 25 percent of aggregate additions to the employee's account. Term insurance sometimes is used to fund death benefits in defined-contribution plans but rarely for defined-benefit plans.

The IRS has not yet ruled on the use of universal life insurance and similar products in qualified plans, but it informally takes the position that the total premiums for such products must meet the same 25 percent limit as that for term insurance. This is almost certainly incorrect, however, since a substantial part of the premium for a universal life policy, as for an ordinary life policy, goes toward increasing the cash value. The limit, therefore, in theory should be higher than 25 percent.

The discussion so far is somewhat simplified, because insurance can be used in qualified plans in many ways, and the IRS has issued many rulings, both revenue rulings and letter rulings, applying the basic 25 percent test to a variety of different fact situations. Thus, there is considerable room for creative design of life insurance-funded death benefits within qualified plans.[3]

If life insurance is provided for a participant through a qualified plan (i.e., by using employer contributions to the plan to pay premiums for the insurance), part or all of the cost of the insurance is currently taxable to the participant. Life insurance provided by the plan is not considered part of a Section 79 group term plan, and consequently the $50,000 exclusion under Section 79 does not apply.

If life insurance with a cash value is used, and if all of the death proceeds are payable to the participant's estate or beneficiary, the term cost or cost of the "pure amount at risk" is taxable to the employee. The term cost is the difference between the face amount of insurance and the cash surrender value of the policy at the end of the policy year. In other words, the cost of the policy's cash value is not currently taxable to the employee, because the cash value is considered part of the plan fund to be used to provide the retirement benefit. The term cost is calculated using either a table of rates (reproduced in Table 10–1) provided by the Internal Revenue Service, known as the "P.S. 58" table, or the insurance company's rates for individual one-year term policies at standard rates, if these are lower and if the insurance company actually offers such policies.

If the plan uses term insurance, rather than cash value insurance, to provide an insured death benefit, the cost of the entire face amount of insurance is taxable to the employee.

If the plan allows employee contributions, the nondeductible employee contributions can be used to offset taxable income resulting from the inclusion of any form of insurance in the plan. However, unless the plan provides otherwise, insurance will be considered to have been paid first from employer contributions and earnings of the plan fund, so this offset is not available unless the plan makes specific provision for it.

Coordination of Death Benefits

A lump-sum insured death benefit is often provided in a plan, in addition to the preretirement survivor annuity required by law in most plans, as discussed earlier in this chapter. In this case, the total death benefit must not exceed the incidental limits.[4] For example, if the lump-sum benefit is at the maximum limit, the lump-sum benefit can be reduced by the actuarial present value of the preretirement survivor annuity.

Survivorship Benefits

In addition to cash death benefits, insured or otherwise, death benefits can be provided in the form of annuity options with survivorship features—that is, an-

---

[3] A good summary of current rulings is found in question 259, *Tax Facts 1* (Cincinnati: National Underwriter Company, 1987).

[4] Rev. Rul. 85–15, 1985–8 IRB 6.

TABLE 10–1. P.S. 58 Rates *(One-Year Term Premiums for $1,000 of Life Insurance Protection*)*

Age	Premium	Age	Premium	Age	Premium
15	$1.27	37	$ 3.63	59	$ 19.08
16	1.38	38	3.87	60	20.73
17	1.48	39	4.14	61	22.53
18	1.52	40	4.42	62	24.50
19	1.56	41	4.73	63	26.63
20	1.61	42	5.07	64	28.98
21	1.67	43	5.44	65	31.51
22	1.73	44	5.85	66	34.28
23	1.79	45	6.30	67	37.31
24	1.86	46	6.78	68	40.59
25	1.93	47	7.32	69	44.17
26	2.02	48	7.89	70	48.06
27	2.11	49	8.53	71	52.29
28	2.20	50	9.22	72	56.89
29	2.31	51	9.97	73	61.89
30	2.43	52	10.79	74	67.33
31	2.57	53	11.69	75	73.23
32	2.70	54	12.67	76	79.63
33	2.86	55	13.74	77	86.57
34	3.02	56	14.91	78	94.09
35	3.21	57	16.18	79	102.23
36	3.41	58	17.56	80	111.04
				81	120.57

*These rates are used in computing the cost of pure life insurance protection that is taxable to the employee under qualified pension and profit-sharing plans.

The rate at insured's attained age is applied to the excess of the amount payable at death over the cash value of the policy at the end of the year.

nuities that continue partial or full payment to a beneficiary after the death of the participant. As discussed earlier, survivorship annuities for the participant's *spouse* are required in certain cases. However, survivorship annuities for the spouse in somewhat different form than the qualified joint-and-survivor annuity, or survivorship annuities for other beneficiaries than the spouse, can be included as benefit options in a qualified plan. These options must not exceed the incidental limits for death benefits in a qualified plan. The design of these optional forms of benefit is covered in Chapter 16.

Designing Incidental Death Benefits

It is relatively uncommon for a qualified plan to provide term life insurance to participants, because the tax treatment provides no advantage to the employee in so doing. It is more common, however, to use cash value life insurance as funding for the plan, because the cost to the employee using the P.S. 58 table or the insurance company's term rates may prove to be a relatively favorable way to provide life insurance.

The decision whether to include life insurance in a qualified plan relates to the employee benefit design objective of efficiency. The employer first must decide whether and to what extent it will provide death benefits to employees. Death benefits can be provided for employees under group term plans and other plans as well as providing them as an incidental benefit in qualified plans. The death benefit should be so designed to produce the lowest employer and employee cost for the benefit level desired. A death benefit should be included in the qualified plan only to the extent it is consistent with this objective.

Disability Benefits from Qualified Plans

A qualified plan may provide as an incidental benefit a pension payable upon disability. This plan must provide a specific definition of disability, and usually some minimum service or age requirements are imposed to appropriately restrict the class of participants entitled to the disability pension. The disability benefit may be the participant's accrued benefit actuarially reduced, because of a commencement date earlier than normal retirement, or the plan may provide some "subsidy" of the disability benefit to be sure that it is adequate for the participant's needs.

It is becoming increasingly common for companies to cover disability through separate benefit programs, often insured. Such programs tend to be fairer and more efficient than providing disability coverage as an incidental benefit under a qualified plan. In all events, the planner should be sure there is no duplication of disability coverage between the qualified plan and any separate short-term or long-term disability plan of the employer.

Even if the qualified plan does not provide immediate disability coverage prior to normal retirement age, it should include some provision for the treatment of the employee's retirement benefit if the employee becomes disabled. Separate long-term disability programs usually cease paying benefits when the participant reaches age 65 or other normal retirement age. After this age, the company's retirement plan must provide whatever income the participant will receive from the employer. Therefore, from an employee standpoint, the plan should be designed so that the retirement benefit will be adequate when long-term disability benefits cease. For example, the plan might provide that, if a participant is disabled as defined in the plan (a definition that should be coordinated with the definition in the employer's long-term disability plan), the participant will continue to receive service credit for purposes of vesting or benefit accrual or both. The plan also should indicate what definition of compensation will be used to determine retirement benefits if the participant becomes disabled before retirement.

Disability Benefit for Smaller Employers

In a small, closely held business, business owners and key employees who are participants are likely to want to be able to receive an immediate benefit from the plan if they become disabled, and such plans are designed accordingly. These plans usually provide for a benefit payable immediately upon disability, or after a waiting period, such as six months, reflecting the expiration of sick-pay or short-term disability payments from the employer.

The definition of disability must be considered carefully. Generally, the social security disability definition, which requires total and permanent disability—the inability to work in any gainful employment—is too stringent. A doctor or lawyer, for example, is likely to consider himself or herself disabled by an inability to work in that specific profession. Disability thus is generally defined in the plan as the inability to work in the participant's current employment. Sometimes, to make such determinations easier and, at least on the surface, more objective, the plan provides that disability is determined by a physician chosen by the plan administrator.

Medical Benefits from Qualified Plans

Medical insurance can be provided as an incidental benefit in a qualified plan, as long as the total cost of all incidental benefits is less than 25 percent of the cost of all plan benefits, as discussed earlier in connection with life insurance benefits. The entire cost of the medical insurance is taxable to the employee, unless the insurance cost can be excluded under Code Section 106 as part of the employer's accident and health plan. Medical benefits are rarely included in qualified plans since there is no significant advantage, tax or otherwise, in doing so.

Summary

All qualified plans, except for certain ESOPs, must provide some form of death benefit for participants' spouses; for pension plans, the benefits required are the qualified joint-and-survivor annuity and the preretirement survivor annuity. Other types of death benefits for spouses or other beneficiaries can be provided as incidental benefits, within specified cost limits. Insurance-funded death benefits are often used. The cost of incidental benefits is generally treated as current taxable income to participants. Disability and medical benefits can also be provided but are less common.

11

Funding a Pension Plan

Objectives of This Chapter
- *Discuss the general purposes of actuarial methods and assumptions in pension plan funding.*
- *Describe the basic mathematical concepts used in actuarial cost methods.*
- *Distinguish between the accrued-benefit and projected-benefit approaches in determining normal cost.*
- *Distinguish between individual and aggregate actuarial cost methods.*
- *Explain how a supplemental liability can be used to increase funding flexibility.*
- *Describe the common actuarial assumptions and how they are chosen.*
- *Discuss the considerations involved in choosing an actuarial cost method.*
- *Describe the minimum funding standards of ERISA.*
- *Discuss the limits on tax-deductibility of pension plan contributions.*

Actuarial Methods and Assumptions

The final or ultimate cost of a qualified plan cannot be determined until the last benefit dollar has been paid to the last surviving plan participant. However, the ultimate cost is not of immediate concern to the employer. Rather, the employer wants to know what the annual cost burden of the plan will be, particularly over the first several years of the plan. For a defined-contribution plan, this is not difficult to determine; the plan document itself specifies the amount of annual contribution that is required, usually in terms of some parameter of business operations, such as payroll or profits. Thus, it is easy to get an idea of the kind of burden the business will be assuming if it adopts this kind of plan. For a defined-benefit plan, however, actuarial methods and assumptions determine the annual cost, since the plan itself specifies only the benefits that will be paid.

In the past, employers had a great deal of flexibility in funding defined-benefit plans. In fact, prior to ERISA it was not necessary even to fund such plans in advance, and benefit payments could be made as they came due. Another method sometimes used was terminal funding—that is, the funding of the benefit in full at the participant's retirement, usually through purchase of an annuity from an insurance company. However, currently all qualified defined-benefit plans subject to the funding provisions of ERISA must provide advance funding over the working lives of the participants using an actuarial cost method and assumptions. The ERISA funding requirements apply basically to all qualified defined-benefit plans of private employers. Certain government and church plans are exempted from coverage, as well as certain types of plans having no employer contributions. Also, fully insured plans are treated under special rules, described later in this chapter in the discussion of minimum funding standards.

An *actuarial cost method* is a method of determining an annual employer contribution for a given set of plan benefits and group of employees. The method produces a schedule of annual contributions aimed at providing a plan fund sufficient to make all benefit payments when they come due without any further contributions by the employer. *Actuarial assumptions* refer to assumptions about future investment return, plan expenses, and the character of the employee group (mortality, turnover) that are made to determine the annual contribution.

Great variety and complexity are possible in actuarial methods and assumptions. Because of this, many people who are otherwise experts in the benefits area tend to regard actuarial methods as a technical subject that should be left solely to actuaries. However, the choice of actuarial methods and assumptions is such an important factor in determining the timing of plan costs (and, therefore, the tax benefits from the plan) that anyone involved in the benefits area should have a basic knowledge of actuarial concepts.

Because of the complexity of the subject and the specialized terminology involved, it is difficult to treat actuarial methods in a brief and concise way. As with so many considerations in the design of qualified plans, there are two interrelated aspects to the issue. First are the basic concepts used by pension actuaries; then there are the limits imposed by the Internal Revenue Code and ERISA on the types of methods and assumptions permitted for a qualified plan.

Basic Pension Calculations

Determining the annual cost for a pension plan may be a complex procedure, but the procedure is based on a few mathematical operations that are relatively simple in themselves. Since an understanding of actuarial cost methods depends entirely on understanding these operations, it is appropriate to begin by reviewing some of them. Three operations or mathematical concepts will be covered here: the annuity purchase rate, present value, and installment savings (level funding).

Annuity Purchase Rate

An annuity purchase rate is a conversion factor that relates a stated monthly or annual benefit to its equivalent lump sum. For example, if the annuity purchase rate at age 65 is $9.50 for $1.00 of annual pension, then an annual pension of $1.00 beginning at age 65 can be purchased with a lump-sum payment at age 65 of $9.50.

The annuity purchase rate depends on the expected (assumed) rate of return and on expected mortality (death rate, based on age and sex) of the group of pension recipients. A higher assumed rate of return will result in a lower annuity purchase rate, since the initial deposit will earn more over the period of the annuity. Likewise, a higher mortality assumption lowers the annuity purchase rate; the rate is lower for male than for female recipients, because of the difference in mortality.

The concept of the equivalence of a periodic pension with a lump sum is important in pension planning for two reasons. First, it enables the plan's funding target to be expressed in terms of a single sum that must be attained by the normal retirement date.

Example

Suppose a plan specifies a normal retirement benefit of $10,000 per year beginning at age 65. By using an annuity purchase rate appropriate for a life annuity beginning at age 65—say $9.50—it is possible to determine that, to fund the specified benefit, this plan requires an accumulation of $95,000 when the participant reaches age 65.

A second significant aspect of the annuity purchase rate is that it can be used to determine the amount of a lump-sum benefit that, if the plan permits, can be provided to the participant as an alternative form of benefit. The annuity purchase rate used for this purpose actually must be specified in some form in the plan document.[1] Also, it cannot be based on sex under current law.

As discussed in Chapter 8, sex-based annuity rates presumably can be used for plan funding purposes, despite the *Norris* decision, as long as the participant's *benefit* is not based on sex. *Note:* using a sex-based annuity rate for a male participant will result in a lower funding target than for a female and, hence, a lower annual deposit to the plan fund. When the plan's objectives are to shelter the maximum amount annually, and most participants are male (for example, the historically typical small professional corporation), it has been customary to use unisex annuity rates to obtain a larger annual contribution.

Present Value

The concept of a present value is a familiar one. In the pension context, the most common application is in determining the present value of a pension payable in the future, such as at age 65.

---

[1] Code Section 401(a)(25)

The concept is based on the idea that an amount, say $1,000, payable 15 years from now is worth less than $1,000 today, because $1,000 today would grow to more than $1,000 after 15 years at compound interest. The present value can be determined based on an assumed rate of return. In the pension context, a mortality assumption can be added if a group of individuals is covered. This reduces the present value still further, because of the possibility that the pension benefit, in some cases, will not actually be paid because of the death of some participants before retirement.

The mathematical formula for the present value (PV) of an amount due in the future (FV), without any mortality factor, where i is the interest rate and n is the number of years (or periods), is:

$$PV = \frac{FV}{(1 + i)^n}$$

Although to make repeated manual calculations using this formula is somewhat awkward, it is simple to program a computer or programmable calculator to do so. Figure 11-1 is an example of a worksheet set up to make this calculation, using the program of 1-2-3® from Lotus®. The Lotus software actually has a present value function, but, for purposes of illustration, it is not used in Figure 11-1.

Tables of present value factors to aid in manual calculation are often useful. Table 11-1 is an example of such a table.

FIGURE 11-1. Present Value Worksheet

E8: +D8/((1+$C$3)^B8)

	A	B	C	D	E	F	G	H
1	PRESENT VAL OF AMT DUE AT AGE 65
2								
3	INTEREST RATE		0.08					
4								
5								
6	NAME	YRS TO AGE 65		AMT DUE	PRES VAL			
7								
8	ABEL	15		1500	472.86			
9	BAKER	25		1500	219.03			
10	CHARLIE	13		2000	735.40			
11	DUANE	22		2000	367.88			
12	ETHEL	16		5000	1459.45			
13	FRITZ	14		5000	1702.31			
14	GIRARD	7		5000	2917.45			
15	HANK	32		5000	426.00			
16	IRA	28		10000	1159.14			
17	JACK	37		10000	579.86			
18	KATE	15		10000	3152.42			
19	LORNA	22		10000	1839.41			
20	MARTHA	41		10000	426.21			

TABLE 11-1. The Present Value of $1 at Compound Interest *(No Mortality Assumption)*

Year	5	6	7	8	9	10	Year
1	.9524	.9434	.9346	.9259	.9174	.9091	1
2	.9070	.8900	.8734	.8573	.8417	.8264	2
3	.8638	.8396	.8163	.7938	.7722	.7513	3
4	.8227	.7921	.7629	.7350	.7084	.6830	4
5	.7835	.7473	.7130	.6806	.6499	.6209	5
6	.7462	.7050	.6663	.6302	.5963	.5645	6
7	.7107	.6651	.6227	.5835	.5470	.5132	7
8	.6768	.6274	.5820	.5403	.5019	.4665	8
9	.6446	.5919	.5439	.5002	.4604	.4241	9
10	.6139	.5584	.5083	.4632	.4224	.3855	10
11	.5847	.5268	.4751	.4289	.3875	.3505	11
12	.5568	.4970	.4440	.3971	.3555	.3186	12
13	.5303	.4688	.4150	.3677	.3262	.2897	13
14	.5051	.4423	.3878	.3405	.2992	.2633	14
15	.4810	.4173	.3624	.3152	.2745	.2394	15
16	.4581	.3936	.3387	.2919	.2519	.2176	16
17	.4363	.3714	.3166	.2703	.2311	.1978	17
18	.4155	.3503	.2959	.2502	.2120	.1799	18
19	.3957	.3305	.2765	.2317	.1945	.1635	19
20	.3769	.3118	.2584	.2145	.1784	.1486	20
21	.3589	.2942	.2415	.1987	.1637	.1351	21
22	.3418	.2775	.2257	.1839	.1502	.1228	22
23	.3256	.2618	.2109	.1703	.1378	.1117	23
24	.3101	.2470	.1971	.1577	.1264	.1015	24
25	.2953	.2330	.1842	.1460	.1160	.9023	25
26	.2812	.2198	.1722	.1352	.1064	.0839	26
27	.2678	.2074	.1609	.1252	.0976	.0763	27
28	.2551	.1956	.1504	.1159	.0895	.0693	28
29	.2429	.1846	.1406	.1073	.0822	.0630	29
30	.2314	.1741	.1314	.0994	.0754	.0573	30
31	.2204	.1643	.1228	.0920	.0691	.0521	31
32	.2099	.1550	.1147	.0852	.0634	.0474	32
33	.1999	.1462	.1072	.0789	.0582	.0431	33
34	.1904	.1379	.1002	.0739	.0534	.0391	34
35	.1813	.1301	.0937	.0676	.0490	.0356	35
36	.1727	.1227	.0875	.0626	.0449	.0323	36
37	.1644	.1158	.0818	.0580	.0412	.0294	37
38	.1566	.1092	.0765	.0537	.0378	.0267	38
39	.1491	.1031	.0715	.0497	.0347	.0243	39
40	.1420	.0972	.0668	.0460	.0318	.0221	40
41	.1353	.0917	.0624	.0426	.0292	.0201	41
42	.1288	.0865	.0583	.0395	.0268	.0183	42
43	.1227	.0816	.0545	.0365	.0246	.0166	43
44	.1169	.0770	.0509	.0338	.0226	.0151	44
45	.1113	.0727	.0476	.0313	.0207	.0137	45
46	.1060	.0685	.0445	.0290	.0190	.0125	46
47	.1009	.0647	.0416	.0269	.0174	.0113	47
48	.0961	.0610	.0389	.0249	.0160	.0103	48
49	.0916	.0575	.0363	.0230	.0147	.0094	49
50	.0872	.0543	.0339	.0213	.0134	.0085	50

Example

Using the table: What is the present value of a pension of $100 per year, payable beginning at age 65 (20 years from now), assuming an 8 percent rate of return? First, the pension must be converted to a lump sum, using an annuity purchase rate; suppose this is $9.50. Thus, the amount needed at age 65 is $950. This is multiplied by the factor from the table, .2145, for 8 percent interest; the result in $203.78. In other words, $203.78 deposited at age 45 and earning 8 percent compound interest thereafter would provide $950 at age 65.

Handbooks of actuarial tables often provide a variety of tables for calculations; for example, some tables automatically might make the annuity purchase rate calculation by giving the present value factor, not for a lump sum due in the future but for a monthly annuity beginning in the future. It is not necessary to discuss these tables in detail, but interested students may wish to pursue this.

Installment Savings (Level Funding)

Pension contributions often consist of equal (level) annual amounts for each participant that are designed to build up to a required sum at retirement age. This is an example of the general concept of installment savings. To illustrate, suppose you want to have a fund of $100,000 available 10 years from now. How much must you put away annually in equal installments to reach your goal? This is determined by the following mathematical formulas. PMT is the installment amount, FV is the amount required in the future, i is the interest rate, and n is the number of periods. The period can be months, years, or any other period, but the interest rate used must be expressed as a rate for the same period.

Each payment made at the beginning of the period:

$$\text{PMT} = \frac{\text{FV}}{(1 + i)} \times \frac{i}{(1 + i)^n - 1}$$

Each payment made at the end of the period:

$$\text{PMT} = \text{FV} \times \frac{i}{(1 + i)^n - 1}$$

Although it is cumbersome to use these formulas for repeated manual calculations, it is easy to program a computer to do this using "worksheet" software. Figure 11–2 is an example of a simple setup of this type using 1–2–3 from Lotus.

Many programmed "business" calculators have a built-in installment savings function that will quickly calculate the annual deposit to a defined-benefit plan for each employee under a level funding method.

An example of such a calculator is the Casio BF–100. Many other calculators are similar in function. Figure 11–3 is from the calculator manual.

This procedure is easily adapted to determine annual pension deposits.

Funding a Pension Plan **113**

FIGURE 11–2. Installment Savings Worksheet

E8: ((D8/(1+$C$3))*SC$3/(((1+$C$3)^B8)-1))

	A	B	C	D	E	F	G	H
1	INSTALLMENT SAVINGS CALCULATION							
2								
3	INTEREST RATE			0.08				
4								
5								
6	NAME	YRS TO AGE 65		TARGET	ANN DEP			
7								
8	ABEL	15		500000	17050.72			
9	BAKER	25		175000	2216.47			
10	CHARLIE	13		50000	2153.79			
11	DUANE	22		135250	2258.18			
12	ETHEL	16		175000	5343.47			
13	FRANK	14		350000	13383.24			
14	GERRY	7		350000	36319.76			
15	HAL	32		175000	1207.31			
16	IRA	28		175000	1699.59			
17	JACK	37		250000	1139.91			
18	KATHY	15		100000	3410.14			
19	LORNA	22		100000	1669.64			
20	MABEL	41		100000	329.77			

FIGURE 11–3. Level Funding Calculation Using a Manual Calculator

Installment savings monthly deposit.

Example—What is the installment savings monthly deposit required to accumulate a savings of $5,000 over a 10-year period when the annual interest rate is 6 percent and is compounded monthly?

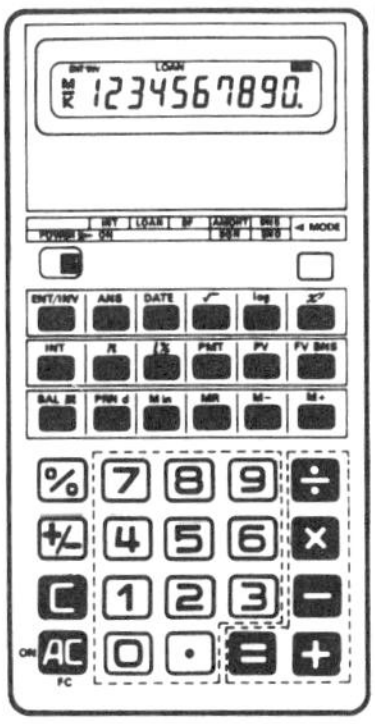

	OPERATION	READ-OUT
"SF, BGN"		
	[INV] [AC/FC]	0.
(period)	10 [×] 12 [=] [ENT] [n]	120.
(interest rate)	6 [÷] 12 [=] [ENT] [i%]	0.5
(total amount of principal and interest)	5000 [ENT] [FV]	5000.
(monthly deposit)	[ANS] [PMT]	30.35845868
"SF, END"		
	[INV] [MODE]	30.35845868
(monthly deposit)	[ANS] [PMT]	30.51025097

Source: Reprinted from Casio BF–100 Operations Manual by permission.

Example

Suppose Abel, age 50, wants to accumulate $500,000 at age 65. Assuming 8 percent interest, what amount must be deposited annually at the beginning of each year? With the calculator in the "SF, BGN" mode, the number of periods, n, is 15, i percent is 8, FV is $500,000, and the PMT is $17,050.72.

Finally, the level contribution can also be computed from a table of factors that are calculated using the above formula. This table, sometimes known as the "temporary annuity due table" is reproduced here as Table 11-2.

Example

Suppose again that Abel, age 50, wants to accumulate $500,000 at age 65. With an 8 percent interest assumption, the factor from Table 11-2 for 15 years is 29.324. Dividing $500,000 by 29.324, we obtain a payment of $17,050.88. (The slight difference from the previous result is due to rounding.)

Actuarial Cost Methods

Basic Principles and Terminology

In an actuarial cost method, the actuary must first determine the amount that will be required at retirement to fully fund each active employee's benefit. For example, suppose that Clutch Company is planning to adopt a defined-benefit plan. The annual retirement benefit will be 50 percent of each employee's salary at retirement, with the benefits payable as a straight-life annuity (equal periodic payments ending at death). Clutch's employee census and projected benefits look like this:

Clutch Company Defined-Benefit Plan

Employee	Age	Current Salary	Projected Annual Retirement Benefit
A	60	$100,000	$50,000
B	50	60,000	30,000
C	45	40,000	20,000
D	30	25,000	12,500

For simplicity, it is assumed in this example that salary at retirement is equal to current salary, even though it is permissible for funding purposes to make certain assumptions about salary changes, as discussed below. At any rate, the actuary's task is to determine an annual deposit to the plan fund ensuring that, as each employee retires, there is enough money in the fund to fully fund the retirement benefit.

Initially, this discussion will focus on methods for determining annual deposits over each employee's working career prior to retirement, designed to fully fund that employee's benefit. The total of such amounts for all employees is the plan's annual *normal cost*. In some actuarial methods, the total cost is divided into two elements. Under this approach, only part of the cost is funded by deposits calculated over employee's working careers (the normal cost), while the remainder of the plan's cost (the *supplemental liability,* which is usually an amount attributable to past service) is funded through deposits over a fixed period of years without reference to participants' retirement dates. This type of funding can provide flexibility in the annual contribution level, as will be discussed below.

The Internal Revenue Code does not specifically prescribe what actuarial methods must be used, only that a method must be "reasonable" (Section 412(c)(3)). However, the Regulations state that, to be reasonable, the actuarial method must determine the normal cost in one of two ways: either (1) the normal cost must be an "amount equal to the present value of benefits accruing under the method for a particular plan year" or (2) the normal cost must be expressed as "a level dollar amount, or a level percentage of pay." Actuarial cost methods used for qualified plans determine the normal cost using one of these two approaches, which can be referred to as (1) the *accrued-benefit* approach and (2) the *projected-benefit* approach.

Accrued-Benefit Approach. Under this method of determining the normal cost, the normal cost for a particular year is the amount needed to fund all the benefits earned for service with the employer that year. The first step in the method, therefore, is to determine the amount of retirement benefit accrued by each employee during the current year. This depends on the plan formula; some formulas may specify the amount accrued for each year of service, while for others the total amount will have to be determined and then spread over the years of service remaining to retirement, usually on a pro rata basis, although the plan can specify otherwise (within the limits of the benefit accrual rules). Pro rata accrual will be used for the plan of the Clutch Company described above. Thus, if normal retirement age is 65, the annual benefit accrual under the Clutch plan would be as follows:

Employee	Projected Annual Retirement Benefit	÷	Years to Retirement	=	Annual Benefit Accrual
A	$50,000		5		$10,000
B	30,000		15		2,000
C	20,000		20		1,000
D	12,500		35		357

TABLE 11–2. Temporary Annuity Due—$1 Annually in Advance
(The Sum to Which $1 per Annum, Paid at the Beginning of Each Year, Will Increase; No Mortality Factor or Salary Scale)

Percent

Years	3½	4	5	6	6½	7	7½	8	8½	9	9½	10	Years
1	1.035	1.040	1.050	1.060	1.065	1.070	1.075	1.080	1.085	1.090	1.095	1.100	1
2	2.106	2.122	2.153	2.184	2.199	2.215	2.231	2.246	2.262	2.278	2.294	2.310	2
3	3.215	3.247	3.310	3.375	3.407	3.440	3.473	3.506	3.540	3.573	3.607	3.641	3
4	4.363	4.416	4.526	4.637	4.694	4.751	4.808	4.866	4.925	4.985	5.045	5.105	4
5	5.550	5.633	5.802	5.975	6.064	6.154	6.244	6.335	6.429	6.524	6.619	6.716	5
6	6.779	6.898	7.142	7.394	7.523	7.655	7.787	7.922	8.060	8.201	8.343	8.487	6
7	8.052	8.214	8.549	8.898	9.077	9.261	9.446	9.636	9.831	10.029	10.230	10.436	7
8	9.369	9.583	10.027	10.491	10.732	10.979	11.230	11.487	11.751	12.022	12.297	12.579	8
9	10.731	11.006	11.578	12.181	12.494	12.817	13.147	13.486	13.835	14.194	14.560	14.937	9
10	12.142	12.486	13.207	13.972	14.372	14.784	15.208	15.645	16.096	16.561	17.039	17.531	10
11	13.602	14.026	14.917	15.870	16.371	16.889	17.424	17.977	18.549	19.141	19.752	20.384	11
12	15.113	15.627	16.713	17.882	18.500	19.141	19.806	20.495	21.211	21.954	21.724	23.523	12
13	16.677	17.292	18.599	20.015	20.767	21.551	22.366	23.215	24.099	25.020	25.977	26.975	13
14	18.296	19.024	20.579	22.276	23.182	24.130	25.118	26.152	27.232	28.362	29.540	30.772	14
15	19.971	20.825	22.658	24.673	25.754	26.889	28.077	29.324	30.632	32.004	33.442	34.950	15
16	21.705	22.698	24.840	27.213	28.493	29.841	31.258	32.750	34.321	35.974	37.714	39.545	16
17	23.500	24.645	27.132	29.906	31.410	33.000	34.677	36.450	38.323	40.302	42.391	44.599	17
18	25.357	26.671	29.539	32.760	34.517	36.380	38.353	40.446	42.665	45.019	47.513	50.159	18
19	27.280	28.778	32.066	35.786	37.825	39.997	42.305	44.762	47.377	50.161	53.122	56.275	19
20	29.270	30.969	34.719	38.993	41.349	43.867	46.553	49.423	52.489	55.765	59.264	63.002	20
21	31.329	33.248	37.505	42.392	45.102	48.008	51.119	54.457	58.036	61.874	65.989	70.403	21
22	33.460	35.618	40.431	45.996	49.098	52.438	56.028	59.894	64.054	68.533	73.353	78.543	22
23	35.667	38.083	43.502	49.816	53.355	57.179	61.305	65.765	70.583	75.791	81.416	87.497	23
24	37.950	40.646	46.727	53.865	57.888	62.251	66.978	72.106	77.668	83.702	90.246	97.347	24
25	40.313	43.312	50.114	58.156	62.715	67.678	73.076	78.954	85.355	92.325	99.914	108.182	25

26	42.759	46.084	53.669	62.706	67.857	73.485	79.632	86.350	93.695	101.724	110.501	120.100	26
27	45.291	48.968	57.403	67.528	73.333	79.699	86.679	94.338	102.744	111.969	122.094	133.210	27
28	47.911	51.966	61.323	72.640	79.164	86.348	94.255	102.965	112.562	123.136	134.788	147.631	28
29	50.623	55.085	65.439	78.058	85.375	93.462	102.399	112.282	123.215	135.308	148.688	163.494	29
30	53.430	58.328	69.761	83.802	91.989	101.074	111.154	122.345	134.773	148.576	163.908	180.943	30
31	56.335	61.702	74.299	89.890	99.034	109.219	120.566	133.213	147.314	163.038	180.574	200.138	31
32	59.341	65.210	79.064	96.343	106.536	117.934	130.683	144.950	160.920	178.801	198.824	221.252	32
33	62.453	68.858	84.067	103.184	114.526	127.259	141.560	157.626	175.684	195.983	218.807	244.477	33
34	65.674	72.652	89.320	110.435	123.035	137.237	153.252	171.316	191.702	214.711	240.688	270.024	34
35	69.008	76.598	94.836	118.121	132.097	147.914	165.820	186.101	209.081	235.125	264.649	298.127	35
36	72.458	80.702	100.628	126.268	141.748	159.338	179.332	202.069	227.938	257.376	290.886	329.039	36
37	76.029	84.970	106.710	134.904	152.027	171.562	193.857	219.315	248.398	281.630	319.615	363.043	37
38	79.725	89.409	113.095	144.059	162.974	184.641	209.471	237.940	270.597	308.067	351.073	400.448	38
39	83.550	94.026	119.800	153.762	174.632	198.636	226.223	258.055	294.683	336.883	385.520	441.593	39
40	87.510	98.827	126.840	164.048	187.048	213.610	244.301	279.780	320.816	368.292	423.239	486.852	40
41	91.607	103.820	134.232	174.951	200.271	229.633	263.698	303.242	349.170	402.528	464.542	536.637	41
42	95.849	109.012	141.993	186.508	214.354	246.777	284.551	328.581	379.934	439.846	509.769	591.401	42
43	100.238	114.413	150.143	198.758	229.352	265.121	306.967	355.948	413.314	480.522	559.292	651.641	43
44	104.782	120.029	158.700	211.744	245.325	284.749	331.065	385.504	449.530	524.859	613.519	717.905	44
45	109.484	125.871	167.685	225.508	262.336	305.751	356.969	417.424	488.825	573.186	672.899	790.795	45
46	114.351	131.945	177.119	240.099	280.453	328.224	384.817	451.898	531.461	625.863	737.919	870.975	46
47	119.388	138.263	187.025	255.565	299.747	352.270	414.753	489.130	577.720	683.281	809.116	959.172	47
48	124.602	144.834	197.427	271.958	320.295	377.999	446.935	529.341	627.911	745.866	887.077	1056.190	48
49	129.998	151.667	208.348	289.336	342.180	405.529	481.530	572.768	682.368	814.084	972.445	1162.909	49
50	135.583	158.774	219.815	307.756	365.486	434.986	518.720	619.670	741.455	888.442	1065.922	1260.299	50

The next step is to compute the amount that must be contributed this year to fund each of these benefits currently—that is, the *present value of the annual accrual*. For simplicity, we will assume that all employees survive and continue in service with the employer until age 65. (Mortality and turnover assumptions, however, are permitted, as discussed below.) The only assumption in the present value calculation, then, is an assumption about the rate of investment return. The factors in Table 11–1 may be used. The Code does not put specific limits on the range of permissible rates, but the rate must be reasonable, as with other actuarial assumptions.

A final concept needed is the annuity purchase rate; as discussed earlier, this is the lump sum needed at retirement to provide a straight-life annuity of $1 per year. For illustration, an annuity purchase rate of $9.50 will be used for the Clutch plan. With that rate, an accrued benefit of $10,000 per year would require an accumulation of $95,000 at age 65. Our calculation under the accrued benefit method, then, is as follows:

Employee	Annual Accrual	×	Annuity Rate	×	Present Value Factor	=	Present Value
A	$10,000		$9.50		.7473		$70,993
B	2,000		9.50		.4173		7,929
C	1,000		9.50		.3118		2,962
D	357		9.50		.1301		441
					Total		$82,325

This calculation shows, for example, that $70,993 must be deposited now to provide a benefit of $10,000 per year for employee A at age 65 (five years from now), $70,993 being the present value of the $95,000 required to purchase the $10,000 annuity at age 65. The normal cost for the current year is the sum of the present values of the annual accruals for all employees, or $82,325.

It will be noted from the present value table (Table 11–1) that the present value factor increases as the participant gets closer to retirement. The accrued-benefit method, therefore, produces a steadily increasing normal cost for a given group of active employees. However, as employees leave the group by retiring or terminating employment, their benefit no longer enters the calculation. Correspondingly, new employees entering the plan will add to the normal cost. Thus, when the accrued-benefit method is used in actual situations, the employer's annual normal cost may increase, decrease, or level off.

Projected-Benefit Methods. The projected-benefit methods determine the normal cost by developing a level annual cost for each employee's benefit, instead of the steadily rising costs resulting under the accrued-benefit method. The concept is that of installment savings, discussed earlier. A simple illustration of this can be provided using the data and assumptions for the Clutch plan discussed above.

(1) Employee	(2) Projected Annual Benefit	×	(3) Annuity Rate	=	(4) Accumulation Required at Age 65	(5) Years to Retirement	(6) Level Annual Deposit (6 Percent) Required to Attain (4)
A	$50,000		$9.50		$475,000	5	$79,494
B	30,000		9.50		285,000	15	11,551
C	20,000		9.50		190,000	20	4,872
D	12,500		9.50		118,750	35	1,005
						Total	$96,922

The calculation of the normal cost under the projected-benefit approach begins with the entire projected benefit at retirement, then a calculation (column 6) of the level deposits necessary each year to provide an ultimate accumulation at retirement age sufficient to provide the projected benefit at an assumed annuity rate. (Column 6 can be calculated from the information in columns 4 and 5, plus an interest assumption—6% was used here—using a pocket calculator having an "installment savings" program, a computer with the same program, or with actuarial tables, such as Table 11–2.) The normal cost for the Clutch plan here is the total of the amounts in column 6, or $96,922. The addition of mortality, turnover, or other actuarial assumptions would complicate the calculation, but the principles are the same. *Note:* the normal cost provided initially under this method is higher than the normal cost using the accrued-benefit method. This is what one would expect, because of the level funding approach in the projected-benefit method.

Several actuarial cost methods use the projected-benefit approach. These can be divided into *individual* and *aggregate* methods. With the individual methods, the plan's normal cost is determined as the sum of separate annual costs determined for each employee. This is the approach used in the example just completed. With aggregate methods, the normal cost is determined by reference to the total benefits and salaries of all employees covered under the plan, rather than on an individual basis. Basically, this is done by determining the normal cost as a percentage of payroll of all employees covered by the plan. The normal cost percentage is defined as:

$$\frac{\text{Present value of projected benefits } - \text{ Plan assets}}{\text{Present value of future salaries}}$$

For a new plan, of course, the value of the plan assets initially will be zero.

An advantage of an aggregate method is that, as the above formula indicates, the value of plan assets is taken into account in determining each year's normal cost percentage; thus, the method automatically makes adjustments for investment results or other fund experience (mortality, turnover, and so on) that deviate from the actuarial assumptions. With individual methods, such adjustments are made after an actuarial valuation and are amortized separately over a period of years, as discussed below.

Amortization of Past Service Cost (Supplemental Liability)

Flexibility in funding is gained by splitting the funding into two elements—the normal cost and a *supplemental liability*. As discussed above, the supplemental liability is usually related to an initial liability for funding past service benefits and, therefore, is often referred to as the *unfunded past service liability*. While the normal cost of a plan is designed to be funded over the period prior to each employee's retirement, the entire supplemental liability may be funded (or *amortized*) over a specified period of years, even if this period extends beyond the retirement dates of some plan participants. Under ERISA, the amortization period (for new single-employer plans) cannot exceed 30 years. A full tax deduction for the supplemental liability amortization, however, can be obtained for an amortization over as little as 10 years, as discussed later under "Deductibility of Pension Plan Contributions."

An actuarial cost method that includes a supplemental liability provides some flexibility in the amount the employer must contribute each year. Once a plan's actuarial methods and assumptions have been determined, the amount of the normal cost has been correspondingly determined, and it may be difficult for an employer to change actuarial methods and assumptions to adjust the normal cost to a more financially comfortable level in the future. However, the portion of the plan funding attributable to amortizing the supplemental liability can be varied by the employer from year to year, as long as the amount is at least enough to meet the 30-year amortization requirement.

Actuarial Assumptions

The importance of actuarial assumptions has been mentioned above. The following are some commonly used actuarial assumptions, with some indication of when and how they are used.

Interest or Investment Return. This is the actuarial assumption that is most basic and must always be used. It reflects the time value of money—the fact that $1 deposited currently will grow over the years to some amount greater than $1. Actuaries typically use conservative (i.e., low) rates of return for defined-benefit plans, because of the plan's long-range nature and the necessity for security. Rates of 5 to 8 percent often have been used, with lower figures being more common in periods of lower current interest rates, such as the 1960s and mid-1980s. The lower the rate used, the greater is the annual deposit required. The use of an unreasonably low rate can result in a penalty tax, as discussed below.

Mortality. A mortality assumption reflects the possibility that some participants in the employee census may die before reaching retirement age, and that the amounts contributed to the plan on their behalf will be available to fund benefits of other participants, assuming the plan does not pay these amounts out fully as a death benefit. A mortality assumption accordingly reduces the current contribution to the plan. A mortality assumption may not be appropriate for a small group—say less than 10 employees. It is hard to predict mortality in such a small group; often, all the members of the group will live to retirement, thus producing underfunding if a mortality assumption has been used.

Turnover. A turnover assumption reflects the possibility that some employees will terminate employment without a fully vested retirement benefit. Again, a turnover assumption tends to reduce current cost for the plan. But, as with mortality, a turnover assumption may not be appropriate for a small group of employees where turnover is difficult to predict.

Salary Scale. If plan benefits depend on future salaries, it is unrealistic to make a benefit projection based on current salaries. Therefore, the plan may include an assumption that salaries will increase at a specified rate over time. Usually it is impractical to assume an increase based on a high inflation rate, because this would produce enormous projected benefits for younger employees. Therefore, a salary scale typically uses a relatively conservative long-term rate based on annual increases of a few percentage points.

Choosing Actuarial Assumptions

The Regulations under Code Section 412 permit assumptions of the four types indicated above, as long as they use "reasonable" factors. Reasonableness is not defined in detail, so considerable flexibility exists. Reasonableness is tested on assumptions in the aggregate; for example, an investment return assumption may be too liberal, but if it is counterbalanced by other too-conservative assumptions the reasonableness test may be met. IRS auditing agents initially test for reasonableness by observing whether the plan is over- or under-funded in actual experience over a period of several years.[2]

Certain types of assumptions that might be considered actuarially appropriate are specifically prohibited by the Regulations. The Regulations do not allow a funding method to anticipate changes in plan benefits that become effective in a future plan year, except for collectively bargained plans. Also, a funding method may not anticipate the future entry of new employees into the plan, except for current employees who have not yet satisfied the plan's participation requirements.

Penalty for Overstatement of Pension Liabilities. If the IRS assesses additional taxes, because an employer's pension plan used unreasonable actuarial

---

[2]IRM 7(10)5(10), *Actuarial Guidelines Handbook* (Department of the Treasury, Internal Revenue Service, December 12, 1984).

assumptions, under Code Section 6659A it can also impose a penalty on the additional tax liability. The amount of the penalty is based on the extent to which the plan's actuary has overstated the pension liability:

Extent of Overstatement	Percent Penalty
150 percent—200 percent	10
More than 200 percent—250 percent	20
More than 250 percent	30

As a result of this penalty, plan actuaries must closely monitor the views of the IRS as to the range of investment return and other assumptions that will be considered reasonable.

Some Specific Permissible Actuarial Cost Methods

As mentioned above, the choice of actuarial cost method is limited only by the Code requirement—that the method be reasonable—and a few corresponding requirements in the Regulations. Thus, a wide variety of actuarial cost methods is available through variations on the concepts discussed above—there is a choice of:

Accrued-benefit or projected-benefit approach for determining normal cost.
Individual or aggregate methods, if the projected-benefit approach is used.
Whether to use a supplemental liability.

Six methods should be discussed briefly here, because they are specifically mentioned in Section 3(31) of ERISA as "acceptable" methods. Because of this legislative endorsement, many plans use one of these methods.

Accrued-Benefit Method. The accrued-benefit method, sometimes called the unit-credit method, is a method under which future service costs are funded using a normal cost determined by an accrued-benefit method, and past service liability is treated separately. This is essentially the method discussed in some detail in the first example for the Clutch plan given above.

Individual Level Premiums Method. This is a method without separate funding for past service benefits, so the entire cost of the plan is funded through the normal cost. In this method, the normal cost is determined on a projected-benefit (level cost) benefit for each participant separately, with the total normal cost for the plan being the sum of the level cost computed for each participant. The second example for the Clutch plan essentially illustrates this method.

Entry Age Normal Method. This is another method under which past service liability is funded separately from the normal cost. The normal cost of the plan each year is the sum of the level costs for each participant. However, the level cost for each participant is determined as if the participant had entered the plan at the age when that participant's benefits began to accrue—the entry age. If entry ages occur before the plan is instituted—that is, if the plan provides past service benefits—then the normal cost will not by itself fully fund the plan. The amount of the past service liability is the present value of the total normal costs (which were never actually paid) between each employee's entry age and the establishment of the plan. This past service liability is then amortized under the applicable rules.

Aggregate Method. This method and the next two methods are aggregate cost methods, since they determine normal cost with reference to total benefits and salaries of all plan participants, rather than making determinations on an individual basis. The "plain" aggregate method does not separately fund past service cost, so there is no initial past service liability. The normal cost percentage is determined from the formula:

$$\frac{\text{Present value of projected benefits} - \text{Plan assets}}{\text{Present value of future salaries}}$$

Attained Age Normal Method. This is a variation of the "plain" aggregate method designed to create an initial past service liability to increase funding flexibility. Under the attained age normal method, the amount of the initial past service liability is determined using the accrued-benefit method. The normal cost percentage is then determined under the following formula:

$$\frac{\begin{pmatrix}\text{Present value of} \\ \text{projected benefits}\end{pmatrix} - \begin{pmatrix}\text{Plan assets} + \begin{matrix}\text{Unfunded initial} \\ \text{past service liability} \\ \text{under the accrued-} \\ \text{benefit method}\end{matrix}\end{pmatrix}}{\text{Present value of future salaries}}$$

Frozen Initial Liability Method. This is a further variation on the aggregate method, and it also determines an initial past service liability to increase funding flexibility. The frozen initial liability method uses a projected-benefit method, such as the entry age normal method, to determine the initial past service liability. As with the attained age normal method, the remaining benefits are funded through future normal cost determined under the aggregate method. Accordingly, the normal cost percentage formula is:

$$\frac{\begin{pmatrix}\text{Present value of} \\ \text{projected benefits}\end{pmatrix} - \begin{pmatrix}\text{Plan assets} + \begin{matrix}\text{Unfunded initial} \\ \text{past service liability} \\ \text{under the entry} \\ \text{age normal method}\end{matrix}\end{pmatrix}}{\text{Present value of future salaries}}$$

The best way to understand how these actuarial cost methods operate is to work through examples of the various types for a given plan and employee group; this is done in "How to Select Acceptable Actuarial Methods for Defined-Benefit

Pension Plans," an article by Kirk F. Maldonado in *The Journal of Taxation* for July 1982.

A comparison of the annual cost for a given plan under the six methods shows how important the choice of method is and how much flexibility is available. In the Maldonado article cited above, the cost for a given plan for each of the six ERISA methods was determined. The plan provides an annual retirement benefit of 40 percent of the employee's salary for his or her final year, and the benefits are to be paid monthly in the form of a straight-life annuity. For simplicity, possible deferred vested benefits for terminating employees were not taken into account.

The employee census data is as follows:

Age	Age when Hired (Entry Age)	Years of Past Service	Current Salary
60	40	20	$100,000
50	45	5	50,000
30	30	0	25,000
25	25	0	10,000

For the first year, the cost comparison from the article is:

Funding Method	Minimum Contribution	Maximum Deduction
Individual methods:		
Accrued benefit	$34,742	$50,162
Individual level premiums	81,938	81,938
Entry age normal	34,546	51,831
Aggregate methods:		
Aggregate	52,318	52,318
Attained age normal	36,594	52,014
Frozen initial liability	34,668	51,953

The column headed "Minimum Contribution" indicates the normal cost plus a 30-year amortization of the supplemental liability, if any, for each method. The column headed "Maximum Deduction" indicates the normal cost plus a 10-year amortization of the supplemental liability. The employee's actual first-year contribution, for a given funding method, could be either amount or any amount in between, as the employer determines.

Choosing an Actuarial Cost Method

The initial choice of an actuarial cost method may be affected by the employer's concerns about how plan costs will be spread over future years. The accrued-benefit method will often produce a lower initial cost than other methods and might be chosen if the employer wishes to minimize costs at the plan's inception with the expectation of increased funding in later years. Sometimes this deferral of funding can be a problem. For example, in the 1950s, plans of large manufacturing companies often used the accrued-benefit method, since they expected continuing expansion of their work force and, thus, increasing contributions. However, with the decline in manufacturing in the 1970s, many such plans became underfunded.

Some employers might prefer to *maximize* initial contributions. This is often the case when a plan benefits mostly key employees and the employer wishes to maximize tax-sheltering effects. In that case, a level cost method, such as the individual level premiums method, may produce the highest annual cost. A very high initial annual cost can sometimes be provided using the individual level premiums method, with past service liability amortized over a 10-year period. However, if high-paid participants are within 10 years of retirement, the individual level premiums method *without* a supplemental liability will generally provide a higher annual tax-deductible contribution.

Sometimes, employers wish to match pension costs as closely as possible to payroll costs. In this situation, the aggregate method is typically used, since it expresses normal cost as a percentage of participants' compensation and, thus, rises automatically with payroll costs. The aggregate method is typically used with larger employee groups for this reason, although it produces the same results with a smaller group of employees as well.

Methods that spread costs over too many years can produce problems of underfunding. For example, using a supplemental liability for past service benefits and spreading these benefits over a 30-year period can result in underfunding if participants with large projected benefits are close to retirement.

If a plan's initial funding method proves unacceptable in practice, the plan administrator can change the method. Code Section 412(c)(5) requires IRS approval for a change in funding method; however, under Revenue Procedure 85–29, such changes will be automatically approved in most routine situations. Changes in actuarial assumptions generally do not require IRS approval.

Ongoing Actuarial Valuations

The discussion so far has focused on actuarial methods for determining plan costs for the initial year. In subsequent years, the plan experience is likely to deviate somewhat from the assumptions made in determining first-year cost. If the deviations are significant enough, one response may be to change the actuarial methods or assumptions. However, other ways deal with variations from the initial assumptions.

The assets of all qualified plans are valued periodically by the actuary; under ERISA, the valuation must be made at least once every three years. If the plan assets are found to be insufficient, there is an actuarial deficiency (or *experience loss*), which is made up with increased contributions that are usually deposited *(amortized)* over a period of years. Similarly, if there is an actuarial surplus (or *experience gain*), contributions are decreased over future years. The minimum funding standards, discussed below, determine how rapidly these experience gains and losses must be amortized.

The valuation of the plan's assets may be made on the basis of any reasonable valuation method, as long as the method takes into account the fair market value of the assets—that is, rather than using cost or some other purely formal method of valuation. The Regulations under Section 412 specify rules that must be used in valuation. For example, debt instruments may be valued by amortizing the difference between initial cost and maturity value over the life of the bond, since it may not be possible to determine current fair market value by market quotations. Also, since valuations are relatively infrequent, the plan can use any reasonable and consistent procedure for averaging actual market value over a period of years or otherwise smoothing out the fluctuations in the market value of assets.

Minimum Funding Standards

The minimum funding standards of Section 412 of the Code and corresponding ERISA provisions provide the basic legal structure for enforcing the advance funding requirement that applies to qualified pension plans. A plan to which the minimum funding standard applies must maintain a *funding standard account*. The funding standard account is annually charged with certain plan costs and credited with certain items that benefit the plan. At the end of the year, if the charges exceed the credits, there may be an *accumulated funding deficiency*. In that case, there is a penalty tax and other enforcement provisions. The penalty tax consists of an initial tax of 5 percent of the deficiency, with an additional 100 percent tax if the deficiency is not corrected after notification by the IRS.

The *charges* to the funding standard account are:

1. The normal cost of the plan for the plan year.
2. The amounts necessary to amortize the unfunded past service liability (usually over a 30-year period, or 40 years for a multiemployer plan).
3. The amount necessary to amortize the net increase, if any, in unfunded past service liability arising from plan amendments.
4. The amount necessary to amortize in equal annual installments the net experience loss, if any, under the plan. The amortization is over 15 years, or, for a multiemployer plan, 20 years.
5. The amount necessary to amortize over a period of 30 years in equal annual installments the net loss, if any, resulting from each change in actuarial assumptions used under the plan.
6. The amount necessary to amortize over a period of 15 years, in equal annual installments, each "waived funding deficiency" (as discussed below).
7. The amount necessary to amortize in equal annual installments over a period of five years any amount credited to the funding standard account as a waived funding deficiency (see item 5 in the list of credits to the account).

The *credits* to the funding standard account for each plan year are:

1. The amount considered contributed by the employer to the plan for the plan year.
2. The amount necessary to amortize in equal annual installments each decrease in unfunded past service liability arising from a plan amendment. The amortization is over 30 years, or, for a multiemployer plan, 40 years.
3. The amount necessary to amortize in equal annual installments each net experience gain for the plan over a period of 15 years, or, for a multiemployer plan, 20 years.
4. The amount necessary to amortize in equal annual installments the net gain from each change in actuarial assumptions, over a period of 30 years.
5. The amount of the waived funding deficiency, as discussed below.
6. If the plan has previously used the alternative minimum funding standard account discussed below, an amount required to provide a smooth transition back to the regular minimum funding standard account.

Obviously, the employer's objective is to *balance* the funding standard account for each year. If the employer is unable to make sufficient contributions to do this, the employer can request a waiver from the IRS of the minimum funding standard for the plan year. The request must show that the employer is unable to satisfy the minimum funding standard without substantial business hardship, and that the application of the standard would be adverse to the interest of the plan participants in the aggregate. If the IRS grants the application, it will waive part or all of the funding deficiency for the year, but it cannot waive the amount necessary to amortize waived funding deficiencies for prior years. Also, the IRS cannot waive the minimum funding standard for more than 5 of any 15 consecutive plan years.

In addition to the waiver provisions, the Code allows an extension of the amortization of certain of the liabilities listed above for up to 10 years. For example, the net experience loss amortization could be extended to 25 years, rather than 15 years, or unfunded past service liability amortization could be extended to 40 years rather than 30 years. Such extensions in the amortization schedules must be approved by the Department of Labor.

The employer is not required to contribute annually any more to the plan than an amount referred to as the *full funding limitation,* even if the funding standard account would then be left with a deficit for the plan year. This important limitation is defined as the difference between the accrued actuarial liability of the plan computed under the plan's funding method (or, if this is not possible, under the entry age normal method) less the value of the plan assets.

Example

Suppose that, after working out a plan's funding standard account, an employer contribution of $100,000 would be required for the plan year to avoid a deficit in the account. However, suppose that, due to investment returns higher than the assumed rate, the value of the plan assets is $1,950,000 but the accrued actuarial liability is only $2,000,000. The full funding limitation, therefore, would be $50,000. The employer need contribute only $50,000, the full funding limitation, to avoid the penalties for a funding deficiency.

Certain plans are allowed to establish an *alternative minimum funding standard account* and then can avoid a funding deficiency by avoiding a deficit in either the funding standard account or the alternative minimum funding standard account, whichever is lesser. The alternative minimum funding standard account may be used only by a plan that uses a funding method requiring contributions in all years at least equal to those required under the entry age normal method. The charges and credits to the alternative minimum funding standard account are somewhat simpler than those for the funding standard account, and it is usually possible to avoid a deficit with a lower employer contribution.

Finally, it is useful to summarize the courses of action open to an employer that is facing a funding deficiency under these provisions. One alternative is simply to pay the initial 5 percent excise tax and attempt to correct the deficiencies before the 100 percent tax or mandatory plan termination by the PBGC results (see the discussion in Chapter 21 of PBGC procedures.) Alternatively, to avoid a funding deficiency, the possibilities include changing the plan's funding method, amending the plan to reduce benefit accrual, and requesting a waiver of the minimum funding standard or an extension of the amortization periods as discussed above.

Exemptions from Minimum Funding Standard

The minimum funding standard rules basically apply to all qualified pension plans. However, governmental plans, church plans that have not elected to be treated as qualified plans, and various types of plans having no employer contributions are exempted in Section 412 of the Code.

More significantly, the minimum funding standards do not apply to profit-sharing or stock-bonus plans. Technically, the standards do apply to defined-contribution pension plans as well as defined-benefit pension plans. However, for defined-contribution pension plans (money-purchase and target-benefit plans) the minimum funding standard will be met as long as the employer contributes each year the amount required to be contributed under the plan's contribution formula.

Fully insured plans—those funded *exclusively* by the purchase of individual insurance or annuity contracts—are specifically exempted from the minimum funding standards as long as the following requirements are met:

> The contracts provide for the payment of premiums in equal annual amounts over a period no longer than the preretirement period of employment.
>
> The plan benefits are equal to those guaranteed by the insurance carrier under the contracts.

The premiums on the contracts have been paid when due or, if there has been a lapse, when the policy has been reinstated.

No rights under the insurance contract have been subject to a security interest at any time during the plan year.

No policy loans are outstanding at any time during the plan year.

Plans that are fully insured under group contracts also are exempt from the minimum funding standard as long as the contracts meet conditions similar to those listed above. These ordinarily would have to be group contracts providing fully allocated funding; these are discussed in Chapter 12.

Deductibility of Pension Plan Contributions

Excessive contributions to a pension plan fund, if they are allowed to be deducted, will accelerate the employer's tax deduction and, thereby, increase the tax benefit of the qualified plan beyond what is considered appropriate. To prevent this, there are specific limits on the amount of pension plan contributions that an employer can deduct in a given plan year.

Unlike the deduction limit for profit-sharing plans, which is a specific 15 percent of payroll (see Chapter 13), the deduction limit for pension plans is based on actuarial considerations. Basically, for a given plan year, an employer can deduct contributions to a pension plan up to a limit determined, in effect, by the larger of three amounts:

The amount necessary to satisfy the minimum funding standard for the year;

the amount necessary to fund benefits based on past and current service on a level funding basis over the years remaining to retirement for each employee (however, if the remaining unfunded cost for any three individuals is more than 50 percent of the total of the unfunded costs, funding for those three individuals must be distributed over a period of at least five taxable years), or

an amount equal to the normal cost of the plan plus, if there is a supplemental liability, an amount necessary to amortize the supplemental liability in equal annual payments over a 10-year period.

In determining the applicable limitation, the funding methods and the actuarial assumptions used must be the same as those used for purposes of the minimum funding standards. Furthermore, the tax deduction for a given plan year cannot exceed the full funding limitation—discussed earlier. Thus, there is little incentive for the employer to contribute beyond the full funding limitation.

Although these limits are expressed in rather complex actuarial language, the implications are relatively easy to understand. First, if the plan is funded on the basis of individual insurance contracts, the second limit will generally be the one applicable to the plan, since most such contracts have premiums determined on the basis of level funding for the years remaining until retirement for each employee. On the other hand, plans funded with group contracts and trust funds using a variety of actuarial methods and assumptions will generally be governed by the third alternative limit.

Note: this limit specifies the *maximum* deductible amount. The amount required to be contributed under the minimum funding standard as applied to the plan may be somewhat less than this limit. Therefore, in a given plan year, the employer's actual contribution and deduction may be less than the maximum limit that applies. This is one of the reasons why a defined-benefit plan with a group pension contract or trust fund can be relatively flexible for the employer. Between the minimum limit required by the minimum funding standards and the maximum deductible limit discussed above, there may be a relatively comfortable range of contributions that can be adjusted according to the employer's specific financial situation.

The rules as stated above technically apply to both defined-benefit and defined-contribution pension plans. However, for defined-contribution plans, the minimum funding standards are satisfied whenever the employer makes the annual contributions specified by the plan document. In other words, the limits on the amount deductible under a defined-contribution pension plan is simply the amount specified in the plan document. For example, the plan document in a money-purchase plan might require that each year the employer must contribute an amount equal to 6 percent of each employee's compensation to that employee's account. The total of such contributions then would be both the amount required by the minimum funding standard and the maximum amount deductible.

If an employer has a combination of defined-benefit plan and a defined-contribution plan covering the same employee or employees, a percentage deduction limit applies. The deduction for a given year cannot exceed the greater of 25 percent of the common payroll (compensation of employees covered under both plans) or the amount required to meet the minimum funding standard for the defined-benefit plan alone. As discussed in Chapter 18, this provision has its greatest impact on highly compensated employees.

Penalty for Nondeductible Contributions. Generally, there is no advantage in contributing more to a plan than is deductible, because not only is the deduction for the excess unavailable but, under Code Section 4972, a 10 percent penalty is imposed on the nondeductible portion of the contribution. However, if nondeductible contributions are made, they can be carried over and deducted in future years. The deduction limit for future years, however, applies to the combination of carried-over and current contributions.

Timing of Deductions

The rules for timing of contributions and deductions for qualified plans are relatively favorable. Contributions will be deemed to be made by the employer for a given taxable year of the employer, and will be deductible for that year, if they are made by the time prescribed for filing the employer's tax return for that year, including extensions. For example, a calendar year corporation's contribution to the plan for 1987 could be made as late as September 15, 1988 (the basic tax filing date of March 15, plus the maximum six-month extension). The rules for timing of contributions and deductions are the same for both cash and accrual-method taxpayers—that is, there is no advantage for this purpose in using the accrual method.

Summary

Actuarial Cost Methods

Actuarial cost methods determine an annual contribution designed to produce a pension fund adequate to make benefit payments as they are due. The annual normal cost is determined by using either an accrued-benefit or projected-benefit approach. The annual normal cost under the accrued-benefit approach is the present value of benefits accrued each year. Under the projected-benefit approach, the normal cost is an amount based on level funding of the total benefits projected to retirement.

If a plan provides past service benefits, plan funding can be split into normal cost and supplemental liability amortization. The supplemental liability is the present value of past service costs currently accrued; this cost can be funded or amortized over a specified period of years ranging from 10 to 30.

Projected-benefit methods can be either individual or aggregate. Aggregate methods are designed to determine plan costs as a percentage of total payroll, rather than as a dollar amount for each individual participant.

Actuarial assumptions about future fund investment return, mortality and turnover of covered participants, and future compensation increases are critical in determining plan funding. Tax deductions claimed on the basis of unreasonable assumptions may result in disallowance and penalty taxes.

Different actuarial cost methods result in somewhat different funding patterns and should be chosen to meet the employer's needs.

Minimum Funding Standards

Employers having a qualified pension plan must make a specified minimum annual contribution to the plan to avoid penalty. Penalties can be avoided by keeping in balance a minimum funding standard account, which is defined in terms of specified credits and charges. Certain exceptions and alternatives apply.

Tax Deductions

An employer can deduct the amount determined by the actuary as the annual contribution, within limits, and can always deduct at least the amount required to meet the minimum funding requirements. A 25 percent of payroll limit applies to a combination of defined-benefit and defined-contribution plans. There is a 10 percent tax penalty for any contributions in excess of the deduction limit. Rules for timing of deductions are the same for cash or accrual method taxpayers.

12

Qualified Plan Funding Instruments

Objectives of This Chapter
- *Describe the types of funding instruments and agencies that can be used to hold qualified plan funds, distinguishing between trusts and insurance contracts.*
- *Explain how plan trusts are organized and operated.*
- *Describe the types of insurance contracts that can be used for qualified plan funding, distinguishing allocated and unallocated contracts, and individual and group contracts.*

Funding Agencies and Instruments

The assets of a qualified plan must be held either by a trustee or by an insurance company. It is also possible to hold plan funds in a bank "custodial account" that is not technically a trust, but under Section 401(f) of the Code such an account is treated the same as a trust for all practical purposes. The trustee or insurance company is referred to as the plan's *funding agency*.

Plan assets are held by a funding agency under a legal document called a *funding instrument*. The funding instrument is either a *trust agreement* or *insurance contract,* depending on the funding agency. There are many legal requirements applicable to a funding instrument; these are discussed in this chapter and in Chapter 17. Within these requirements, however, there is opportunity for flexibility in plan design, in funding procedures, and in investment policy. The employer's choices in these areas are an important part of qualified plan design.

Trusts

The trust is the leading funding agency for qualified plans, both in terms of the number of employees covered and aggregate plan assets.[1] A trust used for quali-

---

[1] At the end of 1985, insurance companies held roughly one fourth and private trustees three fourths of total private plan assets of about $1.3 trillion, according to the Employee Benefit Research Institute Quarterly Pension Investment Report. This percentage has been relatively stable in recent years.

fied plan funding is based on the same general principles of trust law as trusts used for other purposes, such as estate planning and administering the affairs of minors or incompetent persons. Basically, a trust is an arrangement involving three parties—the grantor of the trust, the trustee, and the beneficiaries. In qualified plan funding, the grantor is the employer and the beneficiaries are the employees. The trustee is a party holding funds contributed by the employer for the benefit of employees.

Legally speaking, a trustee is a fiduciary; a fiduciary is a person or organization that holds money on behalf of someone else (here the plan participants and beneficiaries) and must administer that money solely in the interest of those other persons. The trustee's compensation is a fee for services rendered; the trustee is prohibited from personally profiting as a result of investments of the trust funds.

The duties of a qualified plan trustee, like those of any other trustee, are set out in a formal trust agreement. Usually, the duties of a plan trustee are to accept employer contributions, invest those contributions and accumulate the earnings, and pay benefits to plan participants and beneficiaries out of the plan fund. The trustee performs these acts only at the direction of the plan administrator and not at the trustee's own discretion. However, in some cases, a trustee is given direct responsibility for choosing plan investments or choosing an investment adviser. The trustee must account periodically to the plan administrator or the employer for all investments, receipts, and disbursements. The trustee does not guarantee the payment of benefits or the adequacy of the trust fund to pay benefits. That remains the obligation of the employer.

A trustee may be an individual or group of individuals or a corporation, such as a bank or trust company. Often employers name individual trustees, such as the company president or a major shareholder, to obtain an extra measure of control over plan assets. This is permissible under the law; however, when acting as trustee such an individual is legally obligated to act solely in the interest of the plan participants and beneficiaries and not in the interests of the employer or shareholders.

Although a qualified plan trust is created and exists under the laws of the state in which it is established, the most significant provisions of trust law affecting qualified plan trusts have been codified in federal statutes that supersede state law whenever they apply. The area of trust investments and related issues is treated in more detail in Chapter 17.

Insurance Contracts

Allocated and Unallocated Funding in Insurance Contracts

Insurance companies offer a variety of contracts either designed specifically for qualified plan funding or adaptable to it. In theory, an employer could negotiate a contract with the insurance company with provisions specifically tailored to the employer's needs. In practice, however, insurance contracts tend to fall into a number of specific types, with some but not complete flexibility about their terms. This is partly because an insurance contract (particularly a life insurance contract) does not usually result from unfettered negotiation between insurer and contract-holder; often the terms of the contract require state regulatory approval and, consequently, the insurer is not interested in varying them for each individual contract-holder. Also, historical practices and needs in the insurance industry have determined the form of many of the contracts. In addition, administrative costs can be kept lower by minimizing variations from standard forms, and this may be important for smaller employers.

Insurance contracts used in funding qualified plans can be divided into *allocated* and *unallocated* types. Basically, when funding is allocated under an insurance contract, this means that the insurer has assumed the employer's obligation to pay specific benefits to specific participants. The employer is still primarily responsible, but under the terms of the insurance contract participants and the employer can look to the insurance company for payment of specific amounts. With unallocated funding, the insurance company acts basically as a holder of the funds, much like a bank trustee. With unallocated funding, the insurance company, of course, is obligated to deal prudently with the funds, but it makes no guarantee that the funds will be adequate to pay any specific benefits under the plan. An insurance contract used in a qualified plan can be either purely allocated or purely unallocated, or can offer a mixture of both. See Table 12–1 for a comparison of the contracts discussed in this chapter.

Insurance contracts can be classified as follows (and will be discussed in this order in this chapter):

Allocated Contracts

- individual life insurance or annuity contracts:
  —fully insured plans
  —combination plans
- group permanent contracts
- group deferred annuity contracts

Unallocated Contracts

- deposit administration contracts
- immediate participation guarantee (IPG) contracts)

Specialized Insurance Contracts

- guaranteed investment contracts (GICs)
- single-premium annuity contracts

TABLE 12-1. Funding Allocation

Funding Type	When Allocated
Individual policy plans	As benefit accrues
Group permanent	As benefit accrues
Group deferred-annuity contract	As benefit accrues
Group deposit administration contract	At retirement
IPG Contract	Usually never allocated
Trust	Usually never allocated

Insurance Contracts Using Allocated Funding

Individual Life Insurance and Annuity Contracts

For qualified plans of employers with few employees, particularly defined-benefit plans, one of the most common funding methods traditionally has been the use of individual life insurance or annuity contracts. These contracts are typically level-premium contracts—that is, once a benefit level for a given employee has been determined, the benefit is funded using a single insurance or annuity contract, with equal annual premiums paid by the employer until the employee's retirement. It is relatively simple to see how annuity contracts can be used in this manner; the use of life insurance contracts requires some explanation.

The somewhat complex spectrum of life insurance products can be divided into two types of contracts—those providing only term insurance and those with a cash value. Term insurance contracts are not suitable as funding instruments for qualified plans, although they can be used by the plan to provide incidental insurance. Cash value-type contracts, on the other hand, can be used in a qualified plan to provide both retirement benefits and death benefits. This is because these contracts are designed to accumulate a cash value that, if the insured lives long enough, grows to a size sufficient to pay the entire face amount of the contract's death benefit. The purpose of accumulating this amount is to allow the policy to be offered to the insured with the assurance of a level premium for a long time period—the "excess" cost in the early years is used to provide insurance in the later years. Term insurance, by comparison, increases in cost each year as the insured grows older, and there is no reserve to provide insurance for any period longer than one year. A cash value contract, by comparison, is, in effect, an investment medium that can be used in funding a qualified plan.

The most familiar cash value insurance contract, usually referred to as the *whole life contract,* provides increasing cash values up to an advanced age, such as 90 or more. Prior to that age, the scheduled cash value is usually less than the face amount of the death benefit, although many policies provide dividends that accelerate the cash value increase considerably. A whole life policy cannot be used to provide the sole funding for the retirement benefit in a qualified plan with a normal retirement age of 65, because the cash value at age 65 is usually insufficient. Under the "incidental" test for death benefits described in Chapter 10, the death benefit in a qualified plan cannot be more than 100 times the expected monthly pension. So, to illustrate, if the plan provides a monthly pension of $100 per month, no more than $10,000 of whole life insurance can be provided, and the cash value of a $10,000 policy at age 65 is usually insufficient to provide a pension of $100 per month. If whole life policies are used to fund a qualified plan, the plan fund must be supplemented with a side fund or conversion fund, as discussed below under "Combination Plans." To fund a qualified plan benefit with life insurance alone, policies with rapidly increasing cash values must be used; one such policy commonly used is referred to as a *retirement income* policy. The difference in cash value buildup between a retirement income policy and a whole life policy is represented in Figure 12–1.

Use of Retirement Income Policies. The individual retirement income policies used in qualified plans are policies with rapidly increasing cash values, usually similar to such policies offered to the general public for use outside of qualified plans. The plan design options for a plan funded with such policies are somewhat limited, because of the characteristics of the policies themselves. The plans are usually defined-benefit plans providing a life income at retirement in a specified amount, usually expressed in units of $10 per month. When the plan is initially installed, benefit levels are projected for each employee, and a policy is purchased for each employee sufficient to provide these projected benefits. If there is an increase in an employee's projected benefit—for example, if the benefit formula is based on compensation and the employee's compensation increases—then a second, additional policy must be purchased for the employee to provide

FIGURE 12–1. Fully Insured versus Combination Plan

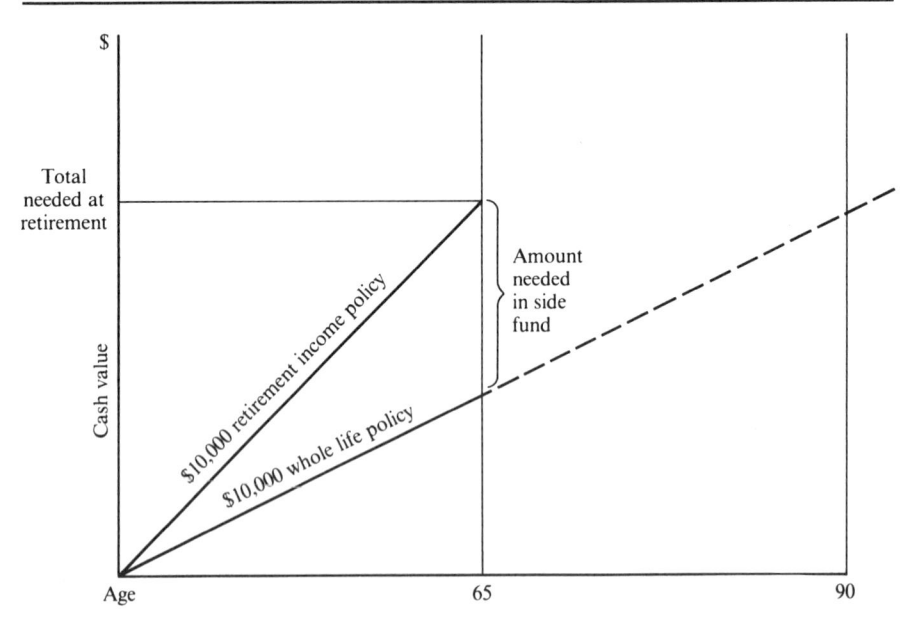

the benefits in excess of the original amount. Thus, the employee's eventual benefit at retirement may be provided under more than one policy.

Since retirement income contracts are basically life insurance policies, the plan provides a preretirement death benefit, usually determined under the 100-to-1 formula. Death benefits may be made subject to medical examinations, or insurance may be made available on a "guaranteed issue" basis (i.e., without medical examinations), usually subject to a minimum number of policies issued, such as five. If medical examinations are required and a participant is uninsurable, the retirement benefit is unaffected, but the death benefit may be reduced or eliminated.

The plan's vesting provisions, of course, must meet the vesting rules described in Chapter 7. To accomplish this, the policies may be distributed at termination of employment to the participant in return for a payment to the plan of the amount of any nonvested cash values in the policy. Alternatively, the plan may retain the policy and use it to provide a deferred vested benefit at the participant's retirement age.

Use of Retirement Annuity Contracts. Retirement annuity contracts are individual contracts used in funding qualified plans in a manner similar to retirement income contracts. However, as the name implies, these are not life insurance contracts, and, therefore, the plan usually provides no death benefit, other than a return of the annuity premiums, or the annuity's cash value, whichever is greater. Thus, the death benefit under a retirement annuity contract is relatively small in a participant's earlier years in the plan.

The employer is the contract-holder under both types of fully insured individual contract plans, although sometimes a trustee is designated as contract-holder for administrative convenience. The employer's sole responsibility for funding the plan is to make the premium payments when due. All benefits are guaranteed by the insurance company, and, if the employer has paid all premiums, it has no further responsibility as long as the insurance company remains solvent.

Under these contracts, the insurance company provides certain credits to the employer to offset premium costs. Because the plan must meet the exclusive-benefit rule applicable to all qualified plans, these credits cannot be paid to the employer in cash. Credits include policy dividends, credits for withdrawal of a participant who is not fully vested, and credits for participants who continue working beyond the normal retirement date.

Combination Plans. A combination plan is a plan that funds a participant's benefit with a whole life policy or policies (i.e., policies whose cash value buildup is relatively slow), plus an additional unallocated trust fund (called a *side fund* or *conversion fund*) to provide the additional amount needed at retirement to fund the retirement benefit. This type of funding is frequently used for defined-benefit plans of small employers, because it combines the advantages of an insured death benefit with some of the flexibility of an unallocated trust fund.

The whole life policies used in combination plans are generally the same as those offered by insurance companies to individuals for purposes other than retirement plans. Almost any type of cash value policy can be used, including some of the newer forms (e.g., universal life policies) that provide substantial investment return, compared with older types of cash value policies. As with fully insured plans, the employer is the policyholder although, again, a trustee can be used to hold the policies, which can be the same person or entity as the trustee of the side fund.

As with fully insured plans, the plan design is to some extent based on the features of the policy used. However, additional flexibility is provided because of the side fund. A whole life policy is purchased for each participant when initial projected-benefit levels are established, and additional policies are provided for each participant if that participant's projected benefit increases because of increases in compensation or otherwise. The employer is responsible for paying premiums on policies, with the insurance company guaranteeing the death benefit and the cash value of the policies. However, the employer is responsible for insuring the adequacy of the side fund. The employer may use its own consulting actuary for purposes of determining funding levels for the side fund, although the insurance company can provide these services if the employer wishes. The employer also determines how the side fund will be invested although, again, the insurance company can hold these funds under a deposit administration type of contract (discussed below).

Table 12–2 illustrates the typical features of a combination plan. *Note:* the amount of life insurance (face amount of each policy) is determined using the 100-to-1 test. The total cost to the employer is the sum of the annual premiums plus the deposit to the side fund. At each participant's retirement, the policy cash value and the balance in the side fund will be combined to provide the retirement benefit. Typically, the plan will provide that an annuity will be purchased from the insurance company at this time at guaranteed rates. If the amount in the side fund is more than is necessary to provide the benefit specified in the plan, the excess remains in the plan, thus allowing the employer to reduce future contributions to the side fund. On the other hand, if the side fund is insufficient at retirement to provide the plan benefit, the employer must make up the difference.

In the event of death before retirement, the combination plan typically provides a death benefit to the participant's beneficiary equal to the policy's full face amount. This is particularly beneficial in the case of a participant who dies early before the cash value or the side fund has built up to significant amounts. These insured death benefits must be coordinated with the preretirement (spousal) sur-

TABLE 12–2. Illustration of Defined-Benefit Combination Plan

	Employee A	Employee B
Age at entry	48	30
Projected monthly retirement benefit	$ 2,250	$ 1,250
Face amount of insurance	225,000	125,000
Gross annual premium	6,399	1,647
Annual side fund deposit	10,174	1,405
Policy cash value at retirement	81,225	65,250
Side fund at retirement (5 percent assumed return)	276,075	133,250

viving annuity required by law and, as discussed in Chapter 10, the total death benefit cannot exceed the "incidental" limit. If the participant terminates employment with a vested benefit, the plan provides a deferred vested benefit using a portion of the cash value of insurance contracts on the participant's life plus a portion of the side fund.

Combination funding can also be used for defined-contribution plans, such as money-purchase pension plans or profit-sharing plans. Since the 100-to-1 test for incidental insurance benefits is difficult to apply in such situations, the amount of whole life insurance is usually designed to meet the other "incidental" test—aggregate insurance premiums less than 50 percent of total contributions, or 25 percent for universal life, as discussed in Chapter 10. In a defined-contribution plan, individual accounts in the side fund must be maintained for each participant. The retirement benefit is usually a lump sum equal to the cash value of the policy or policies, plus the amount in the participant's individual side fund account. Alternatively, this amount could be distributed as an equivalent annuity. If the participant dies before retirement, the death benefit in such a plan usually is the face amount of the life insurance, plus the participant's individual side fund account, although the plan may limit the death benefit to the insurance amount alone.

Group Permanent Contract

To facilitate the use of cash value life insurance contracts in qualified plans of larger employers, insurance companies can write these contracts on a group basis. Such contracts are referred to as *group permanent* contracts. The group permanent contract is used to provide a funding structure similar to that using the corresponding individual contracts, with similar plan design considerations and costs. The major difference is group underwriting. Sometimes a minimum number of employees is required, usually 10 to 25. With group underwriting, the life insurance is written without evidence of insurability up to a limit specified in the plan.

A group permanent (whole life) contract can be designed to provide relatively slow buildup of cash values (and, therefore, lower cost to the employer), so it can be used together with a side fund in much the same manner as a combination plan utilizing individual policies.

Group Deferred Annuity Contract

The group deferred annuity contract is historically an important form of allocated funding contract for pension plans. Under this contract, there is no life insurance. Employer contributions are used to purchase single-premium deferred annuities for employees based on the amount of annuity accrued by the participant each year.

As an illustration, suppose that under the plan an employee earns this year a pension of $10 per month beginning at age 65. The premium for this amount of deferred annuity is determined with similar determinations for other employees covered. The total annuity premium charged to the employer this year is the sum of all such premiums for all employee credits earned during the year. Next year, the premium is the cost of all deferred annuities earned by employees during that year. Thus, unlike the types of contracts discussed so far, the group deferred annuity contract does not generate a level premium but—other things being equal—tends to produce an increasing premium, because the cost of a given amount of deferred annuity increases with increasing age. For an entire employee group, however, the annual premium will not necessarily show an increasing trend, because of retirements, deaths, and terminations of employment.

Since the entire premium under a group deferred annuity contract is determined by the insurance company, the employer has little control over the amount and timing of pension costs. Typically, there are withdrawal credits, deferred retirement credits, and dividends or premium rate adjustments, but these also are largely beyond the control of the employer. Because of the lack of employer flexibility in funding, as well as the availability of better investment results using other contracts, group deferred annuity contracts currently are rarely used.

Insurance Contracts Using Unallocated Funding

The basic characteristic of unallocated funding instruments in a qualified plan is that employer contributions to the plan initially are not allocated to provide specific benefits. In an insurance contract with unallocated funding, the insurance company does not assume the risk of paying specific benefits. Instead, the contributions are held in an undivided fund similar to a trust fund until annuities are purchased at an employee's retirement or until benefits are actually paid to employees. Where long-term investment results are more favorable than the investment assumptions used by insurance companies for allocated contracts, the unallocated type of contract provides an advantage to the employer, because the employer contribution level can be made lower initially and the employer can retain use of the money saved. Thus, unallocated contracts have been developed by insurance companies primarily to compete with other funding agencies, such as bank trust departments.

Group Deposit Administration (DA) Contract

In the conventional type of group deposit administration contract, employer contributions to fund benefits for employees who have not yet retired are held in an unallocated account, referred to as the "active life fund," "annuity purchase fund," "deposit administration fund," "purchase payment fund," or something similar. As each participant reaches retirement age, an amount is taken from the active life fund sufficient to purchase an annuity for that participant in the amount provided by the plan. The annuity purchase rate is determined by the insurance company under the terms of the deposit administration contract. Typically, a deposit administration contract provides a limited guarantee of annuity purchase rates—for example, the contract may guarantee annuity purchase rates for contributions paid during the first five years of the contract, with a year-to-year guarantee thereafter. More liberal guarantees are sometimes made available by insurers to remain competitive.

Under a deposit administration contract, the rate of contributions to the fund is determined by the employer, using a reasonable actuarial method of the employer's choosing, subject to the minimum funding standards and other rules discussed later in this chapter. The employer is entirely responsible for the adequacy of the active life fund and must make contributions accordingly. The insurance company does not determine the premium or funding level. Also, the lack of allocated funding allows the same flexibility in designing the plan's benefit structure as is available under a trust fund plan. Benefit and funding flexibility are the main reasons for the attractiveness of unallocated funding instruments to employers.

In addition to the design flexibility, insurance companies can provide investment features under deposit administration contracts that make these contracts attractive. Most deposit administration contracts provide a minimum investment rate guarantee. As with annuity purchase rate guarantees, the investment rate guarantee will typically apply to contributions paid during the first five years of the contract, with a year-to-year guarantee thereafter; but more liberal guarantees may be made available from time to time to increase the attractiveness of these contracts.

Immediate Participation Guarantee (IPG) Contract

The conventional deposit administration contract described above retains one difference from a fully unallocated fund—the purchase of annuities as participants reach retirement. In determining annuity purchase rates, the insurer includes a factor for expenses and also a factor for a "contingency reserve," to cover the possibility of adverse actuarial experience. This amount must be conservatively determined by the insurance company, because, if the annuity purchase rate turns out to be excessive, the company can return part of the excess through dividends on the contract; but, if the purchase rate is insufficient, the insurance company cannot require the contract-holder to make additional payments.

Many employers, particularly those with many employees, would prefer to assume all of the risks of making postretirement benefit payments to avoid the withdrawal of funds to purchase annuities, thereby maintaining control of the funds for a longer time. The IPG contract was developed to provide for this market.

In most respects, the IPG contract is similar to the conventional deposit administration contract. The principal difference is in the method of providing annuities to participants reaching retirement. Under an IPG contract, there is a single fund into which all plan contributions by the employer are deposited. Under some IPG contracts, no annuity contracts are ever issued; the fund is charged directly with benefit payments as they are made. Under other contracts, the IPG fund is charged as each employee reaches retirement with a single-annuity premium; however, this is done in such a way (e.g., through annual cancellation and reissuance of annuities) as to provide the effect of a trust fund.

Although some insurers offer no guarantees under IPG contracts, principal and minimum investment return guarantees are sometimes made available. As with conventional deposit administration contracts, separate accounts funding can be made available under an IPG contract.

Current Trends in Insurance Contracts for Pension Funding

As Table 12–3 indicates, group contracts cover the largest number of participants in insurance-funded plans and the largest funding total, while individual policy plans account for a larger number of plans, indicating the predominant use of individual policies in smaller plans.

The data in Table 12–3 lumps together all group plans, including group deferred annuity plans, deposit administration plans, and IPGs. However, it is clear from other data that group deferred annuity contracts are a small and declining portion of the market, and that the bulk of group plans are DAs and IPGs.

Separate Accounts Funding and New Money

The investment of qualified plan funds under an insurance contract can involve certain disadvantages relating to the commingling of the employer's pension funds with those of other employers or with other funds of the insurance company. Separate accounts funding and the new money technique are methods by which two of these disadvantages can be mitigated.

Separate Accounts

Separate accounts funding was developed to avoid commingling pension assets with all of the general assets of the insurance company, since an insurance company's general assets have traditionally been invested in long-term, low-return investment vehicles. With separate accounts funding, the insurance company makes available one or more special accounts, "separate" from its general asset accounts, solely for investment of pension money. Such separate accounts may have a specified investment philosophy—for example, one type of account might be invested in common stocks, another in bonds, another in real estate mortgages,

TABLE 12–3. Types of Insurance Contracts Used in Insurance-Funded Retirement Plans

Type of Contract	Number of Plans	Participants Covered (000 omitted)	Fund Total (dollars in millions)
Group (IPG, DA, etc.)	118,120	25,390	$229,490
Individual policy	196,450	1,705	9,440
Keogh plans		475	3,250

Source: Pension Facts, 1986 Update (Washington, D.C.: American Council of Life Insurance).

another in money-market instruments, and the like. The qualified plan sponsor is then given the option to invest various portions of the plan fund in one or more of the separate accounts. Table 12–4 gives the results of a recent informal survey of 12 large insurance companies, indicating the investment options they offer for pension funds.

The funds in separate accounts are commingled with similar funds of other qualified plans, as in a common or collective trust fund. However, if an individual plan fund is large enough, an insurer may also offer the employer an individual separate account only for that employer with whatever mix of assets the employer designates.

New Money

Because many of the insurance contracts available for qualified plan funding involve the mingling of an employer's pension contributions with money invested in previous years, the investment return credited on a given year's contributions is not necessarily equal to the return that could have been earned if the amounts contributed had been newly invested that year. This can present a problem under contracts giving employers discretion on how much to contribute to the fund during a given year, as is generally true under deposit administration and IPG contracts. Where the composite return provided under the insurance contract is greater than that available for new investments, the employer will tend to maximize contributions, while contributions will be minimized when new outside investments can obtain a higher rate of return than under the contract. To alleviate such problems, insurers have developed methods to credit each block of qualified plan contributions with the rate of return at which the funds were actually invested. There are a number of ways of accomplishing this; such techniques are referred to as *new money* or *investment year* methods.

TABLE 12–4. Example of Potential Investment Options—Survey of 12 Insurance Companies, 1986

Company	Fixed Fund New Money Rate	Guaranteed Investment Contract	Money Market	Real Estate	Bonds	Equities	Balanced Account	Services Provided
A	X	X	X			X		No
B	X	X	X			X		No
C	X	X	X	X			X	No
D	X	X	X	X		X		Yes
E		X	X		X	X		Yes
F	X	X	X	X	X	X		Yes (for fee)
G		X	X	X		X		Yes
H	X	X	X			X		No
I		X	X			X		No
J	X	X	X		X	X		Yes
K	X	X	X		X	X	X	Yes

New money methods must not only credit plan contributions for a given year with the current investment rate for that year but must also take account of the fact that contributions from past years are constantly being reinvested at current rates. Thus, a plan contribution made in Year 1 is credited with the new money rate for Year 1. For Year 2, the Year 1 contribution is credited not with the Year 2 rate but with a composite of the Year 1 rate and the Year 2 rate, to reflect the fact that a portion (but only a portion) of the Year 1 money will be reinvested in Year 2.

There are two broad methods of accounting for these changes, the *declining-index* method and the *fixed-index* method. Under the declining-index method, the amount of money associated with a particular year gradually declines as the amount originally invested in that year is reinvested in later years. Thus, under the declining-index method, the amount invested in Year 1 in the example would decline in Year 2 to reflect the fact that part of it was reinvested in Year 2. (See Table 12–5.) Under the fixed-index method, the amount associated with the initial investment year remains the same, and the rate of return credited to that amount is adjusted to reflect reinvestments without changing the original principal amount. The two methods generally produce the same results.

Specialized Insurance Products for Pension Funding

In addition to the contracts, allocated and unallocated, that were described above for use as exclusive vehicles for funding a pension plan, insurance companies offer various types of contracts that are useful for partial funding of a plan—that is, they are treated as investments of the plan, which may hold other types of investments as well. In addition, insurance companies offer other types of specialized funding instruments to meet specific needs of plan administrators and trustees.

Guaranteed Income Contracts. Guaranteed income contracts, also referred to as guaranteed investment contracts, guaranteed interest contracts, or GICs for short, are contracts that offer a guaranteed rate of return for a specified number of years on a lump-sum investment.

From a plan investment point of view, a GIC offers the plan trustee or administrator the opportunity to avoid investment risk on some portion of the plan fund.

TABLE 12–5. Hypothetical Application of Declining-Index New Money Method over Three Years, Assuming 50 percent Reinvestment Each Year *(Ignoring Principal Growth for Illustrative Purposes)*

	Contribution	Total Fund	Year 1 Rate Portion	Year 2 Rate Portion	Year 3 Rate Portion
Year 1	$1,000	$1,000	$1,000	—	—
Year 2	1,000	2,000	500	$1,500	—
Year 3	1,000	3,000	250	750	$2,000

This may be an important element in the overall investment strategy, permitting riskier investments with the remainder of the fund.

There are two basic types of GICs—the bullet and the window contract. The bullet contract involves a single payment by the plan, which is held for a specified period and interest rate. The insurance company repays the funds after the specified period, usually from 2 to 10 years. The window type of contract allows the employer to make deposits over a period of years, with guarantees specified in various ways. For example, the insurer may provide a minimum rate of return, or the company's new money rate.

Single-Purchase Annuity Contracts. Single-purchase or single-premium annuity contracts (SPACs) are typically used to provide annuities for participants in pension plans that have terminated. By purchasing annuities for all participants with accrued benefits or outstanding plan balances, the plan can avoid any further investment or fiduciary problems. However, the plan technically continues to exist and must be administered. The SPAC is a group contract that is generally used where there are a significant number of participants. Since such plans involve substantial amounts, there is an active market for these products.

A smaller terminating plan may find it more advantageous to purchase individual annuity contracts for each participant and distribute these annuities. This is discussed further in Chapter 21.

Summary

Qualified plan assets can be held by a trustee under a trust agreement or by an insurance company under an insurance contract. Trustees can be individuals or corporations, such as banks or trust companies. The majority of pension assets are held by trusts, which offer great flexibility in design. To compete with trust funding, many types of insurance contracts have been developed. Allocated contracts are those in which the insurance company guarantees specific benefits to individuals, whereas, in unallocated contracts, assets are held for all participants as in a trust fund. Insurance contracts can be individual, with individual policies issued for each plan participant, or group, where there is a single contract issued for all participants.

13

Profit-Sharing and Savings Plans

Objectives of This Chapter
- *Describe the purposes for and general characteristics of profit-sharing plans.*
- *Discuss the following specific design features:*
  eligibility and vesting,
  contribution provision,
  account allocation provision,
  forfeitures,
  social security integration,
  withdrawal provisions, and
  incidental benefits.
- *Explain the rules for deducting employer profit-sharing contributions.*
- *Describe how participant account and investment provisions can be designed.*
- *Describe the general characteristics of savings plans, particularly the special features relating to aftertax employee contributions.*

"Nonretirement" Qualified Plans

Qualified plans are a particularly useful employee benefit, because they can be designed for purposes other than simply retirement income. This chapter and the next two chapters will discuss qualified plans that are designed primarily as incentive-type employee benefits, with an element of retirement savings that may in some cases only be incidental. These are:

1. Qualified profit-sharing plans.
2. Savings or thrift plans.
3. Cash or deferred (Section 401(k)) plans (Chapter 14).
4. Employer stock plans (stock-bonus plans and ESOPs) (Chapter 15).

All of the plans discussed in these three chapters are defined-contribution plans, because they inherently have individual accounts for each employee.

Qualified Profit-Sharing Plans

The basic profit-sharing plan is a defined-contribution plan in which employer contributions are typically based in some manner on the employer's profits, although there is no actual requirement for the employer to have profits to contribute to the plan. Even a nonprofit organization may have a "profit-sharing" plan. The general characteristics are:

1. The employer contribution may be specified as a percentage of annual profits each year, or, for even more flexibility, the plan may provide that the employer determines the amount to be contributed on an annual basis, with the option of contributing nothing even in years in which there are profits, or, conversely, making contributions in unprofitable years.

2. The plan must have a nondiscriminatory formula for allocating the employer contribution to the accounts of employees.

3. Since the plan is a defined-contribution plan, the benefit from the plan consists of the amount in each employee's account, usually distributed as a lump sum at retirement or termination of employment.

4. The plan may permit employee withdrawals or loans during employment.

5. Eligibility and vesting are usually liberal, because of the incentive nature of the plan.

6. Forfeitures from employees who terminate employment usually are reallocated to the accounts of remaining participants, thus making the plan particularly attractive to long-service employees.

7. The main price for the advantages of the design is that the employer's annual deduction for contributions to the plan is limited to 15 percent of the payroll of employees covered under the plan.

Eligibility and Vesting

Profit-sharing plans are typically designed with relatively liberal eligibility and vesting provisions, compared with pension plans. This is because the employer generally wishes the incentive objective of the plans to operate for short-term as well as long-term employees, and also because the simplicity of administering a profit-sharing plan makes it less necessary to exclude short-term employees to reduce plan administrative costs. Thus, many profit-sharing plans permit employees to enter the plan immediately upon becoming employed, or after a short waiting period—for example, until the next date on which the plan assets are valued. A great variety of vesting provisions are used, and they are typically tailored to the employer's specific needs.

The restrictions on eligibility and vesting provisions were discussed in detail in Chapters 6 and 7. In summary, a minimum age requirement greater than age 21 is not permitted, nor can a waiting period for entry be longer than one year, or up to 1.5 years if entry is based on plan entry dates. Under the age-discrimination law, no maximum age for entry can be prescribed (and contributions must continue for as long as the employee continues to work). The coverage tests discussed in Chapter 6 apply to a profit-sharing plan as they do to all qualified plans.

The vesting requirements discussed in Chapter 7 are also applicable to profit-sharing plans. A profit-sharing plan is more likely to discriminate in favor of highly compensated employees, as a result of high employee turnover and the use of forfeitures, which are discussed below. Therefore, the IRS may require the more stringent three- to seven-year vesting schedule in new profit-sharing plans. Most profit-sharing plans use a vesting schedule that is at least as generous as this schedule. Even more-stringent vesting is required if the plan is top-heavy (Chapter 18).

Employer Contribution Provision

There is great flexibility in designing an employer contribution provision for a profit-sharing plan. The contribution provision can be either *discretionary* or of the *formula* type.

With the discretionary provision, the company's board of directors determines each year what amount will be contributed. It is not necessary for the company actually to have current or accumulated profits. Many employers will wish to contribute the maximum deductible amount each year, but a lesser amount can be contributed.

Although employers are permitted to omit contributions under a discretionary provision, the IRS requires that contributions be "substantial and recurring."[1] If too many years go by without contributions, the IRS is likely to find that the plan has been terminated, with the consequences discussed in Chapter 21 (basically, 100 percent vesting for all plan participants and distribution under a specified payment schedule). No specific guidelines are given by the IRS about how many years of omitted contributions are permitted, so the decision to skip a profit-sharing contribution must always be made with some caution.

With a formula contribution provision, a specified amount must be contributed to the plan whenever there are profits. Typically, the amount is expressed as a percentage of profits determined under generally accepted accounting principles. There are no specific IRS restrictions on the type of formula, so flexibility is possible. For example, the plan might provide for a contribution of 7 percent of all current profits in excess of $50,000, possibly with a limitation to the amount deductible for the year. There is also considerable freedom in defining the term *profit* in the plan. For example, profit before taxes or after taxes can be used, with before-tax profits being the most common. Profit as defined in the plan can also include capital gains and losses or accumulated profits from prior years. Even an employer that is organized under state law as a "nonprofit" corporation can have a profit-sharing plan funded from a suitably defined surplus account.

The basic advantage of the formula approach is that it is more attractive to employees than the discretionary approach and more definitely serves the incentive purpose of the plan. However, if a formula approach is adopted, the employer must remember that the formula amount must always be contributed to the plan

---

[1] Reg. Sec. 1.401–1(b)(2).

and, therefore, constitutes a continuing legal and financial obligation for the business. It is possible to draft formulas that take into account possible adverse financial contingencies. Without such provisions, the formula may have to be amended in the future in the event of financial difficulty.

Allocations to Employee Accounts

The plan's contribution provision determines the total amount contributed to the plan for all employees. The plan must also have a formula under which appropriate portions of this total contribution are allocated to the individual accounts of employees. Here there is less flexibility, because the allocation provision must meet nondiscrimination requirements. The law provides that contributions must be allocated under a definite formula that does not discriminate in favor of the highly compensated employees.[2] Any formula that meets these requirements can be acceptable; but most formulas allocate to participants on the basis of their compensation, as compared to the compensation of all participants. That is, after the total employer contribution is determined, the amount allocable to a given participant is:

$$\text{Total employer contribution} \times \frac{\text{Participant's compensation}}{\text{Compensation of all participants}}$$

If compensation is used in the allocation formula, the plan must define compensation in a way that does not discriminate. Only the first $200,000 (as indexed) of each employee's compensation can be taken into account in the formula. Compensation might include only base pay, or might be total compensation, including bonuses or overtime. If the profit-sharing plan has discretionary employer contributions, overtime may have to be included in the definition of compensation to avoid a violation of the overtime pay provisions of federal labor law or other labor laws. (Labor-law provisions require a differential for overtime in certain employees' compensation, and such compensation may include discretionary contributions to accounts in a profit-sharing plan). If the plan is integrated with social security, the IRS generally requires that total compensation be used in the allocation formula.

Service is another factor often used in the formula for allocating employer contributions. However, since highly compensated employees are likely to have long service, the IRS will probably require a showing that any service-based formula will not produce discrimination.

Forfeitures

A forfeiture is an unvested amount remaining behind in a participant's account when the participant terminates employment without being fully vested under the plan's vesting schedule. Thus, forfeitures can occur in any defined-contribution

---

[2] Reg. Sec. 1.401–1(b)(1)(ii).

plan that does not have 100 percent immediate vesting. Forfeitures can be reallocated to accounts of other participants or used to reduce future employer contributions. In a profit-sharing plan, forfeitures are usually reallocated to participants to provide an additional incentive for continuing service.

Forfeitures must be allocated in a nondiscriminatory manner. In most plans, forfeiture allocations are made in the same manner as allocations of employer contributions—that is, on the basis of compensation or a combination of compensation and service. The IRS usually will not accept a forfeiture allocation provision based on account balances of remaining participants, because such a provision usually will provide substantial discrimination.

Analysis of profit-sharing plans of smaller employers that have existed for a number of years generally shows that by far the largest account balances are those for highly compensated participants. This is because the combination of higher compensation, longer service (and, therefore, more years in the plan), and low turnover among the highly compensated group eventually produce a great disparity in account balances. This phenomenon is in fact one of the reasons why closely held businesses adopt profit-sharing plans. As such, it is not deemed to be discriminatory. However, if the plan contains any features designed to multiply this inherent discrimination (such as forfeiture allocation based on account balances) the IRS generally will not approve it.

Integration with Social Security

The allocation formula of a profit-sharing plan may be integrated with social security to avoid duplication of benefits and to reduce plan costs to the employer. The integration rules were discussed in detail in Chapter 9. Under those rules, any integration level up to the taxable wage base for the year may be used. The difference between the plan's excess-contribution percentage (contribution percentage for compensation above the integration level) and its base-contribution percentage (contribution percentage for compensation up to the integration level) cannot be more than the lesser of:

> The base-contribution percentage, or
> the nonmedicare social security tax rate, currently 5.7 percent (1986).

The integrated plan, in effect, gives credit to the employer for contributions made to social security as if they had been made to the plan, thus providing overall a nondiscriminatory allocation formula.

Example

Concerning integrated formulas, if the plan uses an integration level of $30,000, it could provide a base allocation percentage of 10 percent of compensation below $30,000, plus an allocation of 5.7 percent of compensation above $30,000. Or, if the plan provided 4 percent of compensation below the integration level, it could provide no more than 4 percent of compensation above the integration level.

Plan allocations counted toward the 5.7 percent limitation must include not only employer contributions for the year but also any forfeitures allocated to the participant's account.

Example

Suppose that, for the year 1987, a plan has two participants with compensation as shown below. For 1987, the employer contributes $5,000 to the plan and a forfeiture of $8,000 is available for allocation to participants' accounts in 1987. The plan's integration level is $20,000. Under the plan's allocation formula, each participant's account is to receive the maximum permitted percent of plan contributions, plus forfeitures for compensation above $20,000 (up to 5.7 percent). The remaining amount of the plan contributions, plus forfeitures, is allocated in proportion to total compensation. Plan allocations would then be as follows:

Employee	1987 Compensation	Compensation above $20,000	5.7 Percent of Excess	Allocation of Remainder	Total Allocation
A	$30,000	$10,000	$570	$8,287	$ 8,857
B	15,000	0	0	4,143	4,143
Payroll	$45,000				$13,000

The amount in the fifth column is arrived at by subtracting the excess allocation (total of column four) from the $13,000 of contributions plus forfeitures; this remaining amount of $12,430 is multiplied by a fraction, the numerator of which is the participant's total compensation, and the denominator of which is the total payroll. This allocation meets the integration rules, since the amount allocated to compensation below $20,000 is more than 5.7 percent.

Deduction of Employer Contributions

The maximum amount that an employer can deduct for contributions to a profit-sharing plan is 15 percent of the compensation paid or accrued during the taxable year to all employees who participate in the profit-sharing plan.[3] This is an employer deduction limit based on compensation of all covered employees; it is not a rule stating that allocations to individual participants' accounts are limited to

---

[3]Code Section 404(a)(3).

15 percent of their compensation. The limitation on annual additions to individual accounts, the Section 415 limit, is the lesser of 25 percent of compensation or $30,000, as discussed in detail in Chapter 18.

An employer can contribute to a profit-sharing or a stock-bonus plan in excess of the 15 percent limit, but the excess is not deductible and is subject to a 10 percent penalty under Section 4972. The excess amount can be carried over to a future year and deducted then, but deductions in the future year for current contributions plus carryovers are still subject to the 15 percent of payroll limit.

Combined Profit-Sharing and Other Plans. If an employer has both a defined-benefit plan and a profit-sharing or other defined-contribution plan covering a common group of employees, the total contribution for both plans cannot exceed 25 percent of compensation of the common group of employees. However, if a greater contribution is necessary to satisfy the minimum funding standard for the defined-benefit plan, the employer will always be able to make and deduct this contribution.

Section 415 Limits

The Section 415 limits (discussed in more detail in Chapter 18) that apply to profit-sharing plans are those applicable to all defined-contribution plans. Basically, the annual addition to any participant's account can not exceed the lesser of 25 percent of the participant's compensation or $30,000. For a profit-sharing plan, the annual addition includes not only the participant's allocable share of the employer contribution but also the participant's share of any forfeitures. This means that, when forfeitures are allocated to a participant's account, the amount of employer contributions that can be allocated may be reduced. The Section 415 limits usually affect only highly compensated employees covered under the plan.

Investment Earnings and Account Balances

As a defined-contribution plan, a profit-sharing plan must provide separate accounts for each participant. However, unless the plan contains a provision permitting participants to direct investments (discussed below) the plan trustee or other funding agent will generally pool all participants' accounts for investment purposes. The plan must then provide a mechanism for allocating investment gains or losses to each participant. Most methods for doing this effectively allocate such gains and losses in proportion to the participant's account balance.

IRS revenue rulings require accounts of all participants to be valued in a uniform and consistent manner at least once each year, unless all plan assets are immediately invested in individual annuity or retirement contracts meeting certain requirements. The plan usually will specify a *valuation date* or dates on which valuation occurs. Investment earnings, gains, and losses are usually allocated to participants' accounts as of this date.

Participant-Directed Investments

Under ERISA, any "individual account" plan (such as a profit-sharing, stock-bonus, or money-purchase pension plan) can include a provision allowing the participant to direct the trustee or other funding agent as to the investment of the participant's account.[4]

If the plan administrator provides a reasonably wide range of investment choices—so the participant's choice has real meaning—then the trustee and other plan fiduciaries are not subject to fiduciary responsibility for the investment decision. A plan can technically allow unlimited choice of investments, but this increases the plan's administrative burdens. Often a family of mutual funds is offered as investment options to increase the administrative feasibility of participant direction.

Investment direction gives the participant a considerable degree of control over the funds in his or her account, and it is frequently used in profit-sharing plans, particularly those for closely held businesses where the controlling employees have by far the largest accounts. On the other hand, to the extent that participant direction of investments removes the security provided by the fiduciary rules (Chapter 17), such a provision is at odds with a plan objective of providing retirement security, and it would not be appropriate if this was a major objective of the plan for a particular employee group.

To prevent certain abuses associated with participant-directed investments, the Code provides that an investment by a participant-directed qualified plan account in a *collectible* will be treated as if the amount invested was distributed to the participant—that is, it is usually taxable income to the participant. Collectible is defined as a work of art, rug or antique, metal or gem, stamp or coin, alcoholic beverage, or any other tangible personal property designated as a collectible by the IRS.[5]

Withdrawals during Employment and Loan Provisions

The incentive (rather than retirement security) focus of profit-sharing plans tends to dictate that participants be given the opportunity to control or benefit from their accounts even before retirement or termination of employment. There are various ways to do this. One such provision is a participant-directed account, as discussed above. Another is a special feature permitted in profit-sharing plans, but not in pension plans—a provision for account withdrawals from the plan during employment.

The Regulations require that employer contributions under a profit-sharing plan must be accumulated for at least two years before they can be withdrawn by participants. However, in some revenue rulings, the IRS has permitted a plan provision allowing employees with at least 60 months of participation to withdraw

---
[4]ERISA Section 401(c).
[5]Code Section 408(m).

employer contributions, including those made within the previous two years. Also, revenue rulings have permitted a plan provision for withdrawal in the case of "hardship," including contributions made within the previous two years. Hardship must be sufficiently defined in the plan, and the definitions must be consistently applied. All these limitations apply only to amounts attributable to employer contributions to the plan. If the plan permits employee contributions, the employee contributions can be withdrawn at any time without restriction.

In considering the design of withdrawal provisions, it is important to keep in mind that the taxation and early withdrawal penalty rules act as disincentives for participants to withdraw plan funds. These rules (discussed in Chapter 16) indirectly reduce the advantages of using a qualified plan as a medium for preretirement savings.

Many plan designers prefer to have a prohibition or at least restrictions on withdrawals from the employer-contributed portion of the account. This is because favorable investment results sometimes depend on having a pool of investment money that is relatively large and not subject to the additional liquidity requirements imposed by the possibility of participant withdrawals. Some typical restrictions found in profit-sharing plans include a requirement that the participant demonstrate a need for the money, coming within a list of authorized needs either set out in the plan or promulgated by the plan administrator and applied consistently. Such needs might include educational expenses for children, home purchase or remodeling, sickness or disability, and so on. Another method of restricting plan withdrawals is to provide a "penalty" on a participant who withdraws amounts from the plan (in addition to the 10 percent federal penalty tax, which also applies). A plan penalty might include suspension of participation for a time, such as six months after the withdrawal. The plan penalty, however, cannot deprive a participant of any previously vested benefit.

Loan provisions as discussed in Chapter 16 are appropriate for profit-sharing plans. Again, however, a generous loan provision in a plan may have the effect of reducing the amount of funds available for other plan investments.

Incidental Benefits

The Regulations permit profit-sharing plans to provide as an incidental benefit life, accident, or health insurance for the participant and the participant's family. Incidental life insurance is the only one of these that is commonly provided. If employer contributions are used to provide insurance, the "incidental benefit" limitations described in Chapter 18 must be met.

If the plan provides incidental whole life insurance, the usual test is that aggregate premiums for each participant must be less than 50 percent of the aggregate of employer contributions allocated to the participant's account. If the plan purchases term insurance or accident and health insurance, the aggregate premiums cannot exceed 25 percent of the employer contributions allocated to the participant's account. The current IRS position is that universal life premiums also must meet the 25 percent limit. *Note:* these tests apply to the *aggregate*—that is, the total contributions made for all years at any given time. If either of these limits is exceeded, the plan could be disqualified. However, insurance premiums paid with employer-contributed funds that have accumulated for at least two years are not subject to these limitations, since they could be distributed to the participant, as discussed above.

If the employee dies before normal retirement age, the plan can provide that the face amount of the policies, plus the balance credited to the participant's account in the profit-sharing plan, can be distributed to him without the life insurance violating the incidental benefit requirement. This can be done even though the amount of life insurance might be more than 100 times the account balance expressed as an expected monthly pension.

If life insurance is provided by the plan, the term insurance cost is currently taxable to the employee under the P.S. 58 table or the insurer's term insurance rates, as discussed in Chapter 10. Accident and health insurance provided by an employer under the plan might not be taxable, because of the exclusion provided for employer provided health insurance. However, there is usually no particular benefit in providing accident and health insurance under a profit-sharing plan. It is usually provided in a separate plan not connected with the profit-sharing plan.

Savings Plans

Almost any qualified plan can have a provision for employee contributions to supplement the plan fund or benefit. A plan that is designed particularly to exploit the possibility of employee contributions is often referred to as a *savings plan* or *thrift plan*.

Mandatory and Voluntary Contributions

In discussing savings plans, or any other type of plan design involving employee contributions, the somewhat complex tax treatment of employee contributions is an essential background. The Code recognizes two types of employee contributions—*mandatory* and *voluntary*. Mandatory contributions are contributions required as a condition for plan participation or for receiving matching employer contributions to the plan. Voluntary contributions are those that do not result in matching employer contributions. Mandatory contributions and voluntary contributions are aftertax contributions. They are not excludible from tax or tax deductible by the employee to any extent.

Design of Savings Plans

A savings plan is a defined-contribution plan so employees can have separate accounts. Usually, qualified savings plans are designed as profit-sharing plans (rather than money-purchase pension plans), because only a profit-sharing plan permits account withdrawals during employment, and this is an important feature of the plan if the plan is to be described to employees as a savings medium. Thus, a savings plan generally can be described as a contributory profit-sharing plan.

The typical savings plan features employer matching of employee contributions. Plan participation is voluntary; employees elect to contribute a chosen percentage of their compensation up to a maximum percentage specified in the plan. The employer then makes a matching contribution to the plan. The matching may be dollar-for-dollar, or the employer may put in some multiple or submultiple of the employee contribution rate. For example, typically a plan might permit an employee to contribute annually any whole percentage of compensation from 1 to 6 percent. The plan might then provide that the employer contributes at the rate of half the chosen employee percentage; thus, if the employee elects to contribute 4 percent of compensation, the employer would contribute an additional 2 percent.

If the plan's maximum contribution level is too high, there is a possibility of discrimination, because only higher-paid employees would be in a position to contribute to the plan, and only they would receive full employer matching contributions. To prevent this type of discrimination, a specific numerical test is applicable to aftertax employee contributions. The test is similar to that applicable to Sec. 401(k) contributions, described in the next chapter. Under this test (Code Section 401(m)), a plan is not deemed discriminatory for a plan year if, for highly compensated employees, the total of employee contributions (both matched and voluntary) plus employer matching contributions does not exceed the greater of:

125 percent of the contribution percentage for all other eligible employees, or the lesser of *(a)* 200 percent of the contribution percentage for all other eligible employees, or *(b)* such percentage plus 2 percentage points.

For example, if employee contributions and employer matching contributions for non-highly compensated employees are 6 percent of compensation, those for highly compensated employees can be up to 8 percent (6 percent plus 2 percent).

The contribution percentage for a group of employees is the average of the ratios for each employee of employee contributions, plus employer matching contributions, divided by the employee's annual compensation.

Example

A plan has two non-highly compensated employees, A and B:

Employee	(1) Employee Contribution	(2) Matching Contribution	(3) Annual Compensation	Ratio (1) + (2) (3)
A	$1,000	$ 500	$15,000	10%
B	4,000	2,000	30,000	20

Contribution percentage for non-highly compensated: 15 percent.
Permitted percentage for highly compensated: 18.75 percent (meets 125 percent test).

To meet this test, the employer may take into account 401(k) contributions to a plan maintained by the employer, or employer contributions to which the 401(k) vesting and withdrawal restrictions apply. The definition of *highly compensated employee* for purposes of these rules follows the definition in Code Sec. 414(q), as with the 401(k) rules.

Apart from the features relating to employee contributions, savings plans generally follow the rules for profit-sharing plans described earlier. In designing a savings plan, emphasis is usually put on features relating to the objective of providing a savings medium for employees. Thus, a savings plan usually has generous provisions for employee withdrawal of funds and for plan loans. In addition, savings plans often have features allowing investment flexibility by participants. This can be done by having either participant-directed accounts or having accounts invested in a number of different pooled funds, with employees having a choice between one or more of the funds. A choice might be offered, for example, between funds invested in fixed-income securities and others invested in equity-type investments. Some savings plans might also provide a separate fund for investment in employer securities or life insurance contracts. Where employees have the option of changing investment elections, there are usually various restrictions on such changes designed to prevent too much movement of funds in response to short-term market value fluctuations.

Savings plans are designed as employee incentives, like regular profit-sharing plans, and, therefore, savings plans usually also have generous vesting provisions. As with all qualified plans, the employee must be 100 percent immediately vested in the employee's own contributions. The rest of the account is subject to usually liberal vesting provisions, typically meeting or bettering the three- to seven-year provision.

Advantages and Disadvantages of Savings Plans

Savings plans have been very popular in the past and continue to be so, despite the advent of other types of plans, such as Section 401(k) plans that provide greater tax leverage. Like all qualified plans, however, a savings plan provides a tax-deferred savings medium, since earnings in the plan fund are not taxable until the employee's account is distributed.

A savings plan usually does not maximize the potential tax deduction available for plan contributions, because it involves mandatory contributions by the employee that are not tax deductible. A greater degree of tax deductibility can be provided with other types of plans, such as regular profit-sharing plans or Section 401(k) plans. However, some of these plans may require a greater employee outlay for the plan itself (although not necessarily for the overall compensation package). These other plans may also entail greater restrictions on the funds, which may make them a less attractive savings medium from the employee's standpoint.

Summary

Qualified profit-sharing plans are designed primarily as a form of incentive compensation, rather than a secure retirement benefit. They tend to have generous eligibility and vesting provisions. Employer contributions can be made on a formula or discretionary basis; profits need not be present. Allocations of employer contributions and forfeitures to participants' accounts must be made under a nondiscriminatory formula. The formula can be integrated with social security under the defined-contribution integration rules. Profit-sharing plans usually have generous provisions for loans and preretirement withdrawals by employees, but some such withdrawals may be subject to the 10 percent penalty tax. The plan can also provide incidental benefits, such as life insurance. Deductible employer contributions to profit-sharing plans are subject to a limit of 15 percent of the payroll of covered employees. Participant accounts in profit-sharing plans share in plan investment earnings, and these plans often use participant investment direction to increase flexibility.

Savings plans are similar to profit-sharing plans but are designed around employee contributions, often with employer matching contributions. If employee contributions are not structured to meet the Section 401(k) rules, they are aftertax (nondeductible). Employee contributions and employer matching contributions must meet specific numerical tests to avoid prohibited discrimination in favor of highly compensated employees.

14

401(k) Plans

Objectives of This Chapter

- *Describe the general characteristics of 401(k) plans, with their advantages and disadvantages.*
- *Discuss the major approaches to 401(k) plan design.*
- *Discuss plan coverage, vesting, and the $7,000 limit on elective deferrals.*
- *Describe the actual deferral percentage (ADP) tests and how they can be met through appropriate plan design.*
- *Discuss the design of plan distribution provisions and the taxation of plan distributions.*
- *Discuss the types of plan investments appropriate to 401(k) plans.*
- *Describe the effect of social security taxes on 401(k) plans.*
- *Explain how the 401(k) rules permit some discrimination in favor of the highly compensated, permitting the plan to provide some tax-shelter benefits to owners of small businesses.*

General Characteristics

A qualified cash or deferred profit-sharing plan, usually referred to as a 401(k) plan, since the special rules for these plans are found in Code Section 401(k), is a qualified profit-sharing or stock-bonus plan that incorporates an option by participants to put money into the plan or to receive it as taxable cash compensation. In other words, a 401(k) plan differs from a regular profit-sharing plan in that employees can participate in deciding how much of their compensation is deferred. Amounts contributed to the plan are not taxable to participants until they are withdrawn; this is a significant advantage over mandatory contributions to a savings plan, which are taxable to the employee before contribution to the plan. However, 401(k) contributions for which the employee has an election to receive cash—*elective deferrals*—are subject to an annual limit of $7,000, indexed for inflation.

A 401(k) plan can be an independent plan, or the 401(k) feature can be included with a regular profit-sharing or stock-bonus plan of the employer. The plan

159

can be designed in a number of ways to combine both employer and employee contributions, or the entire plan can be funded through salary reductions by employees.

Section 401(k) plans can be adopted only by tax-paying private employers; they are not available to tax-exempt or governmental employers. Tax-exempt and governmental employers, instead, may adopt specialized plans, described in Chapter 23, that provide results somewhat similar to 401(k) plans.

Advantages and Disadvantages

Section 401(k) plans are currently very attractive to employees. First, they have the basic attraction of all qualified plans (and IRAs and 403(b) plans as well): they provide a tax-deferred saving medium. But 401(k) plans have an additional advantage in giving employees an opportunity to choose the amount of deferral according to their individual need for savings. From the employee's viewpoint, a 401(k) plan appears much like an individual IRA, but with additional advantages; the 401(k) plan has higher contribution limits than an IRA, it permits five-year averaging on qualifying lump-sum withdrawals, and the withdrawal provisions during employment are slightly less restrictive.

From the employer's viewpoint, 401(k) plans are favorable, because the entire plan can be funded through salary reductions by employees. Thus, the plan provides no direct additional compensation costs to the employer. Because of the popularity of the plan with employees, partly due to good publicity for these plans in the media, the employer can obtain employee goodwill with this type of plan at a relatively low cost. Also, there are some actual dollar savings in using the 401(k) type of design, since salary reductions by employees reduce employer expense for worker's compensation and unemployment compensation insurance.

The 401(k) type of design has some disadvantages; but in reviewing these, it is important always to ask—disadvantages to whom and disadvantages compared with what? First of all, the $7,000 annual limit on elective deferrals is lower than that for other types of qualified plan contributions. However, as a practical matter, this limit primarily affects highly compensated employees. Another disadvantage is that a 401(k) plan is a qualified plan and, as such, is much more complicated than simply leaving savings up to individual employees, either through individual IRAs or otherwise. Also, the 401(k) plan is a qualified profit-sharing plan, not a pension plan, so the employer's deduction is limited to 15 percent of the covered payroll. That is, the total of the employer contribution and nontaxable employee salary reductions cannot exceed 15 percent of covered payroll. Generally speaking, integration of a 401(k) formula with social security is not possible; the 401(k) nondiscrimination rules nevertheless permit significant discrimination in favor of higher-paid employees. Section 401(k) plans are more difficult to administer than regular qualified plans, because of the additional rules (discussed later) that must be satisfied. Deferral amounts must be 100 percent vested; thus, there is no opportunity for the employer to save on plan costs by making use of employee forfeitures on Section 401(k) deferral amounts. Finally, distributions to employees prior to termination of employment are more restrictive than for a regular qualified plan. However, these restrictions are more liberal than those for an IRA.

Major Types of 401(k) Plan Design

There are many possibilities for design variations in 401(k) plans—almost too many possibilities, with the result that plan design proposals can become complex and confusing. The 401(k) plan can be used either as a separate stand-alone plan, or it can be combined with a regular profit-sharing or stock-bonus plan. The major approaches in designing 401(k) plans can be summarized in three categories: the pure salary reduction plan, the bonus 401(k) plan, and the 401(k) thrift plan.

Pure Salary Reduction Plan

The Regulations permit a 401(k) plan to be funded entirely through employee elections to reduce salary by a specified amount and contribute the reduced amount to the plan. The major appeal of this approach is that, based on existing salary scales, the plan can be funded without any specific additional costs to the employer. Also, the plan can be described to employees as a plan somewhat like an IRA.

For purposes of the 15 percent deduction limit and the annual additions limit of Section 415(c), salary reductions are treated as employer contributions to the plan.

Example

Suppose an employer has two employees and, for a given year, their gross salaries and salary reduction contributions to a 401(k) plan are as shown in Table 14–1:

TABLE 14–1

	Gross Salary	Salary Reduction Elected	Salary after Reduction
Pat	$21,000	$1,000	$20,000
Mike	31,000	1,000	30,000
Total			$50,000

Neither participant exceeds the $7,000 limit on elective deferrals. The deduction limit for plan contributions in this case is 15 percent of the payroll of reduced salaries—here, 15 percent of $50,000, or $7,500, which is well in excess of the $2,000 actually contributed to the plan. The annual additions limit for each participant is 25 percent of the reduced salary, or $30,000 if less. For example, for Pat, the annual additions limit is 25 percent of $20,000, or $5,000. *Note:* for both Pat and Mike, the annual additions limit is lower than the $7,000 elective deferral limit, indicating how little impact the $7,000 limit has on lower-income employees. Again, this is much more than the amount actually contributed to the plan.

Salary reductions must be elected by employees before compensation is earned—that is, before they render the services for which compensation is paid. If elections are made after compensation has been earned, the doctrine of constructive receipt would prevent the employee from excluding the salary reduction from taxable income. The regulations indicate that salary reductions must be made before the beginning of the calendar year for which the reduction is effective.

Bonus 401(k) Plan

With this approach, the employer makes an annual contribution to a bonus fund for employees. Employees than have the option to take their share (usually based on compensation) in cash or to contribute all or part of it to a 401(k) plan. This bonus can be communicated to employees either as a cash bonus with an option to put money into the plan or as a plan contribution with an option to take a portion in cash.

While the bonus plan, in substance, is not actually different from a salary reduction plan, the approach is much less popular, because employers view it as lacking the participatory quality of a salary reduction plan. However, the bonus approach is relatively simple technically and may be suitable for adding a simple 401(k) feature to an existing qualified profit-sharing plan.

401(k) Thrift Plan

Under this approach, participating employees can elect salary reductions, with the employer making a matching contribution to the plan. The employer matching can be dollar for dollar, or some specified fraction of the employee's contribution. Matching can be limited to a specified percentage of each employee's compensation. To illustrate, a plan might provide that an employee can elect salary reductions up to 6 percent of compensation, with the employer contributing an additional 1 percent of compensation for each 2 percent of employee salary reduction.

This type of plan is relatively easy to adopt if the employer already has a similar thrift or savings plan. The plan will be mechanically quite similar, but it will provide employees with the advantage of full deductibility (excludibility) of the 401(k) salary reduction amount, unlike the aftertax contributions in traditional savings plans.

A significant advantage to the thrift plan 401(k) approach is that employer matching encourages plan participation by lower-paid employees. This helps to meet the qualification tests for 401(k) plans—the actual deferral percentage tests—discussed later.

Other Possibilities

A 401(k) feature can be combined with many other plan features, and it can offer complex contribution options to the employee. For example, the plan can allow nondeductible employee contributions in addition to the 401(k) amounts. Also, a 401(k) feature can be added to a regular profit-sharing or stock-bonus plan by amending the plan to allow salary reduction or additional employer-bonus contributions.

If a plan is not a pure 401(k) plan, participant accounts based on elective deferrals—referred to here as *401(k) amounts*—must be kept separate for purposes of determining actual deferral percentages, and also because special restrictions apply to 401(k) amounts. These are discussed further below. This is another example of the type of complex administration problems that 401(k) plans can present.

Coverage Requirements

Since a 401(k) plan is basically a qualified profit-sharing plan, it must meet all the coverage requirements of Section 410 of the Code. That is, if age and service are used for eligibility, a plan cannot require an age greater than 21 or require more than one year of service for entry. A 401(k) plan cannot use the two-year waiting period for entry with 100 percent vesting; no more than one year of service can be required for entry. Other plan classifications—for example, a plan covering only salaried employees—are permitted as long as the plan meets the appropriate coverage requirements of the Code. As discussed in detail in Chapter 6, the plan must cover 70 percent of all employees who are not highly compensated, or it must cover a percentage of non-highly compensated employees that is at least 70 percent of the percentage of highly compensated employees covered, or must meet the average-benefits test. In counting employees for these tests, those ineligible under the plan's minimum age or service requirements are excluded, also those excluded because of collective bargaining.

In addition to the regular qualified plan coverage requirements, substantial additional participation by lower-paid employees may indirectly be required to meet the actual deferral percentage requirements applicable under Section 401(k). Since these are critical to the design and ultimate success of a 401(k) plan, they are discussed separately below.

Vesting of Employee Accounts

Vesting requirements in a 401(k) plan may depend upon the source or identity of the plan contributions.

> Nontaxable employee contributions or elective deferrals made under a Section 401(k) cash or deferral option must be immediately 100 percent vested.

Any taxable employee contributions must be 100 percent immediately vested, as in regular qualified plans, such as savings or thrift plans.

All employer contributions to the plan must meet the usual vesting rules for qualified plans, discussed in Chapter 7—that is, the plan must have a vesting schedule meeting at least one of the ERISA minimum vesting standards (five-year vesting or three- to seven-year vesting).

From an employer-cost point of view, the significance of the 100 percent vesting requirement for 401(k) amounts means that the plan will produce fewer forfeitures from terminating employees than can be allocated to accounts of other participants. Thus, a 401(k) plan will provide less benefit for long-term employees than a regular profit-sharing plan with the same employer-contribution level.

Limit of $7,000 on Elective Deferrals

Code Section 402(g) imposes a $7,000 annual limit on elective deferrals for each plan participant. The limit is imposed on the total of elective deferrals under all 401(k) plans, Section 403(b) tax-deferred annuity plans, and salary reduction SEPs (simplified employee pensions) covering the participant. (In the case of a 403(b) plan, a higher limit of $9,500 applies; See Chapter 23.) Any excess over the $7,000 limit is treated as taxable income to the participant. The $7,000 limit is to be adjusted for cost-of-living changes after 1987 in the same manner as the Section 415 dollar limit on annual benefits under defined-benefit plans.

Actual Deferral Percentage Tests

It has long been recognized that, since higher-paid employees have more discretionary income and, in particular, more income to save, any qualified plan that allows employees to choose deferral or cash will be used disproportionately by higher-paid employees. The concept of cash or deferral plans has existed for a long time, but until Congress enacted Section 401(k) in 1978 they were not permitted by statute, because of this potential discrimination problem. The most important provision of Section 401(k) is a series of tests designed to prevent disproportionate use of these plans by higher-paid employees. These are the actual deferral percentage (ADP) tests.

These tests are in the nature of an additional nondiscrimination rule that must be met by 401(k) plans in addition to the usual rules for qualified plans. A qualified 401(k) plan must meet one of the following two tests in actual operation:

The actual deferral percentage for eligible highly compensated employees must not be more than the actual deferral percentage of all other eligible employees multiplied by 1.25 (i.e., must not exceed this percentage by more than 25 percent); or

the actual deferral percentage for eligible highly compensated employees must not exceed the actual deferral percentage of the other eligible employees by more than 2 percent; also, the actual deferral percentage for the highest paid one-third must not be more than the actual deferral percentage of all other eligible employees multiplied by 2.

The actual deferral percentage for a given year is:

$$\frac{\text{Employer contribution to plan for employee (or salary reduction)}}{\text{Employee's compensation}}$$

This amount is computed for each employee and averaged for each of the two groups (highly compensated, non-highly compensated).

A highly compensated employee, as defined in code Section 414(q), means any employee who, during the year or the preceding year:

Was at any time a more than 5 percent owner of the employer, or
received compensation from the employee in excess of $75,000, or
received compensation from the employer in excess of $50,000 and was in the top-paid 20 percent of the employer's employees, or
was at any time an officer and received compensation greater than 150 percent of the Section 415 defined-contribution dollar limit (i.e., for 1987, $45,000).

Current law requires all 401(k) plans to meet one of these two ADP tests. There is no provision for a discretionary test that would allow the plan to qualify without meeting the ADP percentages.

It should be noted that the ADP tests are not licenses to discriminate—that is, a plan cannot be so designed that lower-paid employees, for example, can defer only 6 percent while higher-paid employees can defer 8 percent. It is clear that the amount subject to deferral must be a uniform percentage of compensation for all employees. However, in practice considerable discrimination can exist.

A few examples will illustrate the operation of the ADP tests better than any extended explanation.

Example 1

Ten percent of compensation bonus; only employee A is highly compensated.

Employee	Compensation	Cash	Deferral	ADP
A	$30,000	$1,350	$1,650	5.5%
B	15,000	750	750	5
C	10,000	600	400	4

Test 1 is satisfied; ADP for highly compensated (A only) is 5.5%; ADP for non-highly compensated is 4.5% (average of 4% and 5%) 1.25 times 4.5% is 5.625%.

Example 2

Six percent of compensation bonus; D, E, and F are highly compensated.

Employee	Compensation	Cash	Deferral	ADP
D	$100,000	$ 0	$6,000	6%
E	80,000	0	4,800	6
F	60,000	0	3,600	6
G	40,000	800	1,600	4
H	30,000	600	1,200	4
I	20,000	400	800	4

Plan fails test 1 (1.25 × 4% is less than 6%) but passes test 2 (ADP for highly compensated is no more than 2 percentage points greater and less than 2 times 4%).

Designing a Plan to Meet the ADP Tests

Obviously, it is critical to design the 401(k) plan so that the ADP tests are met; otherwise, the plan will fail to qualify and all tax benefits will be lost. Fortunately, it is not as difficult to do this as plan designers once believed, and disqualifications are rare. Some of the methods used to ensure compliance are:

1. *Mandatory deferral.* For example, an employer contributes 5 percent of compensation for all employees that must be deferred, and allows an additional 2 percent under a cash or deferral option. This plan will always meet the second ADP test.

2. *Limit deferral by higher-paid.* This approach involves administrative problems, because the higher-paid group must be identified and deferral must be monitored, with a mechanism to stop deferrals at an appropriate point during the year if necessary.

3. *Redesignation of 401(k) amounts.* Under this approach, a non-401(k) plan is maintained, and the employer redesignates amounts contributed to the regular plan as 401(k) amounts to the maximum extent, after the year is finished and the plan administrator knows how much can be contributed. The redesignated amounts, of course, will be subject to all of the 401(k) restrictions, such as 100 percent vesting and the distribution restrictions.

4. *Count on the popularity of 401(k).* In actual practice, many companies find that participation by lower-paid employees is substantial. It is not unusual for 75 percent of all employees of an organization to participate in the plan. This may eliminate the problem without any special mechanisms coming into effect.

Because of the ADP tests, not every employer is suitable for a 401(k) plan. Since substantial participation by lower-paid employees is necessary, pay levels must be reasonably high in the organization—at least high enough that some amount of retirement saving is possible by most of the employees.

Distribution Restrictions

Account balances attributable to amounts subject to the cash or deferral election—the 401(k) amounts—are subject to special-distribution restrictions. 401(k) amounts may not be distributed earlier than upon retirement, death, disability, separation from service, hardship, age 59½ or termination of the plan. Also, as with any qualified plan distributions, the 10 percent early withdrawal penalty applies. The proposed regulations define hardship in the following restrictive language:

> For purposes of this Section, a distribution will be on account of hardship if the distribution is necessary in light of immediate and heavy financial needs of the employee. A distribution based upon financial hardship cannot exceed the amount required to meet the immediate financial need created by the hardship and not reasonably available from other resources of the employee. The determination of the existence of financial hardship and the amount required to be distributed to meet the need created by the hardship must be made in accordance with uniform and nondiscriminatory standards set forth in the plan.

The restrictiveness of this definition is not always adequately communicated to employees. Many 401(k) plan participants are under the impression that 401(k) amounts may be withdrawn for such purposes as children's education and purchase or remodeling of a home, but it is not clear that such needs fall within the IRS definition of hardship. Despite this restriction, the withdrawal provisions for 401(k) amounts are still more liberal than those for IRAs, since there is no hardship provision for IRAs. Of course, the 10 percent penalty applies to both IRAs and 401(k) and other qualified plan distributions and, if applicable, reduces the benefits of plan withdrawals.

As discussed further in Chapter 16, the 10 percent early withdrawal penalty applies to any distribution from a 401(k) plan, either 401(k) or non-401(k) amounts, except distributions:

- after age 59½
- on an employee's death,
- upon the employee's disability,
- that are part of a life or joint life annuity payout,
- upon separation from service after age 55,
- to the extent of medical expenses deductible as an itemized deduction under code Section 213.

Note: certain distributions that are permissible under the 401(k) rules nevertheless may be subject to penalty—for example, a nonmedical, nondisability hardship distribution from 401(k) amounts before separation from service or age 59½ is permitted but is subject to the 10 percent penalty.

A 401(k) plan may include contributions by employer or employee that are not subject to the cash or deferral election by the employees; these amounts are referred to as *non-401(k) amounts* for purposes of this chapter. Non-401(k) amounts are treated like any other qualified plan amounts.

The income taxation of distributions from 401(k) plans, including both 401(k) and non-401(k) amounts in the plan, follows the usual rules for qualified plan distributions. In particular, a qualifying lump-sum distribution is eligible for the five-year averaging tax treatment. Also, as with regular qualified plans, periodic payments are taxed under the annuity rules; and the participant's basis in the plan, including nondeductible employee contributions or P.S. 58 costs reported, is recovered tax-free. A distribution of more than 50 percent of the participant's account can be rolled over tax-free to an IRA within 60 days.

Loans from a 401(k) plan are permitted on the same basis as for regular qualified plans—that is, the maximum aggregate loans can not exceed $50,000 or one half of the participant's vested interest in the plan, with a $10,000 floor. The loans must be adequately secured and must bear a reasonable rate of interest. Loans must be repayable within five years, except for loans made to purchase a principal residence.

The qualified plan rules relating to loans and plan distributions are discussed in detail in Chapter 16.

Investments by 401(k) Plans

As with any qualified plan, a 401(k) plan can use a corporate trustee, such as a bank, or an individual trustee or trustees, including the company president or other key employee. The trustee, of course, is governed by the ERISA fiduciary requirements.

A 401(k) plan, like any individual account plan, can allow participants to direct investments in their accounts. This increases the attractiveness of the plan to some participants. The plan can give the participant almost complete choice of investment options, or it can provide for a choice among stated alternatives. As discussed in Chapter 13, participant investment choices can relieve the trustee of fiduciary liability for the investment choice, if the plan offers the participant a broad range of investments. Also, investment in collectibles as defined in Code Section 408(m) can result in a deemed taxable distribution to participants and should be avoided. Investment choices are often provided by using a family of mutual funds for funding the plan.

Life insurance can be used in a 401(k) plan in much the same way as in a regular qualified profit-sharing plan. Participants can be given the option at the time they make their salary reduction election to purchase insurance with plan funds. The purchase of insurance by a participant results in a deemed taxable distribution to the employee to the extent of the pure insurance element involved. The amount taxable is the P.S. 58 costs or the insurer's term rate, if lower.

Life insurance in the plan must meet the incidental limits discussed in Chapter 10. For whole life insurance, aggregate premiums must be less than 50 percent of aggregate employer contributions—meaning, for a 401(k) plan, not only direct employer contributions but also salary reductions contributed to the 401(k) plan. For term insurance, aggregate premiums must be less than 25 percent of aggregate employer contributions, defined in the same way. For universal life policies, the IRS has not taken a formal position, but it has informally indicated that the premiums will be treated the same as term insurance. As with all employee-benefit plans, unisex rates are required for insurance purchased with plan funds.

Social Security and Employment Taxes

Section 401(k) plans are an exception to the general rule—that contributions by an employer to a qualified plan are free of federal employment taxes (social security [FICA] and unemployment tax [FUTA]). The popularity of 401(k) plans when first introduced caused such a noticeable reduction in federal employment tax revenues that Congress made special rules for 401(k) plans. Under current law, 401(k) amounts—that is, amounts in the plan subject to an employee election to defer instead of receiving cash—are subject to FICA and FUTA, whether these are contributed through salary reduction or employer bonuses. FICA and FUTA do not apply to non-401(k) amounts—contributions made by the employer to the plan that are not subject to deferral.

In general, state unemployment compensation and workers' compensation payments are not required for either employer contributions or salary reductions in a 401(k) plan.

401(k) Plans as Tax Shelters for Small Business Owners

The 401(k) approach has been very popular with companies having many employees. However, the 401(k) rules permit the use of this plan by small closely held corporations in a way that not only benefits regular employees but provides some significant tax sheltering for key employees. The rules permit a somewhat greater plan contribution for the highly compensated employees.

Example

Glumm Corporation has a Section 401(k) plan providing for salary reductions and, to encourage participation, a matching contribution from the company up to $1,000 annually. The matching provision does not apply to the company's president and sole shareholder, Al Glumm. For 1987, plan participation and salary reductions were:

Employee	Gross Compensation	Salary Reduction	Reduced Salary	Employer Match	Total	Total as Percentage of Reduced Salary
Al	$50,000	$5,579	$44,421	$ 0	$6,804	12.56
Betty	20,000	1,000	19,000	1,000	2,000	10.05
Chuck	14,000	700	13,300	700	1,400	10.05

Note: the contribution for Al is a higher percentage of reduced salary than for the other employees. This is permitted under the ADP tests. The ADP for the non-highly com-

170 Chapter Fourteen

pensated eligible employees is 10.05 percent; thus, under the first ADP test, Al can provide a salary reduction of up to 12.56 percent (1.25 × 10.5) of reduced salary. The reduced salary then is $50,000 ÷ 1.1256 (100 percent plus 12.56 percent) or $44,421, so the salary reduction is $5,579 ($5.579 is 12.56 percent of $44,421). The plan, therefore, allows the president, Al, to provide a 12.56 percent contribution for himself while providing only 10.05 for the other employees.

Similar discrimination can be obtained with an integrated profit-sharing or money-purchase plan, which can allow a 5.7 percent higher contribution for compensation above the taxable wage base. However, a Section 401(k) plan provides a greater dollar spread, in many cases. Also, a 401(k) plan, such as the Glumm plan, can be used in connection with another fully integrated plan, since it is not considered to be integrated with social security.

Summary

Section 401(k) plans are similar to profit-sharing plans, with the addition of elective deferral, allowing employees to choose within limits between cash compensation and plan contributions (up to $7,000 annually). These plans can be designed as salary reduction plans or as bonus plans. A thrift-plan approach involving employer matching can also be used.

Plan coverage requirements are the same as those for other qualified plans, except that only a one-year waiting (eligibility) period can be used. Elective deferrals must be 100 percent vested. Other employer and employee contributions must meet the regular qualified plan vesting rules.

To prevent excessive discrimination in favor of highly compensated employees, specific limits are placed on the actual deferral percentage (ADP) for highly compensated employees. Since the ADP can be somewhat higher for highly compensated employees, including business owners, some discrimination in their favor is permissible.

A 401(k) plan must meet the usual distribution restrictions for qualified plans, and the 10 percent early withdrawal penalty applies. In addition, 401(k) distributions from elective deferrals are restricted to specific events, such as retirement or hardship. The income taxation of plan distributions is the same as that for other qualified plan distributions. Plan investments and incidental benefit possibilities follow the same pattern as for regular profit-sharing plans.

15

Stock-Bonus Plans and ESOPs

Objectives of This Chapter

- *Outline the ways in which employer stock can be used in a qualified plan and the advantages of doing so.*
- *Describe the technical aspects of a stock-bonus plan, emphasizing the differences from regular qualified plans.*
- *Describe the technical aspects of ESOPs, in particular the leveraging feature.*
- *Explain how stock plans can help create a market for stock of closely held businesses.*

Using Employer Stock in Qualified Plans

For a number of years the Internal Revenue Code has included special provisions for qualified plans that invest primarily in employer securities. Congress wants to encourage these plans, on the premise that it is desirable to give employees some ownership interest in the company for which they work. Therefore, as an inducement to employers to adopt such plans, the Code contains many "sweeteners." The most important of these is the leveraging technique for ESOPs, described below, that allows the employer to use the ESOP as a means of financing corporate growth. Also, there are provisions that significantly enhance the benefit of a stock plan that helps create a market for employer stock.

In recent years, legislation applicable to plans of this type has expanded considerably. ERISA, the Tax Reduction Act of 1975, the Tax Reform Act of 1976, the Revenue Act of 1978, the Economic Recovery Tax Act of 1981, the Tax Reform Act of 1984, and the Tax Reform Act of 1986 all have included significant provisions relating to plans investing primarily in employer securities. This has led to considerable complexity in the law, as well as to a good deal of confusion about terminology.

There are basically two types of qualified plans that invest primarily in employer securities: the traditional *stock-bonus plan* and the *employee stock-*

ownership plan (ESOP).[1] In addition, a regular profit-sharing plan may invest in employer stock without limit, and these plans are sometimes used, formally or informally, for this purpose. Qualified pension plans may not invest more than 10 percent of their assets in employer stock, so these plans are not very useful as employer stock plans.

Advantages of Investing in Employer Stock

There are certain employer and employee advantages to any plan that invests in employer stock, including a regular profit-sharing plan, a stock-bonus plan, or an ESOP.

1. A market can be created for employer stock. This has many planning implications and is discussed in detail below.
2. The employer can obtain a deduction for noncash (i.e., employer stock) contributions to the plan.
3. Employees receive an ownership interest in the company, which may act as a performance incentive.
4. As described below, unrealized appreciation of stock is not taxed to the employee at the time of distribution.

These advantages are available only to a regular or "C" corporation. An S corporation cannot adopt a stock plan because the plan is not a permissible shareholder in an S corporation.[2]

Types of Plans

Stock-Bonus Plan

The stock-bonus plan is the older of the two types. Basically, under the Regulations, a stock-bonus plan is a qualified defined-contribution plan similar to a profit-sharing plan, except that the employer's contributions are not necessarily

---

[1]The history of the terminology for these plans is one of massive confusion. The above terms are those currently used since the 1980 Technical Corrections Act. The employer stock-ownership plan was called a "leveraged ESOP," originally, and its name was changed in 1978 to "leveraged employee stock ownership plan," a name that lasted until 1980. Also, until 1986, there was a third type of stock plan based on a tax credit, rather than a tax deduction. The tax-credit employee stock-ownership plan was originally called a "TRASOP," which stands for Tax Reduction Act Stock Ownership Plan. It was renamed an "ESOP" in the 1978 revenue act, but in 1980 this name was deleted. After 1982, the tax-credit amount was based on payroll, and tax-credit plans were generally referred to as "PAYSOPs." These name changes can make it quite difficult to use prior literature on the subject. The ESOP is also sometimes described as an "ESOT" (for employee stock-ownership trust) or a "Kelso" plan, for Louis D. Kelso, an early advocate.

[2]Code Section 1361(b)(1)(B).

dependent on profits, and the benefits are distributable in the stock of the employer company.[3]

Typically, the plan contribution formula will be based on compensation of employees. Employer contributions to the plan may be made in cash or directly in the form of employer securities, newly issued or otherwise. Shares of stock are allocated to the participants' accounts under a formula that must meet the same nondiscrimination requirements as the allocation formula in a profit-sharing plan. Some stock-bonus plans also provide for employee contributions.

The value of each participant's account in a stock-bonus plan is stated in terms of a certain number of shares of employer stock. The value of the account varies with the value of the underlying employer stock. Dividends on the shares can be used to increase participants' accounts, or cash dividends can be paid through the plan directly to participants as currently taxable income, in which case the employer gets a tax deduction.[4]

Plan Distributions. Distributions from a stock-bonus plan or ESOP are generally subject to the same restrictions applicable to distributions from any qualified plan. Thus, distributions prior to age 59½, death, disability, or retirement are subject to a 10 percent penalty, with some exceptions.[5] However, for a stock-bonus plan or ESOP, there is no requirement of providing a joint-and-survivor annuity or other spousal death benefit.[6]

Since an employee retains the investment risk in the employer company until the stock is distributed, a deferred distribution to a terminated employee would not be appropriate, so payouts from stock-bonus plans or ESOPs have a special earlier beginning date than that for other qualified plans. Distributions from a stock-bonus plan or ESOP must occur no later than one year after the end of the fifth plan year after the employee's separation from service, or no later than one year after retirement, disability, or death.[7]

In general, the plan must distribute benefits in the form of employer stock. However, the participant can be given the option of receiving cash of equal value, subject to a right to receive employer stock. If the participant receives stock that is not traded on an established market, the participant has a right to require that the employer repurchase the securities under a fair valuation formula. This is referred to as the "put" requirement.[8] If an employee exercises the put option on

---

[3]Reg. Sec. 1.401–1(a)(2)(iii) and 1.401–1(b)(1)(iii). See also Rev. Rul. 69–65, 1969–1 C.B. 114, with regard to the purpose of a stock-bonus plan as compared with a profit-sharing plan. Note also Code Section 401(a)(27), was added by the Tax Reform Act of 1986 (profits not required even for profit-sharing plans).

[4]Code Section 404(j). To receive this treatment, the dividends must be paid within 90 days after the close of the plan year.

[5]See Code Section 72(t).

[6]Code Section 401(a)(11)(c).

[7]Code Sections 401(a)(23), 409(o).

[8]Code Sections 401(a)(23), 409(h).

distribution—that is, sells the securities back to the plan—the participant must be paid over no more than five years, and during that time the plan must provide adequate security for the payment.[9]

Voting Rights. If the employer company is closely held, plan participants generally must be given the right to vote with respect to stock held for them in the plan on corporate issues requiring more than a majority of the outstanding common shares.[10] Under most state corporate laws, very few issues require more than a majority vote, so this requirement may not be burdensome. If the employer stock is publicly traded, participants must be permitted to vote on all issues.

Diversification Requirement. Participants in ESOPs who have reached age 55 with 10 years of service are entitled to an annual election requiring the employer to diversify investment in the participant's account.[11] For a 5-year period after becoming eligible for this election, the participant can elect annually to diversify 25 percent of the account balance. In the final year, diversification of 50 percent of the account balance can be elected. The plan must offer at least three investment options, other than employer stock, to the participant for diversification purposes. Alternatively, a plan can meet the diversification requirement by distributing the amount covered by the election within 90 days after the election period.

Taxation of Employees. In addition to the usual tax advantages for qualified plans, the basic employee tax benefit provided by the Code for a plan holding employer stock is the deferral of taxation of unrealized appreciation.[12] When the plan makes a lump-sum distribution, including employer stock, the unrealized appreciation of the stock—that is, the difference between the value of the stock when contributed to or purchased by the trust and its value when distributed to the employee—is not taxable to the employee at the time of distribution to the extent that it (1) represents nondeductible employee contributions or (2) represents employer contributions, and the participant's entire account is distributed within one taxable year as a result of death, the attainment of age 59½, or the employer's separation from the service of the employer.[13]

Basically, this means that the taxable amount of a lump-sum distribution from a stock-bonus plan does not include unrealized appreciation of employer securities if the recipient is entitled to the special tax treatment for lump-sum distributions in general. The unrealized appreciation is taxable only when the employee or

---

[9] Code Section 40(h)(5).

[10] Code Sections 401(a)(22) and 409(e).

[11] Code Section 401(a)(28).

[12] Code Section 402(e)(4)(D).

[13] The favorable tax treatment for unrealized appreciation does not apply to distributions attributable to accumulated voluntary deductible employee contributions (VDECs) made under pre-1986 law.

other recipient sells the securities at a later date. The unrealized appreciation amount is taxable as capital gain when the stock is sold.

Example

An example should make these rules clearer. Suppose that, upon retirement, Farley receives a distribution within one taxable year of his entire account in his employer's noncontributory stock-bonus plan. Farley receives stock from the plan that is worth $20,000 when distributed. At the time the stock was purchased by or contributed to the plan, it had a value of $5,000. (In other words, the plan's cost basis for the stock was $5,000.) The difference of $15,000 between the plan's cost basis and the value of the distribution is not part of Farley's taxable amount; his taxable amount at the time of distribution is limited to $5,000. This $5,000 will be taxable under the rules for lump-sum distributions. If Farley holds the stock for a time and then sells it for $25,000, as a result of this sale he will have to report $20,000 of capital gain.

Comparison with Profit-Sharing Plan. Compared with using employer stock in a regular profit-sharing plan, a stock-bonus plan has a possible advantage. Employer stock held under a profit-sharing plan still must technically produce a "fair return," while that held by a stock-bonus plan need not meet this restriction because of the different purposes for the plan.[14] However, there is a technical disadvantage to a stock-bonus plan as opposed to holding employer stock under a profit-sharing plan. The voting requirements described earlier apply to a stock-bonus plan but not to a profit-sharing plan.[15]

Deductibility of Contributions. As indicated above, the employer can deduct a contribution to a stock-bonus plan in the form of employer securities as well as cash. Deductions for contributions can be taken, even if there are no current or accumulated profits.[16] The deduction limit is the same as that for a profit-sharing plan—15 percent of covered payroll.[17]

Employee Stock-Ownership Plan (ESOP)

The ESOP, first introduced in 1974, is basically a stock-bonus plan with an important additional feature: If certain requirements are met, the plan can be used by the employer company as a means of raising funds on a tax-favored basis. The

---

[14] Rev. Rul. 69–65, 1969–1 C.B. 114.
[15] Code Section 401(a)(22).
[16] See footnote 3.
[17] Code Section 404(a)(3).

FIGURE 15–1. How an ESOP Is Used by an Employer to Obtain Financing with Tax-Deductible Loan Repayments

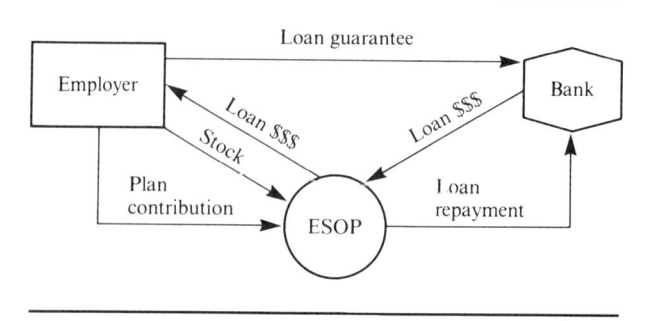

funds can be used for any corporate purposes, which can include acquiring the assets or stock of another company.

In effect, an ESOP allows an employer to indirectly borrow money from a bank and repay the loan with fully deductible repayment amounts. The repayment amounts are deductible in full, because they are structured as contributions to an ESOP; normally, only the interest portion of a loan repayment would be tax-deductible.

This bit of tax magic (see Figure 15–1) is accomplished by first having the plan trustee borrow money from a bank or other lender. The borrowed money is then used to purchase a block of employer stock from the employer. Shares of this stock also will subsequently be allocated to participant's accounts in the ESOP as plan contributions are made. The employer makes periodic plan contributions to the ESOP and obtains a tax deduction for them. These plan contributions are designed to be enough to enable the plan trustee to gradually repay the loan to the bank. The net result is that the employer immediately receives the full proceeds of the bank loan and, in effect, pays off the loan through tax-deductible contributions to the plan on behalf of plan participants.

Since the ESOP normally has no financial status independent of the employer, the employer usually must guarantee the loan to the bank. If the plan gives collateral for the loan, the collateral may consist only of qualifying employer securities.[18]

These transactions are made attractive to lenders by a provision that allows the lender to exclude 50 percent of the interest income from a loan to an ESOP for acquiring employer securities. To qualify for this exclusion, the lender must be a bank, an insurance company, a corporation actively engaged in the business of lending money to ESOPs, or a regulated investment company.[19]

To make these transactions possible, the ESOP must be exempted from certain qualified plan provisions that would otherwise apply. For example, the loan

---

[18]ERISA Section 408(b)(3).
[19]Code Section 133.

guarantee normally would be a prohibited transaction, but there are specific provisions allowing exemptions for loans to an ESOP.[20] The exemption provisions also provide considerable authority to the Labor and Treasury Departments to impose conditions on loans to ESOPs. The current Regulations include such requirements as an arm's-length standard applicable to the terms of the loan, as well as tests designed to ensure that the interest rate for the loan and the price of the securities will not result in a drain on the plan's assets.[21] In another type of exemption, the IRS has held that an ESOP is not subject to unrelated business income tax on its dividend and interest income resulting from investments with borrowed funds.[22]

An ESOP must be invested "primarily in employer securities."[23] The term *primarily* has not been interpreted by the IRS or the Labor Department, but it is clear there is less investment flexibility in an ESOP than in a regular profit-sharing plan.

The stock or other employer securities used in an ESOP must meet a specific definition of "employer securities" found in the Code.[24] Employer securities are defined as common stock issued by the employer that is readily tradable on an established securities market. If such common stock does not exist, employer securities mean common stock issued by the employer having a combination of voting power and dividend rights equal to or in excess of the employer's class of common stock having the greatest voting power and the class of stock having the greatest dividend rates. Employer securities can include noncallable preferred stock, if such stock is convertible at any time into qualified common stock described above at a reasonable conversion price. If the ESOP is established by a member of a controlled group of corporations, the employer securities can be issued by any member of the controlled group.

Contribution Formulas and Accounts. An ESOP's contribution allocation formula may not be integrated with social security, since plan allocations must be based on total compensation.[25] In other respects, contribution formulas and participants' accounts are handled in the same manner as for the stock-bonus plan described earlier.

Deductibility of Contributions. The rules for contribution deductibility for an ESOP are somewhat different from those for a stock-bonus plan or profit-sharing plan. If employer contributions to the ESOP are applied to the repayment of a loan, amounts applied by the plan to repay the loan principal are deductible by the employer up to a limit of 25 percent of compensation of employees covered

---

[20]Code Section 4975(d)(3).
[21]Reg. Secs. 54.4975–7 and 54.4975–11.
[22]Rev. Rul. 79–122, 1979–1 C.B. 204.
[23]Code Section 4975(e)(7)(A).
[24]Code Sections 4975(e)(8) and 409(e).
[25]Reg. Sec. 54–4975–11(a)(7)(ii).

under the plan. Amounts used to repay interest are deductible without any percentage limit.[26]

An ESOP must be a stock-bonus plan under the Code, but it also can include a money-purchase provision.[27] Normally, the only purpose for including a money-purchase feature to the plan would be to increase the deductibility limit above the 15 percent applicable to stock-bonus plans; however, the provision described in the preceding paragraph generally allows adequate deductions, and the money-purchase feature is not commonly used.

Plan Distributions. The distribution rules, voting rights, diversification, and taxation considerations regarding ESOP distributions are the same as those discussed earlier in connection with stock-bonus plans.

Special Annual-Additions Limit for ESOPs. The annual-additions limit of Code Section 415 for ESOPs is higher than for other defined-contribution plans. Instead of the usual limit (lesser of 25 percent of compensation or $30,000), the limit for ESOPs is $30,000 (as adjusted for inflation) plus the lesser of an additional $30,000 (as adjusted) or the amount of securities actually allocated to the employee's plan account.[28] In other words, the limit can be up to $60,000 (as adjusted). *Note:* this provision does not increase the *deduction* limit for the employer, which is still 25 percent of payroll (see above).

This higher annual limit does not apply unless no more than one third of the employer contributions for the year in question go to highly compensated employees, as defined in Code Section 414(q).

Advantages of ESOPs. Basically, the advantages of an ESOP are the same as those of a stock-bonus plan described earlier, with the additional advantage of the leveraging feature. Whether this leveraging feature justifies the additional complexity of an ESOP is a question that has to be decided in light of the employer's objectives. It should be noted that many of the advantages of an ESOP can be obtained more simply by having the corporation borrow the money directly for its needs, pay off the loan regularly in cash, and simultaneously create a regular stock-bonus plan and make regular tax-deductible contributions of employer stock to the stock-bonus plan. As compared with an ESOP, the only limitations on this approach are that deductions to the stock-bonus plan are limited to 15 percent of compensation of covered employees, and the lender is not allowed to exclude 50 percent of the interest income—suggesting that the interest rate under this approach would be higher. Also, with the ESOP approach, the plan acquires a block of employer stock at the outset of the plan. If the company is growing, this means that an ESOP can acquire stock at a lower price than a plan that involves contri-

---

[26]Code Section 404(a)(9).
[27]Code Section 4975(e)(7).
[28]Code Section 415(c)(6).

butions of stock over a period of years. Thus, in a growing company the ESOP approach would be more beneficial to the employees.

Creating a Market for Closely Held Stock

Congress views it as socially desirable for employees to obtain an ownership interest in the company for which they work. Basically, the provisions for stock-bonus plans and ESOPs are Congress's attempt to induce owners of closely held businesses to provide this benefit by tying it to plans that also meet shareholder needs. One of the most important of such needs is the creation of a market for stock of a closely held corporation.

In small companies, it is typical for owners to anticipate that the corporation will redeem their shares at death. Corporate funds to do this must be accumulated out of aftertax income. Alternatively, life insurance can be purchased; but, since the premiums are not deductible, this is also an accumulation from aftertax income. In addition, the accumulation of corporate funds to redeem shares creates potential problems with the accumulated-earnings tax, particularly where the shareholder is a majority shareholder.

If a corporate stock redemption is desired during a shareholder's lifetime, there can be tax problems. A redemption distribution to a shareholder will be treated as a dividend, taxable in full as ordinary income (rather than a purchase taxable as a capital gain) unless the shareholder meets the requirements of Section 302 of the Code. Basically, the redemption must be either a complete redemption or substantially disproportionate redemption under these provisions. Because of the Code's stock attribution rules, it is often very difficult to design a redemption in a closely held corporation that will meet these requirements. However, if the shareholder's basis is low (as is often the case) there may be no significant advantage in redemption treatment, rather than dividend treatment, since the taxable gain will nearly equal the full proceeds and the rate of tax on the gain is the same as on the dividend.

In many cases, an alternative type of planning uses an appropriate form of stock-ownership plan. In the case of an immediate redemption during lifetime, the shareholder's stock can be sold to an ESOP, rather than to the corporation itself. In general, the sale to ESOP will be treated as a sale transaction and will not encounter the problems of complying with the redemption rules of Section 302 of the Code. Therefore, it will result in capital gain to the shareholder.

If a series of stock purchases or a stock purchase in the future is proposed, an ESOP is not appropriate, because of the stipulation that ESOPs acquire a block of stock at the beginning and remain primarily invested in employer securities. For this purpose, a profit-sharing or regular stock-bonus plan can be used. The plan trustee can enter into an agreement with the stockholders to purchase stock in the future. In some cases, the plan may purchase life insurance to obtain the funds to make the purchase.

If the selling shareholder is an employee of the company and a participant in the ESOP or stock-bonus plan, there are certain limitations on the use of this technique. The IRS will not issue a ruling that the sale must qualify for capital-gain treatment (rather than dividend treatment) unless the combined beneficial interest in the plan of the selling shareholder and all related persons does not exceed 20 percent.[29] However, this may not be significant in many low-basis cases, since there is no longer a special tax rate on capital gain, as discussed earlier in connection with redemptions.

Tax Benefits for Shareholder Sales to ESOPs

As a further motivation to encourage shareholder sales of employer stock to ESOPs, the shareholder may elect nonrecognition of gain on the sale under certain circumstances.[30] To obtain this treatment, the seller must acquire replacement securities of another domestic corporation or corporations during a period beginning 3 months before and ending 12 months after the date of the sale to the ESOP. Also, after the sale, the ESOP must own at least 30 percent of the total value of employer stock outstanding at that time. Furthermore, there are restrictions on allocation of stock by the ESOP to the accounts of the seller, a related party, or a more-than-25 percent owner of the employer.

The law also provides a federal *estate* tax exclusion for employee securities transferred to ESOPs.[31] The exclusion from estate tax is equal to 50 percent of the "qualified proceeds" of a "qualified sale" of employer securities. A qualified sale is a sale by the executor of an estate to an ESOP. Qualified proceeds means the amount received by the estate from the sale before the return filing date. Qualified proceeds does not include proceeds from the sale of any stock previously received by the decedent from an ESOP or other qualified plan. The use of ESOPs to help create a market for closely held stock thus may be particularly attractive in cases where a decedent's shareholder's estate holds (or is expected to hold) substantial amounts of stock and there is no marital deduction or the maximum marital deduction will not be used.

Stock Valuation

An essential factor of the success of a stock-bonus plan or ESOP, particularly for a closely held company, is a correct valuation of the stock used. If the plan pays too high a price for the stock, the IRS can impose a penalty (excise tax) on the corporation of up to 100 percent of the amount involved.[32] If employer securities are not readily tradable on an established market, all valuations must be made by an independent appraiser meeting requirements prescribed by regulations.[33] A potential problem in closely held companies may be that other corporate plans—for

---

[29]Rev. Proc. 77–30, 1977–2 C.B. 539.
[30]Code Section 1042.
[31]Code Section 2057.
[32]Code Section 4975(a), (b), and (d)(13); ERISA Section 408(e).
[33]Code Section 401(a)(28).

example, a stock redemption agreement or cross-purchase buy-sell agreement—may specify a different valuation for the stock than that provided in the stock-bonus plan or ESOP.

If the corporation makes its plan contribution by contributing stock, rather than cash, the excise tax problem is avoided, since the company has not actually sold the stock to the plan. The only potential problem is that the company may lose part of its tax deduction, if the IRS disputes the valuation of the stock. Consequently, if valuation is doubtful, stock rather than cash should be contributed. However, this generally can be done only with a stock bonus plan and not with an ESOP, at least at the inception of the plan, because an ESOP must invest in a block of employer stock at the outset with the employer making subsequent cash contributions.

Summary

Substantial holdings of employer stock can be used in profit-sharing plans and in two types of specialized plans, the stock-bonus plan and the ESOP. The use of employer stock provides incentives and tax benefits (on unrealized stock appreciation) to employees. It also helps create a market for employer stock and allows a deduction to the employer for a noncash (stock) contribution to the plan.

The stock-bonus plan is similar to a profit-sharing plan, with accounts and distributions stated in shares of stock. Special distribution rules apply, including a put option feature and a diversification requirement. Employees are not taxed at the time of distribution on unrealized stock appreciation.

An ESOP is similar to a stock-bonus plan, with an additional leveraging feature that allows the employer to borrow money for corporate use indirectly through the ESOP. This allows the loan payoff to be fully deductible. There are also special tax benefits to the lender.

Employer stock plans help create a market for employer stock and, therefore, can be beneficial in financial and estate planning for shareholders in closely held corporations.

Valuation of stock is a critical issue and, if stock is not publicly traded, an independent appraiser must be used.

16

Qualified Plan Distributions and Loans

Objectives of This Chapter
This chapter covers several important and interrelated topics:

- *Designing plan distribution provisions.*
- *Tax treatment of plan distributions.*
- *Plan loans.*
- *Plan benefits in domestic relations disputes.*

Designing Distribution Provisions

A qualified plan must have appropriate distribution provisions to achieve the employer's design objectives. Furthermore, good distribution provisions enable participants to receive maximum tax benefits from the plan while, on the other hand, poorly planned distributions can result in tax disasters to the recipient. Thus, correct design and administration of plan distributions is critical.

A plan's objectives will dictate the type of distribution options to be designed into the plan. There are two typical and somewhat opposite approaches, depending on whether the plan is intended primarily to provide adequate retirement income or, on the other hand, to provide an advantageous means of accumulating savings for further investment and estate planning by plan participants. The first objective will generally lead to annuity-type distribution options, possibly with a choice of options designed to accommodate varying family situations. The second objective, commonly found in plans designed to benefit key employees, may stress lump-sum options, but it also may emphasize methods by which plan funds can be kept within the tax shelter of the plan for as long as possible.

From an employee point of view, maximum flexibility is desirable in plan distribution provisions. However, administrative feasibility is a limit on flexibility, particularly in plans with many participants. Flexibility can increase administrative costs and potentially cause cash-flow problems to the plan fund, so providers of plan investment products and services, such as bank trust departments and insurance companies, may wish to limit payout options.

Flexibility is further limited by a series of complex rules in the Code, Regulations, and IRS rulings. These rules are primarily designed to steer plan distributions in a retirement income direction as much as possible. As discussed in Chapter 4, the use of a plan for investment purposes by key employees, rather than as a vehicle for providing retirement income, is viewed by the government (to some extent) as an abuse.

This discussion will first cover the basic concept of the plan's normal benefit form, then the types of optional benefits that can be used, within the limits referred to in the preceding paragraph.

Normal Form of Benefit

A qualified plan must specify not only the amount of the benefit but the form of the benefit. In a defined-benefit plan, the *normal form of benefit* is the basic "defined benefit," the form that quantifies the benefit due and provides a standard for calculating equivalent alternative benefits. At one time, the normal form was the form a participant received if he or she did not choose an alternative form; but currently, this is not necessarily true, because of the joint-and-survivor provisions, discussed in Chapter 10 and later in this chapter.

The normal form in a defined-benefit plan is usually either a straight-life annuity or a life annuity with period certain. A straight-life annuity simply provides periodic (usually monthly) payments for the participant's life. A life annuity with period certain provides periodic payments for the participant's life, but additionally provides that, if the participant dies before the end of a specified period of years, payments will be continued until the end of that period to the participant's designated beneficiary. Specified periods of 10, 15, and 20 years are commonly used.

In comparing defined-benefit plans, it must be remembered that straight-life and life annuities with periods certain are not equivalent; a plan providing an annuity of $100 per month for life with period certain as the normal form of benefit provides a significantly larger benefit than a plan providing $100 per month as a straight-life annuity. Period-certain annuities as the normal form of benefit are most commonly found in plans using insurance contracts for funding.

As discussed in Chapter 10, if a participant is married, a pension plan must provide a qualified joint-and-survivor annuity for the participant and spouse automatically (i.e., unless the participant elects otherwise). To avoid discrimination against single participants, most plans provide that the qualified joint-and-survivor annuity is "actuarially equivalent" to the normal form. For example, if the normal retirement benefit would be $1,000 per month as a straight-life annuity, the qualified joint-and-survivor annuity might be something like $800 per month to the participant for life, then $400 per month to the spouse for life. However, the plan can partially or fully subsidize the joint-and-survivor annuity; for example, it might provide a straight-life annuity of $1,000 per month or a $1,000/$500 joint-

and-survivor annuity. This might be desirable to the employer, even though it would discriminate against unmarried participants.

Defined-contribution pension plans can provide an annuity as the normal-benefit form. This is particularly common if an insurance contract is used for funding. The amount of the annuity depends on the participant's account balance at retirement, with annuity purchase rates specified in the insurance contract, if any. Optional forms of benefit, particularly a lump sum, are usually provided in defined-contribution plans.

Optional Alternative Forms of Benefit

Participants generally benefit from having a choice of benefit forms as an alternative to the normal form. Participants can then choose a benefit that is structured in accordance with their individual financial needs, family situations, and retirement activities. In defined-benefit plans, the most common alternative forms (assuming a straight-life annuity as the normal form) are, in addition to the qualified joint-and-survivor annuity that must be offered, (1) joint-and-survivor annuities for the participant and spouse or other beneficiary with varying survivorship annuity percentages, such as 50 percent, 75 percent, and 100 percent, and (2) annuities for the participant and beneficiary with varying periods certain, such as 5, 10, 15, or 20 years. The plan also can allow payouts over a fixed period of years without life contingency. All these options are subject to the limitations described below. Table 16–1 gives some indication of the relative usage of various forms.

To avoid undesirable or prohibited discrimination among employees in different situations, the plan should provide that any optional benefit is actuarially

TABLE 16–1. Postretirement-Benefit Options Provided, Medium and Large Firms *(50 Employees and Up)*

Type of Annuity Surviving Spouse	All Partici- pants (Percent)	Professional/ Administrative Employees (Percent)	Technical/ Clerical Employees (Percent)	Production Employees (Percent)
Qualified joint- and-survivor annuity:	90	91	92	89
—50%	20	16	19	24
—51–99%	6	4	3	8
—100%	1	1	<0.5	1
—retiree option %	63	70	70	56
Other survivor annuity forms	10	10	7	11
No survivor annuity or lump-sum death benefit only	<0.5	<0.5	0.5	0

Source: U.S. Department of Labor, Bureau of Labor Statistics. (Profit-sharing and similar plans not included.)

equivalent to the normal form of benefit. Under Code Section 401(a)(25), the actuarial assumptions used for this purpose must be specified in the plan, either by stating the actuarial interest and other factors or by specifying an equivalency table for the various benefits, to avoid employer discretion in favor of highly compensated employees.

Lump-Sum Option. A lump-sum distribution can provide planning flexibility for participants. Lump-sum distribution provisions are most common in defined-contribution plans; in fact, in a profit-sharing plan the lump sum is often the only distribution option. However, even a defined-benefit plan can offer a lump-sum option.

A lump sum may be beneficial for participants, because of the special five-year averaging tax treatment discussed below. However, the same or greater tax saving can often be obtained by a distribution spread over a period of years, so tax saving, as such, is usually not a dominant factor in choosing a lump-sum distribution.

Higher-income participants often would like a lump sum, because they have other sources for retirement income and wish to invest their plan funds in riskier high-return investment vehicles. A defined-contribution plan can be designed to accommodate this need to some extent within the plan, however, by providing participant investment direction. Also, investment results within the plan are enhanced by the tax deferral on plan income and may provide an effective rate of return that the participant cannot match outside of the plan. However, funds cannot be left in the plan indefinitely, and distributions must generally begin at age 70½, under the minimum distribution rules discussed later in this chapter.

In some defined-benefit plans, particularly insured plans, the assumptions used for funding are too conservative. Thus, for example, a plan may have accumulated $140,000 to fund a benefit of $12,000 per year to a retiree. In many cases, however, it might be possible for a retiree to individually invest $140,000 and receive a better return than $12,000 per year for life. Thus, the retiree might rather have a $140,000 lump sum from the plan fund than the plan's annuity benefit. In some cases, this situation results from bad plan design, while in others it is done deliberately to increase the benefit for key employees.

Lump-sum distribution options, particularly those in defined-benefit plans, present a number of design and administrative problems that must be resolved. These include:

- A lump-sum payment to a lower-income employee may deplete the employee's retirement nest egg and be contrary to his or her interests.
- An antiselection problem exists; for example, employees with poor health (and shortened life expectancy) may take the lump sum, while the long-livers take annuities.
- A lump-sum payment to a key employee may deplete the plan's resources enough to impair retirement security for other employees.

Plan provisions and administrative procedures designed to deal with such problems must be nondiscriminatory.

Example

In Rev. Rul. 85–89, the IRS held that a plan could not provide lump-sum payments only to participants earning $50,000 or more. However, the ruling stated that the plan trustees may be given discretion to deny lump-sum payments if the payment was not in the employee's best interest, as long as this discretion does not, in actual operation, favor the prohibited group. Also, a U.S. District Court recently held that medical criteria could be used in determining eligibility for lump-sum benefits from a defined-benefit plan, *Medei* v. *Bethlehem Steel*,—F. Supp.—(E. D. Pa. 1985). These specific cases merely emphasize, however, that lump-sum options must be carefully designed and administered to avoid prohibited discrimination.

Distribution Restrictions

Plan distributions can be designed to provide considerable flexibility, but they must be designed within a rather complex network of rules that have been accumulating in the law over many years. These rules are aimed at protecting the financial interests of participants, but more significantly are designed to limit the use of qualified plans merely as a tax-sheltered investment medium for key employees. The distribution rules must be thoroughly understood by planners and administrators, because a mistake may disqualify the plan or result in tax disaster for participants. Unfortunately, the rules are unclear, overlapping, and not well coordinated. The significant rules are:

> Distinctions between the types of distributions permitted in pension plans, as opposed to profit-sharing plans.
> Rules preventing employers from unjustly delaying benefit payments.
> Minimum distribution requirements.
> Early distribution penalty.
> Incidental-benefit requirements.
> Nonalienation rules.

Pension versus Profit-Sharing Plans. The IRS generally will not allow a pension plan to pay benefits prior to retirement, early retirement, death, or disability, although some limited cashout provisions may be allowed in the event of termination of employment prior to these events, as previously discussed. With a profit-sharing plan, there is much more flexibility and, as discussed in Chapter 13, the plan may allow distributions of employer contributions as early as two years after the contribution. Employee contributions may be distributed to employees without regard to the two-year restriction, and the plan may permit these to be available to the employee at any time without restriction. However, some restrictions on employee withdrawals are often provided in plans to prevent excessive depletion of the plan funds. In addition, the 10 percent penalty (described below) may deter employees from making certain withdrawals.

Delaying Benefit Payments. Under Code Section 401(a)(14) all qualified plans must provide for payment not later than the 60th day after the latest of the following three dates: *(a)* the earlier of age 65 or the plan's normal retirement date; *(b)* the 10th anniversary of the participant's entry into the plan; and *(c)* the participant's termination of service with the employer. The plan may allow the participant to elect a payout that begins at a date later than this maximum limit. However, the extent to which a participant can stretch out payments is limited by the rules discussed in the next paragraph.

Minimum Distribution Rules. Congress does not like qualified plans to be used as tax shelters for funds that are not actually needed by participants for retirement income. Therefore, Section 401(a)(9) of the Code requires plan distributions to begin no later than April 1 of the calendar year following the year in which the employee attains age 70½, even if the participant continues working for the employer.

Furthermore, the distribution must be either in a lump sum or a periodic distribution over a specified period. Basically, the distribution must be paid in substantially equal annual amounts over the life of the employee or the joint lives of the employee and a designated beneficiary. Alternatively, the distribution may be made over a stated period that does not exceed the life expectancy of the employee or the life expectancy of the employee and a designated beneficiary. This permits period-certain annuity payouts, as long as the period certain does not exceed the life expectancy limits. A periodic distribution based on an ongoing recalculation of life expectancy is permitted, which tends to stretch out payments somewhat, since life expectancy is extended by continuing survival. However, life expectancy can be recalculated no more often than annually. Cost-of-living increases in pension payments to retirees are permitted as long as they are not designed to circumvent the minimum distribution rules.

The minimum distribution rules also have provisions applicable to distributions made to a beneficiary if the employee dies before the entire plan interest is distributed. If distributions to the employee have already begun, the remaining portion of the employee's interest must be distributed at least as rapidly as under the method in effect prior to death. For example, if the employee elected a 20-year period-certain annuity and the employee died after 10 years, the remaining interest could be distributed in equal annual installments over a term not exceeding 10 years. The beneficiary, however, could elect to accelerate these payments.

If the employee dies before distributions have begun, the plan's death benefit must be distributed within five years after the employee's death, with an exception. The five-year restriction is not applicable if (1) any portion of the plan benefit is payable to a designated beneficiary, (2) the beneficiary's interest will be distributed over the life of the beneficiary or over a period not extending beyond the life expectancy of the beneficiary, and (3) distributions begin no later than one year after the employee's death. If the designated beneficiary is the surviving spouse, the beginning of the distribution can be delayed to the date on which the employee would have attained age 70½; and, if the surviving spouse dies before receiving distributions, the rules are to be applied as if the surviving spouse were the employee.

Early Distribution Penalty. Section 72(t) of the Code provides a tax penalty for early distributions from qualified plans. This penalty provision was added recently by Congress to encourage plan participants to use qualified plans primarily for retirement and not merely for deferral of compensation. The 10 percent penalty tax applies to distributions from a broad range of tax-advantaged retirement plans, including regular qualified plans, Section 403 tax-deferred annuity plans, and individual retirement arrangements and SEPs. The penalty applies to all distributions, except distributions:

Made on or after attainment of age 59½.
Made to a beneficiary or employee's estate on or after the employee's death.
Attributable to disability.
That are part of a series of substantially equal-period payments made at least annually over the life or life expectancy of the employee, or the joint lives or life expectancies of the employee and beneficiary (separation from service is required).
Made after a separation from service for early retirement after age 55 (not applicable to IRAs).
Certain tax-credit ESOP dividend payments.
Distributions to the extent of medical expenses deductible for the year under Code Section 213, whether or not actually deducted (not applicable to IRAs).

Under this penalty provision, a plan may be permitted to make a distribution to an employee without disqualifying the plan, but the distribution nevertheless may be subject to penalty. For example, many hardship distributions from 401(k) plans or 403(b) tax-deferred annuity plans will be subject to the penalty tax.

Despite the penalty, withdrawals from qualified plans may still be important to participants in many situations—to obtain emergency funds, for example. Therefore, plan designers may wish to provide withdrawals in plans, where permitted, despite the existence of the 10 percent penalty.

Incidental-Benefit Requirements. Some types of optional-benefit forms provide substantial payments to persons other than the participant after the participant's death—for example, a 20-year-certain annuity with payments continued to a beneficiary. Since these are, in effect, death benefits, they must be "incidental," as discussed in Chapter 10.

The IRS has held that a benefit form with a survivorship option is incidental if the participant can expect, actuarially, to receive at least 50 percent of the benefit's present value.[1] For example, if a participant has a 10-year life expectancy at retirement, he or she could not elect a 25-year-certain annuity. This rule appar-

---

[1] Revenue Ruling 72–241.

ently does not apply to the required joint-and-survivor annuity for spouses; thus, for example, a plan could provide a joint and 50 percent survivor annuity for a 65-year-old retiree and his 25-year-old spouse, even though actuarially the participant's present interest in the benefit would be less than 50 percent.

Nonalienation Rules. A qualified plan must provide that plan benefits may not be assigned or alienated (Code Section 401(a)(13)). However, the plan may permit a participant or beneficiary to make a voluntary revocable assignment of up to 10 percent of any benefit payment if benefits are in pay status (i.e., the participant has a present right to receive benefits). On the face of it, this would appear to prevent any levy or garnishment of plan benefits resulting from legal action by creditors or others, because this would not constitute a voluntary assignment to any extent. For divorce, child support, and similar domestic disputes, there are special provisions, discussed later in this chapter.

Examples

The distribution restrictions described in the preceding pages appear so complex as to defy summary. Probably the best way to see how these restrictions work is to look at some examples. Consider the following proposed plan distribution options, offered to a married male participant in a qualified defined-benefit plan retiring at age 65. Assume that the participant and his spouse have waived any required joint and survivor annuity. The following options will be analyzed to see if they are permissible under the distribution restrictions:

- A joint and 100 percent survivor annuity for the lives of the participant and his daughter, age 35.
- A 25-year period-certain annuity for the lives of the participant and his spouse.
- Equal periodic distributions over five years, beginning when the participant reaches age 75.
- Equal monthly payments over a fixed period equal to the participant's life expectancy, but each year if the participant survives, the payout period is extended (the monthly payments are actuarially reduced) to reflect the increased life expectancy.

The first potential distribution would be permitted under the restrictions in Section 401(a)(9), since it extends over the lives of a participant and named beneficiary; but it might not meet the incidental benefit tests, since the participant might not expect to get more than 50 percent of the present value of the benefit. If there is any doubt of this, an actuary's opinion would be necessary; possibly also a ruling could be requested from the IRS.

The second distribution—the 25-year period-certain annuity for the lives of the participant and his spouse—would meet Section 401(a)(9) as long as the joint life expectancy of the participant and spouse is at least 25 years. This annuity will meet the incidental benefit tests, if the participant himself can expect to get more than 50 percent of the present value of the benefit. Again, an actuary should be consulted, but this benefit probably will meet the test.

The third option, a distribution beginning at age 75, is not permitted, because distributions must begin not later than April 1 following the calendar year in which the employee reaches age 70½.

Finally, a fixed-period payout over the participant's life expectancy, with annual recalculations of life expectancy, is permitted. This can be an advantageous way of receiving the benefit, since payments can continue to a relatively advanced age, reducing the danger that retirement income will stop while the participant is still living.

Federal Taxation of Distributions

A qualified plan participant is taxed advantageously on a distribution that qualifies as a *lump-sum distribution,* the definition of which is discussed below. Other types of plan distributions are taxed in accordance with the rules for taxing annuity payments found in Section 72 of the Code. The tax treatment of both types of payments will be discussed here.

This section deals with *federal* income and estate taxation. Some states apply similar tax treatment, but there is considerable variation. Federal taxes are usually the dominant factor in the overall tax burden on plan distributions.

The initial step in determining the taxation of a qualified plan distribution is determining the *taxable amount* of the distribution. For a distribution upon retirement, disability, or termination of employment, the taxable amount consists of the total amount of the distribution less the following amounts, sometimes referred to as the employee's *cost basis* in the plan:

The total nondeductible contributions made by the employee (in the case of a contributory plan).

The total cost of life insurance reported as taxable income by the participant, assuming that the plan distribution is received under the same contract that provided the life insurance protection.

Any employer contributions previously taxed to the employee (e.g., where a nonqualified plan later became qualified).

Certain employer contributions attributable to foreign services performed before 1963.

Amounts paid by the employee in repayment of loans that were treated as distributions.

In the case of a stock-bonus plan or other stock plan, the net unrealized appreciation, as discussed in Chapter 15.

The first two items in the list are the ones most frequently encountered. If the employee is self-employed or was self-employed in the past, the items excludable from the taxable amount are slightly different from the above list. The most important difference is that for a self-employed person who is an owner/employee (a more than 10 percent owner of an unincorporated business), the insurance costs (the second item above) are not part of the cost basis (see Chapter 18).

The simplest way to describe the taxation of qualified plan distributions is to distinguish between those benefits that are paid out fully in a single taxable year of the participant and those that are spread out over more than one taxable year. The latter are discussed first.

Payment over More than One Taxable Year

If the plan distribution is made over more than one taxable year of the employee, the usual annuity rules apply to taxation of the distribution. The distribution will be taxable to the participant or beneficiary in the year received, except to the extent that a cost basis is to be recovered. The cost basis is recovered by calculating an *exclusion ratio* and applying it to each payment to determine the nontaxable amount. The exclusion ratio is defined as:

$$\frac{\text{Investment in the contract}}{\text{Expected return}}$$

"Investment in the contract," in this context, means the amount of the cost basis, while the expected return is determined by multiplying the total annual payment by the participant's life expectancy, according to tables in the Regulations—see Table 16–2.

Example

Employee Green is entitled to a pension at retirement of $200 per month. Green's cost basis in the plan is $8,000. Green retires at age 65. The exclusion ratio will be:

$$\frac{\$8,000}{\$48,000}$$

The numerator is equal to Green's cost basis, while the denominator is Green's annual pension of $2,400 multiplied by his life expectancy of 20 years, as determined from the tables in the Regulations. Thus $8/48$ of each payment that Green receives will be nontaxable, while the remainder will be taxable as ordinary income.

Under the annuity rules, once an exclusion ratio has been determined it continues to apply only until the cost basis is fully recovered (as would be the case if the participant lived longer than the life expectancy described in the Regulations). Payments thereafter are taxable in full. If the participant dies before the cost basis

TABLE 16–2. Life Expectancies, from Prop. Reg. Sec. 1.72–9 *(March 24, 1986—Unisex Tables)*

Age	Multiple	Age	Multiple	Age	Multiple
5	76.6	42	40.6	79	10.0
6	75.6	43	39.6	80	9.5
7	74.7	44	38.7	81	8.9
8	73.7	45	37.7	82	8.4
9	72.7	46	36.8	83	7.9
10	71.7	47	35.9	84	7.4
11	70.7	48	34.9	85	6.9
12	69.7	49	34.0	86	6.5
13	68.8	50	33.1	87	6.1
14	67.8	51	32.2	88	5.7
15	66.8	52	31.3	89	5.3
16	65.8	53	30.4	90	5.0
17	64.8	54	29.5	91	4.7
18	63.9	55	28.6	92	4.4
19	62.9	56	27.7	93	4.1
20	61.9	57	26.8	94	3.9
21	60.9	58	25.9	95	3.7
22	59.9	59	25.0	96	3.4
23	59.0	60	24.2	97	3.2
24	58.0	61	23.3	98	3.0
25	57.0	62	22.5	99	2.8
26	56.0	63	21.6	100	2.7
27	55.1	64	20.8	101	2.5
28	54.1	65	20.0	102	2.3
29	53.1	66	19.2	103	2.1
30	52.2	67	18.4	104	1.9
31	51.2	68	17.6	105	1.8
32	50.2	69	16.8	106	1.6
33	49.3	70	16.0	107	1.4
34	48.3	71	15.3	108	1.3
35	47.3	72	14.6	109	1.1
36	46.4	73	13.9	110	1.0
37	45.4	74	13.2	111	.9
38	44.4	75	12.5	112	.8
39	43.5	76	11.9	113	.7
40	42.5	77	11.2	114	.6
41	41.5	78	10.6	115	.5

has been fully recovered, there is an income tax deduction allowable to the participant's estate representing the unrecovered basis.

The same cost recovery rules apply, with some modifications, if the annuity has a period-certain feature, or is some form of joint-and-survivor annuity. With a period-certain feature, the cost basis in determining the exclusion ratio is reduced in accordance with factors in the Regulations. For a joint-and-survivor annuity, the expected return is adjusted to take the joint life expectancy into account.

Survivorship and period-certain annuities can be paid out in many forms, and the tax consequences of all of these cannot be discussed here.[2] However, the same principles apply in all cases.

Payment in One Taxable Year

If the qualified plan distribution is paid to the participant in a single taxable year, the taxable amount (the amount in excess of the participant's cost basis, as described above) potentially is all taxable to the participant as ordinary income in the year received. Since this can increase the participant's effective tax rate by pushing up the marginal tax bracket in that year, a special one-time relief provision applies if the distribution qualifies as a *lump-sum distribution* and is received after age 59½. A lump-sum distribution must meet all of the following requirements:

It is made in one taxable year of the recipient.
It represents the entire amount of the employee's benefit in the plan.
It is payable on account of the participant's death, attainment of age 59½, separation from service (nonself-employed person only) or disability (self-employed person only).
It is from a qualified plan.
Except for death benefits, the employee must have participated in the plan for at least five years prior to the distribution.

In determining whether the entire amount of the employee's benefit has been distributed, all pension plans maintained by the employer are treated as a single plan, all profit-sharing plans are treated as one plan, and all stock-bonus plans are treated as one plan.

If the distribution qualifies as a lump-sum distribution, the taxable amount of the distribution (the amount remaining after the cost basis is subtracted) is eligible for special tax treatment designed to eliminate the disadvantage of bunching all of the taxable income into one taxable year. This treatment, however, can be elected only if the distribution is received on or after the taxpayer has attained age 59½, and can be made only once.

The special tax treatment for qualifying lump-sum distributions has changed over the years. Prior to 1974, the applicable provision allowed the taxable amount of the lump-sum distribution to be treated as long-term capital gain for tax purposes. After 1973, the taxable amount became eligible for a special provision, referred to as *10-year averaging,* subject to rules somewhat more liberal than the current *5-year averaging* provision that replaced 10-year averaging in 1987. The earlier capital gain treatment was "grandfathered" through 1991; and, if the participant was in the plan before 1974, the distribution is separated into two parts— the pre–1974 and the post–1973 portions. This is done on the basis of the number

---

[2] An extensive discussion is found in *Tax Facts 1* (Cincinnati: National Underwriter Company, 1987), questions 7–20.

of months of plan participation before and after January 1, 1974, rather than by reference to old plan accounting records. The pre–1974 portion of the taxable amount is then subject to tax at a 20 percent rate, to be phased out as follows:

Year	Percent of Pre-1974 Portion Eligible for 20 Percent Rate
1987	100%
1988	95
1989	75
1990	50
1991	25

The remainder of the taxable portion of the distribution is taxed under five-year averaging, if eligible.

The current five-year averaging treatment is a special tax calculation. First, a minimum distribution allowance of the lesser of $10,000 or one half of the total taxable amount is subtracted from the taxable amount. The minimum distribution allowance, however, must be reduced by 20 percent of the total taxable amount in excess of $20,000; therefore, if the taxable amount is $70,000 or more, there is no minimum distribution allowance. The remaining taxable amount after the minimum distribution allowance is, in effect, divided by 5 and a separate tax is determined on this portion; the tax so determined is then multiplied by 5. In making this calculation, the tax is determined apart from the employee's other taxable income, without the usual deductions or exclusions, and the single-taxpayer rate is used. The computation is described on the Internal Revenue form for reporting lump-sum distributions (currently Form 4972) and it is unnecessary to go into the computational details here.

A taxpayer who participated in the plan prior to 1974 has an option to forego capital gain treatment on the pre–1974 portion of the taxable amount and use the five-year averaging method for the entire taxable amount. Normally, such a taxpayer will elect whichever option provides the lowest amount of tax.

The five-year averaging provision is not available unless the employee participated in the plan for five or more taxable years before the distribution. However, if the distribution results from the employee's death, the beneficiary may use five-year averaging, even if the employee was not a participant for five years.

Taxation of Death Benefits from Qualified Plans

The income tax treatment described above also applies in general to plan death benefits paid to beneficiaries of participants—that is, if the death benefit is paid as periodic payments, the annuity rules described above generally apply; while if the death benefit qualifies as a lump-sum distribution, the special favorable tax treatment is available to the beneficiary. Some additional income tax benefits under Section 101 of the Code are also available to the beneficiary, however.

One such benefit is an income tax exclusion of up to $5,000 for a death benefit paid by an employer by reason of death of the employee. If the benefit qualifies as a lump-sum distribution, the full exclusion is available without qualification. However, if the benefit is in the form of periodic payments, the $5,000 exclusion is only available to the extent the employee's benefit was nonvested prior to death.

Another income tax exclusion applies if the death benefit is payable under a life insurance contract held by the plan. The amount excluded from income tax is the pure insurance amount paid—that is, the difference between the policy's face amount and its cash value.

Example

Employee Haines dies before retirement and his beneficiary receives a lump-sum death benefit from the plan consisting of $100,000 of the proceeds of a cash value life insurance contract, the cash value of which was $50,000. The plan was noncontributory and Haines reported a total of $8,000 of insurance costs in his income tax returns during his lifetime as a result of the plan's insurance coverage. The taxable amount of this distribution to the beneficiary is the total distribution of $100,000, less the following:

> The pure insurance amount ($100,000 minus the cash value of $50,000),
> the $5,000 employee death benefit exclusion, and
> Haines's cost basis—in this case, only the $8,000 of insurance cost reported during his lifetime.

The taxable amount, therefore, is $37,000. This amount is taxable income to the beneficiary, subject to the special five-year averaging and capital gain provisions described above.

Excess Distribution Tax

There is a penalty tax of 15 percent, in addition to the regular income tax, on the taxable amount of a distribution that exceeds $112,500 annually (as adjusted in certain cases). Since this affects primarily highly compensated plan participants, it is discussed in detail in Chapter 18.

Federal Estate Tax

The federal estate tax on qualified plan death benefits affects only highly compensated participants (those with a gross estate of at least $600,000) and is discussed further in Chapter 18. There is also an *excess accumulation* tax of 15 percent imposed on estates that is the counterpart of the excess distribution tax.

Qualified Domestic Relations Orders

For many years after the passage in 1974 of the nonalienation rules of Code Section 401(a)(13) (discussed earlier), the state and federal courts were besieged by estranged spouses seeking to reach pension funds to pay alimony and child support. Since there was obvious justice to many of these claims, the courts and the IRS relented somewhat from a strict interpretation of the nonalienation provision, but the law remained unclear in domestic situations. Finally, in 1984, the Code was amended to deal specifically with assignment of qualified plan benefits in domestic situations.

Under current law, the prohibition against nonalienation of benefits does not apply to an assignment of a benefit under a *qualified domestic relations order* (QDRO). Under Code Section 414(p), a QDRO is a decree, order, or property settlement under state law relating to child support, alimony, or marital property rights that assigns a participant's plan benefits to a spouse, former spouse, child, or other dependent of the participant. Currently, therefore, a participant's plan benefits generally become the subject of negotiation in domestic disputes. The pension law itself does not indicate how such benefits are to be divided; this is still a matter of state domestic relations law. The QDRO provision simply provides a means by which state court orders in domestic relations issues can be enforced against plan trustees.

To protect plan administrators and trustees from conflicting claims, a qualified domestic relation order cannot assign a benefit that the plan does not provide. Also, a QDRO cannot assign a benefit that is already assigned under a previous order.

If, under the plan, a participant has no right to an immediate cash payment from the plan, a QDRO cannot require the trustees to make such a cash payment. If a cash settlement is desired, the parties will generally agree to allow the participant to keep the entire plan benefit and pay compensating cash to the nonparticipant spouse. However, if this is not possible, QDROs have been used to segregate plan assets into a subtrust for the benefit of the spouse making the claim, with cash distributions to be made at the earliest time they would be permitted under the plan provisions.

Loans from Qualified Plans

The law permits loans, within limits, to participants in regular qualified plans and Section 403(b) tax-deferred annuity plans. (The latter plans are discussed in Chapter 23.) However, a participant cannot borrow from a plan unless the plan document specifically permits loans, and, as discussed below, loan provisions may not be appropriate for all plans. Loans from IRAs and SEPs (Chapter 22) are not permitted—that is, they are treated as taxable distributions and may be subject to penalties for premature distribution. Also, loans from a qualified plan to an owner/employee (a proprietor or more than 10 percent partner in an unincorporated business) or to an employee of an S corporation who is more than 5 percent shareholder in the corporation are prohibited transactions subject to the prohibited transaction penalties described in Chapter 17.

Limits on Loan Amount

Under Code Section 72(p), loans will be recognized as loans (rather than taxable current distributions) only to the extent that the loan, together with all other outstanding loans, does not exceed the lesser of

- $50,000 reduced by the highest outstanding loan balance during the preceding one-year period, or
- one half of the present value of the vested accrued benefit of the employee under the plan.

A loan up to $10,000 may be made, even if this is more than one half of the present value of the employee's vested accrued benefit. Some examples:

Vested Accrued Benefit	Maximum Aggregate Loans
$120,000	$50,000
40,000	20,000
15,000	10,000

Terms of Loans

To obtain loan treatment, the loan must be repayable by its terms within five years. The rule noted above for reducing the $50,000 limit by the loan balance in the preceding year was designed to prevent avoidance of the five-year limit by simply repaying then immediately reborrowing the same amount every five years. The five-year requirement does not apply to any loan used to acquire a principal residence of the participant.

Transactions with an effect similar to that of loans (e.g., the pledging of an interest in a qualified plan or a loan made against an insurance contract purchased by a qualified plan) are also covered by the loan limitations and rules.

If the plan permits loans, they must be made available on a nondiscriminatory basis. Also, the loans must be adequately secured and bear a reasonable rate of interest. Usually, the security for a plan loan is simply the participant's vested accrued plan benefit. Interest on the loan is consumer interest that is generally not deductible as an itemized deduction unless secured by a home mortgage. However, if the loan is to a key employee as defined in the top-heavy rules (Chapter 18) or is secured by 401(k) or 403(b) elective deferrals, interest is not deductible in any event.

Any loan that does not meet these requirements will be treated as a current distribution and may be currently taxable to the employee when received.

Should the Plan Permit Loans?

Whether the plan should permit loans depends on the employer's objectives for the plan. Plan loan provisions often are desired by the controlling employees of closely held businesses, because a plan loan provides the advantage of tax sheltering the plan funds without losing control of the cash. However, the same considerations may make plan loans desirable for regular employees as well. A disadvantage of plan loans is that, if they are too extensively utilized, they deplete the plan funds available for investment. More fundamentally, however, plan loan provisions are inconsistent with a primary plan objective of providing retirement security. Thus, they are less common in pension plans than in profit-sharing plans. Plan loan provisions are particularly uncommon in defined-benefit plans, because such plans have no individual participant accounts, and it is complicated to convert a participant's vested accrued benefit to a cash equivalent at a given time to determine the amount of loan that can be allowed.

Summary

Qualified plan distribution provisions are designed to meet employer compensation planning objectives or to provide planning flexibility for the employee. In addition to the required joint and survivor and survivorship annuity provisions, plans often offer alternative-annuity or lump-sum forms. However, the law imposes complex restrictions on the types of distributions that are permitted. In particular, there are minimum distribution requirements and rules limiting incidental death benefits. A 10 percent penalty on early distributions also affects distribution planning.

Plan distributions are subject to special, generally favorable, tax provisions. For annuity distributions, an exclusion ratio calculation allows recovery of any nontaxable basis, while, for certain eligible lump-sum distributions, a five-year averaging tax calculation can be elected once after age 59½. However, a 15 percent excess distribution penalty may apply on distributions to highly compensated participants.

Plan loans to participants can be a significant employee benefit. Loans are subject to limits, with a maximum of $50,000, a five-year repayment requirement, and must bear reasonable interest and be adequately secured.

Although plan benefits generally cannot be assigned or alienated, an important exception applies in domestic relations disputes. A qualified domestic relations order (QDRO) issued by a local court under state law relating to child support, alimony, or marital property rights allows assignment of plan benefits to an alternative payee.

17

Plan Investments

Objectives of This Chapter
- *Describe the fiduciary requirements of ERISA and the Code.*
- *Describe the prohibited transaction rules.*
- *Explain how taxable unrelated business income can arise in a qualified plan fund.*
- *Describe some investment vehicles that can be used in trusteed plans and how they are used in connection with investment strategies.*
- *Discuss the basic elements in investment strategy.*
- *Discuss the role of social investing in overall investment strategy.*

● Investment issues may be more important to a plan sponsor than other aspects of the plan. In large defined-benefit plans particularly, the investment performance significantly affects the employer's expense and financial picture. Good investment performance is also important to plan participants, especially those in defined-contribution plans where plan account balances directly reflect investment results.

This chapter will discuss the underlying legal background against which investment issues arise—the fiduciary and related rules of ERISA and the Internal Revenue Code. Investment strategies and specific investment issues are then covered.

Fiduciary Requirements of ERISA and the Internal Revenue Code

A relationship in which one person holds and administers money belonging to another is legally described as a *fiduciary* relationship. A funded employee-benefit plan, therefore, involves fiduciary relationships—plan assets are held by a trustee or insurance company, under the direction of the employer, on behalf of plan participants and beneficiaries. The rules governing fiduciary relationships are generally a subject of state law; however, in the case of qualified plans and other employee-benefit plans, federal law (primarily ERISA) has superimposed specific federal fiduciary requirements that supersede state law where applicable. The federal requirements are usually stricter than the superseded state law requirements. While these rules are applicable to most employee-benefit plans, they have their greatest impact on qualified pension and profit-sharing plans, because the other plans to which they technically apply—welfare-benefit plans—are typically insured or unfunded.

ERISA's fiduciary requirements were not intended as a helpful guide for employers and trustees in administering qualified plans. They do not spell out the specific responsibilities of each person involved in designing and maintaining the plan. Rather, the rules are intended to spread a net of liability over various persons involved with the plan, aimed at maximizing the protection of participants and beneficiaries. Thus, there are not always simple rules about how employers, trustees, and other persons should act on qualified plans; rather, they must be aware of their fiduciary responsibilities and do their best to comply with them or avoid them.

The fiduciary responsibility net is very broad; it includes any person who (ERISA Section 3(21)):

- Exercises any discretionary authority or discretionary control with respect to the management of the plan or exercises any authority or control with respect to the management or disposition of plan assets;
- renders investment advice for a fee or other compensation, direct or indirect, with respect to any plan asset, or has any authority or responsibility to do so; or
- has discretionary authority or discretionary responsibility in the administration of the plan.

This definition of fiduciary certainly includes the employer, the plan administrator, and the trustee. It also includes a wide variety of other possible targets. However, the government has stated that an attorney, accountant, actuary, or consultant who renders legal, accounting, actuarial, or consulting services to the plan will not be considered a fiduciary soley as a result of performing those services. Also, labor regulations exclude broker/dealers, banks, and reporting dealers from being treated as fiduciaries simply as a result of receiving and executing buy-sell instructions from the plan. Furthermore, a person giving investment advice will be considered a fiduciary only with respect to the assets covered by that investment advice.

Every plan must specify a "named fiduciary" in the plan document. The purpose of this requirement is not to limit liability to named persons; rather it is to provide participants and the government with an easy target in case they decide to take legal action against the plan. Other unnamed fiduciaries can also be included in the legal action, of course.

The *duties* of fiduciaries specified in the law are primarily of an investment nature; a fiduciary must (ERISA Section 404):

- Discharge duties with respect to a plan solely in the interest of the participants and the beneficiaries;

(2) act for the exclusive purpose of providing benefits to participants and their beneficiaries, and defraying the reasonable expenses of administering the plan;

(3) act with the care, skill, prudence, and diligence under the circumstances that prevail that a prudent man acting in a like capacity and familiar with such matters would use in the conduct of an enterprise of a like character and with like aims;

(4) diversify the investments of the plan to minimize the risk of large losses, unless under the circumstances it is clearly prudent not to do so;

(5) follow the provisions of the documents and instruments governing the plan, unless inconsistent with ERISA provisions.

In interpreting the "prudent man" requirement, labor regulations indicate that the fiduciary, in making an investment, must determine that the particular investment is reasonably designed as part of the plan's portfolio to further the purposes of the plan, and must consider: (1) the composition of the portfolio with regard to diversification, (2) the liquidity and current return of the portfolio relative to the anticipated cash flow requirements of the plan, and (3) the projected return of the portfolio relative to the funding objectives of the plan.

A major exception to the diversification requirement applies to holdings of employer securities and employer real property. An eligible individual account plan (a profit-sharing, stock-bonus, or employee stock-ownership plan that specifically permits the holding of *employer real property* or *qualifying employer securities*) may hold such property in any amount—and may even hold such property as the exclusive assets of the plan. Other plans can hold such property only up to the extent of 10 percent of the fair market value of the plan assets. The purpose of this exception, of course, is to encourage the adoption of employer stock plans of the type discussed in Chapter 15. A qualifying employer security means employer stock or marketable debt obligations meeting various ERISA requirements (ERISA Section 407). Employer real property is basically real property owned by the plan and leased to the employer, again under limitations set out in Section 407 of ERISA.

The purpose for including employer real property along with employer securities reflects a view that employer real property can serve the same function as a holding of employer securities, and it also reflects the fact that, prior to ERISA, many employers used qualified plans as a means of financing acquisitions of real property.

Fiduciaries can delegate fiduciary responsibilities and, therefore, avoid direct responsibility for performing the duty delegated. For example, the employer can delegate duties relating to the handling and investment of plan assets to a trustee, and the investment management duties can be delegated to an appointed investment manager. The plan must provide a definite procedure for delegating these duties. The delegation of a fiduciary duty does not remove all fiduciary responsibility; a fiduciary will be liable for a breach of fiduciary responsibility of any other fiduciary under the following circumstances (ERISA Section 405):

If he participates knowingly in, or knowingly undertakes to conceal, an act or omission of another fiduciary knowing such act or omission is a breach;

if he fails to comply with fiduciary duties in the administration of his specific responsibilities that give rise to his status as a fiduciary and, therefore, enables another fiduciary to commit a breach; or

if he has knowledge of a breach by another fiduciary, unless he makes reasonable efforts under the circumstances to remedy the breach.

The broad scope of the fiduciary liabilities indicates that, in addition to careful delegation of fiduciary duties to well-chosen trustees and advisors, the employer should take care that its liability insurance coverage adequately covers any liabilities that might arise out of the fiduciary responsibility provisions. ERISA specifically prohibits a plan from excusing or exculpating any person from fiduciary liability, but individuals and employers are permitted to have appropriate insurance, and employers can indemnify (agree to reimburse) plan fiduciaries for losses they might incur as a result of fiduciary duties.

Prohibited Transactions

In addition to the general fiduciary requirements described above, both the Code (Section 4975) and ERISA (Section 406) include a specific list of "don'ts" for employee-benefit plans, including qualified plans. Under these rules, a party-in-interest is forbidden from any of the following, with a number of exceptions described later:

Sale or exchange, or leasing, of any property between the plan and a party-in-interest;

lending of money or other extension of credit between the plan and a party-in-interest;

furnishing of goods, services, or facilities between the plan and a party-in-interest;

transfer to, or use by or for the benefit of, a party-in-interest, of any assets of the plan; or

acquisition, on behalf of the plan, of any employer security or employer real property in excess of the limits described previously in this chapter.

A *party-in-interest* (the Code uses, instead, the term *disqualified person*) is defined very broadly, again to bring the largest possible number of persons into the net to provide the maximum protection for plan participants. A party-in-interest includes:

Any fiduciary, counsel, or employee of the plan.

A person providing services to the plan.

An employer, if any of its employees are covered by the plan.

An employee organization, any of whose members are covered by the plan.

An owner, direct or indirect, of a 50 percent or more interest in an employer or employee organization described above.

Various individuals and organizations related to those on the above list, under specific rules given in Code Section 4975 and ERISA Section 406.

Because of the breadth of the prohibited transaction rules, certain specific exclusions are provided in the law, and the IRS and Labor Department are also given the authority to waive the prohibited transaction rules in certain circumstances.

First, the specific statutory exemptions. Loans to participants or beneficiaries are permitted under the rules discussed in Chapter 16. A loan to an ESOP by a party-in-interest is also permitted under certain circumstances to permit the ESOP to function, as described in Chapter 15. Similar provisions permit such a plan to acquire employer securities or real property without violating the prohibited transaction rules. Also, the plan is allowed to pay a reasonable fee for legal, accounting, or other services performed by a party-in-interest. There are provisions permitting various financial services to the plan by a bank or insurance company that is a party-in-interest. Other provisions exempt normal benefit distributions from any possible conflict with the prohibited transaction rules.

In addition to the specific statutory exemptions, the Department of Labor has broad authority to grant an exemption to the prohibited transaction rules for a transaction or a class of transactions after finding that the exemption is administratively feasible, in the interest of the plan and its participants and beneficiaries, and protective of their rights. There are specific administrative procedures for obtaining such exemptions. Pursuant to this authority, the Labor Department has granted, among others, a class exemption permitting the sale of life insurance policies by participants to the plan or by the plan to participants. Individual exemptions have been granted for a variety of transactions, usually involving a sale to the plan by a party-in-interest of property that represents a particularly favorable investment opportunity for the plan.

Penalties. A violation of the prohibited transaction rules can result in a two-step penalty under the Internal Revenue Code, with the initial penalty equal to 5 percent of the amount involved and an additional 100 percent penalty if the transaction is not corrected within a certain time. A violation of the prohibited transaction rules also can result in penalties for breach of fiduciary liability.

Unrelated Business Income

The trust fund under a qualified plan has a broad exemption from federal income tax similar to that granted to a variety of other institutions and organizations, such as churches, schools, charities, and the like. However, all these tax-exempt organizations are subject to federal income tax on *unrelated business-taxable income* (Code Sections 511–514). Unrelated business-taxable income is income of a tax-exempt organization from a trade or business that is not related to the function that is the basis for the tax exemption. For example, if a charitable organization operates a full-time shoe store in a shopping center, the shoe store income would be taxable to the charity; however, the charity's tax exemption for its other income probably would not be jeopardized unless the effect of operating the shoe store was to shift the focus of the organization totally away from its exempt function.

The basic function of an employee-benefit plan trust is to receive, invest, and distribute plan funds to participants and beneficiaries. Thus, passive investment income of the plan trust is usually not unrelated business income unless the investment is debt-financed, as described in the next paragraph. Problems sometimes arise in distinguishing passive investments from activities that might be considered a trade or business. The law specifically exempts dividends, interest, annuities, and royalties, as well as rents from real property and from personal property leased with real property. However, the wide variety of possible leasing arrangements indicates that each rental arrangement must be looked at on the basis of its own facts and circumstances. For example, a Revenue Ruling held that investments in railroad equipment for leasing constituted an unrelated trade or business, even though such leasing arrangements are usually looked upon by investors as strictly investment activities.[1] Another Revenue Ruling, however, allowed a qualified plan trust to hold shares in a real estate investment trust without incurring unrelated business-taxable income.[2] In short, the possible impact of unrelated business-taxable income is an additional factor that must be taken into account by the investment advisers of a benefit plan trust.

Section 514 of the Code (Section 514) specifies that income from *debt-financed property* is to be treated by a tax-exempt organization as unrelated business-taxable income. There is, however, an exception in Section 514(c)(9) for qualified plans holding certain real estate investments that typically are highly leveraged or debt-financed. Therefore, such investments may still be advantageous to a qualified plan, particularly if they provide long-term growth or other benefits.

Investment Policy

Like all investors, a qualified plan investment adviser or asset manager seeks certain objectives, which depend on the interests of plan participants and beneficiaries as well as those of the sponsoring organization. Some specific investment objectives that make up the parts of an overall investment strategy are: high rate of return, safety of principal, and adequate liquidity.

The pursuit of one of these objectives often will be inconsistent with another; therefore, an overall investment strategy has to strike a balance among them.

Investment Vehicles

The limits set by ERISA allow a qualified plan trustee to invest in a wide range of investment vehicles. Most state laws governing trusts set limits on the types of investments fiduciaries may use in the absence of a specific trust agreement, but allow a trust agreement to expand the permitted category. Qualified plan trust agreements generally are drafted to permit considerable investment flexibility.

---

[1] Rev. Rul. 60–206, 1960–1 C.B. 207.
[2] Rev. Rul. 66–106, 1066–1 C.B. 151.

The most important investment vehicles, and their relation to the objectives listed above, will be briefly discussed here.

Common Stocks. Historically, common stocks have offered a high rate of return, with a relatively larger risk, more so than other investments, although obviously some stocks are much riskier than others. Common stocks can help preserve principal, in that over the long run their value tends to grow as fast as inflation. However, this growth is not always experienced in the short term—for example, throughout most of the 1970s, stock values declined in real terms. Common stocks traded on a stock market provide considerable liquidity and a readily determined market value.

Short-Term Debt. Short-term debt instruments are generally considered to be those maturing in less than a year. Some common short-term instruments include certificates of deposit issued by U.S. or foreign banks, short-term obligations of corporations (commercial paper), and U.S. Treasury bills with 90-day or six-month terms. Such instruments offer significant liquidity, together with a rate of return that is often very high, corresponding to current interest rates in periods when these rates are high—but with correspondingly low rates of return when interest rates decline. The risk involved in such instruments depends on the debtor, but can often be low, particularly for government securities.

Long-Term Debt. Intermediate and long-term bonds and other debt instruments have maturity dates extending from several years to as much as 15 or more years. Corporate bonds are traded on securities exchanges in the same manner as common stocks. The federal government also issues long-term securities. In the long run, long-term securities generally offer higher rates of return than short-term securities, in return for somewhat greater risk. However, U.S. Treasury securities can provide significant returns with relatively little risk. Long-term instruments are not necessarily illiquid, if they can be sold easily on an exchange.

Real Estate. Real estate investments potentially offer a high rate of return. Qualified plans often invest not only in real estate but also in mortgages secured by real estate. Even leveraged real estate investments are possible, because of exemptions from the unrelated business income tax (discussed above). However, because the qualified plan is tax exempt, it gets no benefit from the deduction of interest payments, so leveraged investments must be analyzed somewhat differently than for a taxable investor. Much of the risk typically associated with real estate investments can be reduced by participating in real estate syndications, where the investor owns only a portion of each individual property. Knowledge of the market is essential in real estate investments.

Equipment Leasing. Equipment leasing has been an attractive investment to private investors, because of the available tax benefits; these are less important to a tax-exempt organization. However, the rate of return on equipment leasing can often be very high and, therefore, such investments may be attractive even without tax benefits. As discussed earlier, it may be necessary to obtain a ruling from the IRS to avoid unrelated business income tax in these situations.

Other Investments. Depending on the economic climate, many types of investments are momentarily attractive—for example, gold, antiques, and other collectibles. Such investments are permitted for qualified plans, except for individual account plans with investment direction, as discussed in Chapter 13.

Qualified plans can also make use of investment vehicles, such as options, commodity futures, puts and calls, and other vehicles typically associated with stock market players. These instruments generally do not play a large part in qualified plan investment strategy, but they may be useful for specific needs.

Investment Mix for Private Trusteed Plans. Overall, assets of private trusteed plans were invested as follows:

Equities (primarily common stocks)	35–40%
Bonds (long-term debt)	20
Cash items	5–10
Other (real estate, mortgages, and so on)	35

This investment mix has been relatively stable from about 1981–1985.[3] These are overall figures; there are some differences in asset mix among types of plans. For example, single-employer plans tend to be more heavily invested in equities, while multiemployer plans lean more toward bonds. Defined-benefit plans tend to invest less in cash items than do defined-contribution plans.

Investment Strategy

The policy baseline for the investment of qualified plan funds is set by the ERISA rules discussed above—the exclusive-benefit rule, the prudent expert rule, the diversification requirement, liquidity requirements, the plan document itself, and the additional limitations imposed by the prohibited transaction and unrelated business income provisions. Within these constraints, however, a broad range of investment strategies is possible.

ERISA Section 402 requires every qualified plan to adopt a "funding policy and method consistent with the objectives of the plan." In practice, plan administrators usually adopt a very general written statement to meet this statutory requirement, leaving specific investment strategies to the discretion of the employer or the fund manager.

Growth-Oriented Strategies. Trustees governed by fiduciary rules aimed primarily at the preservation of principal generally do not follow aggressive, growth-oriented investment strategies—and pension trustees are no exception. However, qualified plan design offers a number of opportunities for incorporating

---

[3] *EBRI News*, November 13, 1986 (Washington, D.C.: Employee Benefit Research Institute).

growth-oriented investment strategies without running into fiduciary problems. Investment in common stocks, for example, is permissible and widespread, as well as investment in various types of pooled equity funds maintained by insurance or investment companies.

Defined-contribution plans can provide that part or all of each participant's account be put in a participant-directed account, with the participant then choosing the investment strategy and relieving the trustee of liability for that choice. Also, defined-contribution plan funds can be invested in bank or insurance company pooled accounts that offer participants choices of investment strategies—an equity fund, a fixed-income fund, and so on.

For defined-benefit plans, there is no provision for participant direction of investment; however, as discussed in Chapter 12, defined-benefit plan funds can be invested in insurance company funds utilizing "separate account" funding, with a choice (by the employer) of investment strategies, such as equity, fixed income, and so on. There is also the possibility of structuring the trust agreement to allow the employer to recommend investments, and the employer can pursue a growth-oriented strategy. In such a case, of course, the employer is still responsible for the adequacy of the pension fund and is subject to full fiduciary liability for its investment recommendations. Finally, there is the possibility of designing a plan to invest primarily in employer securities, which can be viewed as a type of growth-oriented investment strategy.

Risk. Most of the ERISA investment rules can be seen as prescriptions for avoiding risk, particularly the risk of large losses; for example, the requirement for diversification of investments. Within the ERISA limits, however, like any investor, the qualified plan investment manager must balance risk and return.

Social Effects. At the end of 1985, private pension funds in the United States totaled about $1.3 trillion, with government-employee funds comprising an additional $400 billion.[4] This is a sizable portion of the nation's capital. If there is any pattern to the investment strategies of qualified plan investment managers, therefore, such a pattern is likely to have an effect on the economy and on society. Because so much pension money is held and invested by large institutions, such as banks and insurance companies, current pension investment policies largely reflect the views of these organizations. In general, such organizations will tend to invest in conventional ways that support the status quo. The question is often raised whether there is a role in pension investing for active attempts to support a particular social result not dictated merely by market conditions.

Existing legislation and other law relating to qualified plan investments focuses primarily on fiduciary aspects of the relationship between plan managers and participants; it does not address issues of social policy. That is, it encourages investment managers to invest and thus prevent direct losses to participants and

---

[4]Employee Benefit Notes, November 1986 (Washington, D.C.: Employee Benefit Research Institute).

beneficiaries, but it does not deal with possible indirect losses that may accrue to participants and beneficiaries as a result of trends in overall pension investment policy that may be contrary to the social and economic interests of plan participants.

Social Investing. In recent years, objections to prevailing pension investment policies have been raised, particularly on behalf of unionized employees in large manufacturing industries. Although these objections are not always clearly stated, four types of arguments can be distinguished. First, it is stated that the usual pension investment policies contribute to the disinvestment in basic manufacturing industries that is now occurring, particularly in certain geographical areas, such as the Midwest. This results in the loss of jobs for persons covered under the pension plans, with the attendant economic and social costs, and also in disinvestment in housing and other facilities in communities where plan participants live. Second, it is stated that pension investors can undercut the union movement by investing in nonunionized corporations. Third, pension investment policies allegedly can affect the welfare of workers adversely by investing in corporations that violate health, safety, or nondiscrimination principles. Finally, objection is made to investment in corporations whose actions are disapproved on moral or political grounds (not directly related to the interest of plan participants), such as environmental pollution, involvement in South Africa, or weapons production. Although advocates of social investment for union pension funds sometimes make common cause with religious and academic groups that advocate social investment policies for church or university endowment funds, it is clear that on this issue the interests of unionized employees are quite distinct.

A decision by a pension investment manager to pursue a social investment strategy that attempts to avoid one or more of these objections raises a number of issues. The first relates to fiduciary responsibility. Does a social investment strategy result in a lower return on the fund? There are some studies indicating that an investment portfolio of "good guy" investments has a lower return. However, such studies usually choose the "good" investments using a broad range of criteria, so they do not indicate the effects of narrower targeting, such as simply excluding nonunion employers. The "efficient markets" theory proposed by some economists would suggest that, in the long run, an investment strategy based on social investing should have no effect on investment return, as long as investments are sufficiently diversified and the market includes other investors who do not use the same social criteria.

Some social investment advocates suggest that, even if the return is lower, the indirect social and economic benefits to plan participants are a compensating factor. However, under current fiduciary law, both state and federal, this argument probably could not protect an investment manager in the event of a lawsuit by a plan participant injured directly by a low return on the fund. Suggestions have been made in Congress to amend federal legislation to permit social investment of various types, but no such provision has yet been enacted. The Department of Labor is reportedly studying the issue, but no regulations or rulings in this area have been issued.

A second problem is, assuming a social investment strategy has been chosen, how does the investment manager evaluate possible investments to determine their compliance with the chosen social criteria? Currently, it is difficult to identify corporations that meet even such simple criteria as compliance with health and safety legislation. Various social investment indices are available, but these are generally inadequate as guidance in any specific program of social investing. Because of these difficulties, social investing usually involves additional administrative costs.

The pension investment community has generally reacted with some hostility to social investing, with most pension advisers taking the view that any considerations other than the tradition ones of risk and return have no part in pension investment decisions, and that it would be violation of fiduciary responsibility to use other criteria.

Summary

ERISA's fiduciary requirements are imposed on a broad group of persons. They mandate a prudent-man investment approach, investment diversification, and investing in the sole interest of plan participants and beneficiaries. Fiduciaries can be sued by plan participants and beneficiaries in federal court for breaching these duties. The law also includes specific prohibited transactions subject to penalty.

Another legal limitation on investment strategy is the unrelated business income tax imposed on business (as opposed to investment) income earned by a tax-exempt trust.

Qualified plan investment policy and strategies must balance return, principal safety, and liquidity, within the limits set by the fiduciary rules and the unrelated business income tax. Typically, qualified plans invest in a mix of common stocks, long-term debt, short-term debt, and cash-type investments, as well as other investments, such as real estate. Certain specific types of plan design and investment strategy can be adopted to meet specific emphases, such as principal growth. Attention also has recently been focused on the social effects of pension investing and the possibility of influencing social goals through investment strategy.

18

Plan Restrictions Aimed at Highly Compensated Employees

Objectives of This Chapter
- Discuss the limitations on annual benefits or contributions of Code Section 415.
- Analyze the restrictions on combinations of defined-benefit and defined-contribution plans, including the tax-deduction limit.
- Describe the limitations on top-heavy plans.
- Discuss the special provisions for owners of unincorporated businesses who are covered under a qualified plan.
- Describe the limit on benefits from terminated plans applicable to an employer's 25 highest-paid employees.
- Discuss the federal estate tax applicable to qualified plan benefits.
- Discuss the excess distribution and excess accumulation penalty taxes.

Significance of the Restrictions Discussed Here

Congress and the IRS have long been convinced that the tax benefits for qualified plans can be abused by plans that confer most of their benefits on highly paid key employees, typically employees who are stockholders or partners in a closely held business. Such plans are inconsistent with the social policy behind the qualified plan provisions, as discussed in Chapter 4. Therefore, the law contains a variety of provisions particularly aimed at this type of abuse. The provisions discussed in this chapter will have little actual effect on plans typically designed for larger employers. However, these rules technically apply to *all* plans and, thus, they must be considered at least in drafting every plan.

There is a large community of pension planners who specialize in designing plans to avoid the provisions discussed in this chapter, so from time to time Congress and the IRS add new rules to close various "loopholes" that plan designers have found. Thus, the provisions discussed here have become the most complex in the entire pension law.

Limitations on Individual Benefits or Annual Additions (Section 415 Limits)

Section 415 of the Internal Revenue Code contains limitations on the amount of benefit or annual account additions that any participant can receive under a qualified plan. These limitations are intended to prevent the qualified plan from being used as an individual tax-sheltering device beyond any reasonable need for retirement savings. They have their greatest impact in planning for small businesses where one or more of the business owners are plan participants. However, the limitations also can have an impact on larger plans that cover high-salaried executives. There are two types of Section 415 limits—one for defined-benefit plans and one for defined-contribution plans.

Defined-Benefit Plans

For defined-benefit plans, the applicable limitation restricts the amount of *benefit* that any individual can receive. Basically, the plan cannot permit a benefit at age 65 (or the social security retirement age, if later) that exceeds the lesser of 100 percent of the participant's compensation averaged over the three years of highest compensation, or $90,000 annually. A pension of up to $10,000 annually can be paid even if it exceeds the 100 percent limit, but this $10,000 floor applies only if the participant has never been covered by a defined-*contribution* plan.

The benefit limit of Section 415 applies to employer-provided benefits only. If the plan provides for employee contributions (which is relatively rare in defined-benefit plans) these employee contributions can be used to increase benefits above the Section 415 limit.

The limits as stated above apply to a benefit in the form of either a straight-life annuity or a qualified joint-and-survivor annuity. However, the limits must be adjusted actuarially if the normal retirement benefit is something else—for example, a 10-year period-certain annuity. No adjustment is made for preretirement death or disability benefits. Also, there is an increase in the limit in the event of late retirement. Table 18–1 indicates the actuarial adjustments required for various benefit forms.

The dollar limit in the Section 415 limitation has been subject to considerable fluctuation since it was originally established in 1974 at $75,000. As a result of cost-of-living indexing, the limit had risen to $136,425 by 1982, but under the Tax Equity and Fiscal Responsibility Act of 1982 (TEFRA) it was cut back to $90,000; see Table 18–3. (TEFRA did not require a cutback in accrued benefits above the current $90,000 limits, if they were accrued prior to the effective date of the lower limit.) After 1987, the $90,000 limit is to be adjusted under a formula based on social security benefit amounts then in effect, a formula that will probably produce a lesser annual increase than the pre-1983 formula.

The $90,000 limit is adjusted actuarially for retirement ages earlier or later than the social security retirement age. This prevents acceleration of the funding (and tax deductions) simply by choosing a normal retirement age earlier than 65. The limit also is increased actuarially for retirement later than the social security

TABLE 18–1. Section 415 Limits-Reduction Factors for Defined-Benefit Plans

Normal Form of Plan Benefit	Reduction Percentage	Dollar Limit/ Percent Limit
Straight-life annuity	0	$90,000/100%
Life annuity—5-year certain	3	87,300/ 97
Life annuity—10-year certain	10	81,000/ 90
Life annuity—15-year certain	20	72,000/ 80
Life annuity—20-year certain	30	63,000/ 70
Life annuity—installment refund	10	81,000/ 90
Life annuity—cash refund	15	76,500/ 85

Where the normal form of retirement benefit is a joint and 50 percent survivor annuity, no reduction is required. Also, a reduction is not required for preretirement death or disability benefits.

retirement age. Table 18–2 illustrates the adjustments for a participant born before 1938 whose social security retirement age is 65.

As indicated above, the Section 415 benefit limitation must be part of every qualified plan document. The plan language, therefore, must prohibit the accrual of any benefit in excess of the limit. For any given employee, however, except an employee who is contemplating retirement in the current plan year, it is impossible to know what the applicable dollar limitation under Section 415 will be in the year of retirement. Nevertheless, the IRS does not allow benefits to be accrued in excess of the Section 415 limits based on current compensation and the current dollar limit, even for a participant far from retirement.

TABLE 18–2

Retirement Age	Maximum Dollar Benefit
55	$ 42,400
60	61,419
62	72,000
65	90,000
70	155,843

Assumptions: 1971 Group Annuity (Male) Table with interest at 5 percent, life annuity. Rev. Rul. 80–253 indicates what assumptions will be considered reasonable for this purpose. For the actuarial increase after age 65, under code Section 415(b)(2)(E)(ii), the interest rate assumption cannot be greater than the lesser of 5 percent or the plan's actuarial interest rate assumption.

Example

The Framp Company plan covers two participants, George Framp, aged 40, who currently earns $200,000 annually, and Fred Lump, aged 55, who currently earns $30,000 annually. The plan formula provides for a benefit equal to 50 percent of each participant's final average compensation averaged over five years, (subject of course to the Section 415 limitation).

For purposes of determining plan funding, the actuary must determine the amount of each participant's accrued benefit for 1987. George's projected benefit on the basis of his current salary is $100,000. However, for the purposes of funding George's benefit, the actuary cannot project a benefit greater than $90,000 annually, the applicable Section 415 limit in 1987, even though it is likely that the limit will be significantly higher 25 years from now when George retires. Fred's benefit is not affected by the Section 415 limit, because the plan's benefit of 50 percent of final average compensation (a projected benefit of $15,000 annually for him) does not bump into the Section 415 limit.

Defined-Contribution Plans

For a defined-contribution plan, the Section 415 limitation is a restriction not on the benefit but on the *annual addition* to each participant's account. The annual addition cannot exceed the lesser of 25 percent of the participant's annual compensation, or $30,000. Like the dollar limit for defined-benefit plans, the $30,000 limit has been frozen through 1987, after which it will be adjusted when the adjusted benefit-defined limit reaches $120,000; the defined-contribution limit thereafter will be set at one fourth the defined-benefit limit; see Table 18–3.

TABLE 18–3

Year	Defined-Contribution Limit	Defined-Benefit Limit
1975*	$25,000*	$ 75,000
1976	26,825	80,475
1977	28,175	84,525
1978	30,050	90,150
1979	32,700	98,100
1980	36,875	110,625
1981	41,500	124,500
1982	45,475	136,425
1983–87	30,000	90,000

*For years prior to 1975 (used in computing the defined-contribution fraction in the combined limit), $25,000 is used.

The annual addition to each participant's account includes three elements:

Employer contributions including employee salary reductions, reallocated forfeitures from other participants' accounts, and nondeductible employee contributions.

The following example shows how the annual additions limit will affect a participant's account in a hypothetical plan. In the example, a forfeiture amount is available that is allocated to the employee's account in proportion to compensation.

Employee Compensation	Maximum Annual Addition	Forfeiture Allocated	Maximum Employer Contribution
$ 20,000	$ 5,000	$ 2,000	$ 3,000
50,000	12,500	5,000	7,500
100,000	25,000	10,000	15,000
200,000	30,000	20,000	10,000

It is important to note that both of the Section 415 limitations apply to individual participants, not to the plan as a whole. Also, it should be noted that the annual addition limit is not a limit on the amount that the employer can deduct for income tax purposes. The deduction limits on a separate set of rules from the Section 415 limits and the two items should not be confused. However, no deduction can ever be taken for an employer contribution that causes an employee's benefit or account to exceed the Section 415 limit.

Combined Limit

Often it is good retirement planning to have both a defined-contribution and a defined-benefit plan covering the same employee, since the different advantages of the two approaches can thereby be combined. If each of the Section 415 limitations were applied separately in this case, the amount of tax benefit to the participant would be far above that available through only one type of plan. Therefore, Section 415 contains special limitations that apply to a participant who is covered under a defined-benefit plan and a defined-contribution plan of the same employer. The purpose of this limitation is to scale back the benefit so that the overall intention of Section 415 is carried out. Even with the combined limit, however, it still is possible for an individual participant to obtain somewhat more tax benefit through a combination of the two plans than would be available through only one type of plan.

The combined rule can be summarized as follows. Two fractions are determined—the *defined-benefit fraction* and the *defined-contribution fraction*. Each fraction more or less represents the benefit or contribution level the participant actually receives in each plan, compared with the maximum amount available in each plan separately. Then, the rule further provides that, where an individual is a participant in both a defined-benefit plan and a defined-contribution plan maintained by the same employer, the *sum of the defined-benefit fraction and the defined-contribution fraction for any year may not exceed one*—that is

$$\text{D.B. fraction} + \text{D.C. fraction} = 1$$

Here is the detailed definition of the fractions:

Defined-Benefit Fraction. *Numerator:* projected annual benefit of the participant under the plan (determined as of the close of the year). *Denominator:* lesser of 125 percent of the maximum dollar limit for the year or 140 percent of average compensation for the three consecutive highest-paid years.

Defined-Contribution Fraction. *Numerator:* total annual additions to the participant's account from the plan's inception to the close of the year. *Denominator:* sum for all years of participation of the lesser of 125 percent of maximum dollar limit for the year (see Table 18–3) or 140 percent of 25 percent of compensation for the year.

The combined limit was changed in 1982, and there are complex transition rules so no benefits will be lost from prior years.

Although the basic purpose of the combined limitation is straightforward, the definition of the fractions is relatively complex, and an example may be helpful showing how the combined limitation operates.

Example

Popps is employed by the Metro Company and earns a salary of $40,000 in 1987. Popps participates in a defined-benefit plan of the Metro Company providing a projected benefit equal to 50 percent of final average compensation. Popps also participates in a defined-contribution money-purchase plan of the Metro Company, and the question is—What is the maximum annual addition that can be allocated to Popps' account in the defined-contribution plan? For simplicity (and to avoid having to calculate the defined-contribution fraction for prior years) we will assume that 1987 is the first year for the defined-contribution plan. Popps' defined-benefit fraction is as follows:

$$\frac{\$20,000}{\$56,000} = 0.357$$

The numerator is the projected annual benefit, 50 percent of $40,000. Current compensation is used for this projection, even though it is likely that final average compensation at retirement will be some different amount. The denominator is the lesser of the two alternatives—in this case, the lesser figure turns out to be 140 percent of high three-year average compensation. Again, $40,000 is used for the high three-year average compensation, on the assumption that Popps' current compensation is as high as it has been so far. Since the defined-benefit fraction equals 0.357, and the total of the two must be less than or equal to 1.0, the defined-contribution fraction can be no more than

0.643. The denominator of the defined-contribution fraction will be $14,000 (140 percent of 25 percent of $40,000, which is less than 125 percent of $30,000). Therefore,

$$0.357 + \frac{\text{Annual Addition}}{14,000} \leq 1$$

The annual addition (the numerator), therefore, cannot exceed $9,002, since this is the amount that would make the defined contribution fraction exactly equal to 0.643.

Combined Deduction Limit. A combined *deduction* limit (Code Section 401(a)(7)) effective after 1986 has the effect of restricting the benefits of many combination plans, even though they meet the 1.40/1.25 rule discussed above. If an employer maintains a defined-contribution and a defined-benefit plan covering the same employer or employees, the employer's annual tax deduction for the plans cannot exceed 25 percent of the compensation of the employees covered under both plans. The 25 percent deduction limit can be exceeded only to meet the minimum funding requirements for the defined-benefit plan. For older plan entrants, the defined-benefit funding level will often exceed 25 percent of compensation, thus (depending on the overall nature of the employee group) potentially eliminating the possibility of adding a defined-contribution plan. For example, if there is only one participant, or only one highly paid participant and a few others (such as the typical plan for a doctor or dentist) this will be the case.

Example

Dr. X, age 55, adopts a plan providing a pension of $75,000 a year (50 percent of compensation) at retirement age 65. Annual cost is $44,428 (8 percent interest assumption), which is 30 percent of Dr. X's compensation. Thus, if Dr. X is the only employee, there is no room for a defined-contribution plan.

Top-Heavy Plans

The *top-heavy* rules are a recent addition to the arsenal of weapons Congress has provided against the use of qualified plans by small businesses that are primarily tax shelters for owners and highly compensated employees. The rules (Code Section 416) provide additional requirements that must be met by all qualified plans meeting the definition of top-heavy. To summarize, the top-heavy requirements:

> Put a ceiling on the amount of a participant's compensation that may be taken into account in plan contribution or benefit formula.

Provide faster vesting of benefits for plan participants who are not key employees.

Provide minimum unintegrated benefit or contribution levels for plan participants who are not key employees.

Reduce the aggregate Section 415 limit on contributions and benefits for key employees in certain situations.

Restrict distributions to key employees.

The top-heavy restrictions must be written into the plan document itself, even a plan for a large employer that is unlikely ever to be top-heavy. The plan document must provide that, if the plan meets the definition of top-heavy on a given determination date, all of the top-heavy restrictions automatically become part of the plan. As long as the plan is not top-heavy, the top-heavy restrictions need not necessarily apply, although, of course, the planner is free to add these restrictions to the plan even if it is not top-heavy.

Definition of Top-Heavy. A defined-benefit plan will be a top-heavy plan for a given plan year, if (as of the determination date—see below) the present value of the accumulated accrued benefits for participants who are key employees is more than 60 percent of the present value of all accumulated accrued benefits in the plan. A defined-contribution plan will be considered top-heavy if, as of the determination date, the sum of the account balances of participants who are key employees exceeds 60 percent of the aggregate value of the accounts of all employees. Benefits and account balances attributable to both employer and employee contributions are to be taken into account, except for accumulated voluntary deductible employee contributions or rollovers from other plans. The present value of a participant's accrued benefit or the value of the participant's account balance is to be increased by any aggregate distributions made with respect to the participant during the five-year period ending on the determination date. Plans of related groups can be lumped together, and, if the contributions or benefits of the overall group are top-heavy, each plan in the group will be considered top-heavy.

Determination Date. The determination date for any given plan year is the last day of the preceding plan year. For the first year of the new plan, the determination date is the last day of the first plan year. The IRS also has the authority to apply the top-heavy provisions on the basis of years other than plan years.

Definition of Key Employee. A key employee is any participant in the plan, including a self-employed person, who at any time in the four preceding years was an officer, an employee owning one of the 10 largest interests in the employer (under attribution-of-ownership rules), a more-than-5 percent owner, or a more-than-1 percent owner earning more than $15,000. Since the term *officer* is not clearly defined, the number of employees who can be treated as officers is limited. No more than 50 employees can be treated as officers, in general, while for small employers the limit on the number of officers is the greater of three individuals or 10 percent of the employees (presumably the highest paid). For example, suppose a small company has 25 employees. In determining who are key employees, the IRS cannot designate more than three of these employees (the greater of three individuals or 10 percent of the employees) as officers.

In determining ownership in the business for purposes of identifying key employees, the top-heavy provisions have rules for attributing stock ownership from related persons, and there are special rules for aggregating commonly controlled groups of employers and affiliated service groups.

A few illustrations of what constitutes a top-heavy plan might be helpful in defining the concept of top-heavy.

Example

Suppose that a corporation with 10 employees has a defined-contribution money-purchase pension plan. The employees include Wolfe, president and sole shareholder; Hare, vice president; and Flynn, foreman. All of the other employers are hourly paid, clerical, or production workers. The IRS would most likely identify the three named employees as the plan's key employees. As of the end of the 1987 plan year, aggregate account balances of all participants in the plan total $200,000. The account balances for Wolfe, Hare, and Flynn total $100,000.

On these facts, the plan is not top-heavy for the plan year 1988, since the aggregate account balances for the three key employees total less than 60 percent of the total account balances as of the determination date, the end of 1987. However, suppose that, in 1986, Wolfe received a distribution of $100,000 from the plan. In this case, the account balances as of the end of 1987 would have to be increased by the amount of this distribution, so they would total $300,000. The account balances for the key employees would then be $200,000, because the $100,000 distribution to Wolfe would have to be included for this purpose. In this situation, the plan would be deemed to be top-heavy for the plan year 1988, since the account balances for key employees would be more than 60 percent of the total.

Although the example above indicated a plan of a small employer that fell somewhat on the line between top-heaviness and avoidance of that status, planners find that virtually all plans of employers with fewer than about 10 employees will be top-heavy at all times. Key employees in such businesses usually have not only higher salaries but much longer service than regular employees, so their account balances or accrued benefits are much higher as a percentage of the total. Therefore, in effect, the top-heavy rules are an additional set of qualification requirements that must be met by all small plans.

Ceiling on Compensation

If a plan is top-heavy, annual compensation taken into account for plan purposes cannot exceed $200,000 for each employee. The $200,000 amount will be adjusted annually for inflation on the same basis as the Section 415 dollar limits. Therefore, the $200,000, like the $30,000 and $90,000 limits, will be frozen through 1987. Beginning in 1989, the $200,000 limit will apply to *all* employees in *all* plans (Code Section 401(a)(17)), and will no longer be a top-heavy limit as such.

Additional Vesting Requirements for Top-Heavy Plans

If a plan meets the definition of top-heavy, the plan provisions must meet one of two special vesting schedules applicable during years in which the plan is top-heavy. One alternative is 100 percent after three years of service. The other alternative is six-year graded vesting, as follows:

Years of Service	Vesting Percentage
2	20
3	40
4	60
5	80
6 or more	100

Minimum Benefit Requirements

A qualified plan must provide minimum benefits or contributions for top-heavy years. For defined-benefit plans, the benefit for each non-key employee must be at least a minimum percentage of average compensation. The applicable minimum percentage of compensation for a given employee is 2 multiplied by the number of the employee's years of service, with a maximum percentage of 20 percent (i.e., 10 years of service or more). The average compensation used for this test will generally be based on the highest five years of compensation.

For a defined-contribution plan, employer contributions during a year of top-heaviness must be not less than 3 percent of each non-key employee's compensation.

A top-heavy plan can consider only nonintegrated benefits in meeting the vesting and minimum-benefit requirements—that is, these requirements must be met based on benefits from the plan itself. Benefits received by the participant from social security cannot be taken into account.

Modification of Section 415 Combined Fraction

If a plan is top-heavy, the defined-benefit or defined-contribution fraction is modified by substituting 100 percent of the dollar limit for 125 percent. The result of this is to increase the fraction of high-paid employees (those affected by the dollar limit) and, therefore, limit total benefits for an employee where the company has both a defined-benefit and defined-contribution plan for that employee. The biggest impact is on very small organizations, such as a self-employed professional. Examples of planning for such organizations are discussed in Chapter 24.

The modification of the fractions does not apply to a regular top-heavy plan, if the plan provides minimum benefits or contributions at least 1 percent higher than the basic minimum—that is, if the plan provides a 4 percent (rather than 3 percent) defined-contribution or a 3 percent per year (rather than 2 percent) defined-benefit. However, if the plan is *super top-heavy* (more than 90 percent of accrued benefits or account balances for key employees), the modified fractions apply regardless of the amount of minimum benefits or contributions.

Effect of Top-Heavy Rules on Integration

If a qualified plan is top-heavy in a given year, one of the restrictions that will apply is that there must be a minimum benefit or contribution level for non-key employees. In such cases, therefore, a pure "excess" type of integrated formula with zero benefits below the integration level cannot be used for non-key employees. For this reason, most planners will prefer to use a stepped-up approach in a plan that either is top-heavy or runs a substantial risk of becoming top-heavy in the foreseeable future. Beginning in 1989, excess-type integrated formulas will no longer be possible in most cases, top-heavy or not (see Chapter 9).

The top-heavy rules do not have much effect on integrated plans in many cases. Many planners already prefer the stepped-up approach in integrated plans, even if the plan is designed primarily to benefit owners and key employees. This is because the percentage benefit permitted in pure excess plans is rather low. To illustrate, in a defined-contribution plan, only 5.7 percent of compensation in excess of the integration level can be allocated to a participant's account. Therefore, to provide a higher percentage of compensation, the stepped-up approach is commonly used in integrated defined-contribution plans. Plans already stepped-up will often meet the top-heavy requirements automatically.

Qualified Plans for Owners of Unincorporated Businesses

The owner of an unincorporated business often works full time or performs substantial services for the business as its proprietor or one of its partners. However, under the law such a person is not technically an "employee" of the business, but is referred to instead as a "self-employed person." For many years, partners and proprietors were not eligible to be covered under qualified plans adopted by their unincorporated businesses. Beginning in 1962, qualified plan coverage was allowed, but only under very restricted conditions. In particular, there was a relatively low limit on the amount that could be contributed to the plan (or on the benefit provided by the plan) for partners and proprietors. The special plans designed under these restrictions were known as *Keogh* or *HR-10* plans. These restrictions were enough to induce many unincorporated businesses to incorporate, simply so the partner or proprietor could become a legally recognized *employee* of the business and be eligible for full qualified plan coverage. However, for plan years beginning after 1983, most of these previous restrictions are eliminated, and partners and proprietors are able to participate fully in qualified plans adopted by their unincorporated businesses.

Earned Income. There remain a few differences in the treatment of unincorporated businesses, most of them related to basic differences in the form of business. For example, an unincorporated business is not treated for federal income tax purposes as a taxable entity but rather as a conduit for passing through the business's taxable income or loss to the partners or proprietor. By comparison, a corporation is a taxpaying entity, and income can be passed through to owners only in the form of salaries representing reasonable compensation for services rendered, or as dividends. Because of this difference, plan benefits or contributions for partners and proprietors are based on a defined amount referred to as *earned income*, which is intended to be comparable to the *compensation* that employees receive.

Basically, earned income means the partner or proprietor's share of the net earnings of the business after taking all appropriate business deductions, and without including nontaxable income. However, earned income includes only earnings with respect to the trade or business in which the personal services of the partner or proprietor are a material income-producing factor. For example, the net profits of an investment-type business could not be treated like compensation to provide a benefit under a qualified plan for a partner who provided no personal services to the business.

The fact that earned income is determined after all business deductions presents a computation problem. The business deductions include deductible contributions to the plan for both the owners and the regular employees. This means that the owner's earned income can be determined only after an algebraic computation. Without going into the complexities, an example will illustrate this sufficiently. Consider a proprietorship with three employees. Suppose that the *Schedule C income* (the business income after all deductions except those for plan contributions) is $200,000. For a plan contribution of 15 percent of compensation or earned income, the result would be as follows:

Employee	Compensation or Earned Income	Plan Contribution (15 Percent Rate)
Owner	$169,086.96	$25,363.04
1	10,000.00	1,500.00
2	12,000.00	1,800.00
3	15,000.00	2,250.00

Total contribution is $30,913.04.

Insurance. Another group of special rules apply to a qualified plan providing insurance for a partner or proprietor. No deduction can be taken by the business for plan contributions that are allocable to the purchase of incidental life, health, or accident insurance. If cash value life insurance is used, the deduction is denied for the portion of the premium allocable to pure insurance protection, but the remainder of the premium is deductible as a plan contribution. The amounts not deducted are in effect taxable income to the business owners, since all taxable income of a partnership or proprietorship flows through to the individual owners. Therefore, there are no PS 58 costs to include in the owner's income if insurance has been purchased, because the full cost of the insurance has already been included in the owner's income. However, unlike regular employees, the owners do not obtain a cost basis for the cost of the insurance to apply to any distribution from the qualified plan.

Aggregation Rule for Unincorporated Businesses. In the past, planners often have attempted to avoid the participation rules for qualified plans by separating a single business into a number of artificial entities and providing plan coverage only for employees of selected entities, thereby excluding large groups of employees. Under current law, this is possible only to a limited extent. As discussed in Chapter 6 and Appendix B, the Code has various provisions under which all businesses (both incorporated and unincorporated) under common control are treated as a single employer for qualified plan purposes. An additional common-control rule that affects primarily unincorporated businesses will be discussed in detail here.

Under this rule (Sections 401(d)-(2)), if a qualified plan covers a partner or proprietor who controls another business (here, control means more than 50 percent ownership) then the plan must either cover the employees of the controlled business or a comparable plan must be provided for employees of the controlled business.

Example

Suppose Fafner and Fasolt are partners in a construction business for which they provide services and which employs one regular employee. Suppose Fafner is a 60 percent partner in a road-paving business with 50 employees. If the Fafner and Fasolt partnership adopts a qualified plan covering Fafner and Fasolt themselves, then the plan must either cover the 50 employees of the road-paving business or the paving business must provide a plan with coverage comparable to that provided for Fafner and Fasolt.

Early Termination Rule for 25 Highest-Paid Employees

Potentially, a qualified defined-benefit plan can be used as a one-time tax shelter for key employees if it is designed with the expectation that most of the key employees will retire within a few years, taking most of the plan assets out for their retirement, and the plan is then terminated. For many years the Regulations (Reg. Sec. 1.401–4(c)) have contained a provision designed to limit this abuse by requiring defined-benefit plans to limit benefits for the 25 highest-paid employees, if they are paid out within 10 years of the plan's establishment or if the plan terminates within 10 years.

In such cases, benefits to the 25 highest-paid employees are limited by limiting the total employer contributions used to fund such benefits. The employer contributions for each such employee cannot exceed the greater of $20,000 or 20 percent of the first $50,000 of employee compensation multiplied by the number of years the plan was in effect prior to the benefit payment or plan termination. Often this will produce a lower limit on benefits than the Section 415 benefit limit. The detailed rules are complex and there is an interaction with the PBGC provisions for plan termination (Chapter 21).

Federal Estate Tax Treatment of Qualified Plan Benefits

The federal estate tax is a tax separate from the income tax that is imposed on the value of a decedent's property at the time of death. Basically, the estate tax is payable out of the decedent's estate and, therefore, reduces the amount available to the beneficiaries. The beneficiaries, however, are not personally responsible for paying the estate tax. Only a small percentage of decedents—less than 5 percent—have enough wealth to be concerned about the estate tax, because of a high initial minimum tax credit applicable to the estate tax. After 1986, no estate tax return need be filed for a decedent whose gross estate is less than approximately $600,000. Also, there is an unlimited marital deduction for federal estate tax purposes—that is, no federal estate tax is imposed on property transferred at death to a spouse, regardless of the amount. However, for business owners and highly compensated executives covered under a qualified plan, the federal estate impact of qualified plan distributions can be a significant factor.

For many years, a total estate tax exclusion was available for insured death benefits paid from qualified plans. Currently, this is no longer available; thus, as a general rule, a lump-sum death benefit, or the present value of an annuity payable to a beneficiary, is includible in the estate of a deceased participant, for federal estate tax purposes. This is of no concern to a participant whose gross estate is so low that no estate tax liability exists. Also, for higher-income participants, in many cases the plan death benefit will be payable to a spouse. The unlimited marital deduction will then avoid federal estate tax on the plan benefit.

For some high-income participants, however, avoiding federal estate taxes on the plan benefit (and also the excess accumulation tax described below) can still be a factor. Their estates generally will be large enough to attract some federal estate tax. The marital deduction may not be significant, since they may not wish to pay the plan benefit to a spouse—they may be widowed or divorced, or may wish to provide for another beneficiary. Also, even if the benefit is payable to a spouse, a spouse is often about the same age as the decedent, and thus, within relatively few years, most of the property transferred to the spouse is potentially subject to federal estate tax again at the spouse's death. As a result, in many cases it is useful to design a qualified plan death benefit that can be excluded from the participant's estate.

The general rule of the federal estate tax is that all items of property are includible, unless a specific Code provision excludes them. Thus, qualified plan death benefits are generally includible, because there is no specific exclusion. However, the estate tax law does have a specific provision dealing with life insurance, Section 2042. Under Section 2042, life insurance proceeds are includible in a decedent's estate only if the decedent has "incidents of ownership" in the insurance policies. An incident of ownership refers to various rights under the policy, particularly the right to designate the beneficiary. Therefore, it seems possible to exclude a qualified plan death benefit if the benefit is provided through a life insurance policy in which the decedent has no incidents of ownership.

There are no clear rules on how to avoid incidents of ownership in a life insurance policy held in a qualified plan for a participant. However, design techniques currently being used for this purpose include the use of a separate trust or subtrust under the plan for holding the policies and a provision for irrevocable beneficiary designations.

Excess Distribution and Excess Accumulation Penalties

To further limit the tax benefits from qualified plans for highly compensated participants, Congress has added penalties for plan distributions in excess of certain specified amounts (Code Section 4981). These penalties apply even if plan contributions or benefits are within the Section 415 limits discussed earlier.

Excess Distribution Penalty. In addition to any regular income tax payable, there is a tax of 15 percent on any excess distribution made in any year from a qualified plan or plans to an individual participant. Distributions from all IRAs, Section 403(b) tax-deferred annuities, and qualified plans of all employers covering the participant are aggregated. A 15 percent tax is imposed on the participant to the extent that the aggregate distributions exceed a specified limit. The distribution limit is $150,000 for individuals participating in plans before 1989 (or in some cases, the participant's accrued benefit as of August 1, 1986). The limit is to be indexed so that it is always equal to at least 125 percent of the Section 415 defined-benefit dollar limit. Since 125 percent of the current $90,000 limit is $112,500, it will require some indexing before the limit catches up with the $150,000 limit for pre-1989 participants; after that, the $150,000 limit will no longer apply.

The excess distribution tax does not apply to the following distributions:

Death benefits paid to a beneficiary (but there may be an excess accumulation tax, as discussed below).
A distribution to an alternate payee under a qualified domestic relations order (QDRO), if includible in income of the alternate payee. However, the alternate payee must then pay the 15 percent penalty.
A distribution of the employee's own aftertax contributions.
A distribution that is not included in income because it is rolled over (see Chapter 22).

For a lump-sum distribution, the limitation is five times the $112,500 limit, or $562,500, subject to indexing as described earlier. If a lump-sum payment exceeds $562,500 (or the indexed limit) then, in addition to the regular tax payable, there is a 15 percent penalty on the amount above $562,500.

The amount of any 15 percent penalty tax is reduced by any 10 percent early distribution tax imposed on the same distribution.

Excess Accumulation Penalty. If an individual participating in a qualified plan dies with an excess accumulation, there is an additional tax, over and above any federal estate tax. The additional tax is equal to 15 percent of the excess accumulation. An excess accumulation is defined as the excess of the value of the qualified plan accumulation over the present value of an annuity paying $112,500 (or the applicable indexed limit) annually over the individual's life expectancy, determined at the date of death.

The additional 15 percent excess accumulation tax is not eligible for the unified credit under the estate and gift tax law, and it cannot be reduced by the marital deduction or the charitable deduction, even if the qualified plan accumulation is actually given to a spouse or a charity. Thus, this tax adds an additional complication to estate planning for high-income individuals participating in qualified plans.

Summary

Qualified defined-benefit plan projected retirement benefits can be no more than an annual pension beginning at the social security retirement age equal to the lesser of $90,000 (to be indexed after 1987 for cost-of-living increases) or the participant's high three-year average annual compensation. These limits are adjusted actuarially for other retirement ages and forms of benefit except a straight-life annuity or qualified joint-and-survivor annuity. For a defined-contribution plan, annual additions (employer and employee contributions and forfeitures) for a participant cannot exceed the lesser of $30,000 (indexed to be one fourth the defined-benefit dollar limit) or 25 percent of the participant's compensation.

If a participant is covered under both a defined-benefit and a defined-contribution plan, the above limits are adjusted under a complex formula. Combined benefits are also subject to a 25 percent of payroll deduction limit applicable to the employer.

A plan is top-heavy if it provides more than 60 percent of its benefits or account balance to key employees, as defined. Top-heavy plans must provide nonkey employees with minimum benefits or contributions and accelerated vesting.

Owners of unincorporated businesses can be covered under qualified plans of the business on much the same terms as regular employees, but some special rules apply. In particular, plan computations are based on earned income, as defined, in place of compensation, and there are special rules for incidental life insurance. There is also a special rule for aggregating commonly controlled unincorporated businesses.

If a qualified defined-benefit plan terminates within 10 years of its inception, benefits payable to the 25 highest-paid employees are subject to specified limits.

In addition to the regular income tax and estate tax payable, annual plan distributions in excess of $150,000 (or $112,500 as indexed to be 125 percent of the defined-benefit dollar limit) are subject to a 15 percent penalty tax. There is also an extra 15 percent federal estate tax on qualified plan accumulations in a decedent's estate over a specified limit.

19

Qualified Plan Installation

Objectives of This Chapter
- *Outline the steps that must be taken to install a qualified plan.*
- *Discuss the significance of advance determination letters issued by the IRS.*
- *Describe how master and prototype plans, pattern plans, and document preparation services can facilitate plan installation.*

Plan Installation: Its Role in the Process

The activities of qualified plan specialists—the qualified plan business—can be grouped in four categories or subspecialties:

Plan design,
plan installation,
plan administration,
plan investment management.

Many firms and individuals specialize only in one or two of these areas. Only a few organizations have found a profitable niche in all areas. At one time, insurance companies were commonly active in virtually all areas, but currently even most insurance companies limit their involvement to some extent.

To be effective in the pension business, pension specialists must learn how to solve their client's problems in all these areas. They generally must not only seek an area in which they can be most effective individually but also must develop working relationships with other specialized professionals to meet all their clients' pension needs.

Although large consulting firms often do plan installation, this particular phase of the process is one of those most likely to involve outside consultants. For example, because of the tax and labor law implications, and because of the direct interaction with the Internal Revenue Service, the employer's attorney will often be involved at this stage.

Steps in Plan Installation

When the basic plan design options have been studied—the type of plan, the benefit formula, and the like—and decisions made, the next step is formally installing the plan. Installing a qualified plan can be fairly complex, particularly if the plan is at all complicated and if the employer wishes to maximize the tax benefits by having the plan effective at the earliest possible date.

The best way to discuss the installation process is to use as a framework for reference the "checklist" for the installation of a hypothetical qualified plan provided in Table 19–1. This checklist should be used for general discussion only; IRS guidelines for plan installation are frequently revised, and procedures may even vary from one Internal Revenue district to another.[1]

Adoption of the Plan

To be effective during a particular year of the employer, the plan must be "adopted" by the employer during that year. For a corporation, the corporate board should pass a resolution adopting the plan before the end of its year for the plan to become effective during that year. It is not proper to "back date" documents for this purpose—the board must actually act legally before the end of the year. It may not be necessary to draft the final form of the plan at this time, however; the board usually can adopt a resolution merely outlining the basic provisions of the plan.

If the plan uses a trust, the trust must be established before the end of the year in which the plan is to be effective. This means that a trust agreement must be executed between the employer and the trustee, and at least a nominal principal contribution may be necessary to establish the existence of the trust. The trust agreement and plan document can be separate, or both can be incorporated in a single document. If the plan uses an insurance contract as a funding instrument, the insurer must have accepted the terms of the agreement before the end of the year, although the contract may not be put into final form until sometime later.

The plan and trust or insurance contract should be finalized prior to the time the employer makes the first plan contribution (other than a nominal contribution required to establish the trust or insurance contract); this usually means the employer's tax-filing date, because, as discussed in Chapter 11, the plan contribution for a given year can be deferred to the tax-filing date for that year.

Plan Year

It is possible to establish a plan with a *plan year* that is different from the employer's taxable year. In that case, one plan year will end and another will begin in the same taxable year of the employer. The employer can then take a deduction

---

[1]Current guidelines on submitting plans to the IRS are found in Revenue Procedure (Rev. Proc.) 80–30 and various addenda and revisions thereto.

TABLE 19–1. Checklist for Installation of Quicklime Construction Company, Inc. *(Calendar-Year Taxpayer)*

EMPLOYEES' PROFIT-SHARING PLAN
(To Be Effective January 1, 1987)

BEFORE DECEMBER 31, 1987
1. Board must pass resolution adopting the Plan. It is sufficient for the Board to adopt a preliminary draft of the Plan, or even a simple resolution listing the major provisions of the Plan.
2. Trust instrument must be executed. (Under state law, a nominal contribution to the Trust corpus also may be necessary in order to establish the existence of the Trust.) If there is a separate group pension contract, the contract need not be in final form before December 31, 1987, but application must have been accepted by insurer and part payment made.
3. Plan should be communicated to employees. (There is no specific statutory deadline for this, but communication before the end of the year is recommended.) Communication can be oral (e.g., at employee meetings) or written. Alternatively the Summary Plan Description (SPD) (see below) can be used for this purpose.

BEFORE EMPLOYER'S TAX-FILING DATE (March 15, 1988; extension to September 15, 1988, is possible)
1. Execute Plan in final form. (Plan may be adopted subject to right to rescind if determination letter is not obtained.)
2. Make 1987 contribution to Trust. (Plan may allow contribution to be returned if Plan does not qualify.)

WITHIN 120 DAYS AFTER PLAN IS ADOPTED BY BOARD OF DIRECTORS (e.g., if resolution adopted December 31, 1987—by April 30, 1988)
1. Furnish Summary Plan Description (SPD) (see "Reporting and Disclosure" in this chapter) to participants.
2. File SPD with Department of Labor.

BEFORE FILING APPLICATION FOR DETERMINATION LETTER WITH IRS
Provide notice to interested parties (i.e., employees) by mail (10 to 24 days before filing) or posting (7 to 20 days before filing).

---

that taxable year for a contribution on behalf of either plan year or for partial contributions for both taxable years; however, the employer must follow a consistent procedure so there is no undue tax benefit. For simplicity, unless otherwise indicated it will be assumed in this chapter that the plan year is the same as the employer's taxable year.

Advance Determination Letter

A central feature of the plan installation process is usually an application to the IRS district director for a *determination letter* stating that the plan as designed is a qualified plan eligible for the accompanying tax benefits. It is not necessary for the plan to have such a letter to be qualified; any plan that complies with the

TABLE 19–1 *(Concluded)*

FILE APPLICATION FOR DETERMINATION WITH IRS

Time
    No statutory deadline. However, should be filed before employer's tax-filing date (March 15, 1988, plus extensions) (the retroactive amendment period). Filing of letter will extend the retroactive amendment date to give time to amend plan to meet IRS objections, if any.

What to file
    Form 5301 (for defined-contribution plan—other forms for other types)
    Form 5302, employee census (data concerning 25 highest-paid employees)
    Other schedules as required under Form 5301 instructions
    Plan—executed
    Trust Agreement—executed (or Insurance Contract)
    Other items (e.g., Power of Attorney)—depending on circumstances

ON OR BEFORE JULY 31, 1988 (AND EACH JULY 31 THEREAFTER)
    File Annual Report (Form 5500 Series) with IRS (see "Reporting and Disclosure" below)

ON OR BEFORE SEPTEMBER 30, 1988 (AND EACH SEPTEMBER 30 THEREAFTER)
    Furnish Summary of Annual Report to participants.

---

applicable Code provisions is a qualified plan. However, if there is no advance determination by the IRS, the IRS will not examine the plan until the time comes for an audit of the employer's tax returns. If the IRS finds at this time that the plan is not qualified, the possible tax consequences can be disastrous: the loss of the employer's tax deductions for plan contributions, the taxation of all plan contributions to participants, and the loss of the trust's tax-exempt status. To avoid this, most employers consider it desirable to have the IRS review the plan in advance and issue a determination letter.

    There are other advantages to the determination letter procedure. The process of IRS review will often reveal drafting problems that might otherwise have gone unnoticed. During the review procedure, the IRS usually will suggest any changes in the plan that are necessary to make it qualify.

    There is a *retroactive amendment* procedure that allows the employer to make amendments to the plan effective for a prior year, if the amendments are necessary to make the plan qualify. In general, retroactive plan amendments may be made up to the employer's tax-filing date for the year in question, plus extensions. For example, if a corporate employer uses a calendar year, the tax-filing date for the year 1986 is March 15, 1987, with possible extensions to September 15, 1987. Thus, an employer could install a qualified plan effective January 1, 1986, and could amend the plan retroactively to January 1, 1986, as late as September 15, 1987. The filing of a determination letter prior to this deadline extends the retroactive amendment procedure while the determination letter request is pending; this is another advantage of requesting an IRS determination letter.

Generally, the employer wishes to make the plan effective as early as possible and thus obtain the maximum tax deduction at the outset. This can present a problem if, upon filing the application for determination, the IRS finds the plan not qualified and retroactive amendments are unavailable or the employer does not wish to make the amendments the IRS suggests. The employer's prior contributions to the plan then might not be retrievable, since the trust must be an irrevocable trust. To avoid this problem, the plan can be drafted making the plan's existence and the employer's contribution contingent on obtaining a determination letter.

The IRS provides various forms for purposes of making an application for determination. Some of these are described in the checklist in Table 19–1. Also, the IRS provides a set of guidelines for examining qualified plans that can be used by the installer to spot possibly defective plan provisions prior to making the application for determination.[2]

One final point should be made concerning IRS determination letters. Determination letters indicate that the IRS has approved the plan on the basis of the plan documents and the facts submitted to it. These are no guarantee that the plan qualifies and will continue to qualify if these facts are not accurate or if the facts change at a subsequent date. Therefore, the continuing qualification of the plan must always be a concern of the employer and its employee-benefit advisers.

Master, Prototype, and Pattern Plans

A qualified plan must be evidenced by a formal written document. Because of the many complex provisions that must be included, it is not unusual for such documents to run to 50 pages or more. If all of the plan language is custom-designed, the drafting expense alone can be considerable.

Various methods have been devised to simplify plan drafting for smaller employers; one of the most common is the use of *master* and *prototype* plans offered by financial institutions and other types of plan advisers. A prototype plan is a standardized form of plan (such as a prototype profit-sharing plan or prototype money-purchase pension plan), usually offering some choice of provisions in the important features—for example, the plan might allow the employer to specify the contribution rate, to choose the vesting schedule, and the like. A master plan is similar to a prototype plan, but the term *master plan* usually refers to a plan form designed by a financial organization and adopted only by employers that wish to use that financial organization for plan funding. The IRS also allows law firms to use *pattern* plans; these are plans using language that has been examined and approved by the IRS, thus allowing speedier IRS approval of plans to the extent they use the pattern language.

---

[2]IRS Alert Guidelines, Forms 5622–5627, Department of the Treasury, Internal Revenue Service.

Most qualified plan consultants use standardized plan language of one kind or another to a considerable extent to reduce drafting costs, even if they do not provide formal master, prototype, or pattern plans. The expense of producing documents is considerable, and many consultants, particularly smaller organizations, use an independent *document preparation service,* which generates documents based on a checklist of desired plan provisions submitted by the plan designer. Using a document preparation service may speed IRS approval of the plan, if IRS district offices have previously approved standardized plan provisions prepared by that preparation service.

Summary

This chapter outlines the steps to be taken in installing a qualified plan, from plan adoption by the employer through application to the IRS for an advance determination letter. An advance determination letter is not required, but is important, because it allows the IRS to raise objections while the plan is still subject to retroactive amendment.

Because of the complexity of plan documents, the cost of installation can be reduced by using predrafted standard forms of various types—master, prototype and pattern plans, or plans drafted by a document preparation service.

20

Plan Administration

Objectives of This Chapter
- *Describe the administrative forms and procedures generally required in plan administration.*
- *Discuss the ERISA reporting and disclosure requirements.*
- *Discuss accounting aspects of plan administration.*

Who Administers a Plan

Plan administration as referred to in this chapter generally means administrative duties not directly related to handling or investment of plan funds. Typically, a trustee, custodian, or insurance company will be appointed to handle plan assets, pay benefits and keep financial records, and protect plan funds and invest them to obtain a good rate of investment return. Administrative activities relating directly to employees and beneficiaries are generally performed separately. The legally designated "plan administrator" has specific duties, as discussed further below. Plan administration considered generically—not restricted only to legal requirements of a plan administrator—includes the following:

Communicating the plan to employees;
determining eligibility of employees for participation and enrolling new participants;
maintaining records of hirings and terminations and communicating these to trustees, plan actuaries, and so on, as necessary;
collecting beneficiary designations, participant investment directions, loan requests, benefit payment requests, optional form of payment requests, and the like, and communicating them to the trustee;
maintaining compensation and other data for computation of plan contributions or benefits;
interpreting plan provisions and initiating plan amendments to correct any defects;
acting as the employer's representative or intermediary in dealing with plan matters with employees;

acting as holder of insurance and annuity contracts as necessary;

hiring professional consultants, such as lawyers, actuaries, and accountants;

establishing a funding method and, in some cases, becoming involved in investment decisions;

amending the plan to meet changing requirements of the law;

conducting hearings on plan claims and other disputes involving issues such as disability or eligibility for benefits;

filing the annual report and other required reports; and

initiating a plan termination where appropriate.

It is cost-effective for some employers to carry out virtually all plan administrative duties through the company's personnel department. Many employers, however, find this difficult. Some types of plans, such as 401(k) plans, involve large volumes of repetitive paperwork, and, as in the case of payroll administration, the company may benefit by contracting this work. Defined-benefit plans involve specialized actuarial skills, and even a large company may not be able to keep an actuary busy full time. Finally, the requirements for administering a qualified plan, as discussed in this chapter, are not only complex but subject to frequent change. It may be difficult for the company's personnel department to keep abreast of all this. The consequences of a mistake can be disastrous—there may be large extra tax costs for employees, or the plan might even be disqualified. As a result, many employers are happy to pass off all or part of the burden of plan administration to an outside administrative firm.

Administrative Forms and Procedures

Qualified plans impose a complicated set of duties on plan administrators. Every plan administrator must adopt a set of forms and procedures appropriate to the plan provisions and employer requirements.

Plan administration must be carried out in such a way that legal requirements are met and that communication with participants and beneficiaries is adequate to avoid unnecessary disputes. Full written documentation of administrative actions is essential.

To get an idea of the scope of plan administration, we will look at the type of forms and procedures that the administrator of a hypothetical profit-sharing plan might use. Other types of plans might require different or additional forms and procedures. In addition to the procedures listed here, plan administration includes the ERISA requirements, discussed in the next section.

Forms and Procedures for Typical Profit-Sharing Plan

1. *Participant's directed investment choice.* If the plan permits directed investments, a participant should file an appropriate form with the administrator that documents the investment choice to relieve the trustee from fiduciary liability (see Chapter 13).

2. Employee contribution election form. If the plan permits employee contributions, the employee should file a written election form indicating the amount of the contribution and the duration of the election.

3. Loan agreement forms. If the plan permits loans, a participant-borrower should file a properly executed note evidencing the loan, and an assignment of the participant's vested interest as collateral. Spousal consent may also be required. (Loans are discussed in Chapter 16.)

4. Income tax withholding notice and election form. As discussed below, the plan must withhold income tax on a distribution unless the participant elects otherwise on this form.

5. Participation application and beneficiary designation. Participants should sign this form to indicate that the summary plan description has been received and a beneficiary designated for the death benefit.

6. Preretirement survivor benefit notices. As discussed in Chapter 10, death benefits must be paid to a participant's spouse unless there is a written election otherwise. Also, a married participant must be notified of this benefit upon entering the plan. Thus, there are two forms involved here: the notice of the preretirement survivor benefit and a form for electing to waive the preretirement survivor benefit with spousal consent.

7. Notice to terminated vested participant. A terminating participant should be given a form indicating what benefits are due and when they begin, and notifying the participant to keep the plan administrator informed of his or her address.

8. Release forms for distributions to participant. When a lump-sum distribution has been made to a participant, the participant should sign a form to document that the plan has no further liability for the amount distributed. Although a distribution up to $3,500 can be made without the participant's consent, the participant should still acknowledge receipt for such a distribution. Where the distribution is over $3,500, the participant's written consent should be obtained and kept on file.

Other Procedures

Qualified Domestic Relations Order (QDRO) Procedures. In addition to the routine forms listed above, a plan should adopt a procedure to deal with qualified domestic relations orders (discussed in Chapter 16). The procedure should include obtaining a written legal opinion that an order presented by a participant or claimant to the plan legally constitutes a QDRO, with procedures for holding the claimed benefit in a suspense account until legal questions are resolved. The procedure should also include a written filing of the claimant's name, address, and other identifying information, and the amount of the claim and how it is to be paid.

Allocation of Plan Contributions and Forfeitures; Account Valuation. For a profit-sharing plan, this is a relatively simple though important procedure, which must be done at least annually. The corresponding requirement for a defined-benefit plan is more complex, since it involves actuarial computations and valuations.

Tax Withholding. Distributions from a qualified retirement plan are subject to federal income tax withholding, in a manner similar to payments of wages or other compensation. However, a recipient can elect not to have tax withholding on the qualified plan distribution, without providing any reason. This, of course, will not relieve the recipient of any obligation to pay whatever income taxes are due. The payor of the plan distribution must notify the recipient of the right not to have taxes withheld.

The withholding requirement applies to both lump-sum distributions and periodic payments. The liability for withholding is imposed on the "payor" of the distribution, but the plan administrator will be held liable unless the plan administrator directs the payor to withhold the tax and provides the payor with the information necessary to make the withholding. If the payor is a different person than the plan administrator, for example a trustee, it is important to have a clear understanding between the parties about the responsibilities for withholding.

ERISA Reporting and Disclosure and Other Requirements

This section will focus on specific obligations imposed by ERISA and the Internal Revenue Code affecting plan administration. Many of the administrative requirements of the law involve penalties for noncompliance, so it is important to impose these duties on specific individuals or groups of individuals to limit the scope of this liability to a known group; otherwise, persons involved with the plan might find themselves held responsible for actions over which they may think they have no control. This problem is greatest in the area of investment decisions; therefore, it is important to be as specific as possible in the plan and trust agreement about who has responsibility for making investment decisions and how these persons are chosen.

Plan Administrator

Any employee-benefit plan subject to ERISA is required to name in the plan document a *plan administrator*. If none is named, the employer will be assumed to be plan administrator. Some employers designate a "plan committee" to be the plan administrator; this committee usually is made up of a group of management and sometimes rank-and-file employees responsible for administering the plan. If this is done, the plan should spell out how committee members are to be named, so there can be no doubt who has the responsibility of plan administrator. Many employers simply designate the employer as plan administrator, with administration duties delegated to specific employees, usually in the personnel department, in the same manner as other management functions are carried out. Where the plan is funded through an insurance contract, some administrative duties may be carried out by the insurance company for a fee; this is particularly likely for smaller employers, where the amount of administrative work involved does not justify the employment of a qualified plan specialist. Plan administrators also often rely on outside benefit consultants for assistance with various administrative duties.

Claims Procedure

One of the plan administrator's duties is to evaluate employee claims for benefits and to direct the trustee or other fund holder to make payments as appropriate. If the plan is properly drafted, there should be little ambiguity about whether a particular participant or beneficiary is entitled to a plan benefit. However, due to the complexity of many plan provisions, disputes sometimes arise.

Every plan must include a written procedure under which a claimant can appeal the denial of a plan benefit to the plan administrator. There are specific time limits (60 to 120 days, generally) within which the plan administrator must make a decision on the appeal. The purpose for the claims procedure requirement is to require plans to develop internal procedures for evaluating claims so that participants will not always be compelled to bring a lawsuit against the plan if a claim is denied. If a claim dispute cannot be satisfactorily resolved internally, however, claimants have the right to sue and many will do so.

Reporting and Disclosure

The reporting and disclosure provisions, enacted as part of ERISA in 1974, impose a variety of duties on employee-benefit plans to report or disclose various plan information to the government and plan participants. The purpose of the reporting and disclosure provisions is to indirectly discourage various plan abuses, on the theory that wrongdoers will be deterred by knowing that their wrongdoing may be exposed to public view. This approach to federal regulation is based on the success of the securities laws of the 1930s and is common in other areas of federal regulation. The statutory format in ERISA for reporting and disclosure is extremely complex and confusing, and many modifications of the original statutory procedure have been since made by regulation, although the underlying statutes remain the same.

The reporting and disclosure requirements currently consist of a series of reports, some annual and some not, that must be provided to the participant or filed with the government or both.

- *Summary Plan Description* (SPD). The summary plan description is a document intended to describe the plan to its participants in plain language. It must be furnished to participants whether they ask for it or not, and it must also be filed with the Department of Labor, within 120 days after the plan is established or 90 days after a new participant enters the plan.

    There is no government form for the SPD; it can be designed according to the employer's specifications. However, the contents of the SPD are specified in minute detail by Department of Labor regulations. These regulations require, among other things, clear identification of the plan sponsor and funding entities, the plan's eligibility requirements, any possibilities of losses or forfeitures of benefits, procedures for making claims for benefits under the plan, and a prescribed statement of the participant's rights under the law.

There is also a "plain language" requirement, and this can be extremely important in practice. If a participant or beneficiary claims a benefit and is disappointed to find that the benefit was not provided under the plan, it is quite likely that the disappointed claimant will find a lawyer who will look closely at the SPD for any ambiguities that might provide grounds for a lawsuit. Such lawsuits often prove successful. The courts usually have not been impressed by mere statements in the SPD to the effect that the language of formal plan documents governs notwithstanding anything in the SPD.

- *Annual Report* (Form 5500 Series). This form is the centerpiece of the reporting requirements. The form is filed only with the IRS but is made available to both IRS and the Department of Labor. The form is filed annually and is due by the end of the seventh month after the end of the plan year (July 31, for calendar year plans). The form includes detailed financial information for the plan, including a signed report by an independent, qualified public accountant, along with any separate financial statements forming the basis of the independent accountant's report. If a qualified plan is subject to the minimum funding requirements, a signed report by the plan's enrolled actuary must be included with this, along with a certified actuarial valuation. If the plan is funded with insurance contracts, specific information about these contracts is required.

   Plans covering fewer than 100 participants are subject to simpler reporting requirements, designed to reduce the cost of compliance for these plans. These plans file Form 5500–C once every three years, and a simplified annual Form 5500–R during the intervening two years. Other plans must file the full Form 5500 each year. To get a better idea of the scope of the reporting requirements, it is useful to obtain from the IRS copies of these forms and accompanying instructions and review them.

   Form 5500 includes schedule SSA, a schedule identifying participants who have separated from service during the year with deferred vested benefits under the plan. It is provided by the IRS to the Social Security Administration so, at retirement, any former participant may be notified of a deferred vested benefit from the plan.

- *Summary of Annual Report* (SAR). The plan administrator must provide participants and beneficiaries with a summary annual report within nine months after the end of the plan year. There is a prescribed format for this SAR, consisting of selected financial information derived from the Form

5500 series annual report plus a prescribed notice that additional information may be obtained from the plan administrator.

- *Report on Termination, Merger, or Other Changes* (Form 5310). The plan administrator of a plan covered under the PBGC plan termination insurance (discussed later in this chapter) must notify the PBGC in advance of the termination. The Code and ERISA also contain a number of other reporting requirements in the event of a plan termination, merger, split up, transfer of assets, and various other similar events. These are generally reported on Form 5310.
- *Individual Benefit Statement.* On written request, the plan administrator must furnish an individual participant or beneficiary with a prescribed statement of his or her current plan benefits (vested and unvested). This need not be furnished more than once a year. Some plan administrators provide these individual statements annually, even without a request from participants or beneficiaries.

The reporting requirements are enforced by various types of penalties, including criminal penalties for willful violations or false statements.

In addition to the specific forms that must be filed or distributed, the reporting and disclosure requirements include a variety of "sunshine" provisions that give government agencies and participants rights to inspect and copy various documents and records relevant to the plan and its operation. It also should be kept in mind that, to obtain an advance determination letter or other IRS ruling, the plan documents must usually be submitted to the IRS.

Accounting for Pension Plans

An accountant's chief responsibility is to represent accurately a client's financial position to an appropriate public, such as shareholders, investors, or the government. Accountants constitute an independent profession and, therefore, generate their own standards for financial disclosure. Thus, accounting for pension plans is an issue independent of the plan qualification and design issues discussed elsewhere in this text.

In the typical pension plan, two entities are involved for which financial disclosure may be necessary: the employer sponsoring the plan and the plan itself. Financial disclosure for the employer has been a much more significant and controversial issue, and it will be discussed here first.

Employers' Accounting for Pensions

Accounting for pensions by employers is not controversial in the case of defined-contribution plans. There, the employer's obligation to contribute each year is defined in the plan, and, once the plan contribution has been made, the employer has no further liability, under normal circumstances. Thus, the only income statement effect is to reduce income by the amount contributed, and there is no effect on the balance sheet unless the employer owes the plan for prior years' contributions that were not made.

For defined-benefit plans, the issue is obviously more difficult. First, there is the question of the amount to report as an annual cost on the income statement; then there is the question of how the plan's various obligations are reflected on the firm's balance sheet. The defined-benefit plan represents a long-term liability of the employer, and, particularly where there is an unfunded past service liability, it has often been argued that something to reflect this liability should be shown on the balance sheet. The problem areas have been:

How much flexibility should the employer have in determining the periodic plan cost charged to expense for the year or other accounting period?

How should supplemental liabilities (unfunded past service costs) of the plan be reflected on the employer's balance sheet?

Until recently, the standard for employers' accounting for pensions was stated in Accounting Principles Board *Opinion No. 8,* issued in 1966. Under *APB Opinion No. 8,* annual pension costs may be determined by any reasonable actuarial method chosen by the employer. *Opinion No. 8* required that any difference between the amount charged to expense under this computation and the amount actually funded should be recorded as a liability on the balance sheet. However, most employers used the same method to measure pension costs for accounting purposes that they used to determine the annual contribution made to the plan. Therefore, since the amount funded and the amount expensed were the same, generally no pension liability was reflected on the balance sheet under *Opinion No. 8.* Also, *Opinion No. 8* did not, in general, require unfunded past service costs to be reflected on the balance sheet; these were treated merely as future contingencies, such as the obligation to pay salaries in the future.

It has long been recognized that the rules of *Opinion No. 8* did not provide adequate disclosure. However, the development of appropriate new standards has involved an extended controversy. The Financial Accounting Standards Board (FASB), the organization designated since 1973 to establish standards of financial accounting and reporting, has had a long-standing project to develop new standards. Various preliminary drafts have been issued over the years, and refined after reflecting the views of critics. The board's rules were put in final form in 1985 as *FASB Statement No. 87,* "Employers' Accounting for Pensions," which supersedes *APB Opinion No. 8.*

First of all, *Statement No. 87* provides a uniform method for determining pension costs; the employer may no longer simply use the amount actually funded for determining this amount. The employer must use the projected unit credit method for allocating the pension costs over the working career of the employee. As discussed in Chapter 11, the unit credit method (accrued-benefit method) essentially relates the cost of an accrued pension benefit directly to the year in which that benefit was accrued. If the expense so determined is different from the employer's actual plan contribution, the difference will be shown as an asset or a liability on the balance sheet. Such entries rarely occurred under *Opinion No. 8,* but are much more likely to occur under *Statement No. 87.* In most cases, the uniform method of determining the expense for accounting purposes under *Statement No. 87* will be different from the method used by the employer for determining plan contributions.

Furthermore, *Statement No. 87* requires that, if the plan's past service costs (referred to as the *accumulated-benefit obligation*) exceed the fair value of plan assets, a liability referred to as the *unfunded accumulated-benefit obligation* must be reflected on the balance sheet. This liability is balanced by an intangible asset on the balance sheet.

In addition, *Statement No. 87* prescribes a specific format for various financial statement footnotes relating to the pension plan, such as the fair market value of plan assets and any unamortized prior-service costs.

Because of the special problems raised by plans that are terminating, in 1985 the FASB also issued *Statement No. 88,* "Employers' Accounting for Settlements and Curtailments of Defined-Benefit Pension Plans and Termination Benefits." Generally, the rules of *Statements No. 87* and *No. 88* are effective for fiscal years beginning after December 15, 1986. These rules have a significant impact on financial reporting and, therefore, on a company's relationship with its creditors and shareholders.

Plan Accounting

Accounting statements by the plan itself, as opposed to the employer, have involved considerably less controversy. The current rules are contained in *FASB Statement No. 35,* "Accounting and Reporting by Defined-Benefit Plans." This statement simply reflects the manner in which plan assets and liabilities are to be reported, and does not directly involve obligations by the employer. It should be noted that a financial statement by the plan itself is generally required as part of the reporting and disclosure requirements of ERISA, as reported on Form 5500, discussed above.

Summary

Plan administration encompasses a variety of procedures required in the practical application of qualified plans. In addition, the law requires each plan to designate a plan administrator, who is legally responsible for a variety of specific acts.

One of a plan administrator's most important legal duties is compliance with the reporting and disclosure requirements of ERISA, including the preparation and filing of the annual report (Form 5500 series), the summary plan description (SPD), and other reports.

The accounting rules for pension plans govern how employers report plan obligations for accounting purposes. For defined-contribution plans, there is no balance sheet effect unless an unpaid plan contribution liability exists. For defined-benefit plans under *FASB No. 87,* any unfunded accumulated benefit obligation must be shown on the balance sheet. Accounting rules also govern internal plan accounting.

21

Plan Termination

Objectives of This Chapter
- *Describe the circumstances under which an employer may terminate a qualified plan.*
- *Describe the distinctions among a premature termination, a regular termination, a partial termination, and a curtailment.*
- *Explain the technique of plan freezing.*
- *Explain the tax consequences of terminating a qualified plan.*
- *Describe the types of plans covered by PBGC insurance.*
- *Outline the two voluntary termination procedures for PBGC insured plans.*
- *Outline the PBGC procedures for involuntary termination.*

Plan Termination

To be qualified, the Regulations require that a plan be "permanent."[1] By this is meant only that the employer must not have an *initial* intention of operating the plan for a few years to obtain tax benefits, then terminating it. Thus, despite the permanence requirement, qualified plans can be terminated and often are.

A plan can be terminated unilaterally by the employer, unless a collective bargaining agreement or other employment contract prohibits it. If an employer does not formally terminate a plan, but merely discontinues contributions to it, the IRS may find that the plan has been terminated, with the same consequences as if a formal termination had been made by the employer. It is also possible to have a *partial termination* of a plan, which usually means that the plan is terminated for an identifiable group of employees, such as employees at a given geographical location, while it is continued for other employees.

---

[1] Reg. Sec. 1.401–1(b)(2).

When Should a Plan Be Terminated?

If a qualified plan ceases to be an effective method of compensating employees, or becomes too expensive for the employer, it should be terminated. However, under the rules discussed in this chapter, a proposed termination may have such undesirable consequences that the employer will decide to continue the plan, possibly in amended form. As discussed below, the substitution of a different plan or plans may avoid some of the undesirable consequences of simply terminating the old plan.

Asset-Reversion Terminations. Defined-benefit plans are sometimes terminated not because they are too costly or ineffective but because the employer wants to take out some of the plan's assets. If the plan is fully funded, excess plan assets will revert to the employer, if the plan so provides. Although the assets that revert are taxable income to the employer, and there is an additional 10 percent federal penalty tax on asset reversions (Code Section 4980), the funds available can be substantial. These *asset-reversion terminations* have become fairly common in industries with declining work forces, which often have overfunded plans.

Questions have been raised about the fairness of asset-reversion terminations, since they deprive plan participants both of future-benefit accruals and possibly part of the security for prior-benefit accruals. These issues led in 1986 to the enactment of the 10 percent penalty tax, mentioned earlier. The penalty tax does not directly benefit employees, however, and its effect is still unclear. Further legislation has been suggested under which employers could get back excess funds from the plan without terminating it, subject to appropriate safeguards.

Premature Termination

The worst kind of termination (because of its bad tax consequences) is a plan termination accompanied by an IRS determination that no bona fide plan ever existed. This is sometimes called a "premature" or "retroactive" termination. If an employer terminates a plan within a few years after its inception, the employer must usually show that the termination resulted from *business necessity*—or the IRS will infer that the permanence requirement for qualification never existed. A business necessity means an adverse business condition that was not reasonably foreseeable when the plan was adopted—for example, insolvency or a sale or discontinuance of the business. If the plan is terminated after many years of operation, the IRS will not raise a presumption of impermanence if the plan is terminated without a business reason so long as the plan is properly funded and termination does not result in prohibited discrimination.

Other Types of Termination

Plan termination or any of a variety of termination-related events in the life of a qualified plan can result in immediate 100 percent vesting for some or all employees. With a defined-benefit plan, 100 percent vesting means that the accrued benefits of affected participants become 100 percent vested at the time of termination, to the extent the plan is funded. Most defined-benefit plans are insured by the PBGC, and the further complications involved are discussed below. With a defined-contribution plan, at termination participants become 100 percent vested in their account balances derived from employer contributions, regardless of where they stand otherwise on the vesting schedule. This precludes the possibility of any future forfeitures (and therefore any future reallocation of forfeitures). Obviously, the purpose of the vesting remedy is to limit the possibility of any discrimination resulting from termination of the plan.

Suspension or Discontinuance of Contributions. One type of event that can result in the IRS asserting a termination without any formal action by the employer is a discontinuance of employer contributions. If the plan is a pension plan, omitting the required contribution will usually result in problems with the minimum funding standards under Section 412 of the Code (Chapter 19), and the IRS probably will not assert the termination remedy immediately, although a termination under the PBGC provisions discussed below might occur. If the plan is a profit-sharing plan, the issue is whether the omission of a few years' contributions is a discontinuance of the plan or merely a temporary suspension. Under the law, this is to be decided on the facts and circumstances of each situation.

Freezing the Plan. A termination-type option open to an employer is to discontinue contributions to the plan, knowing the plan will be considered terminated by the IRS; but the employer does not immediately distribute the plan funds to participants. Instead, the employer maintains the fund and delays distribution of benefits to participants until a later time, such as their termination of employment or retirement. In these situations, the IRS will allow the trust to continue as a tax-free entity until all the trust assets are distributed to participants and beneficiaries under the terms of the plan. In many cases, this may be a beneficial method of plan termination; the participants may not wish to have an immediate distribution, which would be immediately subject to income tax, but may prefer to defer taxes and distributions. However, the participants may be able to roll over an immediate distribution tax free under the IRA provisions discussed in Chapter 22.

A disadvantage of freezing the plan is that it must continue to be administered, including the filing of the Form 5500 series annual report and the updating of the plan to reflect changes in the law. A frozen plan is also subject to the possibility of being disqualified through discrimination in participation, since its coverage will gradually decline over time.

An alternative to freezing that also defers taxation to participants is the purchase of nontransferable annuity contracts from an insurance company and distribution of the contracts to participants and beneficiaries. Income tax is then also payable only as annuity benefits are paid out.

Curtailment. A curtailment is a plan amendment that reduces benefits or employer contributions or that makes eligibility or vesting requirements less liberal. The reason for such amendments is usually to reduce the employer's cost for the plan. The IRS requires the same remedy for a curtailment as for a termination—that is, the affected participants must become 100 percent vested in their accrued benefits or account balances under the plan.

Partial Termination. A partial termination is a plan change initiated by the employer under somewhat similar circumstances as a curtailment, except that a partial termination usually refers to a restriction of coverage of the plan to a smaller group of employees. Simply dismissing or laying off a significant group of covered employees can be deemed a partial termination of the plan. The main result of a partial termination is that the excluded group of employees becomes 100 percent immediately vested in their accrued benefits (to the extent funded) or account balances.

Mergers, Consolidations, and Substitute Plans. Neither curtailment nor partial termination is explicitly defined by the IRS; it is an area deliberately kept vague so as to induce employers to act with caution in this area. This type of plan change, therefore, must be done carefully. Sometimes the IRS will not require immediate vesting if a reduction of benefits in one form is accompanied by an increase in some other form. Also, it is sometimes possible to replace one plan with another comparable plan, or to merge one plan into another comparable plan, without the IRS requiring the termination remedy. In the case of a merger or a consolidation of plans, there is also a specific requirement that, after the transaction, each participant in the plan must be entitled to at least as great a benefit (if the plan had then terminated) as the participant would have been entitled to immediately before the transaction (if the plan had then terminated). A provision to this effect must be included in the plan document, except for a multi-employer plan.

The Pension Benefit Guaranty Corporation (PBGC) and Its Plan Insurance

If an employer encounters financial difficulty and is forced to terminate or curtail a qualified defined-benefit plan, the ultimate payment of plan benefits is often jeopardized. If the plan uses an insurance company contract as the funding medium, the employee's benefit is usually to some extent guaranteed by the insurance company. However, the use of trust funds predominates in defined-benefit plans, and these funds usually involve no insurance company guarantees. Actuarial funding methods assume that plans will be in existence indefinitely; as a result, the plan fund in many cases is, at a given moment, inadequate to fund all of the benefits accrued under the plan if the plan terminates at that moment.

Recognizing this problem, Congress in 1974 as part of ERISA (Title 4—Sections 4000 et seq.) established a scheme of mandatory plan insurance for certain defined-benefit plans, to be administered by a quasi-governmental corporation called the Pension Benefit Guaranty Corporation (PBGC). Defined-contribution plans do not involve the same benefit security problems as defined-benefit plans, because the participant's accrued benefit is always equal to the participant's account balance. Therefore, the PBGC plan insurance scheme does not apply to defined-contribution ("individual account") plans.

Plans Covered

PBGC coverage can be summarized by stating that, in general, all qualified defined-benefit plans are covered, while individual account (defined-contribution) plans are not covered. With respect to defined-benefit plans, the usual exclusions applicable to ERISA provisions apply; there is no PBGC coverage for federal, state, and local government plans, church plans (unless the plan elects coverage), plans with no employer contributions, plans for highly compensated individuals or substantial owners, plans frozen prior to ERISA, and various other exclusions.

Another exception to PBGC coverage is somewhat distinctive: There is no coverage for a plan established and maintained by a professional service employer which, at no time after September 2, 1974, has more than 25 active participants in the plan. A professional service employer means an organization, incorporated or unincorporated, controlled by professional individuals, which includes but is not limited to physicians, dentists, chiropractors, osteopaths, optometrists, other licensed practitioners of the healing arts, attorneys at law, public accountants, public engineers, architects, draftsmen, actuaries, psychologists, social or physical scientists, and performing artists.

Benefits Insured

The PBGC does not insure or guarantee all benefits provided under a qualified defined-benefit plan covered by PBGC insurance. A distinction is made between *basic* and *nonbasic* benefits. The PBGC is required under the terms of its federal charter to insure basic benefits. PBGC is allowed to extend coverage to nonbasic benefits, but it has not yet done so.

There are numerous conditions and limitations on what qualifies as a guaranteed basic benefit, set out in Part 2613 of the PBGC Regulations. The most significant limitations are:

1. The benefit must be nonforfeitable or vested. This refers to vesting that existed under the terms of the plan immediately prior to plan termination, not to benefits that became vested solely on account of plan termination.

2. The benefit must be a "pension benefit," meaning, in general, a benefit payable as an annuity to a retiring or terminating participant or surviving beneficiary, providing a substantially level retirement income to the recipient. Consequently, the PBGC generally does not insure a lump-sum benefit.

3. There is a dollar limitation on the amount of monthly payment the PBGC will guarantee. Regardless of the plan provisions, the insured monthly benefit is limited to $1/12$th of the participant's average annual gross income from the employer during the highest-paid five consecutive calendar years or lesser number of years of active participation. Furthermore, in no event will the insured benefit

exceed a dollar limit, originally $750 monthly in 1974, which is subject to an indexation procedure and for plans terminated in 1987 is $1,857.95 monthly. The dollar limitation applies to a benefit in the form of a straight-life annuity beginning at age 65 and payable monthly. The limit is adjusted actuarially for other forms of benefits.

4. The participant must be "entitled" to the benefit as of the date of plan termination. Generally, this means that the recipient must have satisfied the conditions of the plan necessary to establish the right to receive the benefit (other than mere application for it or satisfying a waiting period) prior to the plan termination date. Also, the benefit must be payable to or for the benefit of a natural person (not, for example, to a corporation).

There are numerous additional limitations on the guaranteed basic benefit, some of which may be significant in specific situations. For example, the full amount is guaranteed only if the plan or plan amendment under which the benefit is provided was in effect for 60 months before plan termination. If this is not the case, only a portion of the benefit may be guaranteed. Also, there is a limitation on guaranteed benefits payable to a "substantial owner" of the business. A substantial owner is one who, at any time within five years of the date of termination, owned directly or indirectly a more than 10 percent interest in the business. Guaranteed benefits of a substantial owner may be reduced, if the substantial owner has less than 30 years of active participation in the plan.

PBGC Funding and Premiums

The PBGC has established several funds to provide benefit guarantees. It has the power to borrow up to $100 million from the U.S. Treasury, if necessary. However, the PBGC is expected to be self-supporting eventually and, therefore, is required to charge insurance premiums for its guarantees. For single-employer plans, the annual premium for 1986 is $8.50 per participant. For multiemployer plans, the current schedule for premium payments provides an annual rate that will ultimately reach $2.68 per participant. Congress has the authority, through a joint resolution procedure, to review and change PBGC rates from time to time, based on various factors set out in the law. Payment of the premiums is mandatory and is enforced by various penalties.

Plan Termination Procedures

Reportable Events. The manner in which the PBGC becomes involved with a plan that is terminating or encountering various difficulties is somewhat complex. First, the plan administrator is obligated to report to the PBGC certain events that could potentially cause financial difficulty. There is a long list of these *reportable events;* some significant ones include:

An IRS or Department of Labor disqualification of the plan.
A plan amendment decreasing retirement benefits.

A decrease in the number of active participants to less than 80 percent of the number at the beginning of the plan year or 75 percent of the number at the beginning of the previous plan year.

A determination by the IRS that there has been a termination or partial termination of the plan.

A failure to meet the minimum funding standards.

An inability by the plan to pay benefits when due.

Certain large distributions to a substantial owner.

A plan merger, consolidation, or transfer of its assets.

The occurrence of another event indicative of a need to terminate the plan—the Regulations refer to such items as insolvency of the employer or a related employer and certain breakups of commonly controlled groups of employers.[2]

If the consequences of these reportable events are significant enough, the plan can be *involuntarily terminated* by the PBGC. Also, of course, a *voluntary termination* can be carried out by the plan administrator under one of the two procedures described below. In any event, the actual termination of a plan covered by PBGC guarantees is carried out under detailed procedures in the law.

Allocation of Plan Assets on Termination. The PBGC termination procedures revolve around the rules for allocation of the assets of a terminated defined-benefit plan under Section 4044 of ERISA. On termination, such plan assets must be allocated in descending order to the following categories:

Benefits attributable to voluntary employee contributions.

Benefits attributable to mandatory employee contributions.

Annuity benefits attributable to employer contributions that were, or could have been, in "pay status" as of three years prior to termination. A benefit in "pay status" essentially means a benefit being paid to a retired (nonactive) employee. The high priority reflects the fact that such employees are least able to protect themselves against a failure of the plan fund.

All other PBGC guaranteed benefits.

All other vested benefits.

All other plan benefits.

Any amount remaining after these categories may revert to the employer, if the plan so provides.

Voluntary Plan Termination. ERISA Section 4041(a) provides for two types of voluntary termination procedures: the *standard termination* and the *distress termination*. A plan is eligible for the standard termination only if assets at the termination date are sufficient to provide for all *benefit commitments* as of the termination date. A benefit commitment to a participant or beneficiary means all benefits guaranteed by the PBGC, as described earlier, but determined without

---

[2]ERISA Section 4043 and PBGC Regs. Section 2615.

certain limitations, such as the maximum dollar limit or the restriction on benefits in effect for less than 60 months before plan termination. Certain early-retirement supplements and plant-closing benefits also come within the definition of benefit commitments. If benefit commitments are not met, a voluntary termination must follow the distress termination procedures.

With a standard termination, the plan administrator must provide 60 days advance notice of intent to terminate to participants, beneficiaries, and other affected parties. In addition, a notice containing certain required information must be filed with the PBGC. The PBGC filing includes an enrolled actuary's certification of the projected amount of plan assets, the actuarial present value of the benefit commitments under the plan, and the plan's sufficiency to fulfill these benefit commitments. The PBGC then has a 60-day determination period under which it may issue a notice of noncompliance, if PBGC finds that the standard termination requirements have not been met.

The plan administrator must begin distributing plan assets at the end of the 60-day determination period, if the PBGC has not issued a notice of noncompliance and if the plan assets are sufficient to meet benefit commitments. The assets are distributed in accordance with the priorities of ERISA Section 4044, described above. Assets must be distributed either through the purchase of annuities from an insurance company to provide plan benefits or in some other manner providing adequate benefit security.

A distress termination is available only if one of three distress criteria is met:

1. Each contributing sponsor of the plan or substantial member of a controlled group sponsoring the plan must be in a liquidation proceeding under federal bankruptcy law or similar state law; or

2. the sponsor must be involved in a reorganization in bankruptcy or an insolvency proceeding; or

3. the plan administrator demonstrates to the PBGC that, unless the termination occurs, the sponsor will not be able to pay its debts and will be unable to continue in business, or the cost of providing benefits under the pension plan have become unreasonably burdensome (e.g., because of a declining work force).

Upon a distress termination, the plan administrator must submit to the PBGC information similar to that required under a standard termination, plus information related to the distress criteria. The PBGC will determine if the distress requirements have been met and whether the plan is sufficient to fulfill benefit commitments and guaranteed benefits. If the PBGC determines that there are sufficient plan assets to fulfill benefit commitments, the plan administrator may begin to distribute the assets in accordance with Section 4044 of ERISA. If the PBGC determines that the plan is sufficient only to provide guaranteed benefits, the plan administrator may distribute plan assets and terminate the plan; but the PBGC will establish a separate trust under ERISA Section 4049 for the terminating plan to pay nonguaranteed benefits. If the PBGC determines that plan assets are not sufficient even for guaranteed benefits, the PBGC will proceed to terminate the plan in accordance with the procedures for involuntary terminations; and it also must establish a separate Section 4049 trust for any benefit commitments under the plan that are not guaranteed.

A Section 4049 trust, as indicated above, is established by the PBGC wherever additional benefit commitments are unfunded under a terminating plan. As long as the employer remains in business, it continues to be obligated to fund these benefit commitments, and the trust is used to receive payments from the employer and to distribute benefits to plan participants and beneficiaries accordingly. The trust continues as long as is necessary to pay all benefit commitments.

Involuntary Termination (Termination by PBGC). The PBGC has broad authority to initiate the termination of a plan. It can do so whenever a plan has failed to meet the minimum funding standard requirements, whenever the plan is unable to pay benefits when due, when there is a distribution to a substantial owner of $10,000 or more, or when, as the statute states, "the possible long-run loss" to the PBGC "may reasonably be expected to increase unreasonably if the plan is not terminated." Presumably, the termination procedures will usually result from receiving bad news from a plan sponsor who has reported under the reportable events provisions, described above. However, the PBGC also has investigative authority that can enable it to invoke its plan termination authority even if the plan administrator has not made any report to the PBGC.

When the PBGC decides to terminate a plan, it notifies the plan administrator and applies to a U.S. District Court for a termination decree. A court-appointed trustee supervises the termination and final distribution of the plan assets. A plan can also be terminated by an agreement between the PBGC and the plan administrator, without court involvement.

Contingent Liability of Employer. In the event of a plan termination covered by PBGC insurance, the employer must reimburse the PBGC for the PBGC's liability for guaranteed benefits in excess of the plan's assets. However, the employer liability to reimburse in full is limited to 30 percent of the "net worth" of the employer. Net worth is determined as of a date chosen by the PBGC, which is not more than 120 days prior to the date of termination. This remedy has proven to be of somewhat limited value, particularly in the case of large bankrupt employers where the PBGC's liability is the greatest, since a bankrupt company has no net worth.

Multiemployer Plans. The previous discussion of termination procedures applies primarily to single-employer plans or plans of controlled groups of employers. The termination problems are somewhat different where contributions to the plan are made by a number of unrelated employers—that is, a multiemployer plan, such as a plan adopted under industry-wide collective bargaining agreements. For such plans, there are different asset allocation provisions and somewhat different provisions for involuntary termination by the PBGC.

The most significant difference from single-employer plans involves the *withdrawal liability* of an employer that completely or partially withdraws from a multiemployer plan. A sale of the employer's assets in an arm's-length transaction will not be treated as a withdrawal as long as the purchaser of the business continues the plan, the purchaser provides an acceptable surety bond or escrow deposit for five years after the sale, and the seller of the business remains secondarily liable for five years. If an employer withdraws from the plan, the employer's withdrawal liability is an amount based on the withdrawing employer's share of unfunded vested benefits under the plan. The withdrawing employer must pay all or a substantial portion of the withdrawal liability to the plan on a periodic basis over a number of years. The law provides for the PBGC to establish a supplemental fund to reimburse multiemployer plans for any uncollectible employer withdrawal liabilities.

Summary

Although a qualified plan must be established with an initial intent of permanence, it can be terminated unilaterally by an employer. If terminated within only a few years, the employer should show business necessity to avoid a finding of premature or retroactive termination. Plans may also be partially terminated with respect to a specific group of employees. When a plan is terminated, all participants must become 100 percent vested in their accrued benefits or account balances, to the extent of plan funds. Any excess funds beyond those needed to fully fund all accrued benefits may be returned to the employer, subject to income taxation plus a 10 percent penalty tax.

On termination, plan assets may simply be distributed to participants in a lump sum, or annuities may be purchased from an insurance company and distributed. Alternatively, the plan can be frozen and continue to exist only for the purpose of paying benefits.

The PBGC is a government corporation funded through employer-paid premiums that insure benefits from certain defined-benefit plans within limits. Defined-contribution plans are not covered. Only basic benefits are insured.

The plan administration of a PBGC-insured plan must notify PBGC if certain reportable events occur, in which case the PBGC can investigate and, in some cases, initiate an involuntary termination of the plan. If a plan administrator wishes to voluntarily terminate a PBGC-insured plan, either a standard or a distress termination procedure must be followed. Asset distributions to participants are permitted only upon favorable PBGC action, and assets must be allocated according to ERISA priorities. Employers remain liable to pay all benefit commitments under the plan even if the fund is insufficient.

22

Individual Retirement Plans and Simplified Employee Pensions

Objectives of This Chapter
- *Describe the role of individual retirement plans in retirement planning for individuals.*
- *Discuss the tax-law treatment of IRAs, in particular the deduction rules and the distribution and taxation rules.*
- *Describe the types of funding that can be used with IRAs.*
- *Discuss the characteristics and planning uses for IRA rollovers and alternative techniques.*
- *Describe the characteristics of SEPs and their planning uses.*

● Complete retirement planning, at least from the employee's viewpoint, requires consideration of individual retirement accounts or annuities (IRAs), which allow individuals to adopt a plan that provides tax-deferral benefits somewhat similar to those available from an employer plan. The role of IRAs is a limited one, however. Individuals who are participants in qualified plans and whose income exceeds specified limits are limited or excluded altogether from eligibility for IRA deductions. And, no employee can contribute more than $2,000 annually to an IRA (or $2,250 including a spousal IRA).

IRAs can be used by employers as part of their employee plan design, either through simply sponsoring an IRA plan or adopting an arrangement known as a *simplified employee pension,* or *SEP*, under which employer contributions or employee salary reductions are made systematically to employees' IRAs. SEPs permit a contribution level similar to that for a qualified plan, and, in fact, are viewed as an alternative to a qualified plan.

IRAs and SEPs involve a variety of planning issues and relatively complex tax-law treatment, as discussed in this chapter.

Individual Retirement Plans

Individual retirement accounts or annuities are plans under which an individual can obtain tax deferral and some of the other benefits of a qualified plan even where there is no employer-sponsored qualified plan. For simplicity, all these plans will be referred to as IRAs, regardless of the funding medium to be described later.

Historical Ups and Downs

The IRA provisions in the Code (Sections 219 and 408) were originally designed by Congress in 1974 to benefit only individuals who were not covered under the qualified plans of their employers. As a result of concern about increasing the rate of savings and investment, effective in 1982 Congress extended the IRA provisions to all employees with earned income, regardless of whether they were covered under other qualified plans. But in the Tax Reform Act of 1986, tax-revenue losses impelled Congress to return in part to the original restrictions, effective January 1, 1987.

As will be seen from this discussion, the IRA provisions are burdened with numerous complex restrictions, and the amount that each employee may contribute and deduct is relatively low. That is, in part, a result of the ongoing policy debate in Congress about the proper tax treatment of retirement savings and concern with the tax-revenue cost of tax-favored plans.

Many of the most complex provisions of the qualified plan law are designed to induce owners of small businesses to adopt plans that cover not only themselves but also provide generous benefits for rank-and-file employees, so the cost-effectiveness of the tax benefits will be maximized, as discussed in Chapter 4. This has considerable policy significance, because small businesses are, collectively, employers of a large portion of the work force.

When the IRA provisions were first enacted, fears were expressed that the existence of tax-favored individual retirement savings plans would discourage the adoption of regular qualified plans, particularly if the individual plans allowed significant contributions and deductions. The concern was also expressed that, if tax-favored retirement savings on an individual basis became dominant, only upper-income people would have retirement savings plans, because they are more likely to have enough discretionary income to put in the plan, and also because the tax benefit of a deduction under the progressive tax system is greater for upper-income persons. The restrictions and low deduction limits for IRAs were apparently intended to address these concerns.

Although there is no clear indication that the IRA provisions have caused a decline in the adoption of qualified plans (primarily because any decline can also be explained by other factors), it is reasonably clear that IRA plans are used predominantly by taxpayers in the upper half of the income distribution. A 1983 study (during the broad eligibility period) indicated that only 11 percent of workers earning less than $20,000 established IRAs, compared with 58 percent of those earning more than $50,000.[1]

---

[1] *Washington Report* 85–43 (Washington, D.C.: Association for Advanced Life Underwriting, 1985). (Report on study by Hewitt Associates.)

Individual Retirement Plans and Simplified Employee Pensions **253**

Eligibility for IRAs

To be eligible for an IRA, an employee or self-employed person must have compensation or earned income.[2] Compensation or earned income means income received from services actually performed by the individual. This includes compensation from self-employment as well as from an employer. The definition has been extended to also include taxable alimony received by a divorced spouse. It does not include investment income, any amount received as a pension or annuity, or any amount received as deferred compensation.

Deduction Limit

The full IRA annual deduction limit is the lesser of $2,000 or 100 percent of earned income. However, deductible IRA contributions are restricted to:

- Individuals who are not active participants in an employer-maintained retirement plan for any part of the retirement plan year ending with or within the individual's taxable year.
- Any other individual, as long as the individual (or married couple if a joint return is filed) has adjusted gross income below a specified limit. If the adjusted gross income exceeds this limit, the $2,000 IRA limit is reduced under a formula that eventually permits no deduction.

The *active participant* restriction applies if the individual (or if a joint return is filed, either the individual or spouse) is an active participant in:

- A regular qualified plan.
- A Sec. 403(b) tax-deferred annuity plan.
- A simplified employee pension (SEP).
- A federal, state, or local government plan, not including a Sec. 457 nonqualified deferred-compensation plan.

Active plan participants can make deductible IRA contributions only if their income falls within certain income limits, as shown by the following table:

IRA Deduction/Compensation Limits (Taxpayer or Spouse Active Plan Participant)

	Full IRA Deduction	Reduced IRA Deduction	No IRA Deduction
Individual	$25,000 or less	between $25,000–$35,000	$35,000 or over
Married couple, joint return	$40,000 or less	between $40,000–$50,000	$50,000 or over
Married, filing separately	not available	$ 0–$10,000	$10,000 or over

---

[2] Code Section 219 covers the IRS eligibility and deduction limits described here.

The reduction in the IRA deduction for those affected is computed by multiplying the IRA limit ($2,000 or 100 percent of compensation) by a fraction equal to:

$$\frac{\text{Taxpayer's adjusted gross income minus full deduction limit}}{\$10,000}$$

There is a $200 floor under this equation—if the result comes out to less than $200, the taxpayer can contribute and deduct $200.

Examples

A married couple, one of whom is an active participant in a regular qualified plan, file a joint return and have an adjusted gross income of $43,000.

$$\frac{\$3,000}{\$10,000} \times \$2,000 = \$600$$

$$\$2,000 - \$600 = \$1,400 \text{ IRA deduction limit}$$

A single person, an active participant in a qualified plan, has an adjusted gross income of $34,500.

$$\frac{\$9,500}{\$10,000} \times \$2,000 = \$1,900$$

$$\$2,000 - \$1,900 = \$100$$

However, the individual may contribute $200, the floor amount.

Spousal IRAs

If an individual has a spouse who has no compensation or earned income, the working individual can also set up an IRA for the spouse. In this case, the total contribution to both IRAs is the lesser of $2,250 or 100 percent of compensation or earned income. If the working spouse is an active participant in an employer retirement plan, the $2,250 is reduced in the same manner as described above, and is thus phased out for joint adjusted gross incomes of $50,000 or more.

A spouse with earned income can elect to be treated as having no earned income, to use the spousal IRA provision; this is useful if the earned income is small (e.g., $250 or less). If both spouses have compensation or earned income, however, it generally is beneficial for each to set up his or her own IRA, within the available deduction restrictions.

Nondeductible IRAs

Individuals not permitted to make deductible IRA contributions may nevertheless make such contributions on a nondeductible basis, up to the usual $2,000/100 percent/$2,250 limit. Nondeductible contributions (but not income on those contributions) are tax free when ultimately distributed to the individual. If nondeductible contributions to an IRA are made, any amounts withdrawn are treated as partly tax free and partly taxable under rules similar to the exclusion ratio calculation for annuities under Code Sec. 72.

The law allows individuals to designate deductible contributions as nondeductible contributions, to be able to receive distributions tax free. This might be a useful technique in a year in which taxable income has been reduced to zero through other deductions or losses.

Other Restrictions

Since the IRA is designed primarily for retirement savings, no IRA deduction is allowed to an individual for the taxable year in which the individual attains age 70½ or any later year.

Contributions to an IRA must be made in cash; contributions of property, such as an insurance policy, are not permitted.

Excess Contributions

A contribution in excess of the deductible limits described above is an *excess contribution* and is subject to an annual nondeductible 6 percent excise tax. The excise tax continues to be applied each year until the contribution is withdrawn from the IRA. Many complex rules apply to excess contributions; their complexity seems out of proportion to the actual issue involved.[3]

Timing of Contributions

An IRA for any given year may be established up to the time for filing the tax return for the given year, not including extensions. Deductible contributions for a given year may be made within the same time limit. This "last minute" feature of IRAs helps to explain a lot of their popularity.

Example

Suppose Frank Filer works out a draft of his 1986 tax return on April 1, 1987, and discovers that he owes the government $600. His local savings bank is running an ad-

---

[3] Code Section 4973.

vertising campaign touting its IRAs and offering to lend money to contribute to an IRA. Frank does some quick figuring and discovers that, if he borrows $2,000 from the bank and contributes it to an IRA, it will wipe out his tax liability and he will be entitled to a $160 tax refund—enough to make the first monthly payment on the loan. This may be a more attractive deal to Frank than borrowing $600 to pay taxes.

Limitations on IRA Distributions

The limitations on IRA distributions are similar to but somewhat more restrictive than those for qualified plans, generally. First, under Code Section 72(t), no distribution may be made from an IRA prior to age 59½ (except for death or disability) without incurring a penalty tax equal to 10 percent of the taxable amount of the distribution, in addition to the regular tax on the distribution. However, distributions in the form of a single or joint life annuity can begin without penalty at any age. For this purpose, an individual is considered disabled if the individual is unable to engage in any substantial gainful activity by reason of any medically determinable physical or mental impairment that can be expected to result in death or to be of long-continued and indefinite duration—a definition similar to the social security disability definition.

Loans from IRAs are treated as distributions and, therefore, are not available for practical purposes. This is another aspect of IRAs that makes them less flexible than regular qualified plans, which allow loans.

There is an *upper* limit on the length of time amounts may be maintained in an IRA. Distributions from an IRA must begin no later than April 1 of the year following the year in which the individual attains age 70½. The distribution may be in the form of lump-sum or periodic payments. The minimum annual distribution is a periodic payment determined on the basis of a period not extending beyond the life expectancy of the individual or the joint life expectancy of the individual and a designated beneficiary. If an individual or beneficiary dies before the entire interest is distributed, the remaining amount, within five years after the death, must be distributed or applied to the purchase of an immediate life annuity for the beneficiary for a term not exceeding the life expectancy of the beneficiary. In general, these rules are the same as the rules under Section 401(a)(9) for distributions from qualified plans, discussed in Chapter 16.

If the assets of the IRA are not distributed at least as rapidly as described above, there is an excise tax of 50 percent of the *excess accumulation*.[4] The excess accumulation is the amount by which the minimum amount required to be distributed during a given year (under the above rules) exceeds the amount actually distributed during the year. The IRS is allowed to waive the 50 percent penalty to avoid penalizing reasonable errors.

---

[4]Code Section 4974.

Taxation of Distributions

The amount distributed from an IRA is taxable as ordinary income in the year of receipt. Lump-sum distributions are fully taxable when received and do not qualify for the special capital-gain or averaging provisions applicable to lump-sum distributions from qualified plans. An IRA annuity is taxed under the Section 72 annuity rules—that is, payments based on deductible contributions and all investment earnings are ordinary income and are taxable in full as received. Nondeductible IRA contributions, if any, are recovered tax free through an exclusion ratio applied to each payment.

The value of an annuity or lump sum received by any beneficiary of a participant in an IRA is included in the deceased participant's gross estate for federal estate tax purposes. However, if the beneficiary is a spouse, there is no estate tax, because of the unlimited marital deduction under the estate tax. Even for a nonspouse beneficiary, there may be no estate tax if the estate is relatively small—less than about $600,000.

Funding of IRAs

The Code provides for two types of IRAs: individual retirement accounts and individual retirement annuities.

Individual Retirement Accounts. An individual retirement account must be a plan established under a written trust created or organized in the United States for the exclusive benefit of the individual creating the IRA. A written custodial agreement can also be used. The written instrument must include the following provisions:

- The contributions must be in cash and not exceed $2,000 on behalf of any individual.
- The trustee must be a bank or "other person" approved by the IRS.
- No part of the trust fund will be invested in life insurance contracts. Annuities, however, can be purchased.
- An individual's account is nonforfeitable.
- The assets of the trust will not be commingled with other property except in a common trust fund or common investment fund.
- The individual's account must be distributed in accordance with certain distribution requirements, such as the age 70.5 provision and the minimum distribution requirement.

Many banks and other savings institutions are actively marketing trusteed IRAs. Brokerage houses and mutual funds also market trusteed IRAs; these technically use a bank as trustee, but the bank's role is purely formal, and the investor views the broker or fund as the sponsor of the IRA.

A bank or institution acting as trustee or custodian may prepare its own prototype trust agreement and submit the agreement to the IRS for approval on Form

5306. Alternatively, the IRS has issued prototype trust and custodial agreements (Forms 5305 and 5305A) which, if used, are automatically qualified. An individual who deposits funds in an IRA that uses an approved form of trust agreement does not have to submit the IRA to the IRS for approval.

Individual Retirement Annuities. An individual may fund an IRA by purchasing an *individual retirement annuity,* which is a contract that is issued by an insurance company and that meets requirements parallel to those listed above for individual retirement accounts. The premium for the annuity may not be fixed, so the only insurance product that can be used is a flexible premium annuity. Both fixed-dollar and variable annuities can be used.

Insurance companies that wish to market individual retirement annuities may apply for IRS approval of their own prototype contracts. As with trusteed plans, an individual who purchases an approved prototype individual retirement annuity contract does not apply separately for IRS approval of the individual IRA plan.

Retirement Bonds. To facilitate the use of IRAs, the federal government issued a special series of bonds designed specifically for funding IRAs. These bonds contain a number of restrictions similar in purpose to those described earlier for individual retirement accounts and annuities. The bonds made no significant impact on the IRA market and sales were suspended in 1982.

Table 22–1 gives some data on the distribution of IRA funding.

Rollovers

To increase the amount of investment flexibility available to participants in IRAs and qualified plans, the Code contains a number of provisions relating to the use of IRAs as vehicles for investment *rollovers*. Three types of tax-favored rollovers are possible.

1. *Rollover from One IRA to Another.* There is no current taxation if an individual withdraws an amount out of an IRA trust fund, IRA annuity, or retire-

TABLE 22–1. IRA Funding

Institution	1977	1984	
	IRA Accounts (000,000 omitted)		
Life insurance companies	$1,875	$12,550	
Mutual funds	178	16,500	
U.S. retirement bonds	33	25	
Commercial banks	n.a.	43,800	(IRA and Keogh)
Mutual savings banks	963	9,644	
Savings & loan associations	2,652	47,500	(IRA and Keogh)
Credit unions	-0-	8,529	
Total	n.a.	n.a.	(IRA and Keogh $150,299)

n.a. = not available.
Source: *Pension Facts,* American Council of Life Insurance, 1986 update.

ment bond plan and invests part or all of it in another IRA plan. To receive this treatment, the amount to be rolled over must be paid into another IRA plan not later than the 60th day after the withdrawal. If such a rollover is made, no additional tax-free rollover of this type is permitted for a period of one year thereafter.

A direct transfer of an account from one IRA trustee to another (with the participant never receiving the money) is not treated as a rollover for purposes of these rules. Thus, a direct transfer can be used as a way of avoiding the one-year rule.

2. *Rollover of Distribution from Qualified Plan or Annuity.* An IRA may be used as a vehicle for receiving the proceeds of a distribution from a qualified plan or a Section 403(b) plan, thereby avoiding immediate taxation on the distribution. The distribution from the qualified plan or Section 403(b) plan must be at least 50 percent of the employee's account balance in the plan to be eligible for rollover. All or any portion of the amount received can be rolled over. The 100 percent/$2,000 limit does not apply to a rollover contribution. The rollover contribution must be made on or before the 60th day after receipt of the distribution. An existing IRA can be used, or a new one may be set up.

The part of the distribution that is rolled over into the IRA will not be currently taxable to the recipient. The usual rules for taxation of IRA distributions will apply when this amount is subsequently withdrawn. Any part of the distribution from the qualified plan or Section 403(b) plan that is not rolled over into the IRA will be taxable at the time of receipt under the usual rules for taxation of distributions, except that the capital-gain and averaging provisions may not be used.

In deciding whether to roll over all or part of the proceeds of a distribution from a qualified plan to an IRA, the alternatives must be considered. A lump-sum distribution from a qualified plan may qualify for the special capital-gain and averaging provisions of the code. Thus, even though a distribution that is not rolled over is taxable immediately, it is taxable under advantageous provisions, if it qualified as a lump-sum distribution. A distribution that is rolled over will not be taxed immediately; taxation will be deferred to the time when it is withdrawn from the IRA. However, this subsequent distribution, like any IRA distribution, is not eligible for the capital-gain or averaging provisions; rather, the taxable amount is taxed as ordinary income. Furthermore, the distribution cannot be made without penalty until age 59½, although it can be deferred as late as age 70½. Also, the $5,000 income tax exclusion for employee death benefits is not available for a distribution from an IRA.

Despite the possible loss of averaging, however, the mere deferral of taxes resulting from a rollover may be advantageous. Furthermore, taxes on investment earnings of the IRA are also deferred until the rollover amount is distributed. Although it is somewhat complex, the tax consequences of the two alternatives can be calculated (under appropriate assumptions) and compared; some financial planners provide such advice to their clients.

Some tax planners have devised methods of obtaining tax-deferral and rollover results in general without using an IRA with all its restrictions. For example, if the plan administrator is willing to cooperate, the plan distribution can be made in the form of a nontransferable deferred annuity instead of cash. This will not result in tax to the recipient until annuity proceeds are withdrawn, just as with an IRA; but this type of annuity does not typically require waiting until age 59½, death, or disability to begin withdrawals. In most of these situations, if there is deferral of the distribution, the averaging and capital-gain treatment is lost, just as with an IRA rollover. Also, careful planning is necessary to obtain the proper tax result.

3. *IRA as Conduit for Transfer from One Plan to Another.* Finally, an IRA may be used as a conduit to carry out a tax-free transfer of cash or property from one corporate qualified plan to another. Basically, if the amount received from the qualified plan is transferred within 60 days to an IRA, the transfer is tax free, as described earlier. In addition, if the IRA plan contains no assets other than those attributable to the distribution from the qualified plan, then the amount in the IRA may subsequently be transferred tax free to another qualified plan—if the transfer is made within 60 days after the property is received. Similar provisions allow an IRA to be used as a conduit between two Section 403(b) annuity plans.

Use of a conduit IRA is subject to some technical limitations.[5] It also is somewhat complex mechanically. In some cases, a simpler procedure known as a *trustee-to-trustee transfer* may be a better way to accomplish the same result. This procedure has been approved by the IRS and is often used by smaller employers to close out a superseded plan.[6]

Example

Suppose Dr. Messer has practiced medicine as a sole practitioner for a number of years and has a qualified ("Keogh") plan. In 1987, he agrees to form a professional corporation with Dr. Couteau. The new company will have a qualified plan. Dr. Messer's account in the old plan may be transferred directly from the trustee of the Messer plan to the trustee of the Messer/Couteau plan without adverse tax consequences. It is important to observe the formalities carefully in a procedure like this, or the IRS might claim that a taxable distribution took place.

Employer-Sponsored IRAs

Although the IRA is viewed primarily as a device for facilitating individual retirement savings, an employer may sponsor an IRA for some or all employees. A labor union also may sponsor an IRA plan for its members. There is no require-

---

[5] Code Section 408(d)(3)(A).
[6] Rev. Rul. 67–213, 1967–2 C.B. 149.

ment that the employer-sponsored IRAs be available to all employees or be nondiscriminatory in coverage.

The contributions to the employer-sponsored IRA may be made as additional compensation or as a salary reduction. Any amount contributed by the employer to the IRA is taxable to the employee as additional compensation income. The employee is then eligible for the IRA tax deduction up to the 100 percent/$2,000 limitation. Since the amounts contributed are additional compensation, they are subject to FICA and FUTA taxes, thereby adding to employer costs. No federal income tax withholding is required, if the employer believes that the employee will be entitled to the offsetting IRA tax deduction.

An employer-sponsored IRA may use separate IRA trusts or annuity plans for each employee, or a single account may be used. However, the single account must provide a separate accounting for each participant's interest. Either a commingled trust fund or a nontrusteed group annuity contract with individual certificates may be used. In an employer-sponsored IRA, the prohibited transaction rules described in Chapter 17 apply to transactions between the employer or other disqualified person and the IRA itself.

An employer sponsoring an IRA may request a determination letter from the IRS, using Form 5306. Furthermore, the same reporting and disclosure requirements applicable to qualified plans under ERISA may apply to an employer sponsoring an IRA plan. The participation, funding, and vesting rules of ERISA, however, do not apply. The latter two are somewhat irrelevant, since the IRA plan may be funded only through the permitted IRA funding vehicles, and each participant is always 100 percent vested. If an employer makes no actual contribution to employee IRAs, but merely provides certain facilities, such as payroll deduction or checkoff, or allows the actual sponsor, an insurer, or labor union, to publicize the program among employees, the reporting and disclosure requirements will not apply to the employer.

Simplified Employee Pensions

The simplified employee pension (SEP) is an expanded version of the employer-sponsored IRA, designed by Congress to make it easy and attractive for employers to adopt a retirement plan which, although not a qualified plan as such, has similar features. A SEP is designed basically like an employer-sponsored IRA, but the deduction limits are much higher—instead of a $2,000 annual deduction limit, the limit on deductible contributions for each employee is the lesser of $30,000 or 15 percent of the employee's compensation. The price for this expanded deduction limit is that the employer loses discretion on who must be covered; there is a coverage requirement that, in some ways, is more stringent than for regular qualified plans.

Eligibility and Coverage

If the employer has a SEP plan, it must cover all employees who are at least 21 years of age and who have worked for the employer during three out of the preceding five calendar years. Part-time employment counts in determining this; there is no 1,000-hour definition of a year of service. However, contributions need not be made on behalf of employees whose compensation for the calendar year was less than $300 (as indexed for inflation). The plan can exclude employees who are members of collective bargaining units, if retirement benefits have been the subject of good faith bargaining, and it can also exclude nonresident aliens. Employer contributions to a SEP can be made for employees over age 70.5; these employees are not eligible for regular IRAs, as discussed earlier.

Contributions and Deductions

An employer need not contribute any particular amount to a SEP in a given year—or even make any contribution at all. In this respect, a SEP is more flexible than any type of qualified plan, even a profit-sharing plan, which requires substantial and recurring employer contributions. However, any employer contribution that is made must be allocated to employees under a definite written formula. The formula may not discriminate in favor of officers, more than 10 percent shareholders, self-employed individuals, or highly compensated employees. In general, the formula must provide allocations as a uniform percentage of total compensation of each employee, taking only the first $200,000 of compensation into account. The SEP allocation formula can be integrated with social security under the usual integration rules for qualified defined-contribution plans.

Each individual in a SEP maintains an IRA, and employer contributions to the SEP are channeled to each employee's IRA. For tax purposes, the employer contributions are treated as if they are paid to the employee in cash and included in income and then contributed to the IRA. The Code provides a deduction to both the employer and to the employee for these amounts.

If the employer maintaining a SEP also has a regular qualified plan, contributions to the SEP may reduce the amount that can be deducted for contributions to the regular plan. A SEP is not subject to the top-heavy rules (Chapter 18) but can be taken into account in determining whether an employer's other plans are top-heavy.

Salary Reduction SEPs

A SEP can be used as an alternative to a 401(k) plan for smaller employers (but not by state or local government employers). If the employer has 25 employees or less during the preceding year, salary reduction SEPs are permitted. Employees may elect to receive cash or have amounts contributed to the SEP. The $7,000 limit for 401(k) plans also applies in this case to the total of the salary reduction SEP and 401(k) salary reductions, if any.

To utilize the salary reduction SEP alternative, not less than 50 percent of the employees must elect to make contributions to the SEP. Also, an average deferral percentage rule similar to the 401(k) rules must be satisfied. The annual deferral percentage for each highly compensated employee who participates must be no more than 1.25 times the average deferral percentage for the year of non-highly compensated employees. For example, if non-highly compensated employees elect salary reductions of 6 percent of compensation, no highly compensated employee can elect more than a 7½ percent salary reduction.

Other Requirements

Except for the contribution, allocation, and deduction provisions, the IRAs maintained as part of a SEP are the same as other IRAs and the rules discussed in the previous section apply to them as well. For example, the rules for taxation of distributions from SEP-IRAs are the same as those for other IRAs. As with regular IRAs, loans to participants from SEP-IRAs are not permitted.

Labor and IRS regulations contain certain reporting and disclosure provisions for SEPs. These are simplified if the employer uses the IRS prototype SEP contained on Form 5305-SEP. This form was designed to simplify the adoption of SEPs by employers; however, it uses a nonintegrated formula.

When Should an Employer Use a SEP?

The term *simplified* in the name of these plans is somewhat misleading; a SEP is not really much simpler than a regular qualified profit-sharing plan, especially where a qualified master or prototype plan is used. However, installation costs are minimal where the government Form 5305-SEP is used; and administration costs are low, since the annual report form (5500 series) need not be filed. Thus, SEPs are attractive for cases where administrative costs must be absolutely minimized, such as a one-person plan. In other specific situations, the special coverage rules for SEPs may be more attractive than the regular coverage rules. Also, a SEP may be useful as a means of meeting the top-heavy requirements. From an employee viewpoint, the complete portability of the SEP benefit is attractive.

Summary

IRA deductions up to $2,000 annually ($2,250 including a spousal IRA) are available for individuals with compensation or earned income, subject to cutbacks where an individual or spouse is an active participant in an employer plan. Nondeductible IRAs also are permitted. Many complex rules and restrictions apply.

IRA distributions before age 59½, death, or disability are subject to penalty. Distributions must begin by April 1 after age 70½ and are taxable in full, except for any nondeductible contributions. IRA loans are not permitted.

IRA plans must be funded using either an individual retirement account or individual retirement annuity.

IRAs can be rolled over tax free to another IRA, or IRAs can be used as a conduit for moving accounts from one qualified plan to another. A direct transfer from trustee to trustee also may be used. Compliance with technical rules is important.

SEPs are employer plans using IRAs for funding, with eligibility, contribution, and other rules somewhat similar to those for a qualified plan.

23

Special Plans for Tax-Exempt and Government Employers

Objectives of This Chapter
This chapter covers two types of deferred-compensation plans for specific employers that have special tax treatment:

- *Section 403(b) tax-deferred annuity plans for tax-exempt organizations.*
- *Section 457 deferred-compensation plans for government and tax-exempt employers.*

● Tax-exempt and government employers can and often do have regular qualified plans, or similar plans, for their employees. However, compensation planning for these employers should always take into account the potential usefulness of these specialized plans as well.

Section 403(b) Tax-Deferred Annuity Plans

Some years ago, Congress was concerned by the possibility that employees of tax-exempt organizations might not have adequate qualified plan coverage, because tax-exempt employers may have relatively little money available for employee benefits and because the tax deductibility of a qualified plan does not act as an incentive, since the tax-exempt employer pays no federal income taxes. As a result, Congress enacted Section 403(b) of the Code which, within limits, allows employees of certain tax-exempt organizations to have money set aside for them by salary deductions or direct employer contributions in a tax-deferred plan somewhat similar to a qualified plan.

Section 403(b) plans are an important consideration in designing the benefit program for any tax-exempt employer. However, today many tax-exempt employers have regular qualified plans for their employees, with the Section 403(b) plan being made available as a supplemental retirement or savings program. In particular, tax-exempt and governmental employers are not permitted to adopt a Section

401(k) plan, so a 403(b) plan is clearly an alternative to a 401(k) plan in such cases.

Section 403(b) plans are sometimes referred to as tax-deferred annuity (TDA) plans or tax-sheltered annuities, but because these terms can also refer to annuities not covered under Section 403(b), the term *Section 403(b) plans* will be used here to avoid confusion.

Eligible Employers

Employees of two types of organizations are eligible for Section 403(b) plans. These employer organizations are:

1. A tax-exempt employer described in Section 501(c)(3) of the Code—that is, an employer "organized and operated exclusively for religious, charitable, scientific, testing for public safety, literary, or educational purposes, or to foster national or international amateur sport competition . . . or for the prevention of cruelty to children or animals." Section 501(c)(3) also requires that the organization benefits the public, rather than a private shareholder or individual, and that the organization refrains from political campaigning or propaganda to influence legislation.

2. An educational organization with a regular faculty and curriculum and a resident student body that is operated by a state or municipal agency—in other words, a public school or college.

Thus, Section 403(b) plans are available to a wide range of familiar nonprofit institutions, such as churches, private and public schools and colleges, hospitals, and charitable organizations.

To participate in a Section 403(b) plan of an eligible employer, the participant must be a full- or part-time employee. This is significant, because tax-exempt organizations often have ties with persons who are independent contractors, rather than employees. To illustrate, many physicians on a hospital staff are not technically employees, but rather independent contractors. A person is an employee when the employer exercises control or has the right to control the person's activities about what is done and when, where, and how it is done. The question of employee status also affects federal income tax withholding, employment taxes (social security and federal unemployment), and participation in other fringe-benefit plans of the employer. If the employer wishes to cover a person under a Section 403(b) plan, it must at least treat that person consistently as an employee for all these purposes.

To be eligible for a Section 403(b) plan, a public school employee must perform services related directly to the educational mission. The employee can be a clerical or custodial employee, as well as a teacher or principal; but a political officeholder is eligible only if the person has educational training or experience.

Coverage and Participation Tests. Section 403(b) plans are subject to the minimum coverage requirements of Section 410(b) beginning after 1988. These are the same coverage tests applicable to qualified plans—the percentage test, the ratio test, and the average-benefit test. Under prior law, no coverage tests were applicable to Section 403(b) plans, and employers could cover even a single highly compensated employee.

A Section 403(b) plan is covered under the age and service provisions of ERISA (ERISA Section 202), which are the same as the analogous age and service Code provisions for qualified plans. Thus, if a Section 403(b) plan uses age or service eligibility, these can be no greater than age 21 and one year of service. However, age and service requirements are rarely used in Section 403(b) plans.

The Annual Exclusion Allowance

An employer may contribute annually to a participant's account in Section 403(b) plan up to that participant's *exclusion allowance* for the year. As in a qualified defined-contribution plan, contributions may not discriminate in favor of highly compensated employees. For example, a contribution equal to a uniform percentage of annual compensation up to $200,000 would be nondiscriminatory. All amounts contributed to the plan must be immediately 100 percent vested.

The formula for the annual exclusion allowance for an employee is:

20 percent of the participant's *includible compensation* (taxable compensation) from the employer, multiplied by:
the employee's total years of service for the employer, minus:
amounts contributed to the plan in prior years that were excluded from the employee's income.

The third item—the amount subtracted from the 20 percent times years of service amount—must include contributions by the employer to regular qualified plans on behalf of the employee. If the qualified plan is a defined-benefit plan, the amount deemed to be contributed for the employee is to be determined under recognized actuarial principles or under a formula provided in the Regulations.

The determination of the exclusion allowance for higher-income employees is complicated by the fact that, although a Section 403(b) plan is not a qualified plan, the Section 415 limitation for defined-contribution plans applies. Thus, the annual addition to any participant's account cannot exceed the lesser of 25 percent of compensation or $30,000, even if the exclusion allowance would produce a higher figure.

Example

Doctor Staph is an employee of the Tibia Hospital and has an annual compensation of $200,000 this year. She has four prior years of service for Tibia Hospital, during which the hospital has contributed $5,000 to her account in a Section 403(b) plan. No amounts have been contributed to any qualified plan on her behalf. The maximum amount that can be contributed to the Section 403(b) plan this year is 20 percent of her includible compensation of $200,000 times her five years of service, or a total of

$200,000, less prior years' contributions of $5,000, or $195,000. Since this exceeds the applicable Section 415 limit of $30,000, $30,000 is the most that can be contributed to the Section 403(b) plan for Doctor Staph this year.

If the participant has more than one employer, all Section 403(b) plans of all employers must be combined for purposes of the Section 415 limit. However, if the employee participates in a regular qualified plan or plans, as well as the Section 403(b) plan, it usually is not necessary to combine the qualified plans and the 403(b) plan for purposes of the Section 415 limit (Section 415(g) and Regulations Section 1.415–8).

Salary Reduction Plans

The preceding discussion of the exclusion allowance assumed a noncontributory plan in which the employer made a contribution to the Section 403(b) plan over and above the employee's regular compensation. Most Section 403(b) plans are *not* designed this way. Instead, such plans are usually *salary reduction* plans. Under a salary reduction plan, the employee is given the option to elect to contribute part of his or her regular salary to the 403(b) plan, instead of receiving it in cash. There is a nondiscrimination requirement: If the plan permits salary reductions of more than $200 by any participant, then all employees in the organization must be given the same option, except for those covered under a Section 457 plan or Section 401(k) plan, or part-time student employees.

There is a $9,500 limit on annual salary reductions for each participant. This limit applies to the total (for each employee) of Section 403(b) salary reductions, salary reduction SEPs, and 401(k) salary reductions under plans of all the employee's employers. The $9,500 is indexed for cost-of-living increases in connection with the $7,000 401(k) limit: Once the 401(k) limit reaches $9,500 through indexing, the two limits will become the same and will be indexed together. The $9,500 limit does not apply to direct employer matching contributions to the participant's account; thus, the total can be more than $9,500 as long as the 20 percent exclusion allowance is not exceeded.

The amount contributed to the plan will not be subject to income taxes, if the salary reduction election is made properly. Basically, for these amounts to avoid taxation the employee must make the election in advance of the period in which the compensation is to be earned, and the salary reduction agreement between the employer and employee must be legally binding. If an employee makes such an agreement after the right to receive the compensation has been earned, the election will not be effective for tax purposes, because of the tax doctrine of constructive receipt.

Although the amounts contributed to the plan under a properly designed salary reduction agreement are not currently subject to income tax to the participant, they are subject to social security and federal unemployment (FICA and FUTA) taxes.

To apply the exclusion allowance formula given above to a salary reduction plan, the amount of *includible compensation* (i.e., compensation included in taxable income) must be used instead of the total salary.

Example

If an employee's stated salary is $30,000, and the employee elects to receive $25,000 in cash and have $5,000 contributed to a Section 403(b) plan, the amount of includible or taxable compensation is $25,000; therefore, the exclusion allowance is 20 percent of $25,000 times the employee's years of service, less prior years plan contributions. In other words, other things being equal, for an employee in the first year of service an employer can contribute up to 20 percent of the full stated salary; but if the employee elects to reduce salary and contribute the reduction to a Section 403(b) plan, then the maximum salary reduction is 16⅔ percent of the full stated salary or 20 percent of the stated salary after reduction.

Catch-Up Alternatives

The Section 415 limit (25 percent/$30,000) may not be exceeded in any year, while the regular exclusion allowance is increased by prior service. This works a hardship on long-service employees who have had relatively low Section 403(b) contributions in prior years. Under the regular exclusion allowance, their prior service would otherwise permit large contributions to catch up for past years. For employees of educational institutions, hospitals, and home-health service agencies—but not other employers—the Code contains catch-up alternatives to the regular Section 415 limitation that are aimed at long-service employees. Under the catch-up alternatives, in some cases the 25 percent of compensation limit under Section 415 is not applied, thus permitting Section 403(b) contributions in excess of 25 percent of the current year's compensation. However, in no event can the $30,000 limitation be exceeded even under the catch-up alternatives.

There is also a catch-up provision to raise the $9,500 salary reduction limit for employees having at least 15 years of service with the employer. The catch-up limit (Code Section 402(g)) allows additional salary reductions above the $9,500 limit (as indexed) equal to the lesser of:

$3,000,
$15,000 less prior catch-up contributions, or
the excess of ($5,000 × prior number of years of service) over prior salary reductions.

Types of Investments for 403(b) Plans

Section 403(b) plan funds must be invested in either: annuity contracts purchased by the employer from an insurance company, or mutual-fund shares held in custodial accounts.

Many different types of annuities may be used for Section 403(b) plans. Thus, the annuities can be individual or group contracts, level or flexible premium annuities, and fixed-dollar or variable annuities. Face-amount certificates providing a fixed-maturity value and a schedule of redemptions are also permitted. In addition, the annuity contract may provide incidental amounts of life insurance for the employee; however, the value of such insurance is taxable to the employee each year under the PS 58 table. The annuity contracts can provide the employee a choice of broad types of investment strategy—for example, a choice between investment in a fixed-income fund and an equity-type fund. However, if the contract gives the employee specific powers to direct the investments of the fund, the IRS will regard the employee as in control of the account for tax purposes, and the employee will be currently taxed on the fund's investment income.

Annuity contracts used in Section 403(b) plans must be nontransferable. This means that they cannot be sold or assigned as collateral to any person other than the insurance company issuing the contract. However, the employee is permitted to designate a beneficiary for death benefits or survivorship annuities. Since similar restrictions apply to annuities transferred to participants from qualified plans, most insurance companies use the same standard provisions for both types of annuity contracts.

Distributions and Loans from Section 403(b) Plans

Beginning after 1988, distributions from Section 403(b) plans will be subject to much the same rules applicable to qualified plans; in particular, those applicable to 401(k) plans.

After 1988, withdrawals are not permitted from 403(b) custodial accounts (mutual funds) or from any salary reduction 403(b) account, except for withdrawals after age 59½, or upon death, disability, separation from service, or financial hardship. The definition of financial hardship was discussed in Chapter 14 in connection with 401(k) plans. These withdrawal restrictions technically do not apply to annuity-type 403(b) accounts funded by direct employer contributions, rather than salary reductions. However, this "loophole" is of limited usefulness, because of the 10 percent early distribution penalty of Code Section 72(t). As discussed in Chapter 16, this penalty applies to most distributions prior to age 59½ from qualified plans, IRAs, and Section 403(b) plans. The penalty applies even to distributions that are permitted—for example, many hardship distributions from Section 403(b) plans will be subject to the penalty.

Other qualified plan distribution rules also apply to Section 403(b) plans. Distributions must begin by April 1 of the calendar year of the year following the attainment of age 70½. The minimum annual distribution thereafter is basically a level amount spread over the participant's life expectancy or over the joint life expectancies of the participant and beneficiary, as discussed in Chapter 16. Failure to make a minimum annual distribution results in a 50 percent penalty under Code Section 4974.

Loans. Section 403(b) plans with either annuity or mutual-fund accounts may permit loans on the same basis as regular qualified plans. Plan loans are discussed in Chapter 16. Because of the restrictions on Section 403(b) distributions, plan loan provisions are particularly important to employees and should be considered in any Section 403(b) plan.

Taxation of Section 403(b) Plans

A Section 403(b) plan provides the same general tax advantages as a qualified plan. Thus, plan contributions within the limits of the exclusion allowance are not currently taxable to the employee. Investment earnings on plan funds are also not currently taxable.

However, the taxation of distributions from Section 403(b) plans is somewhat less favorable than for qualified plans. The full amount of any distribution from a Section 403(b) plan, whether inservice or at termination of service, is fully taxable as ordinary income to the participant, except for any cost basis the participant has in the distribution. A cost basis could result if the employee previously paid tax on any amount contributed to the plan, or reported PS 58 costs if the plan provides incidental life insurance. There are no averaging or capital-gain provisions for the taxable amount of a distribution from a Section 403(b) plan. The bad tax effect of having all of the income taxable in a single year can be alleviated only by having a periodic form of payout from the plan. A periodic distribution from a Section 403(b) plan is taxed under the annuity rules, the same as an annuity from a qualified plan.

Death benefits are also subject to somewhat less favorable income tax treatment than death benefits from qualified plans. The averaging and capital-gain provisions are not available to the beneficiary. Also, the $5,000 employee death benefit exclusion of Code Section 101(b) is available only for a lump-sum distribution from a Section 403(b) plan—and only if the employer was one of a limited subclass. This subclass is defined in a rather complex way, but basically most private religious, educational, and charitable organizations are included; however, it has been held that a state university is included but not a public elementary or high school system.

Section 403(b) death benefits are included in the gross estate of the deceased participant for federal estate tax purposes. However, if they are paid to a spouse, they escape estate taxation under the unlimited marital deduction. Even in other cases there may be no estate tax, because the tax applies only to relatively large estates (those over about $600,000).

Section 403(b) plan amounts are included in determining the excess distribution and excess accumulation taxes (Code Section 4981), discussed in Chapter

16. These taxes can be significant for highly compensated employees. In some cases, the potential effect of these taxes may make it advisable for highly compensated employees to discontinue participation in Section 403(b) or other plans.

Regulatory and Administrative Aspects

A Section 403(b) plan is considered a pension plan, rather than a welfare benefit plan, for purposes of the reporting and disclosure provisions. The reporting and disclosure requirements applicable are similar to those applicable to qualified plans, as discussed in Chapter 20. However, as with qualified plans, Section 403(b) plans of governmental units and churches that have not elected to come under ERISA are exempt from these requirements, unless mutual funds, rather than annuity contracts, are used for funding. If a Section 403(b) plan is purely of the salary reduction type and does not include any direct employer contributions, the reporting and disclosure and other regulatory requirements are greatly reduced.

Section 457 Deferred-Compensation Plans for Governmental Employees

In a nonqualified deferred-compensation plan, an employee may defer tax on compensation income, but with a twofold cost; first, there is a loss of benefit security, because there can be no irrevocable trust fund for the employee, and second, the employer's tax deduction is also deferred. These plans are discussed in detail in Chapter 25.

Neither of these two factors imposes much disadvantage to state and local government employers or employees, because there is little risk of the employer becoming insolvent, and because the employer is nontaxable and derives no benefit from tax deductions. For private tax-exempt employers, the second disadvantage also does not apply, although the first could be significant. To avoid potentially unlimited use of nonqualified deferred compensation by state and local government employees and employees of private tax-exempt employers, Section 457 therefore imposes restrictions on such plans.

Limit on Amount. The amount deferred annually by an employee under these plans cannot exceed the lesser of $7,500 or one third of the employee's taxable compensation, reduced by any salary reductions under a Section 403(b) plan or SEP. However, the ceiling can be increased, in each of the last three years before normal retirement age, to the lesser of $15,000 or the regular ceiling, plus the total amount of potential deferral that was not used in prior years. If an individual has more than one employer, the total deferred for all employers must not exceed these limits.

Example

Fritz is hired by the Suntan, Florida, Municipal Sewage Authority at age 60 and is covered under a Section 457 plan. His compensation is $30,000 annually. Normal retirement age is 65. His actual deferrals and ceilings are:

Year	Ceiling	Fritz's Actual Deferral
1	$ 7,500	$ 5,000
2	7,500	5,000
3	12,500	5,000
4	15,000	5,000
5	15,000	15,000

Other Rules

- Elections to defer compensation under Section 457 are made monthly, under an agreement entered into before the beginning of the month.
- The plan cannot be funded—all deferred compensation and income therefrom remains the property of the employer.
- Plan distributions cannot be made before separation from service or "unforeseeable emergency." Also, plan distributions must meet the rules of Section 401(a)(9) regarding beginning date (April 1 after age 70½). A special incidental death-benefit provision applies—the participant must expect to receive at least two thirds of the total payout where there is a survivor annuity.
- There are no specific coverage requirements—the plan can be offered to all employees, or any group of employees, even a single employee. However, for a tax-exempt organization (but not for a governmental organization) the participation, the fiduciary, and other ERISA rules may apply.
- If the state or local government employer or tax-exempt employer has a nonqualified deferred-compensation plan that does not comply with Section 457—for example, one that exceeds the limits—then it is treated for tax purposes as a funded plan, whether or not it is actually funded. As discussed in Chapter 25, this means that the deferred amount is includible in the participant's income when there is no substantial risk of forfeiture. This does, however, provide some opportunity for governments and tax-exempts to design plans for top executives above the $7,500 limit by including forfeiture provisions.

Summary

Tax-exempt annuity plans under Section 403(b) can be adopted by tax-exempt Section 501(c)(3) organizations and public schools. These plans are generally similar to qualified plans, but they are slightly more favorable for employers and employees. The qualified plan coverage rules apply, and there must be 100 percent vesting. Employer contributions must not discriminate in favor of highly compensated employees. Annual contributions for a participant are limited not only by the 25 percent/$30,000 Section 415 limit but also by a special 20 percent annual exclusion allowance. The plan can be funded through employee salary reductions or elective deferrals, but there is a limit of $9,500 annually, similar to the 401(k) limit.

Section 403(b) plans must be invested either in annuity contracts purchased by the employer from an insurance company or in mutual-fund shares held in custodial accounts.

Distributions from 403(b) plans are subject to basically the same distribution limits and tax rules as other qualified plans, but five-year averaging is not available.

Any nonqualified deferred-compensation plan of a state and local government or tax-exempt organization that provides nonforfeitable benefits is subject to Section 457, which limits annual deferrals to the lesser of $7,500 or one third of the employee's taxable compensation. There are also rules relating to deferral elections and distributions.

24

Qualified Plan Design to Maximize Benefits for Key Employees

Objectives of This Chapter

Most qualified plans—that is, plans considered in terms of numbers of plans, rather than numbers of employees covered—are designed for relatively small businesses. Such businesses often involve active participation by business owners. A few key employees may also make significant and disproportionate contributions to the success of the business.

Plans for organizations of this type are often adopted and designed primarily to provide benefits for the key employees, and only secondarily to other employees—that is, benefits to other employees are provided only to the extent required to make the plan qualified. In some cases, these employers may be interested in providing some degree of retirement plan coverage for all employees, but even then the employer will be concerned to some extent about maximizing benefits for owners and key employees. Therefore, a substantial portion of plan design activity involves techniques for maximizing benefits for key employees.

The qualified plan tax and nontax rules are devoted very extensively to thwarting attempts to provide disproportionate benefits for highly compensated employees. Thus, attempts to maximize benefits for key employees require pushing the law to its limits, which can often be a complex exercise.

This chapter will discuss some of the major techniques for maximizing benefits for key employees within the qualified plan rules. The following are discussed:

- *Defined-Benefit Plans*
    conservative actuarial assumptions
    normal retirement age
    normal form of benefit
    integration with social security
    using life insurance
- *Defined-Contribution Plans*
- *Combination Plans*

Planning to Maximize Benefits

Benefit formulas and other plan features designed to maximize benefits for key employees must be applied, of course, in a nondiscriminatory manner to all employees covered under the plan. If there is a large number of regular employees, some of them are likely to be affected by these generous benefit provisions—considerably increasing the costs of the plan. At some point, therefore, maximizing benefits will increase plan costs for regular employees to the point where the plan provides no net benefit to the business owners. The techniques discussed in this chapter must be viewed with this condition in mind. However, for plans with only a few regular employees—typically, very small corporations, particularly professional corporations—these benefit-maximizing techniques will often be used to the greatest extent possible.

Impact of Excess Penalties. One very significant limitation on all these maximizing techniques must be noted at the outset. The excess distribution tax, a 15 percent penalty on annual distributions exceeding $112,500 annually (as adjusted in certain cases), and the excess accumulation tax, an additional federal estate tax on qualified plan accumulations at death, have their primary impact on highly compensated employees. These taxes are discussed in detail in Chapter 18. The point to note here is that, once a benefit-maximizing technique has been proposed, the impact of these excess penalties must also be analyzed, to make sure that the additional benefits provided through the plan will not simply be taxed away by the penalty taxes.

Maximizing Benefits from Defined-Benefit Plans

Defined-benefit plans provide the maximum possible contribution for an employee who is relatively old at the time the plan is adopted. A defined-contribution plan allows a contribution of no more than $30,000 annually, under the Section 415 limits. There is no dollar limit on the amount of annual contribution under a defined-benefit plan; instead, Section 415 limits the projected *benefit* to the lesser of 100 percent of high-three-year-average compensation or $90,000. Funding the maximum $90,000 benefit for a relatively young employee—say, an employee age 35—generally costs less than $30,000 annually. Thus, for the younger employee, the defined-contribution plan provides a way of sheltering more money from taxes. However, if the plan is adopted when the employee is older—say age 55—the annual funding costs for a maximum $90,000 benefit generally will be greater than $30,000. For this older employee, the defined-benefit plan provides a larger tax shelter.

This "crossover" point—the age at which a defined-benefit plan becomes more favorable—generally occurs somewhere between age 45 and age 55. There is no simple formula for determining the exact crossover point; it depends on the type of plan design and actuarial and funding assumptions. A more conservative actuarial assumption results in greater annual defined-benefit funding at an earlier age, thus reducing the apparent crossover point (see Table 24–1).

TABLE 24–1

Interest Assumption	Annual Contribution (Plan Entry at Age 45, Age 65 Accumulation $850,000)
5%	$24,482
6	21,798
8	17,198
10	13,491

Although the defined-benefit plan may accelerate the funding for older employees, once the plan is fully funded further contributions are not possible. To illustrate, if the plan has a normal retirement age of 62, it often will not be possible to put further contributions into the plan if the employee continues to work after age 62. On the other hand, a defined-contribution plan permits contributions as long as the employee continues working, even to an advanced age. Sometimes it is possible to adopt a supplemental defined-contribution plan after the defined-benefit plan is fully funded; this is limited by the rules discussed below for combination plans.

Conservative Actuarial Assumptions

Conservative actuarial assumptions and methods will accelerate plan funding. Table 24–1 shows the funding required for a $90,000 benefit at age 65 under various interest rate assumptions.

The obvious question for this type of technique is just how far you can go. There are no specific rules for the choice of actuarial assumptions, such as interest rate; the Code (Section 412) and the corresponding regulations simply provide that the method chosen must be reasonable. The IRS has also issued guidelines for its auditing agents that indicate how reasonableness is to be monitored by the IRS.[1] Generally, under these guidelines, the plan is examined over a period of several years; and, if overfunding results consistently, the actuarial assumptions may be deemed unreasonable. For many years, there has been no more specific guidance than this from the IRS; but recently, a number of private letter rulings have been issued indicating that an interest rate assumption of 4 or 5 percent would not be considered reasonable in light of current interest rates in the years at issue in the rulings (1981–82).[2] The rulings suggest 8 percent as a minimum reasonable assumed rate of return. The IRS recognizes that a plan must use a long-term interest assumption, which need not be as high as current short-term

---

[1] IRM 7(10)5(10), Actuarial Guidelines Handbook, Department of the Treasury, Internal Revenue Service, December 12, 1984.

[2] PLRs 8615001–8615007.

rates. Since current short-term rates have declined since the years covered by these rulings, it probably is currently possible to use a rate somewhat less than 8 percent.

Another conservative assumption often used in funding plans for key employees is a unisex mortality assumption. Where key employees are mostly male, a unisex mortality assumption will provide greater contributions than a sex-based assumption. In a very small plan, of course, it may be preferable to use no mortality assumption for preretirement funding purposes, as this will produce the highest possible contribution level and avoid underfunding problems if all participants survive to retirement.

An important limitation on the use of overly conservative actuarial assumptions is the penalty tax for income tax underpayments due to an understatement of pension actuarial liabilities (Code Section 6659A). The penalty is 10 to 30 percent of the underpayment, depending on the degree of understatement. The IRS may waive the penalty if there is a reasonable basis for the valuation and it was made in good faith. This penalty will tend to make actuaries more cautious in suggesting conservative actuarial assumptions to increase plan deductions.

Normal Retirement Age

Funding can be accelerated by choosing a normal retirement age that is as early as possible. Table 24–2 indicates how annual funding for a $90,000 benefit (or actuarial equivalent) varies according to the assumed normal retirement age.

Again, an obvious question is: How early can the plan's normal retirement age be? There are two types of limitations on undue acceleration of the normal retirement age.

First, the Section 415 dollar limits are reduced actuarially for retirement ages that are less than the social security retirement age. The reduction is designed to provide the actuarial equivalent of an annual benefit of $90,000 beginning at the social security retirement age.

Second, the retirement age is considered an actuarial assumption and, as such, must be reasonable.

The methods and assumptions used for actuarially adjusting benefits are not specified in the Code or Regulations, but several revenue rulings list appropriate methods, and other methods may presumably be used if the IRS finds them reasonable.

TABLE 24–2

Retirement Age (Entry Age 50)	Projected Annual Benefit	Annual Contribution
55	$42,400	$87,417
62	72,000	44,312
65	90,000	37,712

There is no specific guideline in the Code or Regulations about what retirement ages are considered reasonable actuarial assumptions. Several recent private letter rulings indicate the IRS position on this issue, however.[3] These rulings viewed the issue as whether the participants could reasonably be expected to retire at the plan's normal retirement age. In the cases considered, 55 was deemed to be unreasonably early. However, the issue is factual in all cases; and, if an earlier retirement can be supported, it is appropriate. For example, a normal retirement age of 40 would likely be reasonable in a plan for professional athletes.

It appears that excessive deductions due to an unrealistic retirement age, like those based on overly conservative interest rates, would be vulnerable to the Section 6659A penalty described earlier. This imposes another limitation on the choice of normal retirement age.

Methods for Increasing Benefits for Late Retirees. For a qualified plan, the maximum normal retirement age is the greater of age 65 or 10 or 5 years after the beginning of plan participation.[4] Thus, unless an employee is over 55, the plan's normal retirement age can't be extended past 65.

Under the age-discrimination law, the plan must give over-65 employees the same benefit accrual that younger employees receive. Many plans, however, provide full benefit accrual after a certain length of service, such as 25 years, with no benefit accrual thereafter. Many over-65 employees, therefore, receive no additional benefit accrual. A plan formula without this service limitation may prove beneficial to business owners who, unlike most employees, plan to continue working after age 65.

The Section 415 dollar limit on the actual benefit payable at retirement is actuarially increased; see Table 24–3. Thus, a key employee may be able to earn

TABLE 24–3

Retirement Age	Maximum Dollar Benefit
55	$ 42,400
60	61,419
62	72,000
65	90,000
70	155,843

Assumptions: 1971 Group Annuity (Male) Table with interest at 5 percent, life annuity. Rev. Rul. 80–253 indicates what assumptions will be considered reasonable for this purpose. For the actuarial increase after age 65, under Code Section 415(b)(2)(E)(ii), the interest rate assumption cannot be greater than the lesser of 5 percent or the plan's actuarial interest rate assumption.

---

[3] See footnote 2.
[4] Code Section 411(a)(8).

benefit credits above $90,000 for working past age 65, and the employer will be allowed to make tax-deductible contributions to the plan to fund these benefits. Also, after 1988, the $90,000 amount will be indexed, which will allow further additional contributions by the employer.

If late retirement is used to improve benefits for key employees, however, it must be made available to all employees on the same nondiscriminatory basis.

Normal Form of Benefit

A defined-benefit plan can provide a normal benefit in almost any form, as discussed in Chapter 16. If maximum tax sheltering for key employees is an objective, this would dictate using a relatively "expensive" benefit form. For example, compared with a $50,000 straight-life annuity, a $50,000 10-year certain annuity would require greater annual contributions. However, if the key employee's benefit is at the Section 415 maximum, there are limits on the extent to which this can be done. The Section 415 limitations are adjusted actuarially to reflect normal retirement benefits that are in other forms than straight-life annuities, as indicated in Table 24–4.

The adjustments summarized in this table have a significant loophole: No actuarial adjustment is required if the normal form of benefit is a qualified joint-and-survivor annuity as defined in Code Section 417(b).[5] A qualified joint-and-survivor annuity can include a survivor annuity anywhere from 50 percent to 100 percent of the joint annuity. As Table 24–5 indicates, funding toward a joint and 100 percent survivor annuity, or even a 50 percent survivor annuity, as the normal form of benefit produces significantly greater annual funding requirements and, thus, a greater tax-deductible contribution.

One problem with using a joint-and-survivor annuity as a normal form of benefit is that, if the participant wants to receive the full amount put into the fund

TABLE 24–4

Normal Retirement Benefit	Reduction Percentage	Maximum Benefit
Annuity—no refund	none	$90,000/100%
Annuity—5-year certain	3%	87,300/ 97
Annuity—10-year certain	10	81,000/ 90
Annuity—15-year certain	20	72,000/ 80
Annuity—20-year certain	30	63,000/ 70
Annuity—installment refund	10	81,000/ 90
Annuity—cash refund	15	76,500/ 85

Source: From Section 9 of Rev. Rul. 71–446. See Rev. Rul. 80–253. Under Rev. Rul. 80–253, the factors in Rev. Rul. 76–47 also may be used, which are slightly different from those in this table.

---

[5]Reg. Sec. 1.415–3(c)(2).

TABLE 24–5. Life Annuity versus Joint and 100 Percent Survivor

Employee Entry Age*	Retirement Age	Annual Cost Life Annuity	Annual Cost J&S (100 Percent)
55	62	$110,000	$145,000
50	62	55,000	72,000

*Male employee with wife five years younger. Computation based on pre–1987 law allowing full $90,000 benefit at age 62; under current law, all annual costs reduced.

on his or her behalf, the benefit must be taken out as a joint-and-survivor annuity. If the participant elects another form of benefit, such as a lump sum, the plan can pay this out only to the extent that it is the actuarial equivalent of a straight-life annuity.[6]

Example

Suppose a plan has accumulated $1,154,000 to fund a joint-and-survivor annuity for Frank Blarp, a key employee and company owner. Frank is retiring at age 65; he does not need the annuity payments for retirement income purposes and is considering electing a lump sum so he can pursue more aggressive investments with the money. Frank cannot take out a lump sum of $1,154,000. Instead, the permissible lump-sum distribution is limited to $854,000; this is the actuarial equivalent of a $90,000 straight-life annuity for Frank under the actuarial assumptions specified in the plan for calculating benefit options. The remaining $300,000 accumulated for Frank must stay in the fund as an actuarial surplus that will reduce future contributions—that is, it will be amortized under the minimum-funding rules. If the plan were to be terminated at this point, the surplus could be returned to the employer and, thus, ultimately to the shareholders of the company, at the cost of the 10 percent penalty (Code Section 4980), described in Chapter 21. Caution should be exercised in any attempt to do this on a systematic basis, because the IRS may attempt to disqualify the plan on the ground that it does not meet the permanence or exclusive benefit requirements for qualified plans.

Using Life Insurance

As discussed in Chapter 10, life insurance can be included in a qualified plan as an incidental benefit. The cost of the life insurance, within the incidental limits, is an additional deductible contribution by the employer to the plan. However, in

---

[6]Reg. Sec. 1.415(3)(c)(1).

a defined-contribution plan, life insurance can be purchased only out of the amount otherwise deductible under the plan. By comparison, in a defined-benefit plan, a life insurance benefit increases the amount of contribution deductible by the employer.

Life insurance is deemed by the IRS to be incidental if the face amount of the insurance does not exceed 100 times the expected monthly retirement benefit. Alternatively, the insurance is incidental if less than 25 percent of the amount allocated to a participant's account is for pure insurance protection. The IRS has ruled that whole life insurance meets this test if the premium is less than 50 percent of the cumulative additions to the participant's account. A defined-benefit plan can use either test to determine whether insurance coverage is incidental. With computerized computation of contributions on behalf of each participant, it is no more difficult to use one test than the other in a defined-benefit plan, but the 100-to-1 test, of course, is more easily explained.

For term insurance, either the 25 percent or the 100-to-1 test can be used in a defined-benefit plan; however, term insurance is used rarely, since it provides no tax advantage. The amount taxable to the participant, as discussed in Chapter 10, is essentially equal to the extra employer deduction, so there is no advantage to having the insurance in the plan, rather than outside the plan.

The IRS has not published a formal ruling on the use of universal life insurance, or products other than term insurance and whole life insurance, in qualified plans. A conservative view is that the premium for universal life insurance should not exceed 25 percent of the total account allocations. This should certainly meet the incidental test, because the amount of universal life premium used for pure insurance protection is less than 100 percent of the premium. It should be possible to make an analogy with whole life insurance and use a percentage greater than 25 percent; in fact, the amount of the universal premium that is added to the plan fund, rather than used to provide pure insurance protection, often may be larger than for a whole life policy, so conceivably it might even be possible to use more than 50 percent of the account allocation for the universal life product. Although it appears that the IRS currently takes the position that the 25 percent limit applies for universal life insurance, aggressive planners might be willing to challenge the IRS on this position and let the courts decide.

The amount of the insurance premium taxable to the participant, as determined by the P.S. 58 table or alternative cost (discussed in Chapter 10), may be less than the cost of similar insurance coverage to the employee outside the plan. Also, except for a self-employed person, the P.S. 58 cost adds to the participant's cost basis in the plan, and is recovered tax free upon a subsequent distribution from the plan.

Maximizing Defined-Contribution Plan Benefits

Defined-contribution plans alone do not offer the opportunities for maximizing that are available to defined-benefit plans. However, certain factors should be considered. To maximize benefits for key employees, social security integration will generally be used, and it can be used to the fullest extent if the employer maintains no integrated defined-benefit or other plan. Choosing an appropriate integration level is significant.

Example

Dr. Brace, an orthodontist, earns more than $200,000 in 1986. (Because the plan is top-heavy, only the first $200,000 of compensation can be used in the plan formula—see Chapter 18—so his compensation will be taken as $200,000 in this example.) Dr. Brace has one employee, a nurse/receptionist who earns $20,000 in 1986. Dr. Brace wants to install an integrated profit-sharing plan for 1986 that will provide the maximum $30,000 contribution that is permitted under the Section 415 limits, at the lowest cost for coverage of the employee. This can be done by appropriately choosing the integration level, as this illustration shows:

Employee	Compensation	Excess Compensation	5.7 Percent of Excess	Allocation of Remainder	Total Allocation
Dr. Brace	$200,000	$180,000	$10,260	$19,740(9.87%)	$30,000
Receptionist	20,000	0	0	1,974(9.87%)	1,974
				Total cost =	$31,974

Note: using the maximum possible integration level (the taxable wage base for 1986—$42,000) does not necessarily provide the lowest plan cost from the doctor's viewpoint. The allocation using an integration level of $42,000 would be as follows:

Employee	Compensation	Excess Compensation	5.7 Percent of Excess	Allocation of Remainder	Total Allocation
Dr. Brace	$200,000	$158,000	$9,006	$20,994(10.5%)	$30,000
Receptionist	20,000	0	0	2,100(10.5%)	2,100
				Total cost =	$32,100

Plan Coverage; Comparable Plans

One way to maximize benefits for key employees is simply to exclude as many non-key employees from the plan as possible. The coverage tests described in Chapter 6 often permit significant exclusions. As an illustration under prior law, Rev. Rul. 83–58 approved a plan covering only 40 employees, 22 of whom were officers or shareholders, where the company had 150 employees. To push exclusion of participation much further, however, may risk disqualification of the plan. Furthermore, there is an inherent instability in plans that have qualified under certain coverage tests, because the IRS determination on coverage applies only to the facts as presented at the time of the application. If the employee census changes significantly and participation drops below the appropriate level, the plan would lose its qualification in operation and risk an IRS challenge at the next tax audit of the employer. This does not happen often, but it is a significant risk.

There are more sophisticated ways of effectively excluding non-key employees from plans designed to maximize benefits for key employees. First, it should be mentioned that, if the non-key employees are covered under a collectively bargained plan, even a very limited plan, they are excluded in the Section 410 coverage tests and, therefore, effectively do not have to be included in the employer's plan for nonbargaining unit employees. In fact, if the employees are in a collective bargaining unit certified under the federal labor laws, they do not have to be considered in the coverage test even if they have no plan, as long as the issue of plan coverage was a subject of good faith collective bargaining. While small employers are not inclined to view unionization of the work force as conferring any great benefit on the employer, this is one instance in which some benefit occasionally is gained. The theory of the pension law is that the collective bargaining process adequately protects employees' interests in pension matters.

Non-key employees can be excluded from a plan for key employees and still be counted in the eligibility and coverage tests, if the non-key employees are covered under a *comparable plan* of the employer, as discussed in Chapter 6. As indicated there, the IRS has ruled in Revenue Ruling 81–202 that two or more qualified plans for different groups of employees can be considered as a single plan for purposes of meeting the percentage or discretionary coverage tests of Code Section 410, provided that the plans are comparable in the sense that, considered as a unit, they do not provide contributions or benefits that discriminate in favor of the prohibited group. Rev. Rul. 81–202 provides a set of methods that may be used to demonstrate comparability; these are not intended as an exclusive set of methods, but they are quite permissive.

Under the methods for testing comparability under Rev. Rul. 81–202, nondiscrimination is established if either the normalized employer-provided benefits, or both (1) the actual employer contributions and (2) the adjusted employer contributions are no greater as a percentage of compensation for the prohibited group and for rank-and-file employees. These amounts are projected to retirement age. The normalized employer-provided benefits basically are the benefits at retirement under a defined-benefit plan. The adjusted employer contributions are the sum of the employer contributions and forfeitures allocated to the account of the participant under a defined-contribution plan.

In determining the employer-provided benefits, social security benefits may be taken into account under a formula provided in Rev. Rul. 81–202. This substantially increases the amount of employer-provided benefit deemed to be provided for lower-paid employees, which makes it easier to satisfy the comparability test. The test in Rev. Rul. 81–202 also provides various adjustment factors for other benefit forms than a straight-life annuity, and for varying vesting schedules.

TABLE 24-6

Employee	Age at Entry	Compensation	Projected Annual Retirement Benefit	Projected Benefit plus Social Security as Percent of Compensation
Dr. Doctor*	48	$300,000	$90,000	33%
Nurse†	31	20,000	26,760	180

*Covered under defined-benefit plan—100 percent of high three-year average compensation or $90,000.
†Covered under 10 percent of compensation money-purchase plan.

Table 24-6 is an example of a hypothetical comparability study for a small employer. Notice that the projected rates of benefit for the rank-and-file employee are very substantial. This is both because of the inclusion of social security benefits and because of the relative youth of the rank-and-file employee; the defined-contribution benefit is very substantial when projected many years forward to age 65.

In general, it appears that the comparability tests in Revenue Ruling 81–202 are relatively easy to meet for a closely held business if the rank-and-file employees are substantially younger than the key employees. In this situation, a relatively beneficial plan can be provided for the key employees, while providing a relatively small defined-contribution plan for the rank and file. Typically, the plan for the key employees is a defined-benefit plan, with a defined-contribution plan for the rank and file. However, the comparability test can also be met with two different defined-contribution plans. If the key employees are sufficiently older, contributions to the plan can be a higher percentage of compensation than for rank-and-file employees.

The use of the comparability technique is restricted by the requirement of Code Section 401(a)(26) that no plan can be qualified unless it covers, on each day of the plan year, the lesser of 50 employees of the employer or 40 percent of the employees of the employer. This means that each plan used for comparability must have substantial coverage; for example, it would not be possible to have one plan for two or three executives and another for 25 rank-and-file employees.

Leased Employees

Under the leased employee rules of Code Section 414(n), an employer cannot generally avoid plan coverage of rank-and-file employees by simply leasing these employees from a leasing organization, rather than hiring them. Otherwise, it would be relatively easy for organizations to technically take employees off their payrolls and, therefore, avoid counting the leased employees for purposes of the various coverage requirements of Section 410 of the Code.

Like so many other Code provisions designed to close loopholes, however, the leased employee provision can actually be turned to the benefit of an employer desiring to maximize coverage for key employees. There is a safe haven in the

Code, under which the leased employees do not have to be considered for coverage purposes if they are covered under a money-purchase plan maintained by the leasing organization that provides a nonintegrated employer contribution rate of at least 10 percent, with immediate participation and full and immediate vesting. All employees of the leasing organization with compensation of $1,000 or more over the past four years must be covered. The safe-harbor exemption may not be used if leased employees constitute more than 20 percent of the recipient's nonhighly compensated work force. Since a 10 percent plan is not a particularly generous one, this safe harbor may provide some help in maximizing benefits for key employees.

Some employers might be tempted to fire employees and lease them back to take advantage of this provision; however, this may not necessarily work, because the employee leasing provisions apply only where the leased employees are not employees in a legal sense. Firing and hiring back the same employees under the same conditions might lead to an IRS conclusion that the lease arrangement was not bona fide, and the purportedly leased employees would be treated as actual employees.

Combinations of Defined-Benefit and Defined-Contribution Plans

It is not possible for an employer to cover a single employee under both a maximum defined-benefit plan and a maximum defined-contribution plan, because of the combined Section 415 limitation, discussed in Chapter 18. However, the combined limit has enough "room" in it that it is frequently advantageous to provide a key employee with both types of plan. The combination may not only increase the funding level but also provide a greater allocation of funds for key employees. An example will show this better than an extended explanation.

Example

Leo Propane, aged 55, is a key employee in an incorporated, closely held oil distribution business. Leo's current salary is $100,000. The company has a profit-sharing plan providing an annual employer contribution of up to 15 percent of compensation (but not more than $30,000 per employee). Leo has been employed and covered under the plan for three years, with contributions as follows:

Year	Salary— L. Propane	Plan Contribution for L. Propane
1985	$ 88,000	$13,200
1986	88,000	13,200
1987	100,000	15,000

It is proposed to install a defined-benefit plan to provide additional benefits for Leo and other employees. Since Leo is older than most employees, funding this plan will provide a disproportionate benefit for Leo. Assuming the plan is not super top-heavy, what projected benefit can be provided for Leo?

The defined-contribution fraction for Leo is, as of the end of 1987:

$$\frac{13{,}200 + 13{,}200 + 15{,}000}{30{,}800 + 30{,}800 + 35{,}000} = 0.429$$

The defined benefit fraction, therefore, must be no greater than $1 - 0.429$, or 0.571. The maximum benefit must satisfy:

$$0.571 = \frac{\text{Maximum projected annual benefit}}{112{,}500}$$

(The denominator is $1.25 \times \$90{,}000$, which is less than 1.4 times 100 percent of Leo's high three-year average compensation—$92,000.)

Leo's maximum projected annual benefit under the plan, thus, is $64,237 at age 65. The cost to fund this over 10 years will be about $37,000 annually. Thus, even with the defined-contribution plan in place, there is room to shelter additional amounts under a defined-benefit plan.

The total amount of possible sheltering, however, must meet the deduction limit for combined plans equal to 25 percent of common payroll, as discussed in Chapter 18. Thus, the defined-benefit level will have to be so adjusted that this ceiling is not exceeded.

Some points in interpreting the significance of this example for other situations:

1. If the company's plan was super top-heavy, the defined-contribution fraction would be somewhat higher, thus reducing the additional defined-benefit plan available to Leo. The super top-heavy fraction would be:

$$\frac{13{,}200 + 13{,}200 + 15{,}000}{30{,}000 + 30{,}000 + 30{,}000} = 0.46$$

2. The example is somewhat untypical, in assuming that Leo has worked for the company only for the three years he was covered under the plan. In many such cases, there would be substantial prior service; this would reduce the defined-contribution fraction. For example, suppose Leo started work in 1983 and earned $60,000 annually in 1983 and 1984. The d.c. fraction would then be:

$$\frac{0 + 0 + 13{,}200 + 13{,}200 + 15{,}000}{21{,}000 + 21{,}000 + 30{,}800 + 30{,}800 + 35{,}000} = 0.299$$

This would permit a projected defined-benefit of $78,862.

3. Even if the defined-contribution plan is super top-heavy and has always provided the maximum $30,000 contribution, pre-plan service will make some room for an additional defined benefit, as long as the 25 percent deduction limit can be met.

Summary

Qualified plans can maximize benefits for key employees through a number of techniques. From this viewpoint, the cost of these techniques is the additional cost of benefits that must be provided for non-key employees as a result.

Defined-benefit plans can exploit the fact that key employees are typically older and have longer service. Conservative actuarial assumptions, within limits of reasonability to avoid penalties, can accelerate funding. A reduced normal retirement age will also accelerate funding. However, late retirement with provisions to continue benefit accrual can also benefit key employees who often continue working in the business after normal retirement age. In many cases, it is advantageous to use a joint-and-survivor annuity as the normal form of benefit. An insured death benefit also increases deductible plan funding.

Defined-contribution plans can be integrated, with a carefully chosen integration level, to maximize key employee benefits. Another use for defined-contribution plans in this context is as part of a combination of defined-benefit and defined-contribution plans for the key employee. Such a combination may increase deductible funding and also the proportion of the deductible funding allocable to key employees.

25

Nonqualified Executive Retirement Benefits

Objectives of This Chapter
- *Describe the planning situations in which nonqualified plans are often used.*
- *Review the general design features of nonqualified plans, explaining how these relate to employer and employee objectives.*
- *Distinguish between funded and unfunded plans.*
- *Explain why nonqualified plans are usually unfunded.*
- *Describe informal funding techniques for nonqualified plans.*
- *Describe the tax treatment of nonqualified plans to employer and employee.*

How Nonqualified Plans Are Used

Although qualified plans have attractive tax benefits, they have certain limitations that, in some cases, indicate the use of nonqualified plans, particularly for compensating executives.

An employer may not have a qualified plan, because it does not wish to provide the kind of broad retirement plan coverage required by the nondiscriminatory coverage requirements. As discussed in Chapter 6, coverage of 70 percent of nonhighly compensated employees, or a similar alternative, is generally required. Thus, if an employer wishes to provide very generous retirement benefits for executives, the employer might not use a qualified plan, because of the requirement of providing the same benefits to a substantial number of nonexecutive employees as well.

Section 415 of the Code, as discussed in Chapter 18, imposes limits on the benefits or employer contributions that can be provided to any one individual under a qualified plan. Annual additions to the account of a participant in a qualified defined-contribution plan are limited to the lesser of 25 percent of the employee's compensation or $30,000. For a defined-benefit plan, the maximum projected annual benefit is the lesser of 100 percent of the employee's compensation or $90,000. For very highly paid executives, these limits can make it difficult to provide appropriate retirement benefits under a qualified plan. For example, a salary of $200,000 is not unusual for an executive. If a qualified plan provides a benefit of 50 percent of final average compensation, a typical benefit level, the executive earning $200,000 could not receive the full 50 percent benefit, because it would exceed the $90,000 maximum limit. Therefore, for very highly paid executives it may be desirable to provide additional nonqualified retirement benefits in excess of the Section 415 limits.

Although nonqualified plans do not receive all the tax benefits of qualified plans—essentially they lack the availability of a current deduction for funding combined with deferred taxation for the participant—there is great flexibility in designing these plans, because the qualified rules do not apply. Some design options will be listed briefly here, followed by a more detailed discussion of design considerations and tax and other legal limitations.

Overview of Nonqualified Plan Design

Overall Design

A deferred-compensation plan can be a pure *excess* plan, by providing benefits keyed specifically to the Section 415 limits and used in connection with a qualified plan. For example, if the qualified plan provides a benefit of 50 percent of final average compensation, for an executive with final average compensation of $200,000, the excess plan would provide a benefit of $10,000 annually (making up the difference between the $90,000 qualified plan limit and 50 percent of final average compensation).

A deferred-compensation plan can also provide a broader range of benefits than a mere excess plan. A nonqualified plan can provide specified retirement benefits for a selected group of executives without specific reference to qualified plan benefits, if any. Such a plan, which can be structured much like the qualified plans discussed in this book, is often referred to as a *supplemental executive retirement plan,* or *SERP.*

Finally, deferred-compensation plans can be used to provide extra compensation or a deferral benefit for a few employees, even one employee, to meet special needs of the employee or employer, and the plan can be structured according to those specific needs.

Contribution and Benefit Formulas

Salary Continuation Plan. A salary continuation plan provides a stated benefit to the employee as an extra fringe benefit, without any specific reduction of current compensation. The benefit is usually designed to begin at a specified normal retirement age.

Deferred-Compensation (Salary Reduction) Plan. This type of design provides deferral of a specific amount of the employee's compensation otherwise payable. Economically, this is essentially the same as salary continuation, but it is much different in terms of communication and employee understanding. This type of design is sometimes referred to as deferred compensation. However, to avoid confusion, the term *salary reduction plan* will be used to describe this approach, with "deferred compensation" being used in its generic sense.

Defined-Contribution versus Defined-Benefit. The plan's deferred benefit can be specified either in terms of a dollar amount or a formula—the defined-benefit approach—or the amount payable can be simply the accumulation in the participant's account—the defined-contribution approach. The "account" can be either a real accumulation of funds or simply a bookkeeping account. A salary continuation plan typically provides a defined-benefit formula, while a salary reduction plan uses a defined-contribution formula, because these benefit approaches best fit the contribution method. However, a different mixture is technically possible.

Funding and Informal Funding

For reasons to be discussed below, most nonqualified deferred-compensation plans are not formally funded, and the employee relies only on the employer's contractual promise to pay benefits. Many approaches have been used to provide some additional benefit security, while retaining the unfunded nature of the plan. Two common approaches are:

Corporate-Owned Life Insurance. Under this arrangement, the employer pays life insurance premiums for a policy of which the employer is owner and beneficiary; the policy is designed to accumulate values sufficient to pay the deferred compensation when due.

Rabbi Trust. A rabbi trust is established by an employer for the benefit of the employee to fund a deferred-compensation plan. Because the trust funds are available to the employer's creditors, the arrangement is not regarded as a formally funded plan.

Designing the Plan

Employer versus Employee Objectives

Certain features of the plan will depend on whether the plan is primarily designed to meet employer objectives or, rather, to meet those of the employee.

An employer's objectives in instituting a nonqualified deferred-compensation plan are typically to provide an inducement to hire key employees, to provide additional inducements to keep key employees working for the employer, and to provide performance incentives. The employee's objective is usually simply to obtain an additional form of compensation payable at retirement or termination of employment, with income tax on the amount deferred as long as possible, preferably until the money is actually received. Generally, only highly paid employees are in a position to defer substantial amounts of compensation. The tax deferral itself is a valuable benefit; in addition, the employee may be in a lower marginal tax bracket when the deferred compensation is received and taxed, although this is difficult to predict as a result of frequent changes in the tax rates.

Employer-Instituted Plan. Eligibility in an employer-instituted plan is usually confined to key executive or technical employees who are difficult to recruit and keep. The plan does not have to specify a class of employees to be covered; it can simply be adopted for specific individuals as the need arises. However, the need for fairness among a similarly situated group of executives often dictates that the plan cover a specific class of employees, rather than individuals.

An employer-instituted plan often will incorporate various incentive features to improve employee performance. The simplest form of incentive provision is a benefit or contribution based on salary. With a defined-contribution formula, the amount credited to the employee's account under the plan will be equal to a percentage of current salary. Then, as the employee receives salary increases reflecting the employee's performance, contributions to the deferred-compensation account increase automatically. In a defined-benefit formula, the benefit can be stated as a percentage of the employee's highest average salary over a period of years—three to five are typical. This will reward performance but, again, by tying increasing benefits to salary increases for improved performance.

The deferred-compensation plan can also provide for incentive increases if specific goals are achieved by the employee. For example, a salesman or sales manager might receive benefits based on a percentage of sales. In other situations, benefits might be geared to percentages of the corporation's profits or to percentages of profits for the employee's department or division.

If the employer's stock is traded on the stock exchange, incentive features can be provided by tying deferred-compensation benefits to the value of the stock. If there is no actual fund invested in employer stock, this is referred to as a *phantom stock* arrangement.

Finally, an employer-instituted plan's termination provisions will reflect the plan's objectives, as discussed below. Often such plans will provide complete forfeiture of benefits, if the employee is terminated before retirement for cause, or if the employee goes to work for a competitor.

Employee Objectives in Nonqualified Deferred-Compensation Plans. If an employee has sufficient bargaining power to dictate the design of the plan, certain different design features will be appropriate. The employee will not be interested in benefits that vary as an incentive, but rather will wish to have the greatest possible degree of certainty and security of the benefit. The employee will not want significant forfeiture provisions, and he or she will want a benefit that is 100 percent immediately vested.

Benefit security and consequently the financial stability of the corporation is an important factor to the employee. Thus, a plan designed with an employee orientation will want to consider some of the informal funding arrangements described here, such as corporate-owned life insurance or the rabbi trust.

Defined-Contribution and Defined-Benefit Formulas

A defined-benefit deferred-compensation formula generally will specify plan benefits as a percentage of compensation measured over a period of years, typically three to five years of highest earnings. Benefits can also be dependent on service, with a specified amount of benefit accruing for each year of service. In general, all the techniques used in benefit design for qualified plans can be used for nonqualified plans as well. However, since the qualified plan rules do not apply, there is more flexibility in design.

A nonqualified plan benefit can be integrated with social security. Typically, this is done using a 100 percent offset. For example, the nonqualified plan might provide an annual retirement benefit of 70 percent of the employee's final average compensation, less social security benefits paid to the employee. Nonqualified plan benefits can also be offset by other retirement benefits payable by the employer to the employee, such as those from a qualified plan. The social security integration rules discussed in Chapter 9 do not apply, so any type of integration formula may be used.

In a defined-contribution approach, usually referred to as a money-purchase formula, the deferred-compensation benefit results from accumulations in an account (real or phantom) set up for the employee with additions or contributions over the employee's working life. The contributions, typically, would be a specified percentage of the employee's current compensation each year. If funds are not actually set aside, the employee may not wish to lose the benefit of investment earnings on the deferred compensation. The employer, therefore, may guarantee a specified minimum rate of interest on plan account allocations. An alternative might be for the employer to make an additional annual allocation equal to a current rate of return on plan funds, determined according to some interest formula or index specified in the plan.

Form of Benefits

Benefits can be payable from the plan at retirement in a lump sum, or the plan can specify a series of annual payments. The most common approach is to specify a fixed number of annual payments, such as 10, but a life annuity or a joint-and-survivor annuity for the participant and spouse can be provided. None of the restrictions in Code Section 401(a)(9) or the incidental benefit rules (discussed in Chapter 16) apply to nonqualified plans, so there is great flexibility. Nonqualified plans, however, have one design problem in the distribution area that qualified plans do not have—that is, nonqualified plans are subject to the constructive receipt doctrine. Nonqualified plan benefits, as discussed below, may be taxable to an employee before they are actually received by the employee. Distribution benefits must be designed accordingly. Thus, while the employee will wish to have maximum flexibility in choosing the form of payment at any time, this is not always possible, as is discussed below.

Termination Payments

The treatment of plan termination benefits is important in nonqualified deferred-compensation plans. Different approaches will be used, depending on whether the employee or the employer has bargaining power in designing the plan. An employer-instituted plan will maximize incentive features and features to deter the employee from leaving, particularly leaving to work for a competitor. Thus, employer-instituted plans may even provide a complete forfeiture on the employee's termination of employment before retirement. If such plans do not have complete forfeiture, they may have a vesting schedule, so the termination benefit is less than 100 percent of the amount deferred or the participant's account balance. If the plan is unfunded, as discussed below, the ERISA vesting provisions do not apply, and any type of vesting schedule can be used.

The plan may have special payout provisions in the event of the employee's disability. In particular, if it is an employee-instituted plan, the employee will generally want benefits paid immediately upon disability. The definition of disability used in the plan need not be "total and permanent" disability, as required for social security disability benefits; a lesser definition may be desirable. For example, a professional would consider himself or herself disabled if unable to continue working in the specific profession, and the definition of disability in the nonqualified plan should be drafted accordingly. To prevent disputes in a closely held business, the determination of any facts related to disability can be shifted to a third party, such as an insurer or physician selected according to some agreed-upon procedure spelled out in the plan.

Funded and Unfunded Plans

In a plan that is formally funded in the tax sense, the employer sets aside money or property to the employee's account in an irrevocable trust or through some other means that restricts access by the employer and the employer's creditors to the fund. With an unfunded plan, either there is no fund at all or the fund that is set up is accessible to the employer and its creditors at all times, so it provides no particular security to the employee, other than the knowledge that the fund exists.

There are significant tax and ERISA *disadvantages* to a funded plan:

> The amounts put into a funded plan generally are taxable to the employee at the time the employee's rights to the fund become nonforfeitable, or *substantially vested*.[1]

---

[1] Code Section 83.

Substantial vesting may occur well in advance of the time these funds are actually received by the employee, thus producing a tax disadvantage.

Funded plans are subject to the ERISA vesting and fiduciary requirements, as discussed later, and this usually is undesirable from the employer's point of view.[2]

As a result of these disadvantages, nonqualified deferred compensation plans generally are unfunded. The employee relies only on the employer's unsecured contractual obligation to pay the deferred compensation. Since such plans provide no real security to the employee, their value as an inducement may be minimal if the company is risky, and employees will probably opt for greater benefits in current cash or property, rather than deferred compensation. To provide some assurance, the employer can informally fund the plan by setting money aside in some kind of separate account, with this arrangement known to the employee but with no formal legal rights on the part of the employee and with the amount in the fund therefore available to the employer's creditors.

Employer-Owned Life Insurance. Several methods are commonly used for this purpose. Life insurance policies on the employee's life (owned by and payable to the employer) are often used to provide this kind of informal funding. Life insurance is particularly useful for this purpose if the deferred compensation plan provides a death benefit to the employee's designated beneficiary, since, if the employee dies after only a few years of employment, the life insurance will make sufficient funds available immediately to pay the death benefit.

Rabbi Trusts. In some situations, an employee's objectives will not be met without providing the funding security (or apparent financial security) of a trust fund for the employee's benefit.

Recent attention has been focused on this area, because of several IRS private letter rulings that have approved a type of trust fund under which the funds were set aside for the employee in a trust but were subject to the employer's creditors first (GCM 39230, Ltr. 8113107). These trusts are often referred to as "rabbi trusts" because one of the earlier cases involved an agreement between a rabbi and his employer. Another IRS ruling approved an arrangement under which only the employer's judgment creditors—those who have won a lawsuit against the employer—had priority over the employee's claim against the trust.

IRS "approval" in these rulings applies only to income tax issues; specifically, that (1) the employee has no constructive receipt of funds in the trust; (2) the trust is a grantor trust—its income is taxable to the employer; and (3) Code Section 83 does not apply. It is also important to avoid ERISA vesting and funding rules. The Department of Labor has recently indicated to the IRS (December 13, 1985) that it will view these plans as unfunded, but the DOL has not yet issued a public ruling.

---

[2] ERISA Sections 201(2), 301(3).

Employers wishing to set up a trust of this type should consider obtaining an IRS ruling. However, from time to time the IRS has suspended rulings in this area, so it may not currently be possible to get a ruling.

Tax Issues in Plan Design

It is essential to obtain the most favorable tax treatment possible in designing and administering a nonqualified deferred-compensation plan, because many of the plan's benefits will be lost if the employee is taxed at the wrong time or if the employer loses tax deductions.

Constructive Receipt

An amount is treated as received for income tax purposes, even if it is not actually received, if it is "credited to the employee's account, set aside, or otherwise made available." Constructive receipt can be avoided if the employee's control over the receipt is subject to a substantial limitation or restriction, such as the passage of time. For example, if an amount is not payable for 10 years or not payable until termination of employment, it will not be constructively received before that time.

Nonqualified deferred-compensation plans must be designed to avoid constructive receipt in a number of different ways. First, if the plan uses a salary reduction approach, where the employee defers specific amounts of compensation that would otherwise be paid currently, the employee's election to defer must be made *before* the services are rendered that give rise to the compensation. If a plan of deferred compensation is installed after the performance of the relevant service, the IRS view is that the plan must have substantial forfeiture provisions to defer taxation—that is, the plan's benefits must be unvested and there must be a substantial risk of losing the benefits.

The constructive receipt problem also exists on benefits paid after retirement or termination of employment. For example, if the plan provides for payment in 10 equal annual installments, but allows the employee to elect at any time to accelerate the payments and receive the balance in a lump sum, the constructive receipt doctrine would require inclusion of the entire amount in the earliest year in which the employee could have elected to receive the balance in a lump sum. Similarly, if the plan has a payout in 10 annual installments, but provides that the employee can elect at any time to spread out the payments further, the constructive receipt doctrine would require the payments to be taxed under the original schedule, unless the act of extending the payment schedule also includes a possibility of forfeiture. For example, the plan might provide that, until the last payment is made, the employee must refrain from competing with the employer and render consulting services at the employer's request. It is a question of fact whether this forfeiture provision is really substantial in a given situation.

Economic Benefit

Under the economic-benefit doctrine, an employee can be taxed currently on the value of an arrangement that provides a current economic benefit, even though the employee cannot receive a current cash equivalent. For example, if a nonqualified deferred-compensation plan uses an irrevocable trust fund for the benefit of the employee—a funded plan—and the employee is fully vested, the employee will be taxed as soon as contributions are made to the fund, even though the employee has no current right to withdraw the fund. The economic-benefit doctrine has relatively little impact in an unfunded plan like most of the arrangements discussed in this chapter. The question has been raised whether the existence of an insured death benefit in the plan creates a current economic benefit equal to the value of the insurance. However, currently the IRS does not appear to take the view that there is an economic benefit in this instance.

Reasonable Compensation

An employer can take a tax deduction for compensation paid, if the compensation was reasonable. In the case of a shareholder-employee, the IRS will often take the position that amounts paid to the shareholder are in excess of the value of the services rendered and, therefore, unreasonable. The excess amount will be treated as a dividend to the shareholder, which is taxable to the shareholder but not deductible to the corporation.

In the case of deferred compensation, the employer's deduction ordinarily is not allowed until the year in which the employee includes the income in receipt. The fact that this occurs in a year later than the year in which the services were performed does not necessarily bar a deduction, because compensation can be deemed reasonable on the basis of prior service previously uncompensated by the employer. However, it is possible that the combination of deferred compensation received and current compensation in a given year could exceed the level deemed to be reasonable.

The determination of reasonableness in deferred-compensation situations is sometimes made more difficult under a plan that allows the benefit to increase independent of the value of the services—for example, if the deferred compensation is geared to employer profits or the value of the employer's stock. By the time the deferred-compensation benefits are paid, they might add up to an amount that is unreasonable as compensation for the services that were rendered.

The IRS frequently litigates the reasonable compensation issue, and there are innumerable cases on the issue that are difficult to summarize. Consequently, no clear guidelines can easily be given on the amount of deferred compensation that will be deemed reasonable.

Taxation of Benefits and Contributions

Benefits from unfunded nonqualified deferred-compensation plans are taxable as ordinary income in the year received or constructively received. The 5-year averaging provision available for qualified plan lump-sum distributions does not apply to nonqualified plans.

Death benefits payable to a beneficiary are taxable as ordinary income to the beneficiary, except for the possible availability of the $5,000 employee death benefit exclusion under Section 101(b) of the Code. For this to apply, the employee must not have had vested rights to the benefit immediately before the employee's death.

Federal Estate Tax Treatment. A deceased employee's estate for federal estate tax purposes includes the value of any death benefit payable to a beneficiary. However, if the decedent never had any right to receive the amount involved while living, this value will be zero. This estate tax result motivates the design of death benefit only (DBO) plans; these are deferred compensation plans that pay only a death benefit to the employee's beneficiary.

Employer's Tax Treatment

In a nonqualified deferred-compensation plan, the employer does not receive a tax deduction for deferred compensation until the year in which the employee must include the compensation in taxable income. This is the case even if the employer has put money aside through formal or informal funding of the plan in an earlier year. For an unfunded plan, the year of inclusion for the employee is the year in which the compensation is actually or constructively received. If the plan is formally funded, the employee includes the compensation in income in the year in which it becomes substantially vested.

Impact of ERISA and Other Regulatory Provisions

To retain design flexibility and keep administrative costs down, most deferred-compensation plans are designed to avoid the fiduciary, vesting, and reporting and disclosure requirements of ERISA to the maximum extent possible. Generally, if the plan is unfunded and is maintained by an employer primarily for the purpose of providing deferred compensation for a select group of management or highly compensated employees, the plan will be exempt from all provisions of ERISA, except for a simple reporting requirement of notifying the Department of Labor of the existence of the plan and some basic facts about it. However, if the plan does not come within this exemption, most of the provisions of ERISA become applicable, and the plan must comply with almost all of the ERISA provisions that apply to a qualified plan. The nonqualified plan could discriminate in participation, benefits, or contributions; but for all other purposes (vesting, fiduciary, and reporting and disclosure) the plan would have to be designed like a qualified plan without the tax benefits for qualified plans. Consequently, most nonqualified deferred-compensation plans are designed to be unfunded and are limited to management or highly compensated employees.

Summary

Nonqualified plans are often used to provide deferred-compensation benefits to executives as an addition to or an alternative to a qualified plan. Benefits do not have to be provided to regular employees in a nonqualified plan, but the employer does not obtain an advance funding deduction.

Benefit formulas and other features reflect the objectives of the employer or employee. The basic formula can be a salary-continuation (defined-benefit) or a salary reduction (defined-contribution) approach. Incentive or other features also are flexible.

Benefit security is important to the employee. Formal funding is rarely used because of unfavorable tax and ERISA aspects; thus, informal funding arrangements, such as corporate-owned life insurance and the rabbi trust, are often used.

Tax to the employee can be deferred to the time of receipt of benefits, if the plan is properly designed. The employer receives a deduction for reasonable compensation in the year the employee includes benefits in income.

APPENDIX A

Pre-1989 Coverage, Vesting, and Integration Rules

Pre-1989 Coverage Tests

As with current law, pre-1989 law includes a set of statutory tests to be applied to the plan in actual operation to determine if coverage is discriminatory. These tests, found in Section 410 of the Code, take the form of two alternative percentage tests, plus a discretionary test, which allows the IRS to approve a plan that does not meet the percentage tests, if the IRS finds that the plan is otherwise nondiscriminatory.

Percentage Tests. The percentage tests are as follows:

1. The plan must cover 70 percent or more of "all employees," or
2. 70 percent or more of all the employees are eligible, and the plan must cover 80 percent or more of all employees who are eligible to benefit under the plan. (This second test is primarily applicable to a plan that allows elective participation by employees, such as a savings plan, described in Chapter 13.)

Although both tests refer to a percentage of "all" employees, one of the most significant aspects of the percentage tests is that "all" does not really mean all. In counting employees, the following employees need not be included:

Employees who have not satisfied the plan's minimum age and service requirements, if any (but those excluded under a maximum age provision must be counted).
Employees excluded by the plan who are included in a collective bargaining unit, if there is evidence that retirement benefits were the subject of good faith bargaining under a collective bargaining agreement.
Employees excluded under a collective bargaining agreement between air pilots and employers under Title II of the Railway Labor Act.
Employees who are nonresident aliens and who receive no earned income from sources within the United States.

While the latter two exclusions are specialized, the first two have a very significant impact on the design of qualified plans. As an example of how these tests work, consider the following.

Example

Axis Transportation Company is a trucking business with 6 office employees and 15 drivers. The drivers are members of a collective bargaining unit with the Teamsters' Union as bargaining agent, and they work under a collective bargaining agreement that requires contributions by Axis to a union-sponsored multiemployer pension plan for the drivers.

The six office employees consist of the president, aged 40, three managers in their 30s or 40s, and two secretaries, one age 30 and the other age 22. Axis adopts a retirement plan for office employees, excluding employees who have not attained age 25. Does the Axis plan meet the percentage test described above? The answer is yes.

"All employees" for purposes of this test is a group consisting only of the president, the three managers, and the secretary who is 30. The secretary who has not met the plan's age-25 requirement is not counted, and neither are the 15 employees in the collective bargaining unit, since there is evidence that they bargained in good faith concerning retirement benefits. (It is irrelevant whether or not they actually have a retirement plan, as long as retirement benefits were the subject of good faith bargaining.)

Since the plan covers 100 percent of "all employees" as so defined, it easily meets the 70 percent test, even though it actually covers only 5 of the company's 21 employees.

The percentage tests apply not only at the plan's inception, but on an ongoing basis. Generally, all of the nondiscrimination requirements must be met by a plan on at least one day of each quarter of the plan's taxable year (Code Section 401(a)(6)). Although the IRS does not perpetually monitor a plan's compliance with the percentage coverage requirements, these requirements give the IRS an ongoing weapon to challenge a plan that may have become discriminatory.

Discretionary Coverage Test

Although it is desirable to design a plan that meets the applicable percentage coverage test (because then it is not usually necessary to demonstrate any further to the IRS that the plan's coverage is nondiscriminatory), the IRS has discretion to approve a plan not meeting the percentage test, if it finds that the plan covers a nondiscriminatory classification of employees.

Although this determination is up to the discretion of the IRS, there are some guidelines for it. One very important guideline is statutory and, therefore, binding on the IRS: Section 401(a)(5) of the Code states that a plan will not be deemed discriminatory merely because it covers salaried employees only. Other guidelines for the discretionary test have been set forth in various pronouncements of the IRS. In general, the IRS will approve a plan if it covers a "fair cross section" of employees. The plan should cover some employees with low wages or salaries, even if the plan as a whole is tilted toward the higher-paid. If there are very few or no low-paid employees covered, the plan probably will not be approved.

A recent Revenue Ruling contains an example illustrating how the IRS applies the discretionary test. This ruling (Rev. Rul. 83–58) involved a profit-sharing plan for salaried employees only. The employer had a total of 150 employees, with only 40 of them participating in the plan. The IRS examined plan participation within various compensation ranges, with the following result:

Group	Compensation Range	Total Employees	Excluded Employees	Participants	Officer or Shareholder Participants
1	$50,001–60,000	4	0	4	4
2	40,001–50,000	0	0	0	0
3	30,001–40,000	25	18	7	7
4	25,001–30,000	45	37	8	8
5	20,001–25,000	50	38	12	3
6	15,001–20,000	14	11	3	0
7	10,001–15,000	9	4	5	0
8	5,001–10,000	3	2	1	0
Total		150	110	40	22

The IRS found that this plan qualified under the discretionary test, even though it did not meet the percentage coverage requirements. This was because the compensation of all but 4 of the 40 participants was substantially the same as that of the excluded hourly paid employees, and also because the plan covered employees in all compensation ranges, with those in middle and lower brackets covered in more than nominal numbers. This ruling and other IRS rulings give a general idea of the types of requirements the IRS will impose in applying the discretionary test. An analysis like this, based on compensation ranges, is usually required.

Pre-1989 Vesting Standards

Under ERISA, as applicable before 1989, a qualified plan must provide that benefits are vested under a specified vesting schedule during the participant's employment so that, if the participant terminates employment prior to retirement age, the participant is entitled to a vested benefit with some stated minimum amount of service.

If the plan provides for employee contributions, the participant's accrued benefit is divided between the part attributable to employee contributions and the part attributable to employer contributions. The part attributable to employee contributions must at all times be 100 percent vested. The part attributable to employer contributions must be vested in accordance with a vesting schedule set out in the plan.

The vesting schedule must be at least as favorable as one of three alternative minimum standards. These are:

10-Year Vesting. The vesting schedule satisfies this minimum requirement if an employee with at least 10 years of service is 100 percent vested in the employer-provided portion of the accrued benefit. This rule is satisfied even if there is no vesting at all before 10 years of service. This rule, therefore, is sometimes referred to as "cliff" vesting.

5- to 15-Year Vesting. A vesting schedule satisfies this minimum standard if the vesting is at least as fast as under the following table:

Years of Service	Vested Percentage
5	25%
6	30
7	35
8	40
9	45
10	50
11	60
12	70
13	80
14	90
15 or more	100

Rule of 45. This is the only vesting alternative that takes a participant's age into consideration. Under this alternative, any employee who has completed at least 5 years of service and who has not separated from service with the employer and for whom the sum of age and years of service equals or exceeds 45, has a vested right to the employer-provided accrued benefit as determined under the following table:

If Years of Service Equal or Exceed	And Sum of Age and Service Equals or Exceeds	Then Vested Percentage Is
5	45	50
6	47	60
7	49	70
8	51	80
9	53	90
10	55	100

The Rule of 45 also imposes an additional requirement: that any employee who has completed at least 10 years of service must be at least 50 percent vested, and he or she must be entitled to an additional 10 percent vesting for each additional year of service thereafter.

As an alternative to the use of a regular vesting schedule meeting one of the three vesting standards, a defined-contribution plan (profit-sharing, stock-bonus, or money-purchase pension plan) may use what is known as *class year vesting*. With class year vesting, a separate vesting percentage is applied to employer contributions for each plan year. For example, a class year plan might provide that employer contributions made in 1986 would vest 50 percent in 1987 and 50 percent in 1988, with similar vesting rules for contributions made in 1987, 1988, and so on. The class year vesting schedule will be permitted as long as the employee is 100 percent vested in the employer-provided portion of the account not later than the end of the fifth plan year following the plan year for which the contributions were made.

In applying the vesting rules, all of a participant's years of service for the employer must be taken into account, even years prior to plan participation, except that years of service prior to age 18 may be excluded. The plan's vesting schedule may also ignore service prior to a break in continuous service with the employer; however, the Code has elaborate restrictions on how this may be done (Code Section 411(a)(6)).

Probably the most common vesting provision in defined-benefit plans has been the 10-year provision, because of its simplicity and because it is generally the most favorable to the employer. Defined-contribution plans are often designed with a more generous (to the employee) vesting schedule, using one of the other two alternatives or an even faster vesting schedule.

4-40 Vesting. The IRS generally requires new plans to adopt a vesting schedule even faster than one of the three specified alternatives. The Code gives the IRS the authority to require more rapid vesting if there has been a "pattern of abuse" under the plan (such as a firing of employees just before they become vested) that discriminates in favor of the prohibited group, or, as the Code puts it, "there has been, or there is reason to believe there will be, an accrual of benefits or forfeitures" discriminating in favor of the prohibited group. In commenting upon this provision, the Conference Committee of the Congress that enacted it in 1974 suggested that any plan which met a nonstatutory vesting schedule referred to as the *4-40 vesting schedule* would satisfy any such objections, except for "pattern of abuse" situations. The 4-40 vesting schedule is as follows:

Years of Service	Vesting Percentage
1–3	0%
4	40
5	45
6	50
7	60
8	70
9	80
10	90
11	100

As a result of this Code provision and statutory history, the IRS has often required new plans to adopt a 4-40 vesting schedule, unless the planner can make a showing that the employer has not had a discriminatory turnover rate in the past. Often this is difficult, for new and for smaller employers particularly, and new plans typically adopt the 4-40 vesting provision to avoid this problem.

Integration of Qualified Plans with Social Security under Pre-1989 Law

The pre-1989 integration rules are mostly administrative, the Code (former Section 401(a)(5)) being very brief on this point. The basic rules are in a 1971 Revenue Ruling—Rev. Rul. 71–446. Under the principles of Rev. Rul. 71–446, as under current law, there are two basic approaches by which a qualified plan can be integrated with social security—the *offset* approach and the *integration level* approach (sometimes called the "excess" approach). Under the offset approach, a specified fraction of the primary social security benefit is subtracted from the benefit otherwise payable under the plan. The offset approach can be used only with a defined-benefit plan. Under the integration level approach, the plan specifies a level of compensation called the "integration level." Benefits or contributions below this integration level are provided at a lower rate than the benefits or contributions for compensation above the integration level. An integration level approach can be used with both defined-benefit and defined-contribution plans.

Integration of Defined-Benefit Plans

Offset Approach. As indicated above, a defined-benefit plan can be integrated with social security using either the offset approach or the integration level approach. Since the offset approach is simpler, it will be discussed first.

With the offset method, the private plan benefit initially is structured to provide the replacement ratio desired, without taking social security into account. Then the benefit formula is modified to subtract a specified percentage of the employee's social security benefit. For example, an offset formula might read as follows:

> Upon retirement, the participant shall be entitled to a monthly retirement benefit equal to 60 percent of the participant's final average monthly compensation, less 70 percent of the participant's monthly primary social security benefit.

Note: in the example above, the reference to the "primary social security benefit."
The amount used in an offset formula must be the participant's primary social security benefit, not the actual social security benefit that the participant and his or her family may receive. The primary social security benefit is basically the benefit provided to a single person, not taking into account any dependent benefits that might be available. The primary social security benefit is used for offset purposes, because otherwise the benefit paid from the plan itself would be less for an employee with dependents than for an employee without dependents.

Full or 100 percent offsetting of social security benefits is not permitted. The maximum percentage of the primary social security benefit that may be used in an offset plan formula is 83⅓ percent. The 83⅓ percent figure refers to a plan with an offset formula using the current social security benefit structure. Higher percentages are permissible if, for some reason, a plan uses for offset purposes the social security benefit as determined under an earlier version of the social security law.

Even though an offset of up to 83⅓ percent of the primary social security benefit is permitted, the typical employer has found that its cost and other planning objectives can be met using a lower offset percentage (and, therefore, providing a more generous benefit from the plan itself). Offset percentages in the range of 50 to 75 percent have been typical.

Social security benefits are currently subject to indexing to reflect increases in the cost of living. However, the benefit paid by a private integrated plan cannot be reduced to reflect postretirement increases in social security benefits, even if an offset formula is used. In other words, the amount of benefit payable to a participant from the plan itself generally will be fixed when the participant retires, regardless of changes in social security benefits paid thereafter to the participant.

As will be evident after reviewing the rules for social security integration using integration levels (discussed next), the principal advantage of a social security offset formula is its simplicity, both in designing the plan and in communicating the plan effectively to employees. Many of the restrictive rules applicable to integration level plans do not apply to offset plans, as discussed later in Adjustments for Additional Benefits and Benefit Forms. A principal disadvantage of an offset plan is the difficulty of determining the advance funding level, because the actuary must make an estimate for each participant of that participant's future social security benefit, and that may not be easily determinable for younger participants.

Integration Level Approach. Using the integration level approach in a defined-benefit plan, a specified level of compensation—the integration level—is defined by the plan. The plan then provides the participant a higher rate of benefits for compensation above the integration level than for compensation for below the integration level. If the private plan provides a zero level of benefits below its specified integration level, the formula is referred to as an *excess* formula. If the formula provides anything other than a zero level of benefits below its integration level, it is referred to as a *stepped-up* formula.

An example of an excess type of integrated formula is:

Upon retirement, the participant will be entitled to an annual retirement benefit equal to 37½ percent of the participant's final average annual compensation in excess of $7,000.

An example of a stepped-up formula is:

Upon retirement, a participant will be entitled to an annual retirement benefit equal to 10 percent of the participant's final average annual compensation up to $7,000, plus 47½ percent of the participant's final average annual compensation in excess of $7,000.

Another way of drafting the same stepped-up formula is:

Upon retirement, a participant will be entitled to an annual retirement benefit equal to 10 percent of the participant's full final average annual compensation, plus 37½ percent of the participant's final average compensation in excess of $7,000.

In both of these plans the integration level is $7,000.

The integration rules of Rev. Rul. 71–446 restrict two parameters of the integration formula: They specify the *maximum integration level* and the *maximum percentage spread* between the benefits provided below the integration level and those provided above. There are separate rules for flat-benefit and unit-benefit formulas.

Integration of flat-benefit plans. For a flat-benefit plan, the *maximum permitted integration level* is the appropriate amount from an IRS table of "covered compensation" (Table A–1). The origin of this table is explained below. The covered compensation is taken from either table I or table II of Table A–1. Since this is an amount that varies with each participant's age, some planners prefer to use a uniform dollar amount as the integration level for all participants to make the plan simpler and easier to describe to participants. Any uniform dollar amount can be used as an integration level, as long as it does not exceed the covered compensation from table I or II for the oldest prospective employee.

Example

Suppose the plan is established in 1986 and excludes persons hired less than five years from their 65th birthday. The oldest prospective employee, therefore, is currently 60; and this employee's covered compensation, based on retirement in five years, would be $18,600 (from table I). Therefore, a uniform integration level of any amount up to $18,600 may be used in this plan.

Notice that this rule refers to the oldest prospective employee, not the oldest actual employee. It is irrelevant that there may be no actual 60-year-old employee hired in 1986.

A uniform dollar amount higher than the maximum described here may be used without disqualifying the plan. However, the use of a higher uniform level will result in a decrease in the maximum percentage spread that is permitted. As an illustration, using the facts in the above example, if a uniform integration level of $37,200 is used, then the maximum allowable percentage will be 18,600 ÷ 37,200 (i.e., half) of that otherwise allowable.

TABLE A–1. Official 1985 IRS Tables of Covered Compensation

Calendar Year of 65th Birthday	Table I	Table II
1985	$13,800	$13,800
1986	15,000	14,760
1987	15,600	15,648
1988	16,200	16,464
1989	17,400	17,244
1990	18,000	17,964
1991	18,600	18,636
1992	19,200	19,272
1993	19,800	19,872
1994	20,400	20,436
1995	21,600	21,432
1996	22,200	22,428
1997	23,400	23,412
1998	24,600	24,408
1999	25,200	25,404
2000	26,400	26,408
2001	27,600	27,396
2002	28,200	28,332
2003	29,400	29,280
2004	30,000	30,192
2005	31,200	31,092
2006	31,800	32,004
2007	33,000	32,916
2008	33,600	33,792
2009	34,800	34,608
2010	35,400	35,364
2011	36,000	36,096
2012	36,600	36,792
2013	37,200	37,452
2014	37,800	38,076
2015	38,400	38,556
2016	39,000	38,940
2017	39,000	39,228
2018	39,600	39,432
2019	39,600	39,540
2020 and later	39,600	39,600

The *maximum percentage spread* in a flat-percentage plan is 37½ percent. The reason for this particular figure is discussed below. As an example of what this means, an integrated flat-benefit formula could provide a zero benefit for a participant's compensation up to the covered compensation level, plus 37½ percent of compensation above the covered compensation level.

The maximum integration levels and integration percentages described above are the same for both excess and stepped-up flat-benefit plans. With a stepped-up plan, the maximum percentage applies to the percentage spread above and below the integration level. For example, a flat-benefit plan could provide a benefit of 10 percent on compensation up to the integration level, and 47.5 percent on compensation in excess of the integration level. Another common way of expressing this same type of benefit formula is a benefit of 10 percent on all compensation, and 37½ percent on compensation in excess of the integration level. The IRS describes stepped-up plans in this manner and treats such a plan basically as two plans: a uniform percentage plan with a 10 percent benefit, and an excess-type integrated plan with a 37½ percent benefit on excess compensation. Described this way, only the excess plan is subject to the integration rules.

Finally, it should be noted that the maximum percentage of 37½ percent applies only to a simple formula with a straight-life annuity benefit and no death or disability benefits, that also meets certain other restrictions. Actuarial adjustments, described more fully below, are provided for more complex benefit forms.

Integration of unit-benefit plans. Unit-benefit plans can be either career-average or final-average types. The basic difference is in the treatment of compensation. For career-average plans, the compensation in effect during each year is taken into account. For final-average plans, only the compensation over a specified period of years is used. Because of this difference, there are different integration rules for the two types of plans.

Career-average plans. For each year of service, the taxable wage base for that year is the maximum integration level. For years prior to 1959, $4,800 may be used. The plan may use any uniform dollar amount that is less than the taxable wage base for the current year.

The maximum integration percentage spread for each year of service is 1.4 percent. Thus, for an employee with 20 years of credited service, the total maximum percentage spread would be 20 × 1.4 percent, or 28 percent.

Final-average plans. For a final-average plan, the maximum integration level is the same as that for a flat-benefit plan—that is, either the covered compensation from table I or II or a uniform dollar amount that does not exceed the covered compensation for the oldest prospective employee.

The maximum percentage spread for final-average unit-benefit plans is 1 percent of final-average compensation. Final-average compensation must be averaged over at least five years to obtain the maximum percentage allowable. A percentage higher than 1 percent per year can be used in a final-average plan, as long as the number of years of credited service is limited so that the total percentage spread does not exceed the flat-benefit limit of 37½. For example, a unit-benefit plan could provide no benefit for final-average compensation below the integration level, plus 1.5 percent of final-average compensation over the integration level, per year, if years of credited service are limited to 25, because the total percentage benefit would then be limited to 25 times 1½ percent, or 37½ percent.

As with flat-benefit plans, reduction in the maximum percentage may be required, if the plan provides certain additional types of benefits or benefit forms, as described below.

Stepped-up plans. The rules described so far apply to an excess-type of unit-benefit plan. A unit-benefit plan can also be stepped-up. In this case, the maximum integration rules would be the same as for the excess plan, and the percentage limits would apply to the percentage spread in the stepped-up plan. Thus, a final-average unit-benefit plan could provide 1 percent of final-average pay for each year of service, plus 1 percent of final-average pay in excess of the integration level for each year of service. (Or, expressed alternatively, 1 percent of final-average pay below the integration level and 2 percent of final-average pay in excess of the integration level.)

Integration of Defined-Contribution Plans

Since the benefits in a defined-contribution plan are based on the participant's account balance, the integration rules for defined-contribution plans apply to the amounts allocated to participant's accounts, rather than to the benefits. Only an integration level approach (not an offset) can be used.

Basically, the maximum allowable integration level for determining allocation in a given year is the taxable wage base for that year. The percentage spread allowable cannot exceed the current social security tax rate imposed on employees for the year, less the amount allocable to medicare. Currently (1986), the social security tax rate is 7.15 percent, or 5.7 percent excluding the medicare portion. Thus, the percentage spread cannot exceed 5.7 percent.

An integration level higher than the current taxable wage base can be used in a defined-contribution plan, but the maximum percentage spread is reduced proportionately. For example, if the actual integration level of the plan is $64,800, and the taxable wage base for the year is $32,400, the maximum percentage spread will be only one half ($32,400 ÷ $64,800) of what otherwise would be allowed. However, a percentage spread *greater* than the social security tax rate is not allowed, even if the plan uses an integration level *below* the maximum.

As an example of an integrated defined-contribution plan, suppose that the integration level of a money-purchase plan is $30,000, and the plan is of the excess type. For an employee earning $40,000, the allocation to the employee's account cannot exceed 5.7 percent of $10,000 (the excess amount), or $570. This small allocation for the excess-type formula shows why the stepped-up approach is common in integrated defined-contribution plans.

The pre-1989 integration rules are summarized in Table A–2.

TABLE A–2. Summary of Pre–1989 Integration Rules

Formula Type	Maximum Integration Level	Maximum Percentage
Flat-benefit	Covered compensation	37½%
Unit-benefit:		
Career-average	Taxable wage base	1.4% per year
Final-average	Covered compensation	1% per year
Defined-contribution	Taxable wage base	OASDI tax rate

Adjustments for Additional Benefits and Benefit Forms

The rules discussed up to this point have referred only to the basic percentages and other limits. These basic rules apply to a plan providing a straight-life annuity as the basic form of benefit, with no integrated death or disability benefits, and satisfying certain other restrictions. Also, the basic rules apply only if the normal retirement age is at least age 65, although earlier retirement is permitted if the benefit is adjusted in accordance with the limits described below.

A large portion of Rev. Rul. 71–446 and other pronouncements by the IRS on plan integration deal with actuarial adjustments that must be made to these percentages if the plan provides alternative benefit forms or additional benefits. Basically, the purpose for these adjustments is to insure that the maximum amount of discrimination permitted in an integrated plan will not be exceeded simply by changing the benefit form or by adding an additional integrated benefit, such as a death or disability benefit. These adjustment rules are extremely complex and, for a basic understanding of pension planning, it is not necessary to memorize the rules in detail. Nevertheless, some of the more significant types of adjustments, and those that are found most often in practice, will be reviewed here.

First of all, if the retirement benefit is not a straight-life annuity, the maximum allowable benefit is reduced to a percentage given in Table A–3, taken from Rev. Rul. 71–446.

In practice, Table A–3 is utilized by appropriately reducing the basic percentage limit. For example, normally a flat-benefit excess plan could provide a benefit of 37½ percent of final average compensation above the integration level. However, if the normal form of benefit under the plan is an annuity for 10 years certain and life thereafter, the maximum benefit would be only 90 percent of this. Since 90 percent of 37½ percent is 33.75, the excess benefit could be no more than 33.75 percent of final average compensation. As another illustration of these reductions, note that a qualified joint and 50 percent survivor annuity as the normal form of benefit would reduce the maximum percentage to 80 percent of that otherwise applicable.

Another rule requires a reduction in the full percentage if the plan provides a full retirement benefit for an employee with less than 15 years of service. To avoid this reduction, the plan must reduce the benefit by at least one 15th for each year of service less than 15.

TABLE A–3. Reductions for Alternate Benefit Forms

Form of Retirement Benefits	Percentage
Annuity for 5 years certain and life thereafter	97
Annuity for 10 years certain and life thereafter	90
Annuity for 15 years certain and life thereafter	80
Annuity for 20 years certain and life thereafter	70
Life annuity with installment refund	90
Life annuity with cash refund (employer contributions)	85
Life annuity with one half continued to surviving spouse of employee	80

A reduction in the percentage also results if the plan provides a benefit at an early retirement date without actuarial reduction. To avoid a reduction in the percentage, generally the minimum actuarial reduction is one 15th of the accrued benefit for each of the first five years and one 30th for each of the next five years, by which payment of benefits precedes age 65, with actuarial reductions for each additional year.

A reduction is also required if the plan provides a deferred vested benefit without a reduction to reflect the accrued benefit at termination of employment. If the employee terminates before normal retirement date with a deferred-vested benefit, the benefit payable at age 65 must be reduced by the ratio of the actual years of service to the years of service that the employee would have had if employment continued to age 65.

Finally, if the plan has an integrated preretirement death or disability benefit, other than the required survivor annuity (Chapters 10 and 16), reduction factors also apply. The reduction factor is one ninth if the plan provides a death benefit using whole life insurance that results in a current tax cost ("P.S. 58" cost) to the covered employee, or provides a death benefit equal to the present value at death of the participant's accrued benefit. Thus, if the maximum percentage was ordinarily 37½ percent, if the plan has this type of death benefit, the 37½ percent would be reduced by one ninth to 33⅜ percent, and this would become the maximum integration percentage for a flat-benefit excess plan. Reductions greater than one ninth are required if the plan has an integrated preretirement death benefit provided without a current tax cost to the employee (i.e., without the use of life insurance).

In the case of disability, the maximum percentages must be reduced unless the plan pays benefits commencing only at age 65. The plan must provide reductions somewhat similar to those required for early retirement, if disability benefits begin prior to age 65.

The reduction factors given above generally apply in reducing all the maximum integration percentages otherwise permitted by the rules. In general, the same factors would be applied to the percentages for flat-benefit plans or unit-benefit plans. However, for offset plans, the reductions differ somewhat. Some of the reductions are not required. For example, it is not necessary to require 15 years of service for a full retirement benefit, nor is there any restriction on the number of years that may be taken into account in determining final average earnings for an offset plan. However, a deferred-vested benefit must be reduced in an offset plan, and reductions are also required if the plan provides death or disability benefits.

APPENDIX B

Controlled Groups, Affiliated Service Groups, and Employee Leasing

Controlled Groups of Corporations and Other Business Organizations

Under Sections 414(b) and (c) of the Code, all employees of members of a controlled group of corporations or controlled group of trades or businesses (whether or not incorporated) that are under common control are treated as employed by a single employer for purposes of Sections 401, 408(k), 410, 411, 415, and 416. This covers most provisions of the qualified plan law. The most important impact relates to the coverage requirements of Code Section 410. Thus, all employees of employers in a controlled group must be taken into account when determining whether a qualified plan maintained by any employer in the controlled group satisfies the percentage participation tests or the discretionary tests.

The existence of a controlled group is determined by applying the rules of Code Section 1563(a), a section originally designed to inhibit corporations from breaking up into smaller units to take advantage of the graduated corporate tax rates. Under this provision, there are three types of controlled groups: parent-subsidiary controlled groups, brother-sister controlled groups, and combined groups.

Parent-Subsidiary Controlled Group

A parent-subsidiary controlled group is one or more chains of corporations connected through stock ownership with a common parent corporation if, with respect to the stock of each corporation (except the parent corporation):

At least 80 percent of the total combined voting power of all classes of stock entitled to vote or at least 80 percent of the total value of shares of all classes of stock is owned by one or more corporations in the group, and
the common parent corporation satisfies the same 80 percent test with at least one other corporation in the group. Stock owned directly by any other corporation in the group is excluded in determining the parent corporation's ownership.

In applying this test to unincorporated trades or businesses, the 80 percent test is applied to an interest in profits or to a capital interest.

Example

Suppose Alpha Corporation owns 80 percent of the total combined voting power of all classes of stock entitled to vote of Beta Corporation. Beta Corporation owns stock that possesses at least 80 percent of the total value of shares of all classes of stock of Gamma Corporation. Alpha is the common parent, and the parent-subsidiary controlled group consists of Alpha, Beta, and Gamma.

Brother-Sister Controlled Group

A brother-sister controlled group is two or more corporations if five or fewer individuals, estates, or trusts own (with attribution, as described below) stock possessing:

At least 80 percent of the total combined voting power or value of all classes of stock (excluding nonvoting stock, which is limited and preferred as to dividends) of each corporation, and
more than 50 percent of the total combined voting power or value of all classes of stock (excluding nonvoting stock, which is limited and preferred as to dividends) of each corporation, taking into account the stock ownership of each owner only to the extent that the owner's interest is identical in each corporation.

Examples

Corporations M, N, and O have only one class of stock, which is owned by five unrelated individuals as follows:

	Percentage of Ownership in			Identical Ownership in
Investor	M	N	O	MNO
Alex	20%	10%	20%	10%
Bartley	20	30	10	10
Clay	20	20	30	20
Davis	20	20	20	20
Ensley	20	20	20	20
Totals	100%	100%	100%	80%

Corporations M, N, and O constitute a brother-sister controlled group.

Another example illustrates some further complexities. Three corporations Q, S, and T are owned by four unrelated individuals as follows:

	Percentage of Ownership in			Identical Ownership in		
Investor	Q	S	T	Q-S	Q-T	S-T
Walt	50%	25%	25.5%	25%	25.5%	25.0%
Xavier	50	25	25.5	25	25.5	25.0
Yolanda	0	25	24.5	0	0.0	24.5
Zorba	0	25	24.5	0	0.0	24.5
Totals	100%	100%	100%	50%	51 %	99 %

Corporations Q and S do not constitute a brother-sister controlled group, because, although four individuals together own 100 percent of each, taking only identical ownership into account, there is only 50 percent common control. However, Q and T are part of a brother-sister controlled group, because the identical ownership in the two adds up to 51 percent. Finally, S and T constitute a second brother-sister controlled group, with identical ownership adding up to a total of 99 percent.

At one time, the IRS included an example in the Regulations which, somewhat simplified, went as follows:

	Percentage of Ownership in			Identical Ownership in		
Investor	A	B	C	AB	AC	BC
1	100%	60%	60%	60%	60%	60%
2	0	40	0	0	0	0
3	0	0	40	0	0	0
Totals	100%	*	*	60%	60%	60%

*100 percent under prior regulations; 60 percent under current regulations. See below.

The Regulations asserted that AB, AC, and BC constituted brother-sister controlled groups, even though some of the owners held no interest at all in A, B, or C. This interpretation was declared invalid by the U.S. Supreme Court in *U.S. v. Vogel Fertilizer Company,* 102 S. Ct. 821(1982). The new proposed regulations reflect this by providing that each person whose stock ownership is taken into account for purposes of the 80 percent requirement also must be a person whose stock ownership is counted toward the 50 percent requirement. Under this interpretation, there are no brother-sister groups in this situation.

Combined Group

A combined group is three or more corporations each of which is a member of a parent-subsidiary group or a brother-sister group and one of which is a common parent of a parent-subsidiary group and also is included in a brother-sister group.

Example

Ken, an individual, owns 80 percent of the total combined voting power of all classes of stock of Steel Corporation and Lint Corporation. Lint Corporation owns 80 percent of the total combined voting power of all classes of the stock of Octopus Corporation. Steel and Lint are members of a brother-sister controlled group. Lint and Octopus are members of a parent-subsidiary group. Lint is the common parent of the parent-subsidiary group and also a member of the brother-sister group. Therefore, Steel, Lint, and Octopus constitute a combined group.

Stock Not Taken into Account in Controlled Group Determination

Under the rules of Code Section 1563, certain stock is excluded from consideration in computing the percentages in the controlled group tests. In general, note that excluding stock from consideration makes it more likely that the tests will be met, because the target shareholder's stock will be a larger percentage of the amount outstanding. This is the purpose of these exclusionary rules; in general, they are designed to thwart attempts to get around controlled group tests by transferring stock to various trusts or other entities, as the rules indicate.

First of all, nonvoting preferred stock and treasury stock are not taken into account.

In addition, the following are not taken into account in determining the existence of a parent-subsidiary controlled group, if the parent owns 50 percent or more of the total combined voting power or value of all classes of stock in the potential subsidiary corporation:

> Stock in a subsidiary held by a trust that is part of a plan of deferred compensation for the benefit of the employees of the parent or the subsidiary.
> Stock in the subsidiary owned by an individual who is a principal shareholder (5 percent or more of voting power or total value) or an officer of the potential parent.
> Stock in the subsidiary owned by an employee of the subsidiary, if the stock is subject to conditions that run in favor of the parent or subsidiary and which substantially restrict the right to dispose of such stock. Stock subject to the typical buy-sell agreement generally would fall within this provision.
> Stock in the subsidiary owned by a tax-exempt organization that is controlled directly or indirectly by the parent or subsidiary or by an individual, estate, or trust that is a principal shareholder of the parent, by an officer of the potential parent, or by any combination of the above.

For purposes of the brother-sister controlled group tests, the following stock is excluded whenever five potential common owners own at least 50 percent of the total combined voting power or value of all classes of stock:

> Stock held for the benefit of the employees of the corporation by a qualified retirement plan trust.
> Stock owned by an employee of the corporation, if the stock is subject to restrictions that run in favor of any of the common owners of the corporation and which substantially restrict the right to dispose of the stock (with an exception for bona fide reciprocal stock-purchase agreements).
> Stock owned by a tax-exempt organization that is controlled directly or indirectly by the corporation, by an individual, estate, or trust that is a principal shareholder of the corporation, by an officer of the corporation, or by any combination of these.

Constructive Ownership (Attribution) Rules

In determining the existence of a controlled group, an individual may be deemed to own not only stock owned directly but also stock owned by certain related parties.

First, an option to acquire stock causes the optionholder to be treated as owning the stock. This rule applies for both parent-subsidiary and brother-sister determinations. Further attribution rules apply in the brother-sister situation. These are:

- Stock owned directly or indirectly by or for a partnership is considered owned by any partner having an interest of 5 percent or more in capital or profits, in proportion to the partner's interest.
- Stock owned directly or indirectly by an estate or trust (including a qualified trust) is considered owned by any beneficiary who has an actuarial interest of 5 percent or more in such stock, to the extent of the actuarial interest.
- Stock owned directly or indirectly by or for any portion of a grantor trust is considered owned by the grantor.
- Stock owned directly by or for a corporation is considered owned by any person who owns 5 percent or more in value of its stock in proportion to the percentage of corporate value owned by the person.
- An individual is considered to own stock in a corporation owned directly or indirectly by or for his spouse (if not legally separated under a decree of divorce or separate maintenance), unless the person's ownership satisfies certain standards of remoteness set out in Section 1563(e)(5).
- A parent is deemed to own stock owned directly or indirectly by or for his children, including legally adopted children, who are less than 21 years of age, and an individual less than 21 years old is deemed to own stock owned directly or indirectly by or for his parents, including legally adoptive parents.
- If an individual owns more than 50 percent of the total combined voting power or value of all classes of stock in a corporation, the individual is considered as owning stock in the corporation owned directly or indirectly by or for his parents, grandparents, grandchildren, and children who have attained age 21.

The above attribution rules all can be used to provide reattribution to another owner, except that stock attributed under the family attribution rules is not reattributed. This can result in very complex attribution patterns, in some cases.

Consequences of Controlled Group Status

Once again, all employees of all corporations that are members of a controlled group of corporations are treated as employed by a single employer for various purposes, specified in Code Section 414(b). Probably the most significant of these consequences is the application of the coverage tests of Section 410 of the Code.

All three tests will be applied to the group as a whole, except to the extent that the tests can be applied to a subgroup constituting a separate line of business under Code Section 414(r). This does not necessarily mean that a plan cannot qualify if it involves employees of only one member of a controlled group. The plan for a single company in the controlled group could qualify if it meets one of the three tests, such as the average-benefit test in particular.

It is also possible that the controlled group aggregation rules can be applied to the advantage of the employer. For example, a plan for a controlled group might meet the average-benefit test, even though in a given corporation included in the group there might be only one or two participants, both among the highest-paid employees of that corporation. Considered separately, the plan for that corporation would fail to qualify.

Affiliated Service Groups

The purpose and effect of the affiliated service group rules of Code Section 414(m) are best understood by looking at the loophole that this provision was designed to close. This loophole typically involved professional corporations or partnerships that desired to exclude rank-and-file employees from qualified plans maintained for the professional owners.

Example

Consider a situation in which two physicians enter into an equal partnership for the practice of medicine. A similar alternative practice was for each doctor to form a one-person professional corporation and then have the professional corporations enter into a partnership. The partnership could then form a separate support business to provide all support services for the medical practice, and the support business would become the employer of all the support employees. Each of the doctors would own just 50 percent of the support organization. Under all the other aggregation rules discussed here, except for the affiliated service group rules, the doctors could each adopt a qualified plan covering only themselves and none of the regular employees. The affiliated service group rules basically eliminate this type of planning or restrict it severely.

The affiliated service group provisions provide complex rules under which the employees of an *affiliated service group* must be included in any qualified plans that benefit the owners. An affiliated service group includes the *service organization* and the professional organization itself. For purposes of most of the pension provisions, including the coverage and nondiscrimination rules, all employees of an affiliated service group are treated as being employed by a single employer.

An affiliated service group means a service organization and one or more organizations that meet one of the following two tests:

1. A service organization that is a shareholder or partner in the first organization and regularly performs services for the first organization or is regularly associated with the first organization in performing services for third persons.
2. An organization in which a significant portion of its business is the performance of services of a type historically performed for the first organization or for a service organization that is the shareholder or partner in the first organization.

    However, this applies only if 10 percent or more of the organization is owned by officers, highly compensated employees, or owners of the first organization or any service organization that is a shareholder or partner in the first organization.

Under the Regulations, the rules apply primarily to service organizations of the type that provide professional services in the fields of health, law, engineering, architecture, accounting, actuarial science, performing arts, consulting, or insurance. However, this list can be further expanded through Regulations.

Example

As an example of the operation of the affiliated service group rules, suppose Dr. VanDerslice incorporates and the corporation becomes a partner with the professional corporations of other doctors. Doctor VanDerslice's corporation regularly associates with the other professional corporations in performing services for third persons—individual patients, a hospital, and the like. Each corporation and the partnership of these corporations constitutes an affiliated service group, because the corporation is a service organization that is a partner with the others and is regularly associated with the partnership in performing services for third persons.

As is readily apparent, the affiliated service group rules go considerably beyond the loophole they were initially intended to close. Furthermore, the complexity of these rules is such that it is often difficult to determine whether they apply. Furthermore, many of the affiliated service group provisions involve a degree of subjective judgment—that is, ultimately they are up to the discretion of the IRS—unlike the controlled group rules which, though complex, are relatively mechanical. Thus, in doubtful cases, it is advisable to obtain a ruling from the IRS about whether an organization is a member of an affiliated service group. A ruling can be obtained pursuant to Rev. Proc. 81–12, 1981–1 C.B. 228.

Employee Leasing

The leased employee provisions of Code Section 414(n) were designed to reduce the discrimination potential from an employer's choosing to lease employees from an independent employee leasing organization, rather than employ them directly. The purpose of this practice is to keep the employees technically off the payroll of the lessee business and, thus, outside the coverage of its qualified plans.

This practice is limited under current law. A leased employee is considered an employee of the lessee organization for which the services are performed if:

> The employee has performed services on a substantially full-time basis for at least one year, and
> the services are of a type "historically performed, in the business field of the recipient, by employees."

This rule does not apply if the leasing organization itself maintains a "safe-harbor" plan for the leased employees meeting certain minimum requirements:

> The plan must be a nonintegrated money-purchase plan with an employer contribution rate of at least 10 percent of compensation, and
> the plan must provide immediate participation and full and immediate vesting.
> All employees of the leasing organization with compensation of $1,000 or more over the past four years must be covered.
> The safe-harbor exemption may not be used if leased employees constitute more than 20 percent of the recipient's (lessor's) work force.

Since 10 percent is a relatively modest plan contribution level, many leasing organizations are adopting this approach. Thus, employee leasing remains a viable method for minimizing plan benefits and contributions for low-level employees, even with the restrictions of Code Section 414(n).

Because of the one-year requirement, the leasing provision has no impact on most short-term temporary help. Attempts to technically exploit this requirement by rotating leased employees may not be effective, because the one-year requirement is determined on the basis of cumulative service for the recipient. The requirement of treating the leased employee as an employee of the recipient does not begin until the leased employee has met the one-year service requirement.

Because of the relatively low safe-harbor provision, some employers might be tempted to convert all their employees to leased employees through some arrangement with a leasing organization. However, the IRS has taken the position that the Code provision applies only to bona fide employee leases. If the lease is not deemed bona fide, the employees will be treated for qualified plan purposes as if they were employed directly.

Bibliography

Periodicals
BNA Pension Reporter. Washington, D.C.: Bureau of National Affairs. (weekly)
Employee Benefit Plan Review. Chicago: Charles D. Spencer & Associates. (monthly)
If Employee Benefits Journal. Brookfield, Wis.: International Foundation of Employee Benefit Plans. (quarterly)
Journal of the American Society of CLU. Bryn Mawr, Pa.: American Society of CLU. (bimonthly)
Journal of Pension Planning and Compliance. Greenvale, N.Y.: Panel Publishers. (quarterly)
Life Insurance Fact Book. Washington, D.C.: American Council of Life Insurance. (annual)
Pension Facts. Washington, D.C.: American Council of Life Insurance. (annual)
Pension World. Atlanta: Communication Channels, Inc. (monthly)
Pensions & Investments. Chicago: Crain Communications, Inc. (biweekly)

Loose-leaf Services
Pension and Profit-Sharing Plans for Small and Medium Size Businesses. Greenvale, N.Y.: Panel Publishers.
Pension and Profit-Sharing Service. Englewood Cliffs, N.J.: Prentice-Hall.
Pension Plan Forms. Jacksonville, Fla.: Corbel & Company.
Pension Plan Guide. Chicago: Commerce Clearing House.
Pension Plans Service. Indianapolis: R & R Newkirk.
Spencer's Retirement Plan Service. Chicago: Charles D. Spencer & Associates.

Books
Allen, Everett T., Jr.; Joseph J. Melone; and Jerry S. Rosenbloom, *Pension Planning*. 5th ed. Homewood, Ill.: Richard D. Irwin, 1984.
Beam, Burton T., Jr., and John J. McFadden. *Employee Benefits*. Homewood, Ill.: Richard D. Irwin, 1985.
Boyers, Judith T. *Pensions in Perspective*. Cincinnati, Ohio: The National Underwriter Company, 1986.
Canan, Michael J., and David R. Baker. *Qualified Retirement Plans*. St. Paul, Minn.: West Publishing Company, 1987.
Dunkle, David S. *Guide to Pension and Profit Sharing Plans*. Colorado Springs: Shepard's/McGraw-Hill, 1984.
McGill, Dan M. *Fundamentals of Private Pensions*. 5th ed. Homewood, Ill.: Richard D. Irwin, 1984.
Osgood, Russell K. *The Law of Pensions and Profit-sharing*. Boston: Little, Brown, 1984.
Slimmon, Robert F. *Successful Pension Design for Small- to Medium-Sized Businesses*. Reston, Va.: Reston Publishing Co., 1985.

Index

A

Accounting rules, 238
Accrued benefit, 67
Accrued-benefit actuarial cost method, 114, 122
Accumulated funding deficiency, 126
Active participant, 253
Actual deferral percentage, 164
Actuarial assumptions, 72, 120–21, 276
Actuarial cost methods, 107, 116
Actuarial deficiency, 125
Actuarial surplus, 125
Actuarial valuations, 125
Administration of qualified plan, 232
Adoption of qualified plan, 227
Advance determination letters, 228
Affiliated service group, 62, 318
Age discrimination, 39, 42, 73
Age requirements, 54
Aggregate actuarial cost methods, 119, 123
AIME, 17
Allocated funding, 134
Allocation of assets on termination, 247
Allocation to accounts, 149
Amortization of supplemental liability, 120
Annual additions limit, 178, 211, 213
Annual report, 237
Annuity purchase rate, 108
Asset reversion, 242
Attained age normal method, 123
Average-benefit test, 58–59
Average indexed monthly earnings; *see* AIME

B

Backloading, 68
Base-benefit percentage, 94
Base-contribution percentage, 96
Basic benefits, 245
Benefit accrual rules, 68
Benefit commitments, 247
Break in service, 56
Business necessity, 242

C

Career-average formula, 83, 308
Cash balance plan, 31–32, 82
Cash or deferred plans; *see* Sec. 401(k) plans
Cashout, 67

Catch-up alternatives, 268
Civil rights, 42, 84
Claims procedure, 236
Code; *see* Internal Revenue Code
Collective bargaining, 3, 28, 36, 53, 58
Combination plans, 136–37
Commonly-controlled employer groups, 62, 222, 312
Comparable plans, 60, 283
Compensation, 218, 253
Compensation policy, 44
Consumer price index, 87
Constructive receipt, 267, 292, 295
Contributory plan, 26
Controlled groups, 62, 222, 312
Conversion fund, 136, 137
Corporate-owned life insurance, 290, 294
Cost basis, 190
Cost of living adjustments, 22, 88
Courts, federal, 41
Covered compensation, 94–95, 306–7
Coverage tests, 26, 58, 265, 282, 299
CPI, 87
Currently insured, OASDI, 14
Curtailment, 243

D

Death benefits, 101, 194
Debt-financed property, 204
Deductibility of contributions, 129, 151, 177, 216
Deferred compensation, 25, 288
Defined-benefit fraction, 215, 219, 286
Defined-benefit plans, 30, 50, 79
Defined-contribution fraction, 215, 219, 286
Defined-contribution plans, 30
Definitely determinable benefits, 74
Deposit administration contract, 140
Determination letter, 228
Disability benefits (disability benefits, social security), 16
Disability benefits, incidental, 105
Disability insured, OASDI, 14
Discretionary formula, 148
Disqualified person, 202
Distress termination, 247
Distributions, 167
Diversification of investments, 174, 201

323

Index

E

Early distribution penalty, 27, 188, 256, 269
Early retirement, 46, 72, 211
Earned income, 220
Economic benefit, 295
EEOC, 84
Elective deferrals, 159, 164
Eligibility, 26, 253, 261
Employee Retirement Income Security Act of 1974; see ERISA
Employee stock ownership plans (ESOPs), 33, 171
Employer securities and real property, 201, 203
Employer-sponsored IRA, 260
Entry age normal method, 122
Entry dates, 54
Equal Employment Opportunity Commission, 84
ERISA, 37
ESOP, 31–33, 47, 171
ESOT, 172
Estate tax, 180, 195, 223, 297
Excess accumulation tax, 195, 225
Excess-benefit percentage, 94
Excess contribution, IRA, 255
Excess-contribution percentage, 96
Excess distribution tax, 195, 224, 275
Excess formula, 91, 304
Exclusion allowance, 266
Exclusion ratio, 191
Experience gain, 126
Experience loss, 125

F

Federal courts, 41
Fiduciary, 26, 37, 199
Final-average formula, 83, 308
5-year averaging, 193
5-year vesting, 65
Flat benefit formula, 80, 306
Flexibility of contributions, 51
Forfeitures, 149
Form 5500, 237
4-40 vesting schedule, 303
Freezing the plan, 243
Frozen initial liability method, 123
Full funding limitation, 127
Fully insured, OASDI, 14
Funding, 26, 37, 206, 293
Funding agency, 132
Funding instrument, 132
Funding limitation, 127
Funding standard account, 126

G

GIC, 144
Government employer, 264, 271
Group deferred annuity contract, 139
Group permanent contract, 139

Guaranteed account plan, 32
Guaranteed income contract, 144

H–I

Hardship, 167, 269
Highly-compensated employees, 26, 58, 156, 164, 262
HR-10 plans; see Keogh plans
Immediate participation guarantee contract, 141
Incidental death benefits, 100, 154, 168, 188, 221, 292
Indexation of benefits, 86
Individual account plans, 30, 245
Individual actuarial cost methods, 119
Individual benefit statement, 238
Individual level premiums method, 122
Individual retirement accounts, 251
Inflation, 8, 22, 85
Installation of qualified plans, 226
Insurance contracts, 135, 227
Integration level, 91, 93, 304–5
Integration with social security, 51, 78, 82, 89, 150, 220, 281, 304
Internal Revenue Code, 40
IPG contract, 141
IRAs, 251

J–L

Joint and survivor annuity, 100, 173, 183
Kelso plan, 172
Keogh plans, 34, 220
Key employee, 217, 274
Labor laws, 41
Late retirement, 73, 212, 278
Leased employees, 62, 284, 320
Letter Rulings, 40
Level funding, 112
Leveraged employee stock ownership plans, 172
Life annuity, 183
Life insurance in qualified plan, 102, 203, 221, 223, 280
Limits on benefits and contributions; see Sec. 415 limits
Loans, 27, 154, 168, 196, 203, 270
Lump-sum distributions, 174, 185, 193, 257

M

Mandatory contributions, 155
Master plans, 230
Matching contributions, 156
Maximum age, 55
Maximum excess allowance, 95
Maximum offset allowance, 92
Medical benefits, incidental, 106
Merger of plans, 244
Minimum age, 54, 58
Minimum distribution rules, 187
Minimum funding requirements, 30, 51, 126

Minimum Universal Pension System; *see* MUPS
Money-purchase plans, 31–32, 75, 178
Mortality, 121, 277
Multiemployer plans, 34
Multiple employer plans, 34, 249
MUPS, 39

N

New money, 143
Nonalienation of benefits, 189
Noncontributory plans, 26
Nondiscrimination, 26, 38
Nonqualified deferred compensation plans, 288
Nonresident aliens, 58
Normal cost, 115
Normal form of benefit, 183, 279
Normal retirement age, 72, 277

O–P

OASDI, 10
Offset, social security, 91–92, 304
Partial termination, 244
Participant-directed investments, 153, 168
Participation tests, 26, 58, 265, 282, 299
Part-time employees, 57
Party-in interest, 202
Past service, 81
Pattern plans, 230
PAYSOPs, 172
PBGC, 41, 244
Penalty, early distribution, 27, 188, 256, 269
Penalty, overstatement of pension liabilities, 121
Pension Benefit Guaranty Corporation; *see* PBGC
Pension plans, 28
Percentage test, 58
Period-certain annuity, 183
Permanence requirement, 241–42
PIA, 17, 18
Plan administrator, 232, 235
Plan termination, 66, 222, 241
Plan year, 227
Predecessor employer, 61
Premature termination, 242
Preretirement survivor annuity, 100
Present value, 109
Primary insurance amount; *see* PIA
Profit-sharing plans, 28, 47, 147
Prohibited transactions, 197, 202
Projected-benefit actuarial cost method, 115, 118
Prototype plans, 230
Prudent man requirement, 201
Public school, 265

Q

QDRO, 196, 234
Qualified domestic relations order, 196, 234
Qualified joint and survivor annuity, 99, 100
Qualified plan, 25
Qualified preretirement survivor annuity, 100

R

Rabbi trust, 290, 294
Ratio test, 58
Reasonable compensation, 296
Reasonableness of actuarial assumptions, 121
Regulations, Treasury, 40
Related employers; *see* Controlled groups
Replacement ratio, 6, 80, 89
Reportable event, 246
Reporting and disclosure requirements, 37, 236
Retirement annuity contracts, 137
Retirement bonds, 258
Retirement income, sources, 1, 48
Retirement income policies, 136
Retirement savings, 252
Retroactive amendments, 229
Retroactive termination, 242
Revenue Rulings, 40
Reverse mortgage, 5
Reversion of assets, 242
Rollovers, 258
Rulings, IRS, 40

S

S corporations, 34, 172, 196
Salary continuation, 289
Salary reductions, 161, 262, 267, 271, 289
Salary scale, 121
Savings, 3, 38
Savings Plans, 155, 162
Sec. 401(k) plans, 31, 33, 48, 159
Sec. 403(b) plans, 264
Sec. 415 limits, 27, 178, 211, 275
Sec. 457 plans, 264, 271
Sec. 501(c)(3), 265
Securities laws, 42
Self-employed persons, 253
Separate accounts, 142
Separate lines of business, 60
SEPs, 251, 261
SERP, 289
Service, 54, 56, 65
Sex discrimination, 39, 83
Side fund, 136–37
Simplified employee pensions, 251, 261
Single purchase annuity contracts, 145
Social investing, 208
Social security, 3, 10
Social security, integration with, 78, 82, 89, 150, 281, 304
Social security taxes, 169, 267
SPAC, 145
SPD, 236
Spousal IRA, 251, 254
Standard termination, 247
Stepped-up formula, 309
Stock bonus plans, 31–33, 47, 171

Stock redemption, 179
Substantial and recurring contributions, 51, 148
Summary annual report, 237
Summary plan description, 236
Super top heavy, 220, 286
Supplemental executive retirement plan, 289
Supplemental liability, 115, 120
Survivors' benefits, social security, 15

T

Target benefits plans, 31–32, 50, 76
Tax benefits, 28
Tax-deferred annuity plans, 264
Tax-exempt employer, 55, 264
Tax expenditure, 38
Tax shelter, 49, 89, 169
10-year averaging, 193
Termination, plan, 65, 222, 241
Termination of employment, 67
3 to 7-year vesting, 65
Thrift plans; *see* Savings Plans
Top-heavy plans, 27, 65, 216, 286
TRASOPs, 172
Trusts, 132, 227
Turnover, 46, 121

U

Unfunded past service liability, 120
Unincorporated business, 196, 220
Unisex, 84, 277
Unit-benefit formulas, 81, 308
Unit-credit method, 122
Universal life insurance, 102, 281
Unrealized appreciation, 172, 174
Unrelated business income, 203

V–Y

Valuation date, 152
Vesting, 27, 37, 46, 64, 163, 219, 242, 244, 266, 293, 301
Voluntary contributions, 155
Welfare and Pension Plans Disclosure Act (WPPDA), 36
Withdrawal liability, 249
Withdrawal penalty, 27
Withdrawals, 153
Withholding, federal income tax, 235
Year of service, 56, 65